RETURN TO THE
CAFFE CINO

EDITED BY
STEVE SUSOYEV
AND
GEORGE BIRIMISA

Moving Finger Press

SAN FRANCISCO

"It is the Off-Off Broadway Theatre Shrine!"
New York Times, 1967

RETURN TO THE CAFFE CINO

First Edition January 2007
Copyright ©2007 Moving Finger Press
All rights reserved

Printed in the United States of America

For information about permission to reproduce selections from this book, write to:
Permissions, Moving Finger Press, 369 Jersey Street, San Francisco, CA 94114,
and see caution statement beginning on this page

Composition and Manufacturing by Falcon Books, San Ramon, CA
Book and cover design by Steve Susoyev
Cover photos by James D. Gossage

Library of Congress Cataloging-in-Publication Data
Susoyev, Steve & Birimisa, George
Return to the Caffe Cino / Susoyev & Birimisa
Includes bibliographical references and index
Library of Congress Control No: 2006096359
ISBN 978-0-9774214-1-1
1. Drama   2. Anthologies   3. The Arts   4. Social Movements

CAUTION: The plays in this volume are protected, in whole and in part, under the Copyright Laws of the United States of America, the United Kingdom, the Dominion of Canada, and all other nations of the Copyright Union, and are subject to royalty for stage production, both professional and amateur, and release in any public or private medium including motion picture, radio, television, recitation, public reading, reprinting, Internet publication, and release through media not yet developed at the time of this publication. Each play in this volume is reprinted by permission of the author and/or rights-holder named below. The English language stock and amateur stage performance rights in these plays are controlled exclusively by such individuals and entities. No professional or nonprofessional performance of any play in this volume may be given without obtaining, in advance, the written permission of the rights-holder and paying any requisite fee.

The playwrights whose addresses appear with their plays in this volume invite readers to contact them directly concerning performance and reprint rights. In all other cases, readers are welcome to contact Moving Finger Press concerning rights.

A *Funny Walk Home* by Jeff Weiss is reprinted by permission of the playwright.

The Bed and *Moon* by Robert Heide are reprinted by permission of the playwright.

The Brown Crown by Haal Borske is reprinted by permission of the playwright.

The Clown *A Fantasy* by Claris Nelson is reprinted by permission of the playwright.

Daddy Violet by George Birimisa is reprinted by permission of the playwright.

Dames at Sea by George Haimsohn & Robin Miller, Composer Jim Wise, is reprinted by permission of Samuel French, Inc.

Good Night, I Love You by William M. Hoffman is reprinted by permission of the playwright.

The Haunted Host by Robert Patrick is reprinted by permission of Samuel French, Inc.

Hurrah for the Bridge (Que Vive el Puente) by Paul Foster is reprinted by permission of the playwright.

Icarus's Mother by Sam Shepard is reprinted by permission of Random House Inc.

I Like It by Michael Smith is reprinted by permission of the playwright.

Medea of the Laundromat or The Stars May Understand by H. M. Koutoukas is reprinted by permission of the playwright.

Monuments by Diane di Prima is reprinted by permission of the playwright.

Now She Dances! by Doric Wilson is reprinted by permission of the playwright.

Sex Is Between Two People by Lanford Wilson is reprinted by permission of the playwright.

The Singing Lesson by Daniel Haben Clark is reprinted by permission of the playwright.

Vinyl by Ronald Tavel is reprinted by permission of the playwright.

Vorspiel Nach Marienstein by Michael Smith, John P. Dodd and Robert Olivo (Ondine) is reprinted by permission of Michael Smith.

Who Killed My Bald Sister Sophie? by Tom Eyen is reprinted by permission of The Tom Eyen 1988 Trust, managed by ICM.

Photographs credited to James D. Gossage are used by permission of the photographer or of the New York Public Library for the Performing Arts. Original negatives are housed at the Billy Rose Theatre Collection at Lincoln Center.

Photographs credited to Fred McDarrah are the property of Fred McDarrah and may not be reprinted without his express permission.

Photographs credited to Conrad Ward are the property of Conrad Ward.

Photographs credited to Marc Cohen are the property of *The Villager*.

Other photographs are the property of the individual photographers and are used by permission.

CONTENTS

ESSAYS, MEMOIRS AND INTERVIEWS

THE PLAYS

CONCERNING ATTRIBUTIONS

Moving Finger Press has made a diligent effort to give appropriate credit, and pay proper royalties, for all intellectual property reprinted in this book.

Still, thanks to the spirit of anarchy that reigned at the Caffe Cino, and because many years have passed, few comprehensive records exists. Where we have been unable to determine who is responsible for a given piece of work, we have noted, for example, "Photographer unknown."

In these instances — or, much worse, where we have given credit to the wrong person — we welcome our readers' corrections for incorporation in future editions, while recognizing that no two people agree about anything that happened forty-plus years ago at 31 Cornelia Street in New York City.

When in doubt concerning photographs, we were tempted to credit them to James D. Gossage, who offered us his entire treasury of Cino-related work, royalty-free, in exchange for our promise to donate any riches we unearthed to the Joe Cino Collection at the New York Public Library's Lincoln Center facility. We readily agreed. The catalogue of Mr. Gossage's Cino photographs runs to ninety-two pages of small print. We wish we could publish all those photographs, and encourage you to visit the Cino Collection at Lincoln Center to see them.

A note about usage: In American writing, "theatre" and "theater" seem to be used interchangeably, and the editors have left the respective spellings intact as they appear in the original memoirs and plays. "Caffe Cino" is neither Italian nor English (in Italian, it would appear as Caffè Cino). Michael Smith, who gave off-off-Broadway its name when he was the chief drama critic for *The Village Voice*, has said he believes the accent mark was never used because 1960s typographers at that newspaper did not have accent marks available. The Caffe Cino's signs, menus, and posters left off the accent mark, and so have we.

Ellen Stewart and Joe Cino accepted the first off-off-Broadway Obie in 1967, ". . . awarded to Caffe Cino and Café La Mama for creating opportunities for new playwrights to confront audiences and gain experience of the real theatre." The *Village Voice* Off-Broadway Awards, nicknamed the "Obies," had been created soon after the newspaper's birth in 1955 to acknowledge and encourage the growing off-Broadway theatre movement.

Photo by, and property of, Fred McDarrah
Moving Finger Press is licensed to reprint this photograph in this anthology only

MAGIC TIME
Steve Susoyev

Why does the theatre thrive when we are surrounded by cheaper alternatives that provide more instantaneous gratification? For the price of a Broadway ticket, people can subscribe to six months' worth of HBO.

One answer may lie in the availability of tickets far from Broadway. For the price of one of the cheaper entrées in a mid-priced restaurant, from which you will awaken hungry in the morning, you can purchase a La Mama E.T.C. ticket, which will nourish your soul.

"Alternative" and "Experimental" theatre venues like La Mama had to fight for legitimacy, even for survival. Beginning in the late 1950s and nearly every night for ten years, Joe Cino stood on an eight-by-eight-foot stage in a Greenwich Village coffeehouse to announce, "And now, before closing, a basket will be passed to accept any contributions for the performers." In this book we have collected a few of the many plays he introduced, and the memories of a few of the people who participated in bringing those plays to life.

This anthology was conceived in 2001, during a production called "Return to the Caffe Cino" in San Francisco, produced by Trauma Flintstone and hosted by the Jon Sims Center. The show featured scenes from plays by George Birimisa, Lanford Wilson and Tom Eyen. I was entranced; these plays were decades old but felt fresh, edgy and important.

For an early draft of this book, we pondered using the words "Dawn of Queer Theatre" in our title, and many participants ganged up to convince us that such a title limited and insulted the work that Joe Cino nurtured on his little stage forty-some years ago. William Hoffman wrote, "I'll be queer if it'll sell books," but in our first meeting he persuaded me that such was not necessary.

Much of the work in this volume does reflect what has come to be called a "gay sensibility." Gay and lesbian history is routinely obliterated from the record of human endeavor. Each generation must reclaim that history. As Bill Hoffman pointed out in our first interview, "The new thing that emerged in the 1960s was not 'gay' theatre, but conscious gay pride. That pride had a profound effect on gay playwrights and their audiences."

All of the work in this volume is important, and worthy of preservation, in part because it often does not represent the playwrights' best-known work. Most Cino playwrights are not in danger of falling out of history. Tom Eyen's *Dreamgirls* is not likely to be forgotten; a major motion picture is due out about a month after the release of this book. Eyen's *The Last Great Cocktail Party*, however, his only overtly gay-themed play, took us nine months to track down, in a fractured, unfinished form. With the help of Tom's brother, Richard Eyen, a third play won a place in this anthology: *Who Killed My Bald Sister Sophie?* is an original, exciting play whose loss would be a tragedy.

But the place these plays hold in history does not date them. In Robert Patrick's *The Haunted Host*, we encounter a familiar twenty-first century theme, the fear of intimacy. *The Bed* by Robert Heide gives us a couple struggling to communicate, with reality-show intensity. Paul Foster's *Hurrah for the Bridge* takes us into the mind of a homeless man. Decades before Will and Grace, William Hoffman wrote *Good Night, I Love You* to explore an intimate friendship between a gay man and a straight woman. Timeless human themes animate all of this work.

Early in the process of collecting plays, we saw that no one could write a definitive "Introduction" to this book. No two people who were involved in the Caffe Cino agree about anything that happened there. And so we asked for short memoirs. The ones we received include stories of cooperation, sacrifice and inspiration — and also of betrayal, assault and battery, and disappointment. But no one accuses Joe Cino, who worked in a laundry during the day to keep his beloved Caffe in business, of harming another human being.

We offer this collection to theatre students and enthusiasts, and to everyone who is interested in the slices of history that are in danger of being lost to future generations. This book celebrates these playwrights, actors and directors who launched a revolution on the eight-by-eight-foot stage in that Greenwich Village dive in the 1960s.

Joe Cino attended nearly every performance of every play that appeared on his stage. He dedicated each performance to the playwrights with the announcement, "Ladies and Gentlemen, it's Magic Time!"

MAKING AMENDS
George Birimisa

I began writing during the Great Depression, trying to tell my story in prose: a story of abandonment by my mother, the death of my Communist father, years in a Catholic orphanage, and brutality at the hands of a homophobic society. I was a miserable and profoundly angry man. After writing five very bad novels with straight protagonists, I had the good sense to write a play with a gay theme. Insecure about my lack of a formal education, I found an art form in which I didn't have to worry about my grammar.

With excellent reviews in *The Village Voice* and *The New York Times* for my play *Daddy Violet*, a world of creativity opened to me. I was no longer a nobody. But I was still angry, and I ridiculed my fellow playwrights, insisting they were brown-noses with no talent.

When Steve Susoyev suggested that we put together an anthology of Caffe Cino plays and memoirs, I jumped at the opportunity. Not only would I see my *Daddy Violet* published, I would get to really know playwrights I hadn't seen in thirty-five years. Having re-read the plays many times, of course I now have a very different opinion of the work. These plays are groundbreaking, courageous and fun to read.

One of the gifts of living as long as I have (I'm writing this six months after my eighty-second birthday) is the opportunity to make amends for my ill-tempered behavior.

Lanford Wilson's *Home Free!* (not included in this collection) opened at the Caffe Cino in 1964 with Joanna Miles and Michael Warren Powell as the incestuous brother and sister Lawrence and Joanna. This shot, taken over the shoulder of an audience member, reveals the intimacy of the Caffe Cino.

Photographer unknown, photo provided through the courtesy of Lanford Wilson

David Christmas and Bernadette Peters performed
"Raining in My Heart" from *Dames at Sea* during Joe
Cino's memorial service at Judson Church, April 10, 1967

DID THEY KNOW THEY WERE MAKING THEATRE HISTORY?

The interior of the Caffe Cino, populated by, from left, Bob Lawlor, Magie Dominic, Charles Stanley, H.M. Koutoukas, and Deborah Lee, in a photograph that many pioneers agree best represents what the Cino looked like

Photographer unknown; photo circa 1964 (but certainly, all parties agree, before the fire of March, 1965), provided through the courtesy of Michael Smith

THE ACCIDENTAL THEATRE
Wendell C. Stone

Fourteen or so times each week, Joseph Cino, short, stocky, and usually in need of a shave, stepped onto the small stage of his coffeehouse to introduce the evening's show: "Ladies and Gentlemen, it's Magic Time!" It is hard to imagine a less likely home for or producer of some of New York's finest theatre during the 1960s. Caffe Cino was a tiny coffeehouse located on quiet, block-long Cornelia Street in Greenwich Village. Joe Cino was a would-be dancer from Buffalo whose career failed, probably because of his short, heavy build. His love of dance, theatre, opera, and spectacle led him to open the Caffe in November 1958, intent on providing an intimate space for his friends and other artists to meet for conversation over coffee and light refreshments. He planned a variety of activities — art shows, poetry readings, and lectures. He never planned on operating a theatre; but the play readings and scene work that he allowed friends and patrons to offer became so popular that he soon found himself offering a new play every week or two.

At the Caffe's peak, performances began at 9:00 p.m. and 11:00 p.m. Tuesday through Sunday and 1:00 a.m. on weekends. The Cino was one of the first and most important venues in the early off-off-Broadway scene, launching the careers of major playwrights (Lanford Wilson), actors (Bernadette Peters), directors (Marshall Mason), and lighting designers (Johnny Dodd). Cino artists explored new styles in the campy productions of H. M. Koutoukas, introduced controversial topics such as sadomasochism in works by William M. Hoffman and Ronald Tavel, and offered playwrights an opportunity to experiment within a noncommercial atmosphere.

Though the Caffe was best known for its exuberant, campy productions, identifying a "Cino style" is nearly impossible. Certainly many of its productions were apolitical, slight nothings taken to the wildest of camp excesses. But it also presented antiwar protests by George Birimisa, realistic renditions of classics by Chekhov, and even an anti-union, conservative work by Terry Alan Smith. Ultimately, Joe Cino's method for selecting works relied less on what the artist had to say than on the fact that the artist had something to say and nowhere to say it because of inexperience, choice of subject matter, or age. As a result, the Cino was not guided by an overarching political philosophy, artistic concept, or box-office strategy, but by the needs of its artists. The dictum that ruled was Cino's phrase, "Do what you have to do." And what it seems that the Cino crowd had to do was to create theatre.

Despite their popularity, the productions brought the Cino into conflict with the City of New York. Codes at the time allowed only two licensing options for venues offering live performance: an expensive cabaret license intended for establishments serving alcoholic beverages, and a theatre license that placed strict requirements on space and physical facilities. Like most coffeehouses, the Cino had neither the financial resources nor appropriate space for meeting either requirement. Thus, it operated without a license, often resulting in legal action from the police, fire, and health departments.

Many of its early shows were drawn from recent Broadway or off-Broadway fare. In 1961, however, that changed when a young redhead walked in with a manuscript in hand. The man was Doric Wilson, the play was *And He Made a Her*, and the event positioned the Caffe as the theatre at which aspiring playwrights could see their work staged. Soon, scripts flowed into the coffeehouse. Over the next few years, Cino produced new works by David Starkweather, Claris Nelson, Lee Kalcheim, Sam Shepard, Ruth Yorck, Robert Patrick, Tom Eyen, Robert Heide, and numerous other figures who would go on to prominence in theatre, television, and film. In addition, the Cino was one of the first theatres in the United States to offer frequent productions by and about gay men, including Lanford Wilson's *The Madness of Lady Bright*, Robert Patrick's *The Haunted Host*, and William M. Hoffman's *Good Night, I Love You*.

Just as it was reaching its peak of success, the Cino burned on March 3, 1965 (Ash Wednesday, ironically enough). Immediately, friends and admirers gathered and staged benefits to rebuild the coffeehouse. Such figures as Ellen Stewart, Edward Albee, and H. M. Koutoukas generously donated time, facilities, and money to the effort. On May 18, 1965, the Cino reopened, presenting Koutoukas's *With Creatures Make My Way*. The following months were the most successful of the Cino's existence. In May 1966, Robert Dahdah, who had directed frequently at the Cino, opened the coffeehouse's most commercially successful production, *Dames at Sea*. It was the only show at the Cino to have an open-ended run.

The success of *Dames* seems to have attracted Andy Warhol's Factory crowd to the Cino, perhaps ultimately leading to its demise. In particular, Warhol film star Ondine (Robert Olivio), known for his heavy drug use, began to frequent the Caffe, appearing in several productions. Perhaps because of this influence, Joe Cino and his lover Jonathan Torrey were both suffering ill effects from drug use by the winter of 1966. Torrey left New York to recover from his addiction, but was killed in an industrial accident on January 5, 1967. Despondent over his lover's death, weakened by his own drug abuse, depressed over aging and solitude, and overwhelmed by the demands of operating a still-illegal business, Joe Cino locked himself in the Cino and committed suicide. He died on April 2, 1967.

First, dancer Charles Stanley, and subsequently the team of *Village Voice* critic Michael Smith and harpsichord manufacturer Wolfgang Zuckermann, attempted to keep the Cino open. It could not, however, survive the mounting legal bills and escalating costs, closing on March 10, 1968 during the run of Diane di Prima's *Monuments*.

Caffe Cino popularized, perhaps even gave birth to, the off-off-Broadway movement; it helped found the contemporary gay theatre; it contributed to the emergence of London's fringe and Paris's café theatre. Thus, its influence is still very much with us. As Ellen Stewart said of Joseph Cino, "Remember that what came from his soul, what came from his heart, what came from his mind contributed in a large degree to everything that we are doing today."

Like all New York City café theaters in the 1960s, the Caffe Cino was illegal. Kenny Burgess, shown above, designed posters that looked like abstract art, to avoid tipping off the authorities. Off-off-Broadway fans knew what to look for. As the Cino became more "legitimate" for the uptown crowd, the plays were reviewed and advertised in the press, but raids still occurred on an arbitrary schedule.

The coded symbols on this poster announced Robert Patrick's 1967 *The Warhol Machine,* starring Magie Dominic, Robert Shields, Haal Borske, and Theodore Morwell, and directed by Andy Milligan

(For a thorough discussion of the politics of the "coffeehouse wars," see Wendell Stone's *Caffe Cino: The Birthplace of Off-Off Broadway,* included in the Bibliography of this volume)

Photos believed to be by Conrad Ward, provided through the courtesy of Robert Patrick

TO CONQUER BROADWAY
Marshall W. Mason

On Friday, September 1, 1961, I arrived in New York City determined to conquer Broadway. The first thing I did was to call the one person I knew in the city, fellow Northwestern graduate Jane Lowry, who had played Varya in Alvina Krause's *Cherry Orchard* in college, and who would, at the end of the decade, play Olga in my production of *Three Sisters* at Circle Rep.

Jane told me that she was currently in a production in the Village, and invited me to come down and see it. About eight o'clock Sunday night, I got on the IND Eighth Avenue subway, and went to West Fourth Street, the gateway to Greenwich Village. Following Jane's directions, I found my way past the Waverly Theater, around the corner to a little street only one block long. Near the end of the block at 31 Cornelia Street, I discovered a storefront with a sign that read "Caffe Cino."

Inside, the intimate room was lighted by strands of Christmas-tree lights, and contained perhaps a dozen small, round tables. I seated myself, and before long, a lithe, elfin creature in an apron approached me, and handed me a mimeographed menu, filled with ornate lettering that advertised various exotic blends of coffee. I ordered a cappuccino, and noticed that the waiter had long, dark hair that reached almost to his shoulders, and that he wore a gold earring in one earlobe. He was the first man I had ever seen with long hair, not to mention an earring, and I soon discovered the name of this magical creature was Johnny Dodd.

Soon after my coffee was served, stage lights went on at the center of the room, and a handsome, chubby man in his early thirties, with curly black hair and a smile as big as Christmas, announced that tonight the Caffe Cino would be presenting a new play by Doric Wilson called *Now She Dances!* The lights went out, and when they came up, Jane entered in a maid's black uniform, with a starched white apron and frilly headpiece. As the play unfolded, it was an amusing retelling of the "Salome" story, as Oscar Wilde *should* have written it — in the style, that is, of *The Importance of Being Earnest*. My only clear memory is that there were a lot of laughs at the sophisticated wit, and that John the Baptist's head was served on a silver platter with a tea cozy! And that I stayed to watch the second performance at eleven o'clock.

The play was over within half an hour, and the actors passed a basket to receive donations from the audience for their artistic efforts. After she was out of costume, Jane joined me at the table, and introduced me to the chubby host of the evening, Joe Cino. The Caffe had begun presenting original plays only recently, beginning with the previous Doric Wilson opus based on Adam and Eve called *And He Made a Her*. Prior to Doric's arrival, they had produced poetry readings and one-act plays by classical authors. But now, it seemed, they were excited by the idea of changing their repertoire to present as many new plays as possible.

In typical fashion, when Joe discovered that I was a director, he immediately said I should direct a play for the Cino.

It was almost a year later when I took Joe up on his offer, directing my New York début production, *The Rue Garden* by another Northwestern friend, Claris Nelson, who also appeared in the cast opposite yet another Northwestern graduate, Ron Willoughby. The cast was rounded out with Lynn McCarthy and the indomitable Linda Eskenas, who would become one of the major stars at the Cino.

As fate would have it, a journalist from *The Village Voice* named Michael Smith caught one of our performances, and his warm review marked the first play from off-off-Broadway ever reviewed by the New York press. As our friend Robert Patrick wryly remarked: "It was the beginning of the end."

With our success, Joe coaxed us into producing another play by Claris, and in October of 1962, we presented *The Clown*, which became Joe's favorite play, and he would request we revive it five years later, under what proved to be ominous circumstances.

We followed *The Clown* a month later with Claris's newest play, *Medea*, which starred Rob Thirkield as Jason. In the week of Valentine's Day 1963, I put together a pastiche of love scenes from Shakespeare, Rostand and Musset, which we presented under the title *Romance d'Amour*.

I spent most of 1964 away from the Cino, raising money for my off-Broadway venture of producing Ibsen's *Little Eyolf* at the Actors' Playhouse on Seventh Avenue, across the street from the Sheridan Square Playhouse, which ten years later would become the home of Circle Rep.

Following my sabbatical from the Cino, I returned to discover there was a new kid in town, a playwright. Michael Smith highly recommended that his readers catch the theatrical coup that ended a new play at the Cino called *So Long at the Fair*. Of course I went, and immediately saw that Lanford Wilson was a major writing talent, and that his actor Michael Warren Powell was electrifying. I saw all of his early productions, which included *Home Free!* and *The Madness of Lady Bright*, the latter with the Olivier of off-off-Broadway, Neil Flanagan.

But it wasn't until the revival of *Home Free!* in 1964 that I actually met the writer who would become the collaborative partner for my whole career. Joe Cino introduced me to Lanford, and so we can hold him responsible for everything that has followed.

In October, I directed Claris's latest play, *Neon in the Night,* and it was around Halloween that I first read Lanford's full-length play *Balm in Gilead* and told him he needed a brilliant director for such a complex play. Lanford took my remark as a criticism, and it took the intervention of Michael Warren Powell to bring us together. He told Lanford I had said it was the best original play I had ever read.

Lanford shrugged this off by saying, "How many original plays has he read?" To which Claris testily retorted: "All of *mine*, for a start."

My next Cino show was the première of Robert Patrick's first play, *The Haunted Host*. I could imagine no better casting for a play about two playwrights, one older and cynical and the other bright-eyed and ambitious, than to cast Robert Patrick opposite William M. Hoffman, who would soon début with his own play, *Thank You, Miss Victoria*.

Late one night in November, after the final performance of the evening, Lanford, Michael, Claris and I sat around the Cino and read his latest play, *The Sandcastle*, for Joe. I thought it was even more sophisticated in technique than *Balm in Gilead*. I loved it so much that when Lanford finally asked me to direct *Balm*, I accepted on the condition that I could follow it up with *The Sandcastle*.

In between, in February, I directed Lanford's professional début with *Home Free!* as part of the Barr-Wilder-Albee series of new playwrights at the Cherry Lane Theater, where it was on a bill with Sam Shepard's *Up to Thursday* with Kevin O'Connor and Stephanie Gordon, and Paul Foster's abstract homage to Beckett, *Balls*, starring two illuminated ping-pong balls swinging back and forth in a chasm of darkness. And Lanford and I spent the rest of 1965 working mainly at La Mama, because she [Ellen Stewart] offered a much larger stage and could accommodate full-length work.

In 1966, I returned to the Cino with David Starkweather's *The Love Pickle*, and Lanford's brief little turn, *Wandering,* in which both he and I appeared.

In April of 1967, Joe requested that we remount his favorite play, *The Clown*, in memory of his lover Jon Torrey, who had recently died in a freak electrical accident in a summer theater. The revival featured an all-star cast of Cino playwrights, directors and actors, that included Lanford Wilson, Robert Patrick, Walter Harris, Neil Flanagan, David Starkweather, Ron Link and me. None of us realized that it was a kind of final curtain call for Joe's Caffe Cino. It was at the end of this run that Joe committed suicide, we were told, with the spectacular phantasmagoria of operatic fashion, accompanied by the recordings of Maria Callas from the Cino juke-box.

Upon learning of Joe's suicide attempt, we all rushed to St. Vincent's Hospital, where we held a vigil outside the emergency room, all of us deeply in shock, until word came that he had died.

It seemed as if our youth was over. All the magic, all the inspiration, all the tireless creativity of the Cino had been centered on this one vibrant person, Joe Cino. It would take a tremendous effort to use his memory alone to spur us on to continue his legacy.

My last production at the Cino was three months later under Charles Stanley's management. His courageous determination kept the doors of the Cino open with the help of Robert Patrick and Michael Smith. It was a revival of *The Sandcastle*, which we'd first done on the larger stage at La Mama two years before. This time the production featured a lovely, sensitive performance by Tanya Berezin, the final piece of the creative puzzle who would join Lanford, Rob and me in founding the Circle Repertory Company two years after Joe's death.

Circle Rep would become an important force in the renaissance of the American theater. But Joe, John, Johnny and Kenny Burgess will always be enshrined in the twinkling memory of our beginnings, in the warm, intimate cocoon of the Caffe Cino, the birthplace of off-off-Broadway, and our artistic lives.

Joe Cino, on the right, with his lover, Jonathan Torrey, in 1963.
A master electrician, Jonathan bypassed the Caffe Cino's electric meter to
connect directly to the city's power supply.

Photographer unknown. Photo provided through the courtesy of Robert Patrick

THE MEMOIRS

Joe Cino in 1965

Photo by James D. Gossage

EDEN
Edward Albee

Caffe Cino: We were all very young; we were all innocent; we knew nothing. We lived in a kind of Eden called Greenwich Village — this was a long time ago.

Greenwich Village then was the center of all the new arts, and everyone was talented, and no one was famous, and we all spent our time with each other's work, learning and cribbing.

And one of the theatre centers was Caffe Cino, where young playwrights who knew nothing about what they were supposed to be doing made exciting work, and the failures were as exciting as the successes.

It was Eden. I miss it.

Joe Cino with Edward Albee at the Writers' Stage Theatre, during the benefit to fund repairs to the Caffe Cino after the fire of 1965

Photo by James D. Gossage

Helen Hanft and Stephen Davis (Van Vost)
in Tom Eyen's *Why Hanna's Skirt Won't Stay Down,*
1965

Photo by James D. Gossage

Helen Hanft in 2006
Photo by Steve Susoyev

TO THINE OWN SELF BE TRUE
A Conversation with Helen Hanft

The editors met with Helen Hanft in May of 2006, during rehearsals for her new film, Noise, *in which she appears with Tim Robbins. Included here are excerpts from their conversation.*

GEORGE BIRIMISA: Helen, we have received memoirs from several people who reminisce about the nurturing atmosphere at the Cino. It sounds like an ideal place for a young actress. Wasn't there any dysfunction?

HELEN HANFT: Well, it's true I was never expected to sleep with anyone to get a part. But the Cino had its share of egomaniacs. A lot of theatre people hate each other, but we don't want to look bad. To look good, especially in that tiny place, we had to make *each other* look good.

    An underlying violence permeated things. That kind of thing trickles down from the top. Joe's drug problem rarely affected the actors directly. But there was a darkness there. I made a decision to keep my distance a little bit.

    I generally don't get along with other actors and I was certainly up and down with Tom Eyen. He was a Leo, I'm an Aries. We fought. We had a terrible fight at the Cino. We were rehearsing *The White Whore and The Bit Player*. Johnny Dodd was lighting me with a putrid green light. I said, "I know I'm supposed to be an ugly nun, but that light makes me look dead!"

    Johnny Dodd, always so sweet. Johnny Dodd had a subtext. He clobbered me in the back of the head.

    Tom Eyen joined in with Johnny Dodd, hitting me. Mari-Claire [Charba] was there. I was thirty, but she was just a kid. I was thinking she would phone for help. She ran into the dressing room and locked the door, so I ran out into the street. I saw two cops at a café on the corner and dragged them into the Cino and told them my story. "Do you want us to arrest these guys for battery?" they asked me. "No," I said, "we're theatre people." So the next day Johnny Dodd brought me flowers. I was black and blue. I never spoke to him again, and I didn't perform under that ghastly green light.

    Joe Cino was a wonderful guy. He really wanted to make peace with people. Didn't want to be in the middle. He loved actors but he was very demanding in a gentle way. I always got the feeling he would protect me. But he couldn't be around all the time, and he was distracted by his relationship with amphetamines.

STEVE SUSOYEV: I got to see you at La Mama last year in the revival of *Why Hanna's Skirt Won't Stay Down*. Ellen Stewart told me that Tom Eyen created the character of Hanna specifically for you to play.

HELEN: He wrote all three of those Hanna plays[1] for me to play. The role of Hanna haunts me. Tom Eyen was a very insightful person. I won't say he based Hanna on me — God, I hope not! — but he knew I would understand her.

In *Hanna's Skirt*, you see a desperately lonely woman. We can laugh at her but we also have to cry for her. Hanna shows her feelings too much, opens her entire life to a narcissistic kid. Together — her with her loneliness, him with his fascination with his own beauty — they become a side-show act without even knowing it. In the second play, *Who Killed My Bald Sister Sophie?*, Hanna and her sister are together, and you see what was wrong. Hanna can't hold her feelings back. Sophie can't show any feelings at all. The terrible sibling rivalry, terrible love-hate. Just like ordinary family life!

When you saw me play Hanna forty years later, I didn't have to study my lines. The role is riveted in my soul, my brain chemistry. This is a woman with more than a blemish. She's deeply wounded.

Outside the role, I was not the easiest person to get along with. I was very envious of people. I always felt I was being deprived, a victim, when I was victimizing people myself. Toxic people are drawn to the theatre. They think they can get away with their toxicity there.

When we asked about her relationship with Tom Eyen outside the theatre, Helen had this to say:

Everybody thought he left me money, but he didn't. If people want to live in a fairy tale, that's their business. Me, I try to be true to myself, and that doesn't always make me popular, but most mornings — not all, but most — I can stand to look at myself in the mirror.

---

[1] *Why Hanna's Skirt Won't Stay Down*, 1965; *Who Killed My Bald Sister Sophie?*, 1968 (included in this collection); and *What is Making Gilda So Gray* (not produced at the Cino) comprise the trilogy Tom Eyen called "The Three Sisters."

FOR THE AUDIENCE
A Conversation with Tom O'Horgan

The editors and Mari-Claire Charba met with Tom O'Horgan in May of 2006. Included here are excerpts from their conversation.

STEVE SUSOYEV: The world credits you with revolutionizing Broadway because you directed *Hair* and *Jesus Christ, Superstar*. Paul Foster describes the night he left the theater, after a preview of *Hair*, and looked up at the stars and said, "He's done it. Tom has gotten rock and roll onto Broadway." Did you know you were starting a revolution?

TOM O'HORGAN: Paul saw stars in the sky over Manhattan? He's such a romantic. My memory isn't what it used to be. I don't remember what I had for breakfast, but I'm good with forty years ago, and I don't think you could see stars in New York back then, either.

No, I didn't set out to start a revolution. I did what came next. I had a night-club act. I hauled around a harp in my station wagon, all over the U.S. and Europe. I wore a tuxedo and told jokes and played my harp. I'm a classical musician. I wasn't interested in rock and roll.

So this idiot drags a harp onto the stage, and plays strange, atonal songs. It was what I could do, so I did it. Certain cities were more open — San Francisco, parts of Chicago, Minneapolis. There were so many clubs, a network all over the country.

Later on, it became more and more difficult to find places to play. Joe Cino opened his coffeehouse, which to me was just a nightclub without alcohol, which meant attentive audiences. His desires were much like mine. I did my harp act there. The Cino was one of the first places that worked for me. It was not perfect, God knows. But the people working there projected an open quality. They inspired me to go to my limit. Joe Cino was a very free soul.

In art you find magical little corners. We were digging into another world of expression. I remember trying to find reasons to do what we were doing, but there was no logic to it.

More important even than helping people mount new work was helping people — audiences — see new work. I remember at the Cino, after a show, the whole audience would be in a state. The whole movement was very spiritual. All art is spiritual. We felt we were breaking through. There was a period when every play you went to gave you a challenge. The audience walked out with some new voice singing in their heads. Paul Foster gave them that challenge. Michael Warren Powell did it too.

MARI-CLAIRE CHARBA: At the Cino there was no payday. Fred Forrest said, "It's better to do a play with two characters. More to share when the basket goes around." Lanford Wilson's plays were wonderful, but too many actors had to share the contents of the basket.

TOM O'HORGAN: The intimacy of the Cino was an accident that happened because the place was so tiny. But I found I had the desire to have the actors touch the audience. The actors resisted, and the audience was repelled.

GEORGE BIRIMISA: It wasn't unusual for an actress to go out and sit on an audience member's lap.

TOM O'HORGAN: Breaking those limits. We did a number of plays that required the audience to participate in the show. The notion developed of a fun-house trip for the audience. Megan Terry set up a wild thing at Cooper Union that was really that, with the audience moving through long, dark hallways, coming across an actor who was in the middle of a scene, then the audience moved on to the next actor. In Paul Foster's *Tom Paine*, the play itself keeps evolving because of the audience's feedback and participation.

In those days, you went to a play with no idea what was going to happen to you. But you knew something was going to happen. My main concern in the theatre is what happens to that audience member. They have to be changed. People give themselves to this event.

Actors and directors sometimes have no idea whose work they are doing. At the Cino we took for granted that the playwright was in the room with us. We often told playwrights, "This isn't what this character is about. Change it." And they did.

I want to think that young playwrights, new actors and directors, have a place where they can experience something like that.

Tom O'Horgan with Mari-Claire Charba in 2005

Photo by Michael Locascio

Tom O'Horgan with George Birimisa in 2006

Photo by Steve Susoyev

LETTER FROM THE REV. AL CARMINES

The Rev. Carmines was an off-Broadway legend in his own right, as explained by the following note from Robert Patrick that accompanies the letter on the opposite page:

"Rev. Al Carmines was Joe Cino's minister, and the world-famed, award-winning composer of scores for innumerable shows and dances, including *What Happened*, *Christmas Rappings*, and *The Faggot*. In 1994 I edited an article about Joe Cino for *Los Angeles Theatres Magazine* (now defunct). Al Carmines sent me the following letter to be used in it. I was able to use only a paragraph. When I called Al in August, 2005, to ask for a contribution for this book, he said I could use this letter. He died three days later."

ROBERT PATRICK
JANUARY 2006

"My biggest pleasure the last two years has come from pop music (the Beatles, Dionne Warwick, the Supremes) + the music of Al Carmines (actor, composer, director, reverend)."

From the notebooks and diaries of Susan Sontag, 1958-67 as published in the New York Times Magazine, *September 10, 2006*

Rauschenbusch Memorial United Church of Christ

I Saw Joe Cino wandering the midtown streets of New York

the day before he committed suicide. He asked me to take a boat trip

to the Statue of Liberty with him . I was too busy; How I regret

that business. The next time I saw him Ellen Stewart and I sat by

his bedside in St.Vincents hospital as he agonizingly died.

Joe Cino was a one man phenomenon —my paragon for the verve,

passion and sheer wonder that a good prudcer must have. Joe was

the virtual foudner of off-off Brodaway. In his tiny Cafe I

saw miriclaes of imgination and power. Landofgod Wilson,

Harry Koutoukas, Dames at Sea and the best Christmas pageant

I have ever seen.

I pwerformed my own brand of blues and songs there several times

and took both male and female lovers there on first dates.

If they like the Cino there was a basis for relationships.

Joe was part of my life too breifly.

He gave till it hurt. He loved till it killed him. He worked

till his face shone with sweat.

He was a roly-poly mench -   and the essenc of amateur -

he loved thea art of te theater simply because it was. Not for

what it cold do for him but for what it did for him - his soul. I

loved him and after 30 years I sitll miss him.

Come back, joe. Lets go on that boat trip toegther.

Al Carmines

Minister: Rev. Al Carmines
400 West 43rd Street #24·N
New York, NY 10036
Telephone 563-5047

Sunday worship 11:00 a.m.
Westside Arts Theater
407 West 43rd Street
New York, NY 10036

I WAS REBORN ON CORNELIA STREET
William M. Hoffman

I guess it was a sign that I had to write this memoir now: yesterday, on a warm early January day in 2006, on Prince Street, in New York City, where I have been living for the last forty years, I ran into Bill Mitchell, who was my first contact with the Caffe Cino.

Bill, a waiter at the Cino and also a dancer, who still lives in Joe Cino's old apartment on Cornelia Street, told me that in 1959 he suggested to Joe, who up till then exhibited paintings in his coffee house and was hosting poetry readings, that he should add plays to the mix, thereby inadvertently setting off a chain of events that led to the founding of one of the most vital theatre movements in America. Most of this I didn't know until yesterday. Damn!

Now Billy was a friend of John Corigliano, the composer, my closest friend and my collaborator on such projects as our opera *The Ghosts of Versailles*. When John and I met Lanford Wilson, who was then called Lance, at a wild party that our brownstone at 25 West 83rd Street collectively threw in 1864, I mean 1964, and Lance mentioned that he had come to New York from Chicago to be a playwright, John immediately thought of his friend Bill Mitchell and the Caffe Cino. Whereupon Lance traveled down to Cornelia Street past the border guards — imaginary — stationed on 14th Street, who guarded the more sedate neighborhoods of Manhattan from the wilder Greenwich Village, and Lance gave unto Joe Cino a manuscript (I think it was *So Long at the Fair*). And applause and accolades soon ensued for Lance, but that is his story.

At the time I was an editor at a small but terrific publisher, Hill & Wang. I was a poet on the side, passionate about the Latin classics, with no interest in writing plays at all, thank you, but I was drawn to the bright lights and the laughter and the applause on Cornelia Street, and before I knew it, I ran away with the circus.

In short order I moved to a tiny studio on Sullivan Street, and wrote lots of intensely lyrical poetry. But one morning I woke up and wrote at one sitting a short story, *Good Night, I Love You*, which was inspired by a conversation I had the night before with Lucy Silvay, who later became an off-off-Broadway star and who is now a brilliant writer. (She was my muse for many years.) The story was almost entirely in dialogue.

If my memory serves me right, Lance was living with me at that moment. He informed me what I had written was a really a one-act play in drag. All I had to do was retype it. I thought he was nuts but I did it anyway.

Which is how I became a playwright. It was that simple. A few months later Joe Cino produced *Good Night, I Love You* on a double bill with my *Saturday Night at the Movies*. I have to tell you I was terrified to see my first play put on. The year was 1965 and I had written about a gay guy who gets all caught up in a fantasy — with a woman he is emotionally but not physically involved with — that he has been knocked up by his boyfriend. Hey, this was five years before Stonewall and forty years before *M. Butterfly* and *Will and Grace*! Gay men were not voicing such things, and many were even not permitting themselves to think such things. I was embarrassed by what I had written and scared to be so publicly queer. But also, dimly aware that I was breaking new ground, I was eager to become one of the performers at the circus on Cornelia Street, no matter what the price.

I don't know where I got the nerve to write such stuff. I was certainly given the courage to do so by the gay material that Lance, in *The Madness of Lady Bright*, and Robert Patrick, in *The Haunted Host*, were turning out. I wouldn't want you to think I was participating in some avant-garde art movement. I had zero interest in avant-garde anything. Invented in 1916 in Zurich, the movement immediately turned to stone. It specialized in nonsense and I wanted desperately to make sense. My heart belonged to the classics, which I saw no reason not to emulate. Nor was I consciously participating in a form of radical politics. I deeply distrusted radical politics. Having grown up on welfare, I couldn't help noticing that the radicals were mainly the richer kids dressing up as the poorer kids. No, I was just trying to portray what I saw around me as best I could.

At the Cino I fit right in, since no one style of writing prevailed. Sure, there were practitioners of the avant-garde, but Lance's and Claris Nelson's lyricism, Bob Patrick's neo-Shavian wit, Bob Heide's pop passion, and Bob Dahdah's brilliant directing of high-gloss musicals were even more popular. And Joe Cino's love of classical music mixed with such old favorites like Kate Smith singing with unashamed patriotic assurance "*God Bless America*" somehow glued what might have been warring factions into a functional family — at least for a while.

I was at home at the Cino and even my dad liked the place. He blended right in. I found out years later that he had been involved as an amateur actor in experimental theatre in Bielsk, a suburb of the legendary Bialystok, in the teens of the last century. He starred in Yiddish in a show called *The Prisoner*. His brother Wolf Younin was also a poet and playwright who was putting on musicals in Yiddish with Molly Picon and Ben Bonus across town on Second Avenue and on Broadway. My dad, a caterer, loved what I was doing and wanted to join in by providing the food. I was too young and shallow to have abetted that. He thought what I was doing was normal! Of course, it was normal, and the Cino was the only place at the time where I felt normal. I loved feeling normal!

Neil Flanagan directed my play. He had starred in *Thank You, Miss Victoria*, a play I wrote after *Good Night, I Love You*. (Bernard Gersten, presently executive producer of the Lincoln Center Theatre, directed him. In my experience there are no degrees of separation.) Linda Eskenas — half wraith, half Medea — created the role of Lisa, and a quintessentially straight actor Michael Griswold was an extraordinarily unlikely Alex. The play was staged on what looked like loft beds at both ends of the shoebox-shaped Cino, with the audience in between them. It was like watching a ping-pong match.

In my recollection, the audience was deeply shocked, but they laughed a lot, or maybe I was shocked, and I was certainly embarrassed to be so "out there."

It strikes me now, on rereading *Good Night, I Love You,* how typical that play is of my work. I still look for lyrical meaning in the small moments of my existence, like a phone call conducted in the dark, and I still like to make people laugh and I still like to write about love. It also strikes me how certain names keep recurring in my history: John Corigliano, Lanford Wilson, Robert Patrick, Lucy Silvay, and, of course, Joe Cino, who gave me permission to be a playwright. These people are the threads of the fabric of my life.

Neil Flanagan in William M. Hoffman's
Thank You, Miss Victoria, 1965

Photo by James D. Gossage

ANGER MANAGEMENT, CINO STYLE
Lucy Silvay

David Starkweather's play, *So, Who's Afraid of Edward Albee?* took full advantage of the Cino's environment as an Italian coffee house with a stage area that moved around, depending on where a given playwright or director wanted it. For the performance, Lee Hickman and I were seated at one of the Cino tables, like any customers. The play began officially when Lee yelled out something like, "When does this damn play start, anyway?" — startling all the real customers. The lights around the Cino dimmed and Johnny Dodd put a spotlight on our table. There was an audible titter, almost a sigh of relief, from the audience, who now understood that Lee's utterance was the opening line of the play they'd come to see.

The play was about the two characters' troubled relationship. The year was 1966, before feminism came into bloom. The female lead was passive and obliging until the play's dénouement when she, played by me, stood up and became angry at the way her boyfriend was treating her. She took the stage and went into a monologue of righteous rage, crying out against all the injustices in her life. It was a feminist play before any of us had heard the word *feminism*.

Here I was, brought up on the tight leash of the '50s, trying to be angry. An angry woman was an anathema. Many off-off-Broadway playwrights had me pegged as an angry woman and cast me in roles where I had to rage at men. I was secretly horrified by this. It was so unattractive. Why was I continually cast in such unappealing parts? What if I got truly angry and people thought I was really like that and were turned off? It was a constant struggle for me. It went against everything I had been trained to be.

All the gay men around the Cino coached me on anger. They explained that the entire one-act piece hinged on the female lead expressing genuine outrage and tried convincing me that I had every right to it. When I finally let loose one night, they were all over me in their praise. It was a release for me the likes of which I'd never known. It gave me a taste for that excised emotion. It also became clear by way of the feelings it awoke how many realities cried for it, how much truth backed it. Unfortunately, for the remainder of the play's run, I wasn't able to recapture the passion of that performance.

Looking back, I see that all those gay men and of course the playwright himself knew more about women's plight than any straight man or woman. They were pushing the envelope toward rabid feminism. Apparently, the gay playwrights, actors, the Cino waiters and habitués were the first to understand that, in our society, a woman getting angry was an imperative. They all sensed the hidden fury of women in general and, in particular, my own.

☙

Once during the run of *The Madness of Lady Bright*, Joe and I were alone together near the espresso machine. I was a twenty-two-year-old actress in my first part. Looking toward the cleavage that I had plumped up under my black scooped dress, Joe said, "Someday, you and I, baby," he pointed back and forth between him and me, "You and I are going to get it on."

With all the gorgeous men at the Cino, this felt like the top compliment. I was also vaguely aware that I wanted his sexual recognition and that Joe sensed that.

Another evening at the Cino, I had just succeeded in filling another monthly scrip for thirty 15-milligram Dexedrine capsules. It was what I needed to get me through the day, no extras. One Saturday after the usual weekend three shows per evening, Joe was cleaning tables and saying to me that he was "wiped." I said, "I have something for you for tomorrow," and withdrew from my purse one 15-milligram Dexedrine capsule. I didn't have a chance to tell him what it was. Without looking at it, Joe popped it into his mouth. It was after one in the morning. "No!" I said, too late.

"No problem, Babe."

"But it's speed!"

"No problem, Babe. Do you have another?"

In a fit of generosity, I gave him two more, thinking they were for tomorrow. He popped them in his mouth, too.

I had never before come across anyone with Joe's sex or drug largesse.

☙

Joe Cino killed himself by committing hara-kiri after his lover's death, and died in 1967. Hara-kiri is done as penance for a shameful act wherein the person committing it cuts himself in several places on the body, including the neck, wrists, belly and genitals. Joe felt he had betrayed his lover. I don't know the details. Despite the tremendous loss of blood, Joe lived for three days at St. Vincent's Hospital in Greenwich Village. The hospital reported that never in their history had they received so many calls inquiring about a patient's status. I myself called twice every day. On the morning of the third day Joe awoke in good spirits and asked for a breakfast of bacon and eggs. Shortly afterward he died.

That night I walked alone over to the Cino and found it filled with other Cino regulars. They were all sitting silently with their own thoughts at the café tables. The only sound in the café was that of people weeping. Someone would put his head in his arms on the table and cry for a while, then sit up and keep sitting there, staring into space. No one on Earth was loved more than Joe.

JOE'S GIFT TO THE WORLD
Magie Dominic

I've written about The Caffe Cino on previous occasions, attempting to illuminate something indefinable — for a 1985 off-off-Broadway exhibition I curated for *Lincoln Center Library for the Performing Arts*; for a Canadian quarterly; and in 2002 I published a memoir, *The Queen of Peace Room*, documenting my life at the Caffe, my friendship with Joe and the people there, and my life as an actress. Kenny Burgess, an artist who worked with Joe and created the only theatre posters to chronicle that era, was my daughter's godfather. Ellen Stewart is her godmother. To say that the Cino was like family would be inaccurate. The Caffe Cino *was* my family. I've maintained friendships with designers, actors, and playwrights for forty years.

Joe Cino arrived in New York from Buffalo in 1948, during a blizzard, worked two jobs, and opened the Caffe in December 1958. He was 26. The Caffe was Joe's gift to the world. At 31 Cornelia Street.

One morning Joe called me at home.

"They're doing the umbrellas for *Dames at Sea*," he said, "and I won't let anyone touch them until you get here. Come in now," and he hung up.

I took the subway not knowing what "*umbrellas*" meant. It could have been like "*Ella*," Joe's word for everything. Anything could be *Ella*.

Dames at Sea was a thirty-minute musical directed by Robert Dahdah, on an eight-foot stage with a very young Bernadette Peters. I spent hours gluing silver sequins to open plastic umbrellas.

Open umbrellas were forbidden, but plastic bubbles with magic raindrops were allowed, for "Raining in My Heart," Bernadette's signature song. Thousands of umbrellas in other productions, in other countries, had sequins glued to plastic. This is how it originated.

Dames at Sea played to packed houses for two months. The room was officially full when two people were seated on top of the cigarette machine. It was the longest run in Cino history. Financial success for an entire summer. Eight weeks later a producer moved it to a large theatre, Carol Burnett saw it, invited Bernadette on her show and the rest is history. Joe would have let *Dames at Sea* run for fifty years if he'd been given a choice. But he wasn't.

One summer Charles Stanley came flying from the Caffe as I walked up Cornelia, said the night's production had canceled. We were doing the comic book *Snow White*, and I was in it. I asked what part he wanted me to play. "*Snow White*," he

Magie Dominic surrounded by *(clockwise, from top left)*:
Steve Van Vost (Davis), Joe Cino, Helen Hanft, Jack Quinn, Tom Eyen,
John (now Genji) Schmeder, and Charles Stanley
on Josef Bush's set for *Why Hanna's Skirt Won't Stay Down*, 1965

Photo by James D. Gossage

said, as we ran through the middle of the street. The playwright Harry Koutoukas was in costume and make-up as the wicked stepmother. I entered the comic book as one would enter a building. In the fleeing through the forest scene, Robert Patrick, hiding behind a white curtain, waved plastic ferns in my face with sheer franticness, as if he were being chased by demons. Charles created a lightning storm, accompanied by a blaring aria, and I raced from one end of the tiny stage to the other, back and forth and back and forth, until I collapsed, to the floor, fourteen times a week, for two weeks. And every night, Kenny, as a forest creature, knelt beside me as I moved silently and slowly, with my right hand, imaginary branches, so we could see the imaginary house in the imaginary clearing. I was never taught how to do this. I knew it instinctively. BUT THAT'S ANOTHER STORY.

JOE CINO'S KALEIDOSCOPIC STEWPOT
Dan Leach

Memory is a trickster, more so after forty years, particularly when swathed in the romanticism of youthful endeavor and layered beneath a lifetime of quite disparate pursuits. Perhaps no harm is done delving, but only so long as the findings aren't identified with objective fact.

The aura of phantasmagoria that the Caffe Cino exuded epitomized the '60s. Physically, I recall a long, narrow street level "cave" encrusted, ceiling and walls, with layers of Christmas lights in which "floated" a moveable platform stage amenable to whatever configuration the featured playwright/director needed, surrounded variously by small café tables and chairs. Situated amidst the twinkling lights were theatre spots controlled from a booth at the rear of this storefront psychedelia. It was probably a fire hazard. It was definitely a benevolent witches' cauldron that brewed, nightly, magical potions of varying intensities. The major conjurer was Joe Cino, who, because he wanted the theatre artists to do their thing, rarely intruded. As a budding actor focused primarily on my role in the play at hand, I have only the vaguest memories of him.

The play was George Birimisa's *Daddy Violet*, a one-act meditation on the personal sources of the then-raging war in Vietnam, that had evolved from improvisations on Birimisa's ideas, which our three-person cast (that included the author as actor and director, myself, and an actress) had wrestled with over a period of several months. Birimisa's final script and direction was, in language and form, quite set, although there were moments throughout of direct audience engagement. The casualness of the beginning, with George (as The Director) sweeping the stage and calling to us, the actors, to come onstage to start working on our acting exercises — exercises that led us into quite personal insights — lured the audience into believing they were simply watching actors improvise. As our emerging personal realizations provoked us to confront our own responsibility in the Vietnam debacle, the audience members were hit, as the play climaxed, with their own culpability.

The theatrical device of audience participation may go back to early cabaret and vaudeville, but I suspect that at least one of our thrusts in that direction might have been a first. At one point, due to a "discovery" engendered by an acting exercise, my character (The Actor) realizes his homosexuality, flits into the audience, flings himself onto the lap of the straightest-looking guy visible, and, running his hand through the unsuspecting guy's hair, commences a seduction. That we didn't get punched or walked out on or arrested is a testament to either the liberality of the times or the certain shock and seduction of the piece. This was, after all, pre-Stonewall.

Aside from the Caffe Cino stint, we played across the country and in Canada, in everything from legit theatres and university festivals to Protestant churches, without any violent confrontation. Only once, at the University of British Columbia in Vancouver, did students, armed with the published script, challenge our faux improvisation by calling out our lines from the audience just before we said them.

Our run at the Caffe Cino, which was one of the four "name" off-off-Broadway venues along with Ellen Stewart's La Mama E.T.C. (then on 2nd Avenue near 8th Street, one flight up), Al Carmine's Judson Church, and Ralph Cook's Theatre Genesis at St. Marks-in-the-Bowery, followed close on the heels of *Dames at Sea* starring the then unknown (though not for long) Bernadette Peters. The Caffe Cino was also the testing ground for the early work of Lanford Wilson, Leonard Melfi, Ron Tavel, Ron Link and a host of others.

This kaleidoscopic stewpot, itself an "installation" before the art world had even coined the term, bubbled up from Joe Cino's imaginative fantasy and spilled the riches out into a larger world of American theatre. And, in the process, became theatrical history.

CINO PEOPLE
Robert Patrick

For all the glory of the work done there, it was people who made the Cino my heart's home. Joe himself, all smiles and smells and wry compassion. Neil Flanagan, slick and flip, secretly fatherly. Andy Milligan, sharp and gruff, at heart an insecure puppy. Kenny Burgess, who seemed a drawling hick but was so sophisticated it took time to sink in. Pixie-pretty Johnny Dodd, with hands strong enough to hang big light-pipes yet sensitive enough to tint actors without your noticing. Bob Dahdah, a one-man university of acting, directing, good manners. Painter neighbor Esther Travers, who inspired us by finding us inspiring. Dancer Tommy Garland, so disciplined that he indulged his alcoholism only with his pay as a Cino waiter.

Graceful camel Charles Stanley; when I called men and women to tell them he had died, fully half gasped, "He was my lover, you know." Charles Loubier and Joe Davies, ancient friends of Joe's carrying an air of an unknowable private past. Matt Baylor, movie-star handsome and hound-dog loyal to Joe. Dishwasher Janet Hessler sang like Judy Garland but disdained any career. Show-business critic Judith Gayle Harris gave Joe all her evening gowns for costumes. German countess and silent-film actress Ruth Landshoff Yorck breathed intoxicating old-world ennui. Claris Nelson, protectively pert, had eyes sharper than baby teeth. David Starkweather, isolated by an immeasurable I.Q. Johnny Torrey, Joe's stunning, cunning lover, hooked us up a free phone and electricity for Johnny Dodd's lights. Michael Smith, worldly in a brand-new world he helped make. Beautiful boys Keith Carsey, Jim Jennings, Michael Warren Powell, John Gilman who became an authority on collectibles, Louis Waldon who went on to Warhol, Dean Selmier who claimed to have been a C.I.A. hit-man, and most beautiful, Steven Davis (Van Vost), who looked like the "Oscar" and could steal a show from even prima diva Helen Hanft, whose perfectly ordinary New York accent escalated onstage into an idiom that inspired writer Tom Eyen, whose plays were as angry as he was suave. Dreamboat dramatists Doric Wilson, Lanford Wilson, Paul Foster, Sam Shepard, William Hoffman, Daniel Clark ornamented the room like their plays ornamented the stage.

Gorgeous Magie Dominic, Connie Clark, Mari-Claire Charba, Lucy Silvay, Deborah Lee, quietly became, respectively, a poet, a scholar, two psychotherapists, and a producer. Great actresses Jacque Lynn Colton and Mary Boylan, whose professionalism shone like gemstones. Eccentric Cino literary originals, H. M. Koutoukas, Donald Kvares, Bob Heide, and Haal Borske, whose conversation sparkled like their plays. Prematurely mature Marshall Mason and eternally childlike Rev. Al Carmines, who both cared so much for Joe. Visitors like Ellen Stewart who gave Joe strength and support, and Jerome Ragni whom Joe talked into doing *Hair*. And I? I reveled to be let work for and among these living myths. Magie Dominic described me, "on the phone, at the door, beside a table, and writing a play all simultaneously."

There were as many Cinos as people who came there. It was a kaleidoscope. It will take a lot of these "memoirs" to give any coherent picture of what the Cino was like. This Ground Zero of the 1960s was a coffee-house, a theatre, a brothel, a temple, a flophouse, a dope-ring, a launching-pad, an insane asylum, a safe-house, and a sleeper cell for an unnamed revolution.

RUNNING THE BALLS
Michael Warren Powell

Michael Warren Powell, in addition to creating roles in dozens of plays by some of America's major playwrights, was Artistic Director of the Circle Repertory Lab, then of Circle East Theater Company, as well as of the El Tribu Theatre Company on Ibiza. In this memory of the Cino, he puts to rest a rumor concerning a backstage encounter between himself and Joe Cino.

The composer John Corigliano brought me and the future playwrights Lanford Wilson and William M. Hoffman to the Cino in 1963. We saw Ionesco's *The Lesson* or *The Chairs*. In Chicago, Lanford and I had been freelance designers, I of clothes and Lanford of packaging. We didn't want to be designers, so we came to New York. After seeing the Ionesco, I decided I wanted to be an actor and Lanford that he wanted to be a playwright. Joe Cino said to Lanford, "Okay. You write a play for him and do it here." We thought that was the most marvelous suggestion. It would never have occurred to us. So Lanford wrote *So Long at the Fair* for me. The two of us and Robert Patrick moved director Glenn DuBose's couch in a truck to the Cino for scenery. The play is about a girl trying to seduce a shy boy (me). Instead he kills her and folds her body up in the hide-a-bed sofa. One snowy night there were only three people in the audience — a sailor who was drunk, a woman, and her teenage son. The play was filthy. Sample lines:

GIRL: I'm still a virgin. No one can break my titanic membrane.
BOY: That's "tympanic." And it's in your ear.

The woman put her hands over her son's ears and left. The sailor fell asleep. We looked over at Joe and he made a motion, "Continue on." We continued.

Lanford and I had no money, so we lived at the Cino and slept on the couch until I gave in and took a job with the interior decorator, Leona Kahn (mother of the actor Irving Metzman), and Lanford as a clerk at the Americana (which he described as "the box that Disneyland came in").

At the Cino, everyone did everything. I acted in lots of plays, designed costumes for some. Paul Foster's *Balls* was a sort of puppet show with recorded dialogue. All the audience saw was two illuminated ping-pong balls swinging in darkness. I stood behind a black scrim and operated the balls. Their moves were rigidly choreographed. Once the play started, neither of my hands was ever free. I could see the audience through the scrim, but they couldn't see me.

Joe Cino came up to me one night and pulled my pants down. I didn't wear underwear in those days. I was naked from the waist down. I couldn't let go of the balls. Joe Cino blew me. When I came, the balls went wild, swinging every which way. It was supposed to be a very somber show, you see. Lanford said afterward, "What happened?" and Paul Foster was puzzled.

I didn't blame him. But I couldn't tell them then what had happened.

ON AGGRESSION
Ronald Tavel

Vinyl was the first of a projected eight plays inspired by the then-current subject *On Aggression*, and principally a speculation on how the atrocities of WWII could have taken place and just what would it take to get people to torture each other (and get tortured). Answer: have someone in authority (like a director) simply tell them to do it.

Of the eight planned plays, using the same characters (roughly, members of an S-M club) appearing in different guises, only *Vinyl* and *Vinyl Visits an FM Station* were written and produced before I turned to other assignments.

I also knew that the audience and critics would blithely watch performers get tortured right in front of them and assume it was all a harmless ritual. It wasn't — a number of the actors had to go to St. Vincent's Hospital amidst complaints that the doctor character (Mary Woronov) got continually carried away.

Under Harvey "Doc Harv" Tavel's precise direction at the Caffe Cino, the one-acter was choreographed by the late Ron Pratt and highlighted by a breathtaking dance in which Raymond Edwards, at its climax, executed a daring spin and threw a dart at a board inches above the front row seats. My heart in my mouth every night, I asked Ray what would happen if he missed one night and the dart hit a spectator in the face. He said, "I never miss."

And at one performance, a young audience member stood, lifted his chair, and screaming, "She's not real! She's not real," flung it at Mary. But she was, and still is, real.

The two-week show sold out to standing room only at the Caffe Cino and Charles Stanley asked the cast to extend the run. But since he was pocketing the contributions intended for the cast, and they were nursing more tangible wounds, they declined. Near the end of the run, Harvey Tavel crossed Washington Square on his way home and when he bent to drink from a water fountain, two shadowy figures approached him. One seethed, "Fifty cent! No scream!" He turned toward them with all of *Vinyl* in his face and both wannabe muggers dropped back and took quickly to their heels.

SUCCEED OR FAIL
WITHOUT RECRIMINATION
Jennie Ventriss

My memories of the Cino are very joyful. Joe Cino was an honest and loving man. The Cino's policy was to pass the hat after each performance. Several years after appearing there, I was an audience member at the Cino when Joe came up to me with an envelope containing about $10 — money which he said was due me from *Ludlow Fair*. He said after tabulation it was money I earned, and he had kept it in trust for me. This was a complete surprise as every evening we collected our money. I always felt protected and cared for at the Caffe. Gay or straight, everyone was an equal and I never felt any animosity from anyone. There were a lot of flamboyant characters but they were fun and basically sweet. Oddly perhaps, the early '60s were an era of innocence. I was a middle-class woman from Chicago, separated from my husband and seeking a career in the professional theatre. The Cino was a warm and safe haven that prepared me for my subsequent life in the theatre.

The play was the début of *Ludlow Fair* and I played Agnes, a girl lost because of her lack of self esteem. Agnes was constantly saying "fuck." Neil Flanagan, the director, saw I was having a difficult time saying the word. He sent me home with an assignment: to repeat the horrid word until it rolled easily and unselfconsciously off my tongue. I was diligent to the point that it became an integral part of my vocabulary. The play was a success and I garnered some personal accolades and made some wonderful friends.

At the Cino testing ground we could succeed or fail without recrimination. Thank you, Joe. Thank you, Neil.

CINO CUISINO
Walter Michael Harris

The Harris family moved to Florida in 1957 because Dad had been there in the Army and it seemed like a nice place to live.

My parents, actors with the local little theater, encouraged us kids to become thespians, which we did with great enthusiasm. Before long we were cultivating home-grown musical comedies in our Florida garage, which we transformed into a popular neighborhood theater. Our first scripts were based on the liner notes from Broadway show albums. Soon we moved up to the harder stuff — writing our own.

Hard bit by "the bug," we made a family decision to head North and find the bright lights of Broadway. My Dad was the advance scout. He went ahead of the family by several months, saving money by writing home on anything handy — placemats, the backs of envelopes, and Caffe Cino menus.

Dad's lack of proper stationery exposed our young imaginations to the rococo nomenclature of the Caffe Cino. The language of espresso was fascinating: "Cappuccino!" "Grenadine!" "Antipasto!" and my personal favorite, "Doppio!" The Greco-Roman illustrations brought an exciting, enticing touch of old Europe to our Florida home.

Soon we followed Dad to the Big Apple. We arrived in New York a band of gypsies, the youngest barely walking, the oldest barely a teen. It was early autumn 1964, Kennedy was gone, and the Beatles were burning up the charts. Arriving in New York in late October, we saw autumn leaves and subways for the first time. We set up camp in a one-room, fifth-floor walkup apartment, enrolled in school and pounded the pavement with our portfolios.

One evening, with the first breath of winter in the air, Mom led us on the first of many cross-town walks from the Lower East Side. Like ducklings, we six kids followed her up St. Marks Place, past The Five Spot, where Dave Brubeck held forth nightly, past Cooper Union, where our great-grandfather taught — past the "art movie house" on 8th Street, and across the borderline of 5th Avenue. There "The Village" proper began, past Washington Square and across legendary Bleecker Street and, finally, to the place with the funny menus.

We could see it from the end of the block — twinkle lights and a warm orange glow spilling out into Cornelia Street in the night air. Inside was a world of wonder. The delicious aroma of coffee, the lilt of opera, the strange hissing sound of Joe Cino's magic espresso machine and millions of colorful twinkle lights gave the place

A Caffe Cino Menu, illustrated and illuminated by M. Wiley
Menu provided through the courtesy of John Borske

Walter's mother, Ann Harris, as Starina in son George III's show,
Angels of Light, in 1974

Photogrrapher unknown

the air of Charlie's Chocolate Factory, or Café Society in Paris. The efficient, effeminate waiters deftly maneuvered around the tiny tables, swishing by with giant platters of food and exotic drinks. The tiny stage in the middle of the room made us feel right at home. The play that evening was *Balls* by Paul Foster. We thought it was about ping-pong balls and enjoyed it very much.

Thinking this must be one of those grown-up liquor places where an eleven-year-old kid like me had to order Shirley Temples or hot chocolate, I ordered the chocolate. A steamy, creamy concoction laced with some exotic flavor (hazelnut?) which conjured up images of grinning, coal-black natives harvesting cocoa beans on some far-off plantation and singing work songs. All this from the first sip! The whipped-cream topping was sprinkled with nutmeg, garnished with chocolate sprinkles and topped off with a twist of orange and a huge maraschino cherry.

Now, THIS was *CHOCOLATE!*

Eager to learn more about the menu, we ordered sandwiches. Mine was ham, which came with curled edges. I thought it was great that they had somehow developed a method of curling the edges of the bread in such a way that it seemed lightly toasted. The sandwich came with thin slices of Roma tomatoes and mustard that was not French's. Washed down with a gulp of Congo chocolate, it was nothing short of divine.

Last came the splendid dessert tray, displayed with a flourish by our waiter. We gleefully sampled the exotic pastries we read about on the funny menus. My favorite was the Napoleon, with its layers of crunchy crust and swizzly icing on top. In Florida we had Ho-Ho's and Ding Dongs, but they paled in comparison to the real deal.

Over the course of the next year I would become an expert on the Cino cuisine. In winter it was hot chocolate and Napoleons. In the summer it was the delicious Orange Blossom drink that captured my imagination. I could not believe anything could taste so good. I slurped them down in frenzied gulps, pulling at my straw to capture the last few sweet drops of chilled nectar. The curly-edged ham sandwich remained my favorite no matter the season.

That first night we learned about olives and opera, grenadine and gender fuck. The food was an integral part of the wildly creative atmosphere. Having seen the Cino at age eleven, how could I go back to the Catholic Church? Joe Cino became our swishy High Priest, celebrating his counterculture Mass from behind the counter, dispensing culture, a generous man who accepted us as family.

A lingering image of our first night at the Caffe Cino also had to do with food. Walking east from the Cino, we passed the Zemperelli Brothers Bakery. The smell of fresh-baked Italian bread welcomed us to Greenwich Village as we made our way home in the chill night air.

Right: Walter's father, George Harris II, the man who ran away with the circus and brought along his wife and six children, in a "Beyond the Fringe" skit, 1966 *Spring Horror Show* at the Cino

Left: Walter appeared as Kenny in Lanford Wilson's *The Sandcastle* at the Cino, 1965

Photos by James D. Gossage, provided through the courtesy of Robert Patrick

Walter Michael Harris, on the right, with his brother George Harris III, during Ellen Stewart's Young Playwrights Series, 1966

At 16, Walter was the youngest member of the cast of *Hair* on Broadway, cast by Cino colleague Tom O'Horgan to sing "What a Piece of Work is Man"

As "Hibiscus," George III later founded San Francisco's Cockettes

At 18, George III was, in Robert Patrick's words, "the famous blond sticking the famous flower into the famous rifle at the Pentagon"

Bernie Boston Photography, 1967

By 1968, Hibiscus had completely (if temporarily) taken over George Harris III

Photo by Ingeborg Gerdes

Photos provided through the courtesy of Ann Harris, mother of Walter and George III

THIS IS CRAZY
Larry Loonin

Letter to Robert Patrick,
October 10, 2005

Dear Robert,

This is crazy. Really crazy. I directed *Hello Out There* with Roy Levine at the Cino. I had done the show at Brooklyn College and Joe gave me two weekends to do it at the Cino. Roy, who later directed *MacBird* at Luggoff's place on Bleecker, was a little nuts. He didn't show up for the second performance on a Saturday night during the first weekend. The stage manager of the show was Joel Zwick, who stage managed the show at Brooklyn College. I was doing another show elsewhere and Joel stepped in and took over the show for the second weekend. (Joel became a TV director and later directed *My Big Fat Greek Wedding*, and many other things). Anyway, Joel got this actor (I didn't know until you wrote this note to me that it was Pacino) and the show went on. Wow!

I got to know Al because of other events. He dated Jill Clayburgh for awhile and I was directing her at the Brooklyn Academy of Music in *The Innocent Party*. The other actress in the show was Stockard Channing. Anyway, one night Pacino tells me that he was once in a show I directed and he and I try to figure out what the show was. We concluded that we must be making a mistake. This is incredible. Do you have the program for that show? You will see that I was the director.

I can recall my conversation with Pacino in 1969 when he was trying to recall how he might have known me. I'm now wondering if Joel Zwick knows that the "kid" he got to go on during that weekend was Pacino. Roy Levine actually died in California after meeting with Joel sometime in the early 70's.

I do come in contact with Pacino (though never at an arranged meeting) and can't wait to tell him.

Larry

PLAY IT FOR THE WALLS
Crystal Field

I never performed at the Caffe Cino, but I attended many performances there. I remember that Joe said, when there was no audience, "Play it for the walls," and as far as I know, there never was a cancellation of a performance at the Caffe Cino. I did a fundraiser for the Cino, once, at La Mama. I saw the première of *Dames at Sea* with Bernadette Peters, which I loved very much. I saw Charles Stanley perform and we actually named one of our Theaters after him, for about ten years.

But the most important person I found there was John P. Dodd (Johnny Dodd), Lighting Designer extraordinaire. He lit all my shows (the ones I directed) at TNC and before that at the Judson Church. He was a genius with light. He could light a show with clip lights and make it look like a Broadway production. He could light with anything from a computer board to a flashlight. He made light magic. Johnny died young, of AIDS, the Twentieth-Century plague. But before he left us, he had put his mark on stage lighting in the USA. I shall never forget him. Every beam of light, from a firefly, to a 6 x 12 Leko, to the beam of light from the clouds to the Earth, spells Johnny Dodd in my book.

CRYSTAL FIELD
EXECUTIVE DIRECTOR
THEATER FOR THE NEW CITY

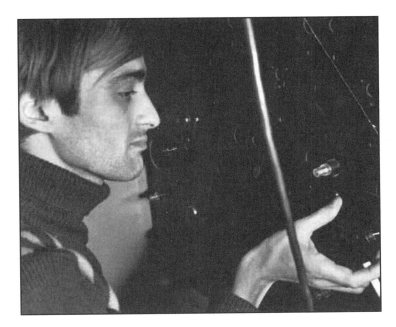

Johnny Dodd at his lightboard

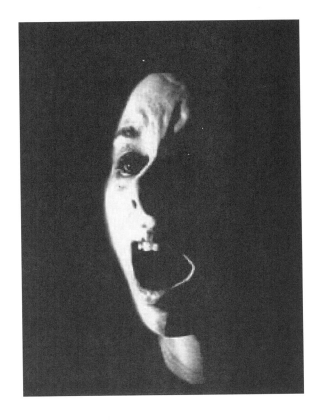

Linda Eskenas, lit by Johnny Dodd
with one bulb

Photos by James D. Gossage

ABOUT JOHNNY DODD
Michael Smith

Lighting designer extraordinaire John P. Dodd worked with a matchless range of artists in the downtown performance world in the '60s when theatre and dance were being made new. Light is the medium of performance, which cannot be seen without it. He made it intensely expressive with intuitively conceptual designs that challenged convention and made a virtue of a necessary minimalism.

Dodd came to New York after putting himself through high school in Indianapolis and naturally gravitated to Greenwich Village. Exploring the streets he encountered Joe Cino standing outside his café on Cornelia Street and immediately recognized a soulmate. Going to work as a waiter at the Caffe Cino, he soon started doing the lights whenever resident designer Jon Torrey was otherwise engaged. This brought him into collaboration with a generation of directors and playwrights who were freshly empowered by the availability of the Cino's modest stage.

Building on an apprenticeship with light-master Nikola Cernovich, Dodd branched out to light a season of plays for Albee-Barr-Wilder's Playwrights' Unit, ground-breaking plays at Judson, La Mama, and Theatre Genesis and dance at Judson and beyond, touring Europe and North America with La Mama Troupe and Tom O'Horgan's New Troupe. As the scene expanded, so did he. The catalogue of his oeuvre fills many pages.

To the outsider, light is like magic, bathing the stage as if emanating directly from the auteur's intention. Lighting work is often seen as "tech," more craft than art. It was especially hard work in the early days, when venues were ill-equipped and setting up lights for a show involved staying up all night running cable, improvising circuits, hefting heavy instruments onto precarious pipes. Anyone who worked with Dodd can attest to his intensity and commitment, and he pushed many small theatres to improve their equipment. As a designer he had strong ideas, sometimes at odds with directors' preconceptions, and put himself on the line to realize them. Seldom an easy collaborator, he contributed a wild lyric energy that could drive the performance to unanticipated levels.

Most of his work was done in the days before computer lightboards, when the long mechanical levers of autotransformer dimmers permitted a hands-on finesse and precision that is now largely lost. Dodd's great innovation was to support the performance with moment-to-moment light changes, some so subtle as to be unnoticed, others bold and in-your-face. Color could bloom with the dynamics of music, light intensify with rising emotion or linger on a captivating image. Sympathetic actors could feel him responding to their impulses, and his approach opened the door to an exhilarating immediacy.

He went on to light Robert Wilson's memorable *Deafman Glance* at BAM, rock tours with Tim Curry and the New York Dolls, Black New World, industrial shows, shows on Broadway and in London's West End. His generosity was legendary: when Judith Malina and Hanon Reznikov opened a new Living Theatre on East 3rd Street, he set them up with lights and dimmers in memory of Julian Beck's inimitable artistry. Throughout a creative career spanning three decades, he fearlessly embodied the anarchic free spirit of pure visionary spontaneity, respecting no authority but the quest for beauty.

> *One of the most gratifying moments of my life was when Johnny let me run his lights for Robert Heide's* Moon *one night when he had to be away. He returned halfway through the second show and stood in the street-door watching. One of the actors played a scene with a little less intensity than usual, so I found myself raising the light level to "goose" the moment up. Having done that, I found it was necessary to make small adjustments throughout. I was terrified after the show as Johnny walked the length of the Caffe back to the lightboard. I had visions of him thrusting my treacherous hands into the jerry-rigged lightboard and electrocuting me for deviating from his meticulous lighting plot. Instead, he took my hands, turned them over, said, "You have beautiful hands," and tore his lighting-plot into confetti. It was the first time that I felt I might not be entirely out of place among the masterful Cino artists whom I worshipped.*
>
> *Robert Patrick*

George Linjeris in Robert Patrick's *Indecent Exposure*, directed by Lanford Wilson, lit by Johnny Dodd with one bulb, September 1966

Photo by James D. Gossage

ABOUT MICHAEL SMITH
Larry Loonin

Michael Smith has been described as the father, and the godfather, and the grand patron, of off-off-Broadway. He is even credited with naming it. When he wrote drama criticism for The Village Voice *during the 1960s, he broke new ground, not only following the standard route of making and breaking others' careers, but writing plays as boldly experimental as those anyone else was writing. The following letter, which reads like the kind of tribute you would like someone to deliver at your funeral, is the text of a letter written by Larry Loonin to Robert Patrick on December 19, 2005, the morning after Michael Smith's presentation at the Coffeehouse Chronicles at La Mama. Michael remains, as we go to press, very much alive. Two of his short plays appear later in this volume.*

THE EDITORS

Robert,

I just wanted to let you know how wonderful Michael was yesterday at La Mama. We all learned so much about him and the funny thing is we all thought we knew so much before.

But the biggest impact for many, as we heard him talk, was the role he played in off-off-Broadway. Yes, that was the way it happened and how it happened.

Michael didn't see himself as a critic (yes, we knew that, but didn't really appreciate how this was working in the scheme of things). He made a great effort to see everything and report on what he saw from his own perspective and not pretend to be some sort of *tabula rasa*. He wasn't warm and fuzzy about what he saw, but he tended to want to have a good time when he went to the theater, and often remarked about what "worked" for him.

Michael was very generous (as always) with his give-and-take from the audience and, in particular, toward Jerry Tallmer who had served as an early mentor.

He put his slides to great use. Many were of plays he wrote or directed "out of town," but he always had something interesting to say about the production without bragging or celebrating a brilliant production.

The afternoon was indeed different and very special.

LARRY

THE HYMN OF THE EVENING
Sandra Bigtree

Norma Bigtree, who played Mona in *Dames at Sea* throughout the play's Cino run (and my older sister) phoned home to Syracuse one night telling Mom to get me on the next bus to New York. Bernadette Peters had left the show and a replacement was needed to play Ruby, the show's romantic lead, within forty-eight hours. I blinked, and there I was straddling that Greyhound (as Chuck Berry once said *en route* to that Promised Land), staring wide-eyed into the seat ahead for six hours before pulling in to the Port Authority. I arrived at the Cino by late morning. The audition was a blur, for Bob Dahdah and James Wise had swept me right into the swirl of rehearsals for a show opening that next evening — even though, like Ruby, the character I was to play, I was already a day into its plot.

The Caffe was reminiscent of a 1930s movie set: everything was black and white, shadows settling everywhere, but the sparkles made everything glitter. Arriving guests seated themselves in a room that wrapped around a small square stage; mirrors served as its backdrop leaving everything exposed, for there were no curtains behind which to hide. The audience was unwittingly reflected back onto themselves, while at the same time "appearing" with us on stage — dissolving any distance that safely divided the audience from the performer. Senses were piqued with the smell of fresh-ground espresso beans, and visually enhanced by the sweet delights of sculpted Italian pastries. On one occasion, I remember watching Joe carefully balance a tray of those luscious goodies in one hand — ready to serve the uptown crowd — while flicking off a cockroach with his other. He then emerged from his kitchen, reached up into the ceiling, setting into motion and clatter all his hanging paraphernalia to announce the evening's performance. Turning around he passed that big poster with the unsettling gaze of Jean Harlow — her eyes frozen in a decade we could only imagine through movies.

The black-and-white mentality of the post-war 1950s was my childhood (quite a stretch for a Mohawk), and I literally grew up inside those black-and-white studio sets. I performed with my older sisters, Jeanne and Norma, as "The Bigtrees," singing and dancing on local TV and radio from 1951 to 1962. I was the good little Bigtree girl who sang the hymn of the morning each week — right in the "heart" of the traditional Iroquois. I watched the transformation from a local, somewhat diversified community expression as it collapsed into one collective syndicated media voice, not really belonging to anyone. By 1966, I was already pretty jaded.

But something was new and exciting at the Cino. There obviously was a sense of purpose to the shows other than being there for sheer entertainment, although entertained we were!

I've since heard the stories of drug use and conflict, but this was never displayed in front of me. It may be true. Oppression is effective in bringing out the very worst in people. Once identities have been mutilated, subdued and ridiculed, people are left broken and it's a long fight scrambling to reassemble the pieces. Being an urban Mohawk woman, I understand oppression. Joe Cino, however, took that courageous first step to finally provide the gay community with an outlet to start speaking — speaking to everybody. Thereby enriching our WHOLE community. His brilliance was in sharing it over a cup of coffee.

THE PLAYWRIGHT WAS ROYALTY
Bob Shields

I should point out that my role in this project is as a straight actor working in what is, apparently, now perceived as the Birthplace of Gay Theater. Who knew? Let me assure my heterosexual brethren that I never, personally, experienced a bunch of guys, in rubber pants, running around going "Woo-Woo." It was a theater. I was in love with the room. Who you walked out the door with was your business. And still is. Anyone who was there to work was treated with respect.

I had more fun acting at the Caffe Cino than at any other time, or place, in my career. In the off-off-Broadway scene of the 1960s, the playwright was royalty. The entire movement was one big workshop for writers, and their words were what stirred our blood. It was a happier time when creators with something to say put it on a page and let interpreters discover the truth in front of an audience. We were treated as (kind of) equal collaborators, exploring the human condition, not as spokespersons for a social cause. I wanted to be part of the playwright's work, not use it to land a part in a TV series. I was. And I did not. And I wouldn't have it any other way.

That said, of the five-and-a-half productions in which I performed at the Cino, two were scripted (Robert Patrick's *The Warhol Machine* and Haal Borske's *The Brown Crown*). The others were on a different kind of page. These were: *Snow White,* script by Walt Disney Comics; *Faust,* script by Classics Illustrated Comics; *Archie*, script by Archie Comics, and *Vultures Over Miami*, script by the genius that was Charles Stanley.

In 1980, I was working on Buck Henry's film *The First Family*. I played the White House photographer (seven paid weeks, edited to thirty seconds of screen time) and got to work with, among others, the comic actor Fred Willard. We were talking one day about our backgrounds in New York in the 60s and, when I mentioned the Cino, he said, "Oh yeah, I went to see *Snow White* there one night and ended up being a dwarf." I recruited him that night. That's what it was like. This production was *Snow White And The Anywhere From Four To Sixteen Dwarves*. I don't know what this show was like for the audience since, at any given performance, we shanghaied as many of them as we could. Magie Dominic played the title role, Bob Patrick was Doc and David Starkweather sneezed, inspirationally, as, well — who else? I was Grumpy. (For today's actors: I was doing a mood piece about a vertically-challenged miner with rage issues.) The rest of the group were "Hey, you wanna be a dwarf?" respondents. I'm hoping the full cast is listed elsewhere because I'm running out of space but, to this day, whenever some other ass tries to out-pompous me, I channel Tommy Garland (as the Huntsman) bowing to Queen Koutoukas and say "Yes, Your High Nose."

Basic rules of doing a comic-book show:

1. Always keep the comic book in sight;
2. Never do a comic book that is written to be "funny" (such as *Archie*);
3. Get Bob Patrick out of his apartment and get him involved;
4. And, finally, have Magie Dominic play the lead.

This was as close as my real world ever came to "Come on, kids, let's put on a show."

A KID AT THE CINO:
A DISTANT, DISTINCT MEMORY
Perry Brass

Going into the Caffe Cino was like entering an Aladdin's cave of treasures. The walls glittered with selected ephemera, effeminata (images gilding the glamour of starlets, fabled celluloid queens and gods, including vintage *Photoplay* spreads of marabou mules, Grable gams, torpedo cleavage, assorted eyeball candy and anatomical bulges; the whole voluptuous schmear of American pop culture before it became marketed all the way down to worthlessness: this was a genuine altar of worship); and, inside, an effusion of low-lit, real-flesh NewYorkiana. Its characters, its players. New York; the '60s. Where all was possible.

It was.

I was barely nineteen; it was 1966, and I remember virtually every remarkable moment of it, as you will from that nascent epoch in your life. The sounds when you entered: anything that struck Joe Cino's fancy, from opera to Elvis. Joe himself, dark, handsome, behind the espresso machine, making coffee, dishing out cannolis; and the plays. Vividly I remember them; strikingly, like nothing else: this rumbling detonation of talent. Lanford Wilson's *The Madness of Lady Bright*, I saw it twice with Neil Flanagan as the Lady; Robert Heide's *Moon*, with that tense, bewitching silence of gay becoming in it; Wilson's genius in *The Rimers of Eldritch*; Tom Eyen's *Sarah B. Divine*; and numerous gay plays by a young, shy Robert Patrick, a grinning, hunky Doric Wilson, and a young playwright from New Orleans named Charles Kerbs who became my friend. But most breathtakingly, I recall Jeff Weiss's *A Funny Walk Home* which I saw several times, absorbing his performance as if he were doing it only for me, because it was all about being a young gay man; a small-town adolescence; his coming fully, rebelliously into himself.

It was my story. I knew it. Honest, flagrant, spitting in lots of faces. I loved it because it talked loudly about being attracted to men, when most people could barely whisper about it. But it could be more than whispered about at the Cino: it could be celebrated. It was part of the bigger life of New York, this life with its youthful, undeniable glamour, from the walk-ups of the Lower East Side to the penthouses of the Upper; I was starting to figure some of that out, with boyfriends in both places. But you could have both easily then, if you were part of the wondrous country of New York art. If you were openly curious: and the Cino with its wise, unflinching eyes, welcoming, smiling, was one magnetic, bull's-eye center of that country.

It really just clicked, this strange, marvelous little theater, and it did all of it on passion, not money. The stage at the Cino was about as big as a card table, and it traveled. Sometimes it was up front, and sometimes in the back, and sometimes it had a Kabuki-style walkway, and you always looked up and over from your seat at what was going on, even if it were only a foot away from you, because it was always poetry, the poetry of the most commonplace, or the most exalted, but the language of all the Cino poet-playwrights was so intensely real that only the keenness of poetry, its precision and crystalline focus, could hold it. So, although there was a camp aura to the wall decor and music, the plays were not exactly campy. They were too straight on, dealing with real life. The life I was leading, working for a pretentious, uptight ad agency in the day, and living to be at places like Cino at night.

It was all so available. You didn't need reservations, you just walked in. Joe or one of the kids would welcome you and take your order. Lights went down. Joe'd make an announcement about the play, the actors, and any significance of the evening:

> "We're dedicating tonight's performance to Busby Berkeley.
> Walt Disney. And Yma Sumac on her birthday."

Prices were ridiculously low. For a few dollars and change, you could get a cup of coffee and a slice of cake, and see something that drove you crazy. You'd babble about it afterwards. Pure magic; theater incarnate, yet real: you didn't just dream it, yet left in that daze of happiness — and the whole machinery of it was so powerful in its effect, its pulsing, splendid energy, that it was easy to forget how fragile it was.

Then, just before one of my night-school advertising art classes at the School of Visual Arts, I opened *The Village Voice* and read that Joseph Cino had killed himself. I still remember the pain of that; I cried. Through Kerbs and his boyfriend Shawn, I'd gone to parties with actors and playwrights, and felt humbly delighted to touch the hem of all that sparkle: I was an innocent then, and they were opening up the cave. Just for a peek. This was real theater, what Shakespeare did. There was nothing amateur about it. It might have been in a coffee shop on Cornelia Street, not on Broadway, but the drive, the outrageous commitment, was holy, truly. Broadway was corrupt, laugh-track Neil Simon, but this was real poverty and obedience to the Muse. There were big theatrical egos in this small place, and I knew it. But also an extravagance of talent and insight we will not see again.

Still, I'd love to be proven wrong at that.[1]

---

[1] Poet/novelist Perry Brass has published thirteen books, been a finalist six times for Lambda Literary Awards, and won an Ippy Award for his novel *Warlock*. You can learn more about his work through www.perrybrass.com.

Part of the cast of the 1966 "Spring Gala," familiarly called "The Spring Horror Show," quickly organized when the cast of another show walked out. It featured pre-existing scenes and songs as well as quickly-written skits by Lanford Wilson, Robert Patrick, and others. The performers are (top, left-to-right) Bob Dahdah, George Harris II, Freddie Dundee, Mary Boylan, unknown, unknown, and bottom (left-to-right) Claudia Tedesco, Walter Harris, Jeanie Lanson, John Herbert MacDowell, and Deborah Lee.

Ducking behind Walter in a moment of uncharacteristic shyness is his brother George Harris III, not yet incarnated as "Hibiscus."

Photographer unknown

THE SPRING GALA 1966, OR
THE HORROR SHOW
Genji (formerly John) Schmeder

The following is an email exchange between Robert Patrick and Genji Schmeder, who in the Cino days went by the name "John." The material in bold italics is from Mr. Patrick.

THE EDITORS

Robert Patrick —

Thanks for your pages of photos and descriptions of the Caffe Cino years. I may be able to help in the smallest way to complete the caption for the photo of the Spring Gala of 1966.

The woman standing between George Harris and Mary Boylan seems to be Freddie Dundee, a singer and guitar player from Scotland. I recall Joe Cino disliked her performance for being folk music and outside the milieu of the rest of the Gala. Freddie Dundee began by singing *Ochin Chornii*, the Russian Black Eyes song. Joe demanded something else so she sang the same song with different words. Again the demand to change, and again another variation. The duel could have gone on forever. I found this very amusing, and was glad Freddie always found a way around Joe.

My brief involvement in Caffe Cino and Cafe La Mama E.T.C. are still vivid memories. I was recruited by John Herbert McDowell to be stage manager of that Spring Gala. Having no experience working in theatre, everything and everybody made lasting impressions.

I think you were doing a two-person skit with a very pretty blonde woman whose name I don't recall. (I think she also was in the sleeping bag with you) *[Jeanie Lanson]*. In the Spring Gala skit, you both had taken some psychedelic and imagined yourselves immersed in something like strawberry shortcake *[Cheesecake, the title of the skit]*. It ended with one of you going offstage to find a way out while the other bid farewell with "Write to me from the whipped cream!" Maybe you did this skit on another occasion since I did see several of your plays.

One night of the Spring Gala after I'd composed the schedule of acts, you objected that I'd put yours between two incompatible acts. I had no idea what the problem was, but you were so irritated that you walked out of the Cino. You returned a while later as if nothing had happened between us and went on stage in the second session that night.

I was confused by such behavior, but soon got used to volatile theatre person-alities. *[I don't recall this incident, but it's certainly typical of my arrogant behavior.]*

GENJI SCHMEDER

Mari-Claire Charba and Helen Hanft in Tom Eyen's 1965 première of
The White Whore and the Bit Player

Photo by James D. Gossage

YOUNG AND IN LOVE WITH THEATRE
Mari-Claire Charba

I lived at 11 Cornelia Street, a few doors down from the Caffe Cino . . . and before I ever performed there I would notice the exotic "Lady" Hope Stansbury (her shiny, long, blue-black hair, white skin and thinness) open the Cino doors and set up for the evening. I thought, "this must be some dark den of intrigue." Quite the contrary . . . once inside I discovered a room of glittering . . . tinkling . . . twinkling . . . giggling theatrics.

The Room was alive . . . organic . . . a shape shifter . . . expanding and contracting to accommodate the production . . . transmuting from an intimate cloistered cell or existentialist interior into the spaciousness of Radio City Music Hall. How did it do that????????????????????

But what never changed was one's entrance. Making your way from the closet of a dressing room (tiny, white and bright) through the chiffon drape that served as a door . . . brushing against the audience, past the steaming espresso machine, tinkling cups, Joe's smile and nod of encouragement (Joe served art with his coffee) and onto the magical performance box. Intimacy with the audience is hard to explain. I performed in many small theatrical spaces, but except for one performance of *The White Whore and The Bit Player* (the first) in my bedroom where Jacque Lynn Colton and I, seated upon two hampers, performed to a packed room, no other space was as intimate *and* pure as the Cino. I can easily summon the feeling of performing there . . . the little platform in the light . . . the audience . . . their eyes . . . so close. Yes, it was special . . . a stage like no other. The muses were there and Joe gave them the freedom to fly about. The Cino, where there was no proscenium and the fourth wall was absent.

The shows consisted of dialogue and costume (usually our own clothes) and if there was a set it was foraged from the street . . . reconfigured, painted and sometimes glittered (lotsa glitter and glamour). We were ahead of our time when it came to recycling.

The Caffe Cino was one of the theatrical incubators of off-off-Broadway. Joe, a former dancer, knew the importance of artistic freedom and dispersed it generously to all of the artists that worked there. Unbeknownst to us we were in the middle of an American theatrical revolution.

The country was in the midst of the Vietnam War, many of our friends were drafted or fighting the draft. We were on the Art Front fighting the war of ideas, identity and civil rights. Consciousness was rising. Drugs . . . Yoga . . . Zen . . . everyone was becoming enlightened. WHAT A TIME!!!!!!!! The street and the stage were converging. Shaking out the Play . . . finding new life in an old form . . . a life reflecting our experience . . . Theatre Born Anew . . . goofy and wacky and meaningful . . . filled with surprise and not afraid to fail.

. . . First Love. A night out at the Cino, a rare event for me . . . I was performing most nights somewhere . . . and on the stage I saw Frederick Forrest in a white T-shirt . . . I was smitten . . . I didn't know his name . . . we would meet a few months later and spend two years together. Love was in the air.

. . . There was a terrible rainstorm. I got a call from Bob Heide, his play *Moon* was running at the Cino. "Lucy (Silvay) can't do the show tonight." "Bring over the script," I said. He arrived . . . I looked it over and out the door . . . schlepping through the rain toward my new role. We were a loosely connected collective . . . always on call.

. . . Summer. Hot. Helen [Hanft] and me. A new production of *The White Whore* . . . what carryings on, but in the end always a brilliant performance. Tom [Eyen] bringing us new lines every night . . . so excited . . . the beautiful pearls he gave me from the Five and Dime . . . everything was real. Still rehearsing . . . midnight . . . 12 a.m. . . . Johnny Dodd gelling lights . . . Cornelia Street . . . quiet . . . empty . . . our church . . . the Altar where we left our offerings.

There was Light and there was Darkness. Darkness came too soon to the Cino.

And now . . . here in my Bleecker Street kitchen, a hop, skip and jump from the old Cino door . . . I remember. We were young and in love with Theatre.

THE POINT OF ACTING
Claris Nelson

When I moved to New York in March, 1962, my fellow Northwestern University graduate Marshall W. Mason took me to the Caffe Cino. At Northwestern, I acted in and wrote plays and Marshall directed plays, so the plan was for him to direct my plays at the Cino. We walked through the carved double doors into that magical space lit only by twinkle lights, probably saw a show, and Marshall introduced me to Joe. I was a Sagittarius; Joe was on its cusp. Joe gave us a date for *The Rue Garden*. I had a theatrical home in New York. I had no earthly idea how rare that was.

At Northwestern, the décor was far more normal, but the lab theater system was the same. A student asked for a slot to direct something, and got one. Students did everything on the show. Acting teacher Alvina Krause led a discussion of the work and passed final judgment on it. At the Cino, we passed the hat, which was a sort of judgment but far less stressful. For me, the move from Northwestern to the Cino was seamless.

Later, I changed my name when acting at the Cino to avoid being tossed out of Actors' Equity, which believed the point of acting was to make money. The point was not making money, but making magic. And behind the twinkle lights and opera music and wonderful, free, astonishingly diverse plays, real magic was at work — economic magic that made it possible for Joe to rent a performance space through the sale of coffee and a sometimes day job, and Joe's personal magic that let him give the space to us to use with no strings attached — no rent, no script approval, no content approval, no anything. Today a sometimes day job doesn't rent you a closet in Manhattan. Anyone looking to revive the off-off movement needs to do it in another, very different city.

I was born in 1940 and brought up a vegetarian, a believer in reincarnation and astrology, in Chicago (hog butcher of the world) and its suburbs. Our religion did not believe in meeting. Apart from my family, I knew no one who was like me. I never belonged to a group. I knew nothing of groups. I went to school to learn. Then for my junior year of high school, we moved to Evanston and I found the high school drama club. From then on, I was part of a group — theater people. In all other respects, I had no expectation that anyone would be like me. I dealt with others on a case-by-case basis, as individuals, never as part of any group except theater people. Until the recent resurgence of interest in off-off-Broadway, it had not occurred to me that the majority of people I knew at the Cino were gay men. To me,

Cino people were, and are, theater people. They're my people. As far as I was concerned, we were there to do theater, and we did it very darn well.

Claris Nelson and Frank Manuela in Claris's 1964 "revenge comedy," *Neon in the Night*, directed by Marshall W. Mason

Photo by James D. Gossage, provided through the courtesy of Claris Nelson

WHO IS THIS GUY CINO?
Jerry Cunliffe

In late March of 1967 I ran into Tom O'Horgan, an old friend from Chicago theatre days, and now a neighbor in Greenwich Village, as were Joe Cino, Michael Smith and others involved in theater and music.

Tom told me he was very excited about the play he was doing at La Mama, E.T.C. I went to see Rochelle Owens's *Futz* and was thrilled by it. I congratulated Rochelle and Tom, who commented, "Rochelle and I have the same chemical imbalances." I asked Tom if I could work with his company. The next day I began rehearsing Paul Foster's *Tom Paine*, initiating three years with "La Mama Troupe."

Two or three days later, we were warming up for a rehearsal when O'Horgan asked us to sit down. He told us of Joe Cino's self-inflicted injuries — the response was a mixture of shock and controlled hysteria.

That afternoon I went to my waiter's job at a restaurant on 13th Street, often frequented by nurses and interns from nearby St. Vincent's Hospital. As I passed the bar where they were gathered I overheard remarks: "Who is this guy Cino?" and "The hall at the hospital is mobbed with people lined up to donate blood for that guy."

Indeed, it was a record number of blood donors for that venerable Village institution, not for a beloved priest, a politician or anyone's grandmother, but for "that guy" who produced plays at a café on Cornelia Street in Greenwich Village. I realized as I was serving lasagna that I had become part of a devoted and powerful community of artists — "Off-Off-Broadway."

This was confirmed when we learned that Joe Cino was dead. Tom O'Horgan prepared a piece with us for the Cino Memorial at Judson Church. Slow, sculpted movement and various vocal and instrumental sounds, without words, carried us from our seats to the stage where everyone subsided into still silence.

I have no idea if our piece was effective as I was engulfed in the charged atmosphere of so many people in palpable pain, yet bonding together to mourn the loss of a friend and mentor. I recall a very young Bernadette Peters trying to hold back her tears as she sang a winsome song from *Dames at Sea*, which had premièred at the Caffe. That afternoon was one of the most moving experiences of my life.

Hopefully, the greater availability of the fine plays in this collection will inspire young theater artists to revive them, knowing they were born in a small space, with small casts and little money, but with an enormous amount of resourcefulness, skill, imagination and love.

GEBONDORETTA
Glenn DuBose

It was the fall of 1959, I was fresh out of the Army, and had just made my move to Manhattan via a summer-stock stint at Kennebunkport Playhouse. My new boyfriend, the late film writer Carlos Clarens, introduced me to the Caffe Cino just a few days after we met. It was his hang-out and a favorite of the semi-intellectual, semi-gay, wholly impoverished artistic set in the West Village.

"The Cino" — mismatched chairs and tables, worn velvet drapes, random photographs of Maria Callas, a coffee bar framed by twinkling lights. To me, a Northern California boy starved for Eastern "edge," Joe Cino's unfashionable boho café was utter perfection, and I immediately felt at home. Carlos introduced me to Joe, who pulled me aside and proffered "the best blow job you've ever had." I was rather taken aback but also rather flattered — until I came to understand that Joe made this proposal to lots of young men and that he frequently followed through behind the espresso machine while customers awaited their cappuccinos.

Once Joe learned I was an aspiring actor-director, he insisted that I direct something, anything, for "the room" (as Joe always called it). He wanted to sell more coffee, of course, but I think he was equally interested simply in fostering a bit of action for the regulars. Often, Carlos and I were the only customers, and I don't ever recall a full house until we began producing plays.

Even in the quietest times, the mood at the Cino was zany. With his deep voice, shaggy beard and mellow, matter-of-fact delivery, Joe was warm and funny and a true character. He and Charles Loubier, Joe's closest friend and occasional waiter, talked in a pidgin Anglo-Italian all their own: "ella" was a surrogate for any and all pronouns, "Maria" was everyone's name, "high koo-kaia" meant "certifiable," "full mala" was "troubled," and "put your faccia in my crotcheria," no translation needed. I loved picking up what Carlos and I came to call "Cino Talk," and I was truly honored when Joe incorporated "gebondoretta," my own silliness for "dick."

Before long (April 24, 1960), my production of Edna St. Vincent Millay's *Aria da Capo* was up and running on weekends at the Caffe Cino. Carlos's roommate, Billy Mitchell, played the lead, and Billy had drafted his cousin Kitty MacDonald, an exceptional actress, to play Pierette. Anticipating my audience, I transformed a couple of Joe's young hotties into winsome, half-naked shepherd boys. In the context of the Cino's edgy history, it seems ironic that *Aria da Capo*, written in 1919, was one of its first shows, if not the very first. On the other hand, Millay's poetic anti-war, anti-greed message may have been right on the mark for the dawning of the Age of Aquarius.

Aria da Capo attracted an audience, and Joe was delighted that people, besides the regulars, had appeared at his door. I followed Millay with another one-act play, *Love and How to Cure It,* by Thornton Wilder; and that was followed by the *Red Peppers* one-act from Noel Coward's *Tonight at 8:30.* Pretty square stuff, but people came and never complained. Carlos's and my "double-dates," Susan Sontag and Maria Irene Fornes, were faithful attendees, and many uptown theater people showed up as well. It was a fresh experience seeing good acting and good plays in a funky cafe setting, and all one had to do was buy a cup of coffee and throw a little change in the hat after the show.

The Cino was always on the verge of closing. Every month or so an inspector from the city would write up a violation, ordering Joe to close because the toilet was too close to the cannolis or some other such infraction. Joe would tell Josie, an elderly Italian woman who owned many properties on Cornelia Street and apparently had "connections." The licensing problem would cease and the Caffe Cino sailed on.

I left the Cino scene for several months in 1960-61, when I was hired to direct Imogene Coca and King Donovan, her difficult husband, in a summer stock tour of *The Fourposter.* Midway through that stormy gig, Josh Logan cast my stripped-to-the-waist torso in the national touring company of *The World of Suzie Wong;* and six highly educational months later, I returned to Kennebunkport Playhouse for another summer of acting.

That's where I met Bob O'Connor (a.k.a. Robert Patrick), fresh in from Roswell, New Mexico. Bob knew the complete lyrics, including verse, to more songs than anyone I've ever known. He taught me the words to "A Couple of Swells," and he and I performed it, including the Judy and Fred moves (I generally did Judy), for anybody who would sit still. I also met James Arntz, who has been my partner ever since, going on forty-five years. Jim had written a musical during his senior year at Bowdoin College, and Bob Currier, madcap proprietor of the Playhouse, presented Jim's show as a "pre-Broadway" special. It was a great summer, a life-changing summer for all of us.

Back in New York in '62, after a lengthy "honeymoon" with Jim in Europe, I landed a steady job at CBS-TV, working as production assistant on "Calendar," a live, daily, news-and-chat show hosted by Harry Reasoner. The new job supported a relatively roach-free two-bedroom apartment (ninety dollars a month) on East 13th Street and left me with enough spare time and money to consider directing another play at the Cino.

That's about the time two handsome young transplants from Chicago — Lance (Lanford) Wilson and Michael (Warren) Powell — bounced into the Cino and became instant pals with Jim, me and the soon-to-be-rechristened Robert Patrick. The five of us hung out at the Cino, ate potluck in our East Village apartment and talked about theater and writing and who was doing whom. Lance was way ahead of the rest of us in terms of career-focus, and he often tried out his plays on us, reading them aloud and asking for our opinions. Bob, who had an amazing gift for language, offered breathtakingly epic poems about the street life of the city.

When Lance asked me to direct *So Long at the Fair*, we worked up the script at my CBS midtown offices. And because the play ended with a troubled young man killing his girl friend and folding her into a sofa-bed, Michael, Lance, Bob and I borrowed a van and loaded the lead-weight sofa from Jim's and my parlor.

During the drive across town toward the Cino, the four of us were sitting on the floor of the van's enclosed cargo space. A tiny pinhole in the rear door created a perfect camera obscura effect on the opposite wall, revealing the most vivid moving pictures of the street scenes outside. It seemed to us a miracle at the time, and over the years we have often reminded one another of the magic of that moment and of the images which remain indelibly in our minds to this day.

When *So Long at the Fair* opened, Michael Powell's performance as the young man received much praise from the audience, as did the play itself. We got a positive review in *The Village Voice* and the play was held over for several performances. Joe was thrilled, and I think it motivated him to go out of his way to encourage new dramatic works.

Soon, Robert Patrick was writing for the Cino, as were Sam Shepard, Doric Wilson, William Hoffman and so many others. And I think it was Lanford's *The Madness of Lady Bright* that put Caffe Cino on the cultural map, attracting the famous like Edward Albee, and establishing the concept of a vital off-off-Broadway scene. Joe Cino became a real impresario, and the theatre has been all the better for it.

By early 1964, I was busy rehearsing and then performing (swimming, dancing and bouncing basketballs) four shows a day in the Billy Rose Pavilion at the New York World's Fair. Whenever I had a night off, which was rare, I dropped by the Cino; and every time I saw Joe, he would greet me with a kiss (and a grope) and would say "Write something for the room, Maria! Direct something! I don't care what it is." Haven't run into that attitude much in the forty-two years since.

SO, WHO'S AFRAID OF DAVID STARKWEATHER?
Richard Smithies

"David Starkweather is the great,
unsung genius of off-off-Broadway."
Ellen Stewart
Founder of La Mama E.T.C.

David Starkweather, an essential Caffe Cino playwright, has declined to have his early work included in this anthology. The editors were enthusiastically encouraged to obtain rights to reprint Family Joke, The Poet's Papers, *and* You May Go Home Again. *Richard Smithies, a director of one of Mr. Starkweather's plays at the Caffe Cino, here recalls the experience of working with him. In the subsequent essay, Phoebe Wray of the Boston Conservatory includes reflections on her work with Mr. Starkweather, directing his play* So, Who's Afraid of Edward Albee? *in her reminiscences.*

By the time I was twenty-five, I had performed many of the great roles for men over fifty, including Ephraim Cabot, Big Daddy and Polonius, and it was still my ambition to play Hamlet and Macbeth. It was therefore something of a surprise to find myself appearing as an adolescent David Starkweather returning home for his sister's wedding in *You May Go Home Again.* Where else but at the Cino?

Leigh Dean, who had played opposite me in *The Chairs*, had been at college (the University of Wisconsin, if I'm not mistaken) with David, and she eagerly brought me the play, which I think was his first to be done in New York.

David's nubile sister was played by Lucy Martin, a beautiful brunette from Mississippi, who was still at the point in her career (which later led her to Broadway in *Children of a Lesser God*) where she embraced with enthusiasm any opportunity to act. The other two men, however, were a problem. The plump young playwright whom I originally cast as the brother took an unreasoning, but passionate, dislike to the role and was replaced just in time by a friend-of-a-friend called Jim who had recently arrived from Kentucky. Jim was nicknamed "Tiss," the gay argot of the moment for one of those little bags woven of metal beads, which Edwardian ladies were fond of, but he was strapping, red-haired and willing.

The father turned out, after long searching, to be a fellow-Australian. I was slightly disturbed when he informed me that he was going to play it in a "singlet," which is Brit-talk for "tank-top," but he was capable of learning his lines, so I wasn't about to argue.

So the Starkweather family, as seen at the Cino, was a somewhat rare combination: an Australian father and son, a Jewish mother, a Southern belle and a brother from Kentucky.

I can't remember David ever coming to rehearsals, which took place in the living room of an elegant brownstone that Lucy's parents owned in the East 60s, but I never encouraged anyone to attend rehearsals, so that was probably my fault.

At all events, the production got itself quite smoothly together — even the inevitable wait for Joe and Johnny to appear at the tech rehearsal was shorter than usual — and we arrived without further mishap at opening night.

As David the Executioner, I stood in splendid isolation, dressed all in black with a mask, on a wooden box one-and-a-half feet square under a single glaring P.A.R.[1] The "family" was a couple of yards away on their own, considerably larger, platform: Lucy in ankle-length bridal satin, Leigh washing imaginary windows with the faultless technique she had learned from Margery Butterworth, Jim soothing an imaginary baby, and Papa longing for an imaginary beer.

My opening speech, delivered in what everyone has now learned to call my "stentorian" voice, was full of Ancient-Mariner-type threats of revenge. Then the family took over with their fond expectations of David's arrival. Finally, I crossed the two-yard divide, pulled off my mask and revealed my own fair, rather babyish face, to be welcomed with enthusiasm by the others. *The End.*

I'm afraid, from Starkweather's point of view, I didn't get it right, for he never congratulated or thanked me that I can remember. Joe, however, must have seen something in the play, for one night, when no audience showed up for the 1:00 o'clock show, he insisted on us giving a performance just for him and the lighting man, and we all found it magical!

---

[1] The P.A.R., or Parabolic Arc Reflector, is better known as a "spotlight."

A PLACE TO SAY SOMETHING
Phoebe Wray

The Cino was a dark, glittering space occupied by a tribe of aggressive talents. Rehearsals were at odd hours in odd places; the dressing room was a closet; the work was uneven; tempers flared, hearts broke, triumphs were expected. Looking back, the off-off-Broadway scene has a pleasant, nostalgic, glow about it. I've largely forgotten the dark side: the disheartening hostility of Actors' Equity, the crummy backstages, the sometimes dangerous neighborhoods, the indelicacy of passing the hat for the players. I have not forgotten the gifted, beautiful, young people who abused their bodies, or flew out windows and were lost, from messing with drugs. It bothered me then and it bothers me now. But that was part of the whole society, not just the Cino.

We all loved Joe, and, mostly and intermittently, each other. No one questioned the validity of what we were doing: Theatre. We workshopped nothing. The plays opened, stood, or died.

I directed a revival of David Starkweather's multilayered play, *So, Who's Afraid of Edward Albee?* — a play about relationships, structured as a sort of fractured mirror. The audience was challenged to reassemble the shards to see its own image. I remember David's encouragement and support, and very little else about the production. I was temporarily emotionally shattered myself, a Cino hazard. Working with all those temperaments, talents, and appetites was akin to the perils and pleasures of swimming the rip tide. But the play worked. David said he liked it, and audiences looked in the mirror.

Bob Patrick's trenchant short play, *Indecent Exposure*, was written and rehearsed in three days to replace a no-show production. The night before opening, we were up until dawn. We rehearsed, then the men went off to steal pallets (heavy things with splinters) to build a high platform in the middle of the room. I helped Johnny Dodd take down every light in the Cino. He lit the play with one dangling overhead lamp: stark, disquieting, a police interrogation room. I played The Girl, there to bail out her artist lover, and to explain to the NYPD why he had walked naked through the Village with his draft card taped to his wrist. The play says many things about war, art, and the artist's obligation to the truth. It ran eleven minutes, so we did it four times a night. Audiences stayed to hear it a second time, not because they hadn't finished their coffee, but because they wanted to hear things said.

That was it. It was all about the plays. Plotz. Succeed. Didn't matter. The space was a place to say something. It took theatre seriously, lovingly. It was immensely rewarding. Dionysus smiled on us, and his Temple began to change. It has taken too long for its beauties to be revealed.

A RECOLLECTION
David Christmas

David Christmas starred with Bernadette Peters in the première of Dames at Sea *at the Caffe Cino in 1966, at age 24, and submits the following to further enhance his reputation:*

The Cino *Dames* got me the lead in *The Butter and Egg Man* (off B'way). Then *Dames* again Off B'way in 1968 with Bernadette. I continued my acting career appearing in the nude (can you believe it?) in *Grin and Bear It* at the Belasco Theatre (I was young then) and *Very Good Eddie* at the Booth. Worked at the Goodspeed Theatre in Connecticut. Lots of road shows and stock. *Hello, Dolly!*, *The Matchmaker*, *Side by Side by Sondheim*. I quit the Biz about 1980 and really can't remember all the shows I have done. They would usually put me in a sailor suit or tuxedo and push me on stage. I was very good at playing the naïve young fellow from Oswego, New York or Centerville, Utah.

Were there drugs at the Cino? Fuck my reputation. I was tired, young and needed a "lift." Little did I know the lift that I would get. Lovely!!!!!! Joe gave me a potion one night that lifted me up to the sky. I thought I'd died and gone to heaven.

After working all day, and knowing I had to get through three shows that night, I whined to Joe that I was really dragging. He said, "I'll give you some coffee. It'll fix you up." After maneuvering around his big espresso machine, he handed me a cup. I noticed some white specks sinking down through the coffee. What could that be, I wondered? I stirred and I sipped. Well, in a few minutes I was up and ready to tap my little butt off. I did the three shows and was still perking. Went out for drinks with Jim Wise and a friend. I then went home — cleaned my apartment, did my nails, had a few more drinks and (luckily) fell asleep. It felt like I was sleeping about five inches off the bed that night.

The next day dawned and I went to work. Felt great. I got to the Cino for my three shows. The memories of the night before were, of course, bopping around in my head. (I really liked the way that felt!) So I sat down near Joe and, feigning tiredness, said "God Joe, I'm so beat tonight. Could I have some of that coffee you gave me last night?" Joe handed me a cup with those same little white specks sinking down to the bottom. I stirred and drank. Instant replay. I did my three shows like it was nothing. I was brilliant! However, I didn't have anything to do after the show that night. No friends to have drinks with. So home I went. But there was nothing to clean. No nails to do. I'd done it all the night before. I just sat there watching TV and jumping out of my skin. I had an audition the next morning, early, and needed to get some sleep. Well, sleep didn't come that night. As dawn broke, I thought, why is this not like last night? Everything was so fantastic! Everything was so "interest-ing." I dragged myself to the audition. I didn't get the job. I never asked Joe for coffee again.

David Christmas and Bernadette Peters in *Dames at Sea*, the Cino's longest-running show, 1966

TRIBAL RENAISSANCE
Francis Medicine Story Talbot

F. Story Talbot, author of two Cino plays, Sometime Jam Today *(1966) and* Herrengasse *(1961), wrote the following in response to Robert's Patrick's request for plays and show photos for this collection:*

Dear Robert,

Yes, I AM HE. That is a wonderful project, and I wish I could contribute — unfortunately, when my stepfather died in 1972 his sons threw out my trunk that was stored at my mother's, containing all my scripts, photos, reviews and other memorabilia. I still haven't gotten over that loss — as though a whole life was lost.

What remains is only the first act of *Sometime Jam Today* which is preserved in the New York Public Library Lincoln Center theatre collection, as you probably know. I regret not having a script of *Herrengasse*, which was the first play I did at Cino's, and the first musical he did there. That was a really nice production, and given a nice notice in *Time* Magazine — do you remember when *Life* had all of us on the roof there for a photo shoot that never got printed? Years later I learned there had been a San Francisco production I hadn't known about, but I don't know who did it.

I am also very sad not to have *The Ash Tray*, which I rather liked, that I did in our own Off Bowery Theatre in 1961, and *In The Beginning*, which we did with the New York Community Church Theatre sometime in the 50s.

When I left the New York theatre scene in 1967, I went to San Francisco where I acted in a production of Michael McClure's *Blossom* at the Straight Theatre, then directed a modern musical of Artistophanes's *Peace* and fulfilled an old dream of playing the Stage Manager in *Our Town*. (Wilder was my mentor in college — it is a curious twist that I wound up living for the past thirty years here in the Monadnock area — *Our Town* country.)

I was searching for understanding of what makes human society so inhuman, and finally found the wisdom that made sense when I sought elders of my native traditions from the First Nations of Canada and the U.S. I came back east to help edit *Akwesasne Notes*, the Mohawk journal, toured with the Mohawks telling stories of my grandfather, who was Wampanoag, came back to help with our tribal renaissance in Massachusetts, and began to write and teach what I had learned. I have published four books under my native name Manitonquat (Medicine Story) and will soon be coming out with others.

With my Swedish wife, Ellika Lindén, I spend every summer in Europe, making international family camps of tribal living, and in winter we are settled into a small handmade house in the New Hampshire woods where I write, play in a small band, and bring native spiritual circles into six prisons every week, and where we teach and help with a nature school for young children.

You can check on what we are up to on our website: www.circleway.org. Also, you can Google my native name Manitonquat for more info.

I remember you well, the charm and wit of your writing and performing, and often wonder how the paths of your journey since then have been. I would also love at some time to know about your archive project and how it goes.

WISHING YOU THE BEST,
FRANCIS MEDICINE STORY TALBOT

TOM EYEN, THE BEGINNING
by His Brother, Richard Eyen

Looking back today at what came to be known as the off- and off-off Broadway phenomenon of the early 1960s and 70s, it is not at all difficult to recognize that this period had a major impact on theater as we know it. But, at that time, few of the participants suspected that they would have such an impact. They, and in particular the playwrights, were just doing what they deeply felt they wanted to convey to all who would listen.

My brother Tom was a part of that group, often presenting plays at the Caffe Cino, La Mama and any other venues available. There was no shortage of willing actors, and Tom was able to form his own group, "The Theater of the Eye," with over a dozen regulars. As for budgets, I recall some plays with a $15.00 budget for sets and costumes with, of course, anything that could be begged, borrowed . . . never stolen. I remember that when Tom came to my gallery or apartment, a number of items might disappear, only to be seen again on a stage somewhere. But mainly, I remember the excitement of the times — the complete devotion to a movement that no one realized at the time was a movement.

I felt *Who Killed My Bald Sister Sophie?* was the right choice for this anthology. Tom completed it in 1968 as a follow-up or possible second act to *Why Hanna's Skirt Won't Stay Down*. While the better-known *Hanna*, first presented in 1963, is most often performed alone, the inclusion of *Sophie* in this anthology will give it a much-deserved second look. I am grateful to Moving Finger Press for their revisit to the Caffe Cino and the playwrights who gave it sound and soul.

We are never certain where even the smallest incident will lead. Tom was ten years my junior. When I was nineteen, I saw Carol Channing in *Gentlemen Prefer Blondes* in New York, and brought the cast album home to Ohio. He had many albums available, but Tom played this one over and over until he knew every line and had all the timing down. The next year, Carol Channing was appearing at the Palace Theater in Columbus, Ohio with the touring company. I knew I had to take Tom to see it. And so, a ten-year-old, sitting in an orchestra aisle seat, entered a world in which he would dwell his entire life. Thirty-three years later, the curtain would rise in the same theater on the touring company production of Tom's Broadway hit, *Dreamgirls*.

GREENWICH VILLAGE — THE GLORY DAYS
Robert Heide

I first became interested in the prospect of a theater life at Northwestern University, where the great drama teacher Alvina Krause felt I should devote myself to becoming an actor. I moved out of my hometown of Irvington, New Jersey and into a two-room flat in Greenwich Village.

I studied with Stella Adler thinking I might be on my way to becoming the next Marlon Brando. I remember reading in *Confidential Magazine* that Marlon shared a flat in the Village with esoteric TV actor Wally Cox. The two of them had started to paint the apartment walls a putrid purple color. Another crazy reason was that I wanted to live near a cellar dive on Tenth Street — a watering hole called Lenny's Hideaway. It was at Lenny's that I first met the young and handsome Edward Albee and his companion William Flanagan. Both were at the bar nightly, always in leather jackets and khaki pants. A few years later the gay Bohemia hangout went from Lenny's Hideaway to the Art Deco glow of the more atmospheric San Remo at the corner of Bleecker and MacDougal — this was the spot where Jack Kerouac and Allen Ginsberg chose as their stomping ground.

Jimmy Spicer and Lee Paton produced my play *Hector* and *West of the Moon* at the New Playwrights on Third Street and Thompson. The subject of *West of the Moon* involved a gay, drug-addicted, male hustler who meets a naïve minister's son just newly arrived in town. The Pinocchio Bad-Boy at Pleasure Island syndrome was apparently too much for the conservative critics of the day when one of them suggested that the author (myself) break his typewriter over his hands and never write again. Jerry Tallmer in the *Voice* wrote that he had never seen such barbaric attacks on a writer. In the audience during this short run was Joe Cino, who told me he loved *West of the Moon* and asked if I would write a play just like it for his Caffe. "Make it a play for two blond men," he said with a mischievous grin. "Write it exactly the way you want it and fuck the critics."

Having thoroughly read and digested *Being and Nothingness*, Sartre's philosophical work, I experimented with concepts of slowed down time, infinite space, and the existential despair happening in the lives of two young men bent on self-destruction with booze and drugs. The two-character play that I gave to Joe Cino was entitled *The Bed*. I envisioned the stage as one gigantic bed. However, the initial production was postponed due to a fire at the Cino apparently set by Jon Torrey, the brilliant lighting designer who was Joe Cino's out-of-control lover. People from all over town came to help re-open the Caffe Cino, and a benefit was sponsored by director Ron Link and Ellen Stewart. *The Bed,* directed by Robert Dahdah, was scheduled for a full run at the Caffe Cino. Ron Link created a white-on-white bed set that looked like either a room in a mental ward or perhaps a big slab in the city morgue. Like the Queen of Clean, Joan Crawford, Ron Link hated filth and took to washing the sheets and pillowcases every day as well as scrubbing the floor which he had given a coat of white enamel paint.

Eleanor Lester gave my play a great review in *The Village Voice.* Andy Warhol saw *The Bed* and decided to make a film version of it. The film opened at the Cinematheque under the auspices of Jonas Mekas.

When Joe Cino committed a hara-kiri type suicide during a drug-induced "trip" at his Caffe, I was devastated. Some have since likened Joe to a Saint who helped open up the doors for a great many who were in a desperate creative life struggle. At the funeral at Judson Church, actor John Gilman appeared dressed all in white. Looking like an angelic astronaut, he said, "My friend is Joe. He's asleep."

I will always remember Joe behind the coffee machine, happily preparing a steaming hot cup of cappuccino as he listened to the voices coming out of the loudspeaker system, usually his special favorites like Kate Smith's "When the Moon Comes Over the Mountain" or Rudy Vallee crooning "I'm Just a Vagabond Lover."

When Joe first heard the Beatles singing their '60s anthems to love, love, love, he was enchanted. The year Joe died by his own hand in his beloved Caffe was 1967, the year that the Beatles recorded the "Magical Mystery Tour" album: "I've got an invitation to make a reservation . . . the 'Magical Mystery Tour' is coming to take you away . . . is hoping to take you away . . . is dying to take you away . . . take you today."

Certainly Joe and his magical Caffe Cino took all of us for a glittering ride that will never end. Yet today I can still see Joe under one of those Johnny Dodd spotlights wrapped in an American flag, radiant like some larger-than-life, unshaven, elfin love-god ringing a tinkling bell and proclaiming at the start of each evening's performance, "It's Magic Time!"

Robert Heide in 1965

Photo by James D. Gossage

MAGIC, MYSTERY AND MADNESS
FROM SAN FRANCISCO TO THE CAFFE CINO
John Gilman

The Black Cat was an infamous bar on a block-long stretch of Pacific Street in San Francisco's North Beach. Animal cravings and moral weaknesses were encouraged at the Black Cat; during World War II the place was off limits to Naval personnel. This bohemian dive is where my parents met in the 1930s.

I grew up on the West Coast and received some experimental theater training, and had landed roles in several Golden Gate Park summer Shakespeare festivals and other San Francisco theatrical venues. I decided to go to New York, where I thought I could discover more about myself and find work as an actor.

I found my own "Black Cat Café" one night in the Village when I wandered into the mad, glittering arena of the Caffe Cino. Joe Cino welcomed me and I eagerly joined in, becoming a part of the life of this fascinating enclave of playwrights and actors. I vividly remember the Christmas lights and pictures of Tab Hunter, Guy Madison and Rock Hudson stuck on the walls. My first role off-off-Broadway at the Caffe was offstage as the voice of the "Captain" in William M. Hoffman's play *Saturday Night at the Movies.*

I was hanging out with Cino writers and artists like Charles Loubier, H. M. Koutoukas and Sam Shepard, and I was elated to find myself in the Village, experiencing the creative, bohemian life I had inherited from my burn-your-candle-at-both-ends parents. One day after a night of debauchery I was sitting with Joe Cino at Mother Hubbard's Restaurant on Sheridan Square when in walked a tall blond man, whom Joe introduced as Robert Heide, the author of *The Bed*. That night I saw a performance of *The Bed* at the Caffe Cino. I wanted to leave because my table and chair were practically in the set, which was a gigantic tilted-forward bed with two handsome young men in their underwear. The tangled white sheets were close enough to touch and for a moment I thought it was myself in the play. I started to look for an exit. I thought that everyone in the audience realized that the play was somehow about me. As the play progressed my panic subsided and I realized that this was the kind of theater that made sense to me. And yes, the author of *The Bed* and I became inseparable.

My own experiences at the Cino were crystallized when Robert Heide cast me in his play *Moon*, which opened at the Caffe on Valentine's day, 1967. *Moon* was a hit; we did it again at the Cino a year later, and at Brecht West in New Brunswick and at the Manhattan Theatre Club.

A strange man named Alan James often showed up at the Cino late shows claiming to be Oscar Wilde; he also wrote plays and performed Wilde at the Cino. At the beginning of each performance Joe Cino would ring his bell and announce "It's magic time," and indeed it was.

I met Andy Warhol, Edward Albee and his producer Dick Barr at the Caffe. When Dick Barr invited me to a New Year's Eve Party, I found myself seated on a couch between John Gielgud and Noel Coward.

I often wish I could go back in a time machine to a dime store to buy a Mickey Mouse *Big Little Book*, and I would also like to stop off in the late 1960s at the Caffe Cino to have a cappuccino and a cannoli, and watch a new and exciting play. In the firmament of the great people who died young there are James Dean, Marilyn Monroe, Elvis Presley, and for us in the underground theater there is Joe Cino, a shining star if there ever was one.

John Gilman and Robert Heide in the Caffe Cino block of Cornelia Street in 2006
Photo by Steve Susoyev

THANK GOD I'M A PISCES
Robert Dahdah
(Excerpts transcribed from a tape submitted by Mr. Dahdah)

When I met Joe Cino, he was working at the American Laundry on East 42nd Street in the daytime and running the Caffe Cino at night. The first thing Joe said when we met was, "What's your sign?" And I said, "Pisces." His face lit up and he said he wanted me to do a play at the Cino.

At that time I had a floating repertory company called "Bob Dahdah and His Group," and we played one-act plays all over the city — At Bellevue, the Seaman's Church Institute and many other venues. He suggested I direct a production of Sartre's *No Exit*, because the director had walked out. That was the first show to be reviewed by *The Village Voice* and it got an excellent review. So I started doing all my one-act plays from my repertory company at the Cino. During the week it was two shows a night, but on the weekends it was three. I don't know how many plays I directed in the next two years but it was a lot.

One day I came into the Cino and Joe was cleaning his files. On top of the garbage he was throwing away was a script called *Dames at Sea*. It was yellow around the edges and had been submitted two years before. So I said, "What's this? And Joe said, "Oh, probably nothing." Well, I hate to see a script thrown out. At one time I had thousands of scripts in my apartment. Finally I put them in shopping carts and took them to the public library at 10th Avenue and 50th Street. The library accepted them and catalogued them and I didn't have to throw them out.

I took the *Dames at Sea* script with me on the subway and as I was riding uptown I thought, I can do this like a Busby Berkeley musical, in black and white and silver and platinum, just like an old movie. And then I started casting it for the Cino. So Ron Price, who was my choreographer at the time, said he knew a girl named Bernadette Peters. When Bernadette showed up, she was perfect for the role. During rehearsals, one of the writers, George Haimsohn, said Bernadette was "blah." He said, "I want her to play bitchy." Well, I loved Ruby Keeler, and I wasn't going to make this kid play a part based on Ruby Keeler as bitchy. Anyway, we opened and the play was a big hit and Joe open-ended the run. It attracted a lot of famous people, and Bernadette got a lot of attention. She ended up going on tour with Robert Alda, Alan's father, playing a child — she was only fifteen and could pass for twelve. Her sister, Donna, a terrific tap-dancer, took over the role and later she left to get married. And then Sandy Bigtree took over the role and saw it through to the end of the run at the Cino.

Now, the real monster in this situation was Jim Wise, the composer. If ever there was a monster, he was a monster. He had a big hit on his hands, he could see it was going places, and he wanted to get rid of me. He felt obligated to me because I expanded the play; I added "Raining in my Heart," which was the hit of the show. I co-wrote the lyrics for it and then I added the title song "Dames at Sea." I made a lot of character changes, and lyric changes, and added a lot of dialogue that I knew from the old movies. It started out as a half-hour show and we developed it into a full-length production.

Joe was broke all the time, and worked like a maniac. He had lost his apartment and was living on a mattress at the Cino, and he had a key to my place so he could take a shower. Now, if Joe had a dispute on his hands between a writer and a director, he closed the show. He never took sides. But for the first time he had a show that was making money and he couldn't close it. And I wasn't compassionate enough to understand. When he refused to close the show, I stopped speaking to him for almost a year. I finally went and saw him after his friend Jon Torrey died, and gave him back the key to my place.

Stupidly, I never had anything on paper. All of us involved in *Dames* did sign a paper that said I had co-written the music, but it disappeared after Joe died. If people say: "Don't you trust us?" you say, "It's not about trust. It's just good business to have things on paper."

So when Jordan Hart decided to produce *Dames at Sea* for an off-Broadway run, he got another guy named Jacob Milstein to co-produce with him. They decided to do it without me. I went to lawyer after lawyer but I didn't have anything in writing. They finally made an offer. They said if I would sign away any claim to co-writing the lyrics they would let me direct *Dames at Sea*. And I realized that if I went along with that, after a week they could fire me and then I'd have nothing.

After going to a few more lawyers I gave up on *Dames at Sea*. They went on to make a lot of money, millions I guess, because it was done all over the world. I got absolutely nothing. When I found out that Jim Wise had died, I called his collaborator, George Haimsohn, and I said, "Jim Wise is dead. Good." And he said, "Why good?" and I said, "Because he stole my talent, and he never recompensed me for it. And he's burning in hell." And, do you know, two weeks later I read George Haimsohn's obituary in *Variety*. So they're both burning in hell but that doesn't do me much good.

I had some successful shows after *Dames at Sea*, including *Curly McDimple*, and at this point in my life I have no regrets.

Incidentally, Bernadette Peters always kisses me when she sees me. Her manager isn't very nice to me, but she always kisses me.

THE PLAYS

November 27, 2005
6 A.M.

Steve Susoyev
Moving Finger Press
San Francisco, California

Dear Steve,

Enclosed "A Funny Walk Home."

All the errors in spelling, punctuation, egregious typos are mine or the doleful state of my old Royal.

Since I am computer illiterate

No fax

No e-mail

No website

No processor

No education

No mind to speak of

I'm forced to have you take me as-is.

The lower case "n" is on the fritz, that's why in ten pages I switched to upper case.

I made as many corrections as I could by hand to make the November deadline.

Please understand, caring for my partner, in the midst of his worsening Parkinson's, and my sister with lung cancer has somewhat muddled my mind while manually preparing the copy of what, for me, is an ancient text.

Here she be, though, warts and all — written in a fever, decades ago.

ALL THE BEST, STEVE
JEFF WEISS

A FUNNY WALK HOME
Jeff Weiss

FOR CARLOS RICARDO MARTÍNEZ
HOW COULD SOMEONE LIKE ME
BE SO BLESSED TO HAVE A FRIEND LIKE YOU?

(Before the play begins, ESTELLE and BILL, the Mother and Father, mingle with the audience, handing out invitations, seating people, distributing streamers for the homecoming, seeing to it that everyone is comfortable. As the house lights dim and the recorded music begins, the parents return to the stage.)

TEXT OF INVITATION:

Mr. and Mrs. William Kleppinger
have the honor of welcoming you
to the official homecoming for their son Stephen Kleppinger,
who has been away from his home,
family and friends for thirteen years.

Refreshments will be served (Dutch Treat).
Appropriate recorded music* for your
diversion and amusement
will be played while we wait.

We thank you so much for attending
these festivities
and God bless you all.

(*Note: Player-piano recordings of director's choice.)

ESTELLE: This won't take long.

BILL: I shouldn't think so.

ESTELLE: It's simple enough. Is everyone comfortable? Can you see all right, sir?

BILL: I think we should start.

ESTELLE: Can you hear us all right? You all have your party-favors?

BILL: I think we should begin now. He'll be here soon and there's some background to cover.

ESTELLE: Alright, dear. Now?

BILL: Yes. Now.

ESTELLE: Our oldest child, Stephen, has been "away" thirteen years. In an asylum . . .

BILL: An institution.

ESTELLE: A rest home for disturbed children.

BILL: He wasn't ever violent or anything like that.

ESTELLE: Heavens no! He was just . . . ah . . . Bill?

BILL: Well . . . gosh, now . . . How would you say it?

ESTELLE: He wasn't, I would say, a very "serious" boy.

BILL: Hell no!

ESTELLE: Heavens, no!

BILL: He was always a happy child.

ESTELLE: Laughter and songs . . . singing, dancing and always and ever . . . grinning.

BILL: Was very hard talking to him, seriously, about . . . anything.

ESTELLE: Every time he spoke, he giggled. Life tickled him.

BILL: But life isn't all that funny, Estelle.

ESTELLE: Don't I know it. *(To audience.)* Don't we all? But for Stevie . . . well . . . Bill?

BILL: No, no one liked him.

ESTELLE: Was embarrassing when Bill brought customers home.

BILL: He was always making funnies and smiling strangely. But jokes don't sell cement. There's no comedy in construction products. Deadly serious business.

ESTELLE: Even as a baby, I can't remember his ever having cried. When I dropped him on his head.

BILL: Not even then, not a peep.

ESTELLE: I was just gonna say, not a peep. Through all childhood's traumas . . . from diaper rash to swollen glands . . . always and ever, that silly grin.

BILL: He became intolerable . . .

ESTELLE: To the church . . .

BILL: To the community . . .

ESTELLE: To my Bridge Club . . .

BILL: To friends and business associates . . .

ESTELLE: And finally . . .

BILL and ESTELLE: *(As one.)* To us.

ESTELLE: We loved him.

BILL: He was our boy.

ESTELLE: We taught him . . .

BILL: With love . . .

ESTELLE: What it means to care about serious things.

BILL: Politics.

ESTELLE: Music.

BILL: Self-defense.

ESTELLE: Art.

BILL: War.

ESTELLE: Peace. We'd all listen to the Longine Symphonette together.

BILL: I tried to teach him how to be moved by great moments . . . in a manly way, of course.

ESTELLE: How to say "Thank you very much," in French.

BILL: How to shake hands firmly with the grip of a man.

ESTELLE: We discussed all our problems openly.

BILL: I taught him how to clean leaves from a clogged rake, in autumn, by dragging it upside down along the ground.

ESTELLE: How to talk loud in an interested way to my mother. His Granny's ninety-two, with Bright's Disease.

BILL: All the time . . .

ESTELLE: The effort . . .

BILL: Years of instruction . . .

ESTELLE: And loving understanding . . .

BILL: So what do *we* get when he's thirteen? His teeth grinning through the night.

ESTELLE: He was exhausted in the day from laughing all night.

BILL: He was arrested once for giggling hysterically at a Memorial Service for our Home Town War Dead.

ESTELLE: What could we do?

BILL: He was our boy . . .

ESTELLE: We loved him, honest.

BILL: Sure we did . . . anybody can see that.

ESTELLE: So what could we do . . . Oh Bill . . .

BILL: Go on hon.

ESTELLE: You tell them.

BILL: We put him away.

ESTELLE: He was thirteen. We haven't seen him in all these years.

BILL: We haven't written . . .

ESTELLE: We haven't called . . .

BILL: We both felt it would be better for *him* if he came through this alone, like a man.

ESTELLE: He wrote us.

BILL: He had to. Every Saturday the inmates . . .

ESTELLE: *Patients*, Bill . . .

BILL: Right. The patients are required to write their folks . . .

ESTELLE: We *did* sign the releases . . . I don't want you folks to think we weren't "hands on" in our duties.

BILL: These people don't know about that, Estelle.

ESTELLE: Oh, right. The sixteen releases, over the years, for the fifteen sets of shock treatments, sixty jolts in each set . . .

BILL: You said "*sixteen* releases" and "*fifteen* sets" of shock . . . you're forgetting the pre-frontal lobotomy . . .

ESTELLE: I was just about to say, with the lobotomy, that's sixteen releases, right, hon?

BILL: Uh huh.

ESTELLE: And oh Bill . . . I'm so excited. Tell them.

BILL: Our Stevie's well and serious as hell.

ESTELLE: Committed . . . spiritually, politically, intellectually . . .

BILL: An example to this community.

ESTELLE: And his family . . .

BILL: Got to be quite an athlete at the asylum. Wrestling, gymnastics . . .

ESTELLE: He can lick his own behind I'm told . . . he's that flexible.

BILL: But I bet you a plug nickel he can't take his old Dad at arm-wrestling.

ESTELLE: Yes, dear. And he wrote a whole book of poetry too.

BILL: *And* he's a Republican.

ESTELLE: Yes, he is, I hear . . . but he's very interested in the Peace Movement, like his Mom.

BILL: That's true, but he's not snowed by the niggers any more than his Daddy is.

ESTELLE: He reads Simone Weil and Bertrand Russell.

BILL: Has a photograph of Joe McCarthy hanging in his cell.

ESTELLE: And Senator Fulbright.

BILL: John Foster Dulles.

ESTELLE: And Leadbelly.

BILL: General Westmoreland.

ESTELLE: Mao Tse Tung.

BILL: William Buckley.

ESTELLE: Steve Reeves and Gorilla Monsoon.

BILL: Who?

ESTELLE: Well, he's still reaching, I'd say, wouldn't you, dear?

BILL: Feeling his way in and around and back into the world that's changed so much while he's been away.

ESTELLE: And he is coming back . . . to his friends, his mummy and daddy . . . tell them, Bill . . .

BILL: Yes he is . . . today. Within the hour.

ESTELLE: And that's why we're so happy and smiling.

BILL: And drunk . . .

ESTELLE: With expectancy . . .

BILL: Because today . . .

ESTELLE: Thirteen years later . . .

BILL: On this crisp, cold, beautiful Sunday morning in autumn . . .

ESTELLE: Our son . . .

BILL: My boy . . .

ESTELLE: Oh, Bill . . .

BILL: Our Stevie . . .

BILL and ESTELLE: IS COMING HOME.

THE LETTERS

(The lights full up. The Player Piano tinkles away madly while the parents dance. When the music ends they take chairs, one to stage right, one to stage left and sit stiffly across from one another, waiting. On tape three letters are read by STEVE, flanked by happy music.)

STEVE: Dear Folks:

This place is terrific! I've met the funniest people in the world here. What a great bunch! There's a lady named Mrs. Vlakas who has visions in Safeway supermarkets. The bleeding heart of Betty Crocker. A watermelon with stigmata. Holy Mary, mother of Mrs. Grossinger. She lisps and loves to sing. She's right across the hall from me. She ought to be shot.

Dick Grammes wears white floor-length surgical gowns, has a bag for a bladder and shrieks, "Cardinal Spellman sucks bananas."

Only one bad thing here. I wish you'd do something about it. My doctor is some kind of degenerate monster. He's a Jew and, what's worse, from Israel. He is more insane, brutal and moronic than the worst SS inclined ex-Nazi fascist bastard could possibly be. He wears a little Hitler shrubbery on his upper lip. The mustache is phony baloney. I know this 'cause yesterday, when he thought he'd bullied me into a corner, he started to sweat, quite overwrought . . . peed his pants and the whole lip piece fell into his mouth. Do something, please! He has big hairy veins on his arms . . . he's very strong, likes to knead my shoulder muscles with his hands. He says he took a course in Jewish massage, but what I want to know is, are they known for that? Don't Jews stop with knishes and the Old Testament? At this point I'm with the Arabs one hundred per cent. Also, the food here stinks, but the interns are sexy.

> Love,
> Your Son,
> Stevie

(Happy music. As music fades, second letter is read.)

STEVE: Dear Mumsy and Dah-Dah:

I got the books and all for X-mas. Wish you sent a note or something . . . but I understand. It isn't recommended, right? Ain't I understanding? Ha Ha. Thanks Mom for *The Village Voice*, the issues of *The Realist* and *Ramparts* and the subscription to *The Peacemaker*. Andy Warhol and his freaks smell bad and I'm not talking about their movies. I sent Paul Krassner mouthwash for the New Year and tried to burn a psychotic child in Section 6 to protest the war in Vietnam. The kid wouldn't hold still. The bully boys threw me into cold pack. Ain't life swell? Dad, it's so nice to see you've made a decision for Christ and Ronald Reagan. I read every right-wing rag you send me.

Stick with it, you might succeed in smothering the life force in the whole community.

The liberals had their go, now it's our turn. "Masturbation and the Conservative in America," a new book by George Murphy. I'm writing it for him now. You'll love it, Pop. Full of good old American folk tunes, raw pornography and Senate scandal. Up the flag!

My eleventh set of shock treatments and boy, do I feel serious! No tears yet, but the more my doctors mumble "Lobotomy," the seriouser and seriouser I get. By the time I get out I should qualify as the new W.A.S.P. Arthur Miller.

"The world is a hell of a place, folks, but the universe is a fine thing."

> Serious love, etc.
> Your son,
> Steve

(Another blast of mad Party Piano. Third letter is read.)

STEVE: Dearest Mother and Father:

I had the lobotomy Tuesday. I remember everything: my home, my parents, my school and friends . . . my coming here . . . but all, I can assure you, without joy. I am so moved by my joylessness! I know you'll be more than pleased when you see me. I wept all day yesterday. The interns don't have to stick their fingers in my eyes to make me cry anymore. I was tremendously moved by our President's Report to the Nation and Christ is such a wonderful way to spend your time. I can't wait to read the Bible from beginning to end . . . twice. There is so much to read and talk about and cry over and hope for. There is so little, really, to laugh about. Being serious is oh so very very fulfilling . . . I can't tell you how solemnity touches my heart. Everyone listens to me now, so I don't have to listen to anyone. It is the way of the successfully committed person. One must talk a lot, persuasively, about a great many things . . . with a strong voice and few, but telling, gestures. That is the way for me now. I am here, I am well, and I am waiting, waiting, waiting to come home.

> I am your affectionate
> and humorless son,
> Stephen Kleppinger

(One last blast of whoopee tunes, then silence. The parents rise from their seats, look anxiously about the room, pull the drapes aside from the window, look. They make another drink. Play "Deep Purple" on the Victrola. When the tension threatens to shatter the mood of the play, the door bursts open and their son STEVE arrives.)

ESTELLE: My baby.

BILL: My son.

(The parents stand, arms outstretched to receive their son's embrace. He stares at them solemnly. Looks at the room full of people . . . does not move or speak.)

ESTELLE: Stevie? *(No response.)* Hon? Honey? All your friends are here. Say hello!

STEVE: *(Inertly in a toneless voice.)* Hello.

ESTELLE: *(Weeps, blows her nose in a big, red hanky.)* I'm . . . I'm so sorry . . . I'm so happy. Forgive me.

STEVE: Of course, Mother. I forgive you for being happy.

BILL: *(To guests.)* Well, I guess you can throw the streamers, confetti now. And don't forget to pop your balloons.

(The guests follow instructions, followed by a dead silence.)

ESTELLE: *(Tentatively.)* Gee. Boy. What a homecoming, huh? We've all been waiting so long . . . and . . . well . . . now you're here. Welcome home!

BILL: Okay. All together now . . . c'mon everybody . . . "For he's a jolly good fellow," *(And so forth, till the guests stop or fade away.)*

STEVE: They don't seem very enthusiastic.

ESTELLE: Well, they're tired. Been a long wait, Stevie.

STEVE: I missed the bus. My legs are swollen from the walk here. It rained. Was cold. I haven't eaten since yesterday.

ESTELLE: I'll make some nice hot soup.

STEVE: Thank you all for coming. I don't know any of these people.

BILL: They're all your old friends . . .

ESTELLE: Grown up . . . like you . . .

STEVE: Oh? Old friends? So.

BILL: Let me just see now how my boy feels. Off with the coat. Feel this kid's arms, Estelle. Built like a wrestler. Look at those shoulders. Good solid legs. The place must have agreed with you, son. You're built like your old man, how 'bout it?

STEVE: Physical therapy. You get two months of training after every shock treatment. Getting the nerves and muscles to work together again.

ESTELLE: You look real good, Stebo. And *well*.

BILL: Nice sensible business man's haircut.

ESTELLE: Nice strong features . . . fine nose, sensual lips . . .

BILL: He's a handsome young man, Estelle. We won't be ashamed to take *him* bowling.

ESTELLE: I'll be so proud when you carry my groceries to the parking lot. "Why, Mrs. Kleppinger, who's that hunk carrying your bags," and I'll say . . .

STEVE: *(Interrupts.)* I'll be pleased to bowl and bag with both of you.
      (Awkward silence.)

BILL: Well, gee . . . I think we oughta just sit down here now and fill each other in on how we are and what we are and where we're going. I think you'll be pleased to know son, there's a position for you at Allentown Portland Cement, whenever you're ready to take it.

ESTELLE: And you can help me nights canvassing for civil rights.

BILL: I don't think we should discuss that right now, dear. Your mother's still pushing the niggers into every respectable neighborhood.

ESTELLE: Bill, you promised.

BILL: Okay, hon . . . I don't interfere with your Mom's ineffectual liberalism and she doesn't dispute my membership in the John Birch Society. And she's still my girl. Right, hon?

ESTELLE: Your Dad. I'm telling you . . . he's a pistol . . .

BILL: Still, just for the record . . . the first time I saw a nigger with his big black blubbering lips, on T.V., in a Schlitz commercial no less, was the last time I watched the Friday night fights.

ESTELLE: It's true, Stevie. Your father may be a reactionary and we disagree on some things . . . but I have to admit he's a man of principle when it comes to his beliefs and ideas. And I've always respected that and loved him all the same. Right, Bill?

BILL: Right, hon.

ESTELLE: Ask your son how *he* feels about the Negro question, he'll give you an earful, I bet.

BILL: How 'bout it boy, where do you stand?

STEVE: I love their feet. The entire problem and whole solution is in the feet. They are flat, long, wide and black. The skin is dry and cracks easily. Determines how they move, at what rate. Their attitude and rhythm . . . defenses and strength start in those miraculous black feet. Now if you would bind those feet at birth, like the Chinese do, you wouldn't have a Negro problem and the world's shoe-leather surplus would accordingly increase. Consequently, we could then afford to bomb China with big shoes which they can't use, their feet are so tiny, we would confuse and totally disarm them and thereby stabilize the world situation.
      (Silence.)

ESTELLE: *(To the guests.)* You'll have to admit, he has a quick mind.

BILL: Veeeery interesting.

ESTELLE: Good heavens, Bill, he's joking . . . isn't he?

BILL: It's all in the feet, huh?

ESTELLE: You are sympathetic with the black man's struggle, though . . . aren't you?

STEVE: I'm for socialized medicine, school prayer, birth control, unlimited welfare and the Warren Report.
        (Silence.)

ESTELLE: Did you get "out" much while you were "in," hon? I mean, was there any recreation . . . you know, field trips?

STEVE: A beach party three years ago . . . they wanted to see how we would react to the bodies there . . . all that flesh . . . skin and muscle, half-naked, baking in the sun . . . Coppertone and baby oil . . . hair and sweat in the sand . . . greasy brown thighs . . . the interns kept watch on our bathing suits . . . I wasn't excited at all . . . I stayed in the water on a raft and caught a cold.

ESTELLE: Shh, baby, shh. It's all over, you're home now.

STEVE: My last doctor was a coon. Very well-dressed, cultivated, each word articulated carefully, like a white man in black face. All that surface poise and style. Was he queer or just well educated? He was gaga over Garbo and Vivaldi. I slept with him for a year. Ouch.

ESTELLE: You mean now, don't you, you mean he kept you company on occasion, perhaps, when you were feverish, hysterical or depressed, right? He comforted you, kept you warm like your Daddy used to do.

STEVIE: No mother. I slept with him. You know, slept with him? Sex. Remember sex?

ESTELLE: *(In a sudden panic.)* Bill?

BILL: It's all in the feet.

STEVE: Do you mind if I smoke, Mother?

ESTELLE: Bill? *(Then to STEVE.)* Of course not, dear.

BILL: Yes, Estelle?

STEVE: *(To ESTELLE.)* Oh well then, of course, I won't.

ESTELLE: He's talking so funny, Bill.

BILL: I don't know. I think we've got quite an original young thinker on our hands, dear. I'm a pretty proud Papa, let me tell you. Let's have a drink on that. Big black feet! Wow!
        (At this moment, RICHARD enters. The brother he's never seen. Very much the bland, infant American Protestant product. Blonde, beautiful, inert.)

STEVE: What's that?

ESTELLE: Oh Richy, Sunday School's over? Ah . . . uhm . . . ah . . .

RICHARD: Reverend Duncombe'll be here in a jiff, Mom, right after he enters the collection in the books.

ESTELLE: Fine, son.

BILL: Steve?

ESTELLE: Dear, this is Richard . . .

BILL: We never mentioned it but . . . well, the doctors thought it might upset you . . . so we never told you . . . now look here . . . this fine, tall, handsome young boy here, Steve, is . . . well now . . . just after you left thirteen or so years ago . . .

ESTELLE: Oh, for heaven's sake, tell him.

BILL: Meet your little brother . . . Richy . . . ah . . . Richard . . . Ah, Richard Nixon Kleppinger. Richy, shake hands with your big brother. He's all better now and he's come home to be with you . . . with all of us . . . forever. He won't be going away again, so now you have yourself a big, strong, older brother to take care of you, be your buddy . . .

RICHARD: Hi, you must be Steve. How are you?

STEVE: Oh, fine, Richard.

RICHARD: *(Extends his hand.)* Pleased to meet you.

STEVE: *(They shake hands stiffly.)* Hello. Likewise, I'm sure. He's my brother, huh?

ESTELLE: You two just get acquainted now . . .

BILL: Pretend we're not here.

STEVE: I can't believe this. You're my little brother. Blonde like I used to be. Makes me very happy to know you.

RICHARD: Mom and Dad talk about you all the time . . . how you used to sing and dance and tell funny stories. Where have you been? They said you were sick and would be away till you were all better. Your blood's all okay now?

STEVE: My blood? Well yeah . . . blood's right as rainwater, now, I feel fine . . .

RICHARD: Yeah? You don't look very happy.

STEVE: Oh but I am . . . I'm *so* happy.

RICHARD: Your mouth turns down at the corners like a sad clown.

STEVE: I'm grinning from ear to ear, Richard.

RICHARD: Aw, come on, you're making a joke.

STEVE: Me? A joke? I don't know how to make a joke.

RICHARD: Oh, you wanna come upstairs and see the room Mom fixed for us?

STEVE: We have a room together?

RICHARD: Dad says I'll have to watch you awhile, make sure you don't bleed through the night.

STEVE: I see. That's very thoughtful of him.

RICHARD: Should I take you up?

STEVE: I . . . I . . . Oh . . . Richard . . . Richy . . .

RICHARD: Ow. You wanna let go my hand? You squeeze too tight.

STEVE: Oh, sorry. (*Lets go of RICHARD's hand.*) Can I look at your palm and the veins in your wrist?

RICHARD: Can you tell fortunes?

STEVE: Some. Yeah.

RICHARD: Could you tell if I'll get the Junior Achievement Award this year?

STEVE: Let me see, I don't know. You have beautiful hands. Smooth.

RICHARD: I'm going out for track this spring. Should I try out for speed events or the mile relay?

STEVE: What's that?

RICHARD: What should I try for in track?

STEVE: The one that takes you farthest away in the shortest time.

RICHARD: Yeah? Where d'ya see that?

STEVE: Oh, around in there someplace. How old are you?

RICHARD: I'll be fourteen in April. I'm the tallest in my class.

STEVE: (*After a long pause.*) Say something else. Keep talking to me. I love to watch your mouth move.

RICHARD: I'm a good basketball player.

STEVE: That's nice. Tell me about yourself. Personal things. Anything you want to say, I'll listen. We all need someone to explain ourselves to. Did you ever have the twenty-four-hour virus?

RICHARD: I guess so. Is that the one you take Pepto Bismol for?

STEVE: Yes. The one for the shits. That would be it. Do you have a girl friend?

RICHARD: Some girls are okay . . . but . . . I don't know . . .

STEVE: I do.

RICHARD: What?

STEVE: Talk to me. Don't you have anything you want to say to me? Isn't there something you want to show me, share with me?

RICHARD: I can show you my report card. I was on the Honor Roll twice.

STEVE: Shh. Alright. Let me show you, then, how much I love you. I never knew you, but now I do, I love you. You're my brother, my beautiful brother, with beautiful hands and slender wrists . . . puffy lips and azure eyes . . . someone I can love . . . at long last . . . love.

(STEVE embraces his little brother and begins to turn slowly round and round in a kind of emotionally charged dance. He touches RICHARD's hair now, presses his body against his brother ever more closely, as if to absorb the boy's body into himself. The parents are moved by this singular display of sibling affection. RICHARD begins to gasp in his brother's grip, tries to free himself from what has become a bear hug. RICHARD's body is off the floor now, dangles helplessly in STEVE's iron grip. STEVE stares up into the stage lights, sobs, blinded, turning and turning, in a trance.)

BILL: Estelle! Is he . . . oh, God . . . is he weeping?

ESTELLE: I can't say for sure . . . I can't see . . . his face is turned up to the lights.

BILL: He seems to be sobbing.

ESTELLE: I won't be convinced he's totally sane till I see the tears streaming out of his eyes . . .

BILL: Dripping off his face onto his shirt . . .

ESTELLE: His face is wet, but that might be sweat. His mouth is open . . . he seems to be in pain. Oh, Bill . . . maybe he is alright.

BILL: I'll get you a chair, hon. *(He does.)* You go on up first, dear, you're the mother.

(ESTELLE climbs up onto the chair, looks down into STEVE's upturned face.)

ESTELLE: Bill, oh Bill, come quick. Get on up here. I want you to share this moment with me. I don't want to say for sure, I'll need your confirmation, but if I'm not mistaken I think we've got real tears here, hon. Emotion, genuine feeling pouring out of him.

(BILL joins his wife on the chair. With one thick finger he touches STEVE's cheek and tastes his son's tears.)

BILL: Salt, Estelle, real tears.

ESTELLE: They are *real* then? No fraud? *Actual* sentiment?

BILL: Honest, hon. Taste for yourself.

ESTELLE: *(Sucks on her husband's finger.)* Oh Bill . . . these are serious tears . . .

(They embrace. Look at one another like kids, awash in avid glee. Nod their heads, and giggle. They begin licking STEVE's face with wild abandon, sheer innocent joy.)

ESTELLE: Yummy, yummy in the tummy! Tears!

BILL: Hold it a second, dear. I think this moment requires some explanation for our guests.

ESTELLE: *(To the guests.)* Things like this can happen when a person is genuinely moved. That's why the most intense religious experiences are often accompanied by violence and passion.

BILL: *(To guests.)* Thirteen years ago our son Steve would have been incapable of such deep feelings. I'm telling you this to put your minds at ease, allay your fears. Richy'll be okay. I think even he, as young as he is, understands the significance of this moment. It means for us . . . for Steve . . .

ESTELLE: Let me tell them, Bill . . .

BILL: Okay, sweety.

ESTELLE: Frightening as this may seem to all of you, for us this is an epistemological experience. We know now, for sure, that our son . . . our eldest . . . our Stevie . . . can weep with the best of them. No giggling and grinning . . . real tears, real emotion, the real McCoy.

BILL: And what's more, it proves he's a Christian, because . . .

ESTELLE: Only Christians . . .

BILL: Kill their own . . .

ESTELLE: For love.

BILL: Take Richy up to bed now, hon. He needs some rest. We can tape his ribs in the morning. I want to have a real man-to-man talk with our boy here.

ESTELLE: C'mon, Richy, up you go, nighty time. You don't want to be spitting-up and carrying-on when Reverend Duncombe gets here.
(ESTELLE and RICHY exit.)

BILL: Steve. *(No response.)* Stevie. Stephen . . . Stebo?

STEVE: I think these doctors . . .

BILL: What was that, son? You wanna tell your Dad how you feel, dontcha? We're very proud of you, boy. *(Belches.)* Oops. What d'ya know, I'm a little drunk. What was I saying?

STEVE: The doctors should stop . . .

BILL: The doctors what? Wait a minute. What was I talking about? Your sadness, that's it. Your sadness makes your Mom and I very happy. It gives both of us something to play off of. You understand what I mean?

STEVE: I understand the doctors should stop all this nonsense about finding a cure for cancer. Diseases, epidemics, plagues, these are terribly important, useful tools. Doctors should be prevented, by law, from easing pain. It's the only thing left in this world capable of ennobling us. Pain. Rather they should devote each day, every moment to finding new horrors . . . a bacilli that can swell to the size of an elephant inside us . . . oozing out of us everywhere . . . sucking at our tissues perpetually . . . Then to become plump and firm like the head of a boil, or better, a cyst . . . to burst and consume us utterly after, at the very least, a decade of unceasing torment.

ESTELLE: *(Enters.)* And what are my two big boys talking about so secretly?

BILL: You don't want to upset your mother, we'll skip to something else.

ESTELLE: If it's about Christmas, I don't want either of you to spend any extra on me. I'm not going to fuss and I don't want you guys to. *(Aside to guests.)* I say the same thing every year and each year the Christmas gets more elaborate than the last one. I don't know why I even bother opening my mouth. *(Back to the boys.)* I'm so happy *and* a little tipsy too, so if it's about Christmas . . .

BILL: Why no, dear, we were discussing politics . . .

ESTELLE: Oh. Not Christmas. Well, sorry, I didn't mean to interrupt you.

BILL: I was just gonna ask Steve . . . I'm sure our friends are eager to hear his thoughts on the matter . . . what he thinks of our new President.

STEVE: He gives me great joy. And all those degenerates in the press try to break his great heart. Well, once you arrive at the pinnacle of political life, it seems swarms of maggoty freaks ooze out of your nights and days to waste your time. So many pressure groups, so many scurvy nobodies savaging his great plans for America. I can hardly wait for his next cerebral hemorrhage. Manfully thrusting a catheter into his throat on coast-to-coast television.

BILL: Stephen!

ESTELLE: You know his policy on Vietnam is monstrous.

STEVE: Indeed it is. One should deal with him the same way he dealt with Kennedy, the same way Kennedy dealt with Eisenhower.

ESTELLE: Whatever do you mean, hon?

STEVE: Kennedy flooded the White House with threatening postcards from all over the world. He was directly responsible for Ike's gradual hardening of the arteries to his brain.

ESTELLE: Well, I . . . gee . . .

STEVE: Come on, Mom. Politics is nothing more or less than the application of terror in the right place at the right time.

BILL: But the Commies . . . if they're not contained in Vietnam will . . . well . . . they'll just . . .

STEVE: Build a mammoth toilet in an open-pit mine somewhere in Pennsylvania . . . One enormous flush and there goes the Eastern Seaboard. There's no room for Protestants in a Chink universe. We should bomb them to memory tomorrow. Right, Dad?

BILL: Well, now, I don't know if I'd go quite that far . . .

STEVE: Why not? How much imagination does it take to shove any position one short step further into global collapse? We're so close to it anyway, every day of our lives.

BILL: Yes, but it's such an extreme position, son . . .

STEVE: Why? Blow them all up. Then we could begin what we do best . . . reconstruction. But first, reduce all museums to ashes . . . burn the Rembrandts, Goyas, Manets, Da Vincis . . . all those objects whose very existence negates the greatest treasure of all . . . the people . . . the American people . . . free those legions of Americans from the dead cultures that surround us . . . sink Europe in the sea where it belongs. If only World War II had ended that continental cancer for all time. Hang de Gaulle. Tear down Notre Dame, Chartres, the Sistine Chapel . . . all that moribund architecture, and crush it, stone on stone. Build a world of plastic and Saran Wrap . . . aspirin bottles and colored glass . . . Christmas lights and angel hair. Then throw the old, the black, the sick, the warped into them and burn them to the ground and then begin again. Now. Again. New materials. New construction. Human hair and lengths of copper wiring. Time tables and rubber cement. Then "in" with the freckled, faded who knows what? All and everything out of step and burn *it* to the ground and then begin again and again . . . simplify . . . reconstruct . . . destroy . . . begin again . . .

ESTELLE: Steve! Stop!

BILL: Please son, you're upsetting your mother and your friends.

STEVE: And you, Pop?

BILL: I can take it.

ESTELLE: Let's not get too serious now. I'm pleased to see you care . . . but well . . . why not sing us all a song! Remember? You used to perform for the P.T.A. . . .

BILL: Stag night at the Elks Club . . .

ESTELLE: All those songs and funny stories. "When You're Smiling."

STEVE: *(In a fury.)* Power. It's all power. If you don't create your own justice, you're a moron. You want victory? You gotta smash heads to get it. Want to become famous? Learn to swim in other people's blood. You gotta have money and power. If you have neither, you must commit murder and mayhem to get it. If you don't have the balls to beat a child to death or knife a stranger . . . be a thief, steal till your muscles are developed. Exercise twice a day, an hour in the morning and at night . . . turn your body into an army of destruction, a beast to contend with . . . tendons of titanium . . . distended veins, raw muscle for crushing other people, stomping beggars, kicking little kids till they explode . . .

*(At this point STEVE, suddenly light-headed from lack of breath, falls
backward onto the floor. The parents rush over to him. He sits up and giggles softly.)*

ESTELLE: Stevie, are you alright? Help him up, Bill. He didn't hurt his head, did
he?

BILL: He's alright. Just got carried away is all.

ESTELLE: I don't know, Bill . . . why is he . . . ?

BILL: Aw, he's okay . . . why look, he's laughing.

ESTELLE: I know, Bill, that's just it . . . he's laughing.

BILL: Why not? It *is* kinda funny.

ESTELLE: What is?

BILL: His falling over.

STEVE: I'm fine, I needed to faint . . . the anarchy of too many people in one
room looking at *me*. Listening to *me*. Blew me away!

BILL: I don't get you, son.

(STEVE hops off the stage and begins sniffing the guests.)

ESTELLE: What are you doing, Stevie, don't smell your friends, it's not polite.

STEVIE*: (Hops back onto the stage.)* Hey Maw!

ESTELLE: Huh?

STEVE: Do ya smell ma berries?

ESTELLE: Your what?

STEVIE: Ma berries.

BILL: He said, do you smell his berries.

ESTELLE: I know what he said. What does he mean, though?

BILL: I'm drunk. Somebody make me a bourbon and water.

ESTELLE: *You're* drunk? *I'm* drunk. Somebody make me a scotch and soda.

STEVE: *(Lights an enormous cigar.)* He's drunk. *She's* drunk. I'm delighted.
Somebody make me.

ESTELLE: Tired? Beat. That's what I am. But I told myself this morning, this
would be a party we'd all remember.

BILL: And all for you, son. Your Mom broke her back getting all your old friends
here. We're having a buffet when the Reverend arrives. She's been working
for two weeks to make this the most fulfilling homecoming any kid fresh
from a madhouse could possibly hope for.

ESTELLE: Well, I wanted to do it right. I like things to be nice. I wanted to make
my Stevie happy and now I see you smile, I know you are and, drunk or not,
I'm pleased.

STEVE: *(To the guests.)* My parents are of that far-off generation that says what they mean but, as the years flow by, have less and less to say.

BILL: *(To ESTELLE.)* C'mon, sexy, I wanna dance with ya.

STEVE: Go on, Maw, dance with Papa. I'll sing both of you an old song, how 'bout it? I want to see you guys ripe and sentimental, like in the old days. I feel so . . . what? Theatrical right now. And you're a perfect set-up for some nostalgic drivel. How 'bout it, kids?

ESTELLE: I always liked hearing you sing, son.

BILL: Boy oh boy, me too.

ESTELLE: Oh, Stevie, we had some good times, didn't we? When you were little and we'd go in the basement and play records, sing and dance. You were always so warm, so bright and always, always smiling.

BILL: Some of our happiest times were when you sang, Mummy danced and I tapped out the rhythm on an ashtray.

ESTELLE: We only carried on like that when we were drunk. I don't want our friends to think we were silly when we were sober.

BILL: Hell no, we cling to the strait and narrow, but it's kind of a kick to let your hair down once in a blue moon . . .

ESTELLE: And kick the gong around every once in a while.

STEVE: Okay. Attention, please. Mother. Father. Friends. Stay alert, 'cause ready or not, your Stevie's coming home.
   (STEVE sings "Left All Alone Again Blues" with tape. BILL dances with ESTELLE. For these brief moments there is a warm, familial feeling amongst them.)

STEVE: Mom, you make Vera-Ellen look like a cunt.

ESTELLE: Now stop that. No dirty talk. Like I always say . . . I wanted to be in show business and would have if your grandmother hadn't decided I should be a dressmaker.

BILL: I always had a lot of natural rhythm.

STEVE: *(Downs a shot of scotch.)* I know you did, Pop. Remember when you'd have me nap with you on Saturday and Sunday afternoons when your work-week was through? I'm sure it's okay with you if your deadbeat son has another shot, right? *(He downs two shots in as many seconds.)* All the doctors and interns would ply me with hooch. Your little boy's a wild one when he's smashed. 'Member Pop, you'd stick your nose in my navel and bite my belly and then roar, "Bore a hole, bore a hole, bore a hole"? Then you'd have me lay naked on top of you and you'd roll over on top of me and then to the edge of the bed and you'd say it was the crest of a cliff and "You're gonna fall off the mountain. You're gonna fall off the mountain. Hang on to Atlas. Atlas will save you. Hold on!" And I'd hold onto you as tightly as I could, curl my child's legs around your thighs . . . and you'd roll back over onto me, cover me with your big body, press down on me so the avalanche wouldn't crush me. You taught me the value of drama and panic, for which I'll always be grateful. We'll have to have a go at that mountain again sometime. How 'bout it, Atlas?

(The parents are stunned. BILL makes an effort to speak, but instead starts laughing. So does STEVE.)

ESTELLE: *(Giggles nervously.)* All fathers should play little games with sons. I think that's very healthy, don't you folks?

BILL: I . . . I . . . I . . . had almost forgotten our . . . ah . . . well . . . you have one swell memory, boy. Well now, how 'bout a drink for my girl?

ESTELLE: I think I've had it. I'm three sheets to the wind as it is.

BILL: You reeling around like a fart in the fog, Mom?

ESTELLE: Oh hon, how you talk.

BILL: Aw, c'mon Estelle. Today it's "No holds barred," how 'bout it? We'll all get drunk and be together. Being together and feeling it strongly, that's the reason America is the greatest country on God's footstool.

STEVE: C'mon, Mom, you don't wanna be unpatriotic, do ya?

BILL: *(Makes a drink for ESTELLE.)* A light one, little Mother, for the days when we were young and strong and on our way.

ESTELLE: You characters. *(Then to guests.)* Is there anything wrong with having a little party fun once in a while?

STEVE: *(Takes the bottle from BILL.)* Let her make her own. Come on, Dad. Down on the floor. Let's arm-wrestle.

BILL: Gonna see if you can take your old man, huh? I'm game.

ESTELLE: I'll referee.

(BILL and STEVE arm-wrestle. ESTELLE makes herself a long one and, while drinking, watches the contest on her knees. She sings and hums "Always" as her boys continue to arm-wrestle.)

STEVE: *(Wins the contest.)* The cement king loses, at long last he loses!! Hey, Pop, how 'bout it, what d'ya say? Time to take a nap with Daddy!?!

(STEVE jumps on top of BILL, yanks BILL's shirt out of his pants, buries his head in BILL's stomach.)

STEVE: Bore a hole. Bore a hole. Bore a hole!!!!!

BILL: Stop, stop it, Daddy. I'm ticklish. It tickles. Stop. Estelle! Tickle him! Tickle him! Get him off me!

ESTELLE: *(Jumps on STEVE. Tickles him.)* Stop. Let your Daddy go. He's ticklish. Let him up. It's my turn. I wanna be the baby on the mountain. Come on, Atlas . . . give me a turn . . . pleeeeze!

STEVE: Right you are, baby doll. It's Mommy's turn!
　　(STEVE vacates the carpet. ESTELLE and BILL on the floor roll to the apron of the stage, laughing, while STEVE on his hands and knees urges them on.)
　　Save the baby, the mountain's crumbling!
　　(REVEREND DUNCOMBE has arrived. Stands at the door, watching.)
STEVE: *(Sings.)* Wrap your legs around him Mommy
　　Squeeze him tight
　　Muddle-up and cuddle-up with all your might.
BILL: You're gonna fall off the mountain.
ESTELLE: Atlas! Help! Atlas!
STEVE: *(Sings.)* Oh, Babe, when you roll those thighs
　　Thighs that we just idolize
　　When you press on him his dick begins to bloat
　　Till you've got him sexed-up like a billy goat.
　　(Stops singing.)
　　Here comes the avalanche. Save her, Atlas!!
　　(STEVE drops magazines and sections of the N.Y. Sunday Times on BILL's back. Makes crash sounds.)
ESTELLE: Save me, Atlas!
STEVE: *(Sings.)* Oh, babe, he never knew
　　Any lay like you.
BILL: *(Sees the good REVEREND DUNCOMBE.)* Ah . . . ah . . . Estelle, stop, wait a second, hon.
ESTELLE: Let's do it again. This time I'll be the Daddy. Bill, let Stevie be the baby this time. Stevie, you be the little baby boy, I'll be Atlas!
BILL: Estelle, we have a guest . . .
ESTELLE: We have socks full of guests. Oh, Stevie, c'mon down here. I want so much to feel you close, now I'm so happy and need you so badly. Please, Stevie, please.
BILL: Later, dear. Reverend Duncombe's here.
ESTELLE: Who?
STEVE: *(Points at DUNCOMBE.)* What in Christ's name is that?
　　(DUNCOMBE wears a phony Jewish nose and is in full blackface.)
BILL: We were just playing charades, Reverend.
ESTELLE: Oh my, ha ha, Reverend Dunky . . . ah . . . Duncombe. We were . . . gee . . . getting reacquainted with our son.
STEVE: Actually, Mummy had an epileptic convulsion, we were trying . . .
BILL: Shut up, Steve.

STEVE: I was just gonna say, it's tough to get a grip on a mother's tongue.

ESTELLE: He's making a funny, forgive him. This is Stephen.

BILL: Our son. Formerly nuts, but now doing really well.

DUNCOMBE: *(Crucifix in hand.)* Young man, I have come to give you Christ.

STEVE: You've come to give me *what?* I need cock and cocaine, you bring me Christ?

ESTELLE: He has a cold. He's not himself.

BILL: He walked home from the asylum.

ESTELLE: He missed the bus and caught the flu.

BILL: He's feverish with excitement.

DUNCOMBE: *(Moves toward STEVE.)* This is the way. *(DUNCOMBE extends the large brass cross toward STEVE's now ashen face.)* There is no other that leads to purity of vision.

STEVE: Couldn't I just buy a new pair of glasses instead? What's that shit on your face?

ESTELLE: He's a Negro, sweetie.

STEVE: So where did he get the nose?

BILL: His mother was Jewish.

DUNCOMBE: As long as you live and have breath in your body, do not sell yourself to anybody.

STEVE: How can he say that? I can't wait to peddle my ass. What's he talking about?

BILL: He thinks in terms of all religions . . .

ESTELLE: All the time. He sees a little bit of Christ in everyone.

BILL: He's all scripture, chapter and verse.

ESTELLE: He offers his complete self to all those in need, regardless of race, color or creed.

STEVE: In other words, he's a goddamned fool, right?

DUNCOMBE: Fodder and a stick, burdens for an ass, bread and discipline, work for a servant.

STEVE: What the hell does that mean?

ESTELLE: He's come to give you Communion.

STEVE: You've got to be kidding!

BILL: We know how long it's been since you've had the sacrament.

ESTELLE: We thought you'd be pleased. You wrote us how "God was such a wonderful way to spend your time."

DUNCOMBE: *Anni novi rediit novitas*
  Hieman cedit asperitas
  Breves dies prolongantur
  Elementa temperantur.

STEVE: *(Skitters under an end table.)* Take him away, will ya? He'll tear me apart with that mouth of his.

ESTELLE: He's so full of goodness. He'll perk you up.

STEVE: I don't need perking up!

DUNCOMBE: There is no room for God in him who is full of himself.

STEVE: How could you sic a Jewish jigaboo on me? He's so scary.

  (STEVE starts to crawl quickly across the floor toward his parents.)

STEVE: Save me, Atlas . . . *save me!*

  (DUNCOMBE hops on STEVE's back, riding STEVE as he crawls. STEVE stands, DUNCOMBE still on him.)

STEVE: *(Frantic with fear.)* Will somebody please get Jesus off my back!?

ESTELLE: Hold on, Reverend, you're getting to him.

BILL: He's buckling, sinking at the knees.

  (With a shriek, STEVE flips the minister over his shoulder and onto the floor.)

STEVE: Stop. Hold it. Don't come at me again, Padre, or I'll kick you in the face. You barreled in here and busted up our party. My parents and I were on the brink of bonding when you and Christ came nosing around. I'm for putting God and his sacrament aside till we finish what we started here. I need to feel the weight of all the years I've come through. I wanna play with my parents, okay, is that so bad? They had their chance, thirteen years worth, now it's my turn. Mine! Crawl over there by the wall, I'll call you if I need you. Go on. Heel!

  (DUNCOMBE crawls to the wall and prays on his knees.)

BILL: What happens now?

ESTELLE: I'm dizzy. I think I'm going to be sick.

STEVE: Not yet, you're not. We have years to go before we sleep. Tell you what, let's make a play together, the three of us, unashamedly.

ESTELLE: A play?

BILL: I don't understand, and I don't feel well either.

STEVE: Come on. We all act out our lives. The only thing missing is the form, the honesty of a totally theatrical performance. The President walks those corridors all day, overhearing conversations, counting paper clips . . . But where is his mind? . . . Fucking around on a concrete floor with some big, muscular nigger. He rapes himself every night. Close your eyes and you'll see him, an old man, maybe eighty, bigger and fatter than the city of Washington, straddling the White House dome with his great flabby legs, his beard full of brains, playing with himself, cracking between his teeth the bones of every dark race in the world. Bring that vision down to these toilets where we play out our lives and I'll show you horror . . . terror . . . real screams in the night . . . and you don't have to leave your bedroom for it . . . I'll bring it to you, right here, in this room, with our friends.

ESTELLE: *(To the guests.)* Go home, all of you. Please, go home. If we could start again . . . if we could . . . get the hell out of here!

BILL: Let them stay, Estelle. We'll be done soon enough. They haven't come to a homecoming or a play.

STEVE: *(On the lip of the stage, staring at his friends.)* Indeed not, Pop. They're attending a street accident. Right? You want the hell of seeing that everything remains the same . . . that no matter how we pray or rage at things as they are, they will never change . . . not even after the blood has dried on the walls, right? You can comfort yourselves by repeating play is play, play is play. And you won't leave till we need you, will you? And we will need you. You're the only ones able to stop us if you care enough to make the effort. Of course you'll stay, because you're curious, you want to know how the story ends . . . else why read books, why see plays?

ESTELLE: Don't talk to your friends that way . . .

BILL: *(To the guests.)* Please don't go. Don't leave me alone here.

ESTELLE: I need something to steady me.

STEVE: You don't need any more booze for what's coming up, cookie.

ESTELLE: Gimme that bottle, you little son-of-a-bitch!

STEVE: *(To guests.)* Ha. Ha. See what I mean? Scratch a blue-haired mother, you get a Medea every time.

ESTELLE: Oh, God, is this the son I bore?

STEVE: You certainly do, Mother.

BILL: Don't leave me alone.

STEVE: Why are you a fascist, Pop? All that liberal breast-beating, why for, Mama? Do you find each other sexually repellant, need something to do with your minds and hands? Or is it some obscure device to forestall a performance you know will have to end, violently, tonight within the time given to us on this platform? What is it? *(STEVE grips his head with his hands.)* Oh boyo boyo boy! We're gonna do it! Now! All over again. Out of love turned in on itself, we're gonna write a poem, the only one worth writing anymore. A poem of anarchy and passion, sickness and death. No going back now. Listen. Listen. I'm gonna be the Daddy. You're gonna be me, Pop. You'll remain the same, Mama. A man can change, adjust his age, his sex, cut off his cock and start from scratch. A woman is trapped in her body, forever. I'm gonna make you inside your mother. You'll be born for me, Papa. You'll be the scapegoat this time, Balaam's ass on a budget. Think about me while I'm inside her. Study this face. Watch me move. Hear my voice and remember. Remember. C'mon Estelle, let's make a tax deduction!

(STEVE drags ESTELLE across the carpet and fucks her on the floor.)

ESTELLE: Bill oh Bill! Stop! Stop him!

STEVE: Don't do it for me, hon. Think of the company pension plan and give, give!

BILL: I'm sorry Steve. I can't permit the community to witness such a disgraceful performance. If this gets back to the Elks Club or my bowling partner . . .

(BILL rips a drape off the living room window and covers the writhing bodies on the rug.)

STEVE: *(From under the drape.)* Shut your mouth and curl up on the floor. You're not supposed to talk. You haven't been born yet. Shut up and gestate. *(STEVE crawls out from under the drape.)* That's it. The little shit is in the can. Freeze. Both of you. During your pregnancy I'm gonna deal with Jesus over there. *(Moves to DUNCOMBE.)* New York is a Chanukah Festival, right, Krishnamurti?

DUNCOMBE: *Hari hari ailee ailee yama sue bah can.*

STEVE: I'm gonna murder you, Ducky. Gonna tear religion's heart out and make you eat it. What's the difference between a truck load of bowling balls and a truck load of dead babies?

DUNCOMBE: *Quo Vadis, Domino.*

STEVE: You can't unload bowling balls with a pitchfork.

(STEVE kicks DUNCOMBE in the side.)

ESTELLE: *(Screams.)* Ahhhhh! the baby's coming! The baby!

STEVE: Hold it a second, will ya, Moldy Mary, I'll be with you in a jiff.

(STEVE sits on DUNCOMBE's chest. Starts to strangle him. The black face comes off on STEVE's hands.)

STEVE: Look at this, you black-faced bastard! Now for the nose.

(DUNCOMBE starts yowling like a whooping crane, twisting his head from side to side. STEVE tears off the rubber nose, stands up and tosses it into the audience. STEVE whips off his belt and flails at DUNCOMBE, driving the good Reverend out the door.)

DUNCOMBE: *(Looks in through the window as snow falls.)* I am but a slave freed from servitude. A bird uncaged. Freed to flee. Let me go. Let me go, lover.

(DUNCOMBE vanishes, as though he had never existed. STEVE whips the drape off ESTELLE and gives his parents final instructions.)

STEVE: It's time. Everything moves toward the birth of our poem. *(To BILL.)* Get in there, baby, you're about to be born. Now push, Estelle. Push.

(BILL obeys. He tucks himself between ESTELLE's outstretched legs. STEVE covers them with the drape. ESTELLE heaves in her birth throes. STEVE stands over them in near total darkness except for his illuminated face.)

STEVE:
Was so tight inside
Round and hot
My toes on your heart
My legs bent against your bladder
Fingers gripping the tubes
That led to your belly, Mama
No more than a lump with tentacles
My head seeping out of your body
Kicking at your organs, Mama
The hard muscles of your cunt
Let me go, Mama
I'm drowning in your blood
My head battered by my Papa's thrusts
If I had teeth
I would have bitten off his cock
If I could speak
I would have screamed
Shit! I don't want to live!
I don't want to live!

(The "baby" is born, comes out from under the blanket singing "You Are My Sunshine.")

ESTELLE: *(Staggers about, frantic and enraged.)* Steve. Bill. Stop this. For Christ's sake, stop. We're killing ourselves. Stop that singing, you shithead. *(ESTELLE throws a drink in BILL's face.)* Shut up! Shut up!

(BILL stops, looks about, bewildered. His mouth moves without sound. Then to ESTELLE.)

BILL: I didn't want to be left alone. I thought we could be a family again if . . . oh, my God, Mama, he's mad. He's lost to us . . .

ESTELLE: He's always been.

STEVE: *(In his mother's voice.)* Now what are my two big boys talking about so secretly?

ESTELLE: *(Turning to her son, snarls.)* Stop grinning, you mindless animal.

BILL: You've embarrassed everyone.

ESTELLE: Look at these people, your friends. They don't know what to make of you.

BILL: After all, we have to live in this town. We cannot allow one member of the
family unit to cast aspersions on the rest of us by erratic behavior and foul
language.

ESTELLE: *(Cracks STEVE across the face.)* Stop smiling.

STEVE: *(Softly.)* I can't.

BILL: *(Slaps STEVE.)* Pull your face together.

STEVE: *(Whispers.)* I can't.

ESTELLE: *(Slaps STEVE again.)* Liar!

BILL: *(Punches STEVE in the stomach.)* Sodomite.

> *(STEVE goes to his knees, still grinning up at them. ESTELLE hammers away
> on his back with her fists.)*

ESTELLE: Dicky licker!

BILL: *(Kicks him in the head.)* Pervert. Communist.

ESTELLE: *(Stomps on him.)* Fascist pig!

> *(Exhausted, the blows begin to lose force. They stop. There is silence except
> for the parents' labored breathing. BILL stumbles across the room and
> drags two chairs back. The parents slump in their seats, then speak, quite
> calmly now.)*

ESTELLE: I'll give you one minute to pull yourself together and make a serious
statement on a subject of your choice.

BILL: You've heard your mother's ultimatum, kid. This is your chance to redeem
yourself. If you're not totally corrupt, you'll do it. If not, you'll be back in
the madhouse by this afternoon. And this time, as sure as Christ made little
apples, we'll have them burn your brains out. It's your call, buddy boy.

ESTELLE: Talk.

BILL: Apologize to these people.

ESTELLE: Make your peace with this community.

BILL: And, for God's sake, be a man!

> *(STEVE walks to the edge of the platform and looks earnestly at the faces of
> his friends. When he speaks, and it takes some time for him to begin, he's
> very calm.)*

STEVE: I want to say something, then I'll be done with this long poem. Let me
ask you, though, before I go on, before it's too late to turn back and make
things right, I ask you now, if anyone here be moved by what might come of
us in the next few moments . . . I ask for help and peace and solace in our
crisis. Truly, I shall have need of kindly friends on that journey when I go to
my long home. This present life of men on Earth, in comparison with the
time that is unknown to us, seems to me as if we were sitting at a homecoming with our friends in the wintertime with the fire burning and the room

not too warm, and outside the storms of winter rain or snow were raging; and there should come a sparrow swiftly flying through the room, coming in by one door and flying out through another. During the time it is inside, it is not touched by the storms of winter, but that little moment of quiet having passed, it soon returns from winter back to winter again, and is lost to sight. So this life of ours seems like a short interval: what may have gone before or what may come after, we do not know. I'm done now. The rest of this play is up to you. You will write this last poem for me. You. Will have to be you, if only *one* of you, caring enough to stop us . . . that's love . . . that's thea-ter . . . that's life.

(STEVE looks out into the dark house.)

BILL: They don't know what you're talking about.

ESTELLE: Turn around. I want to see your face.

BILL: Your mother said, turn around.

(STEVE looks at the guests, still searching for a face, a pair of eyes, a hand . . . someone to stand in the house and come to him, hold him, rescue him. If not that, some sign that the play might end happily for someone. He shrugs his shoulders, grins hideously, flings his arms wide as if to take mad flight and turns to his parents.)

ESTELLE: Bill! Look at his face!

BILL: My God, he's insane. I'll call the asylum.

(BILL goes for the phone. STEVE is on him before he can get to it. STEVE locks BILL in a full Nelson. He pushes BILL's head down, applies more and more pressure. BILL's feet are off the floor now; he dangles limp and dead in STEVE's arms. During the killing, ESTELLE ignores BILL's murder and goes for the phone herself.)

ESTELLE: This is Mrs. Kleppinger. Bring a straitjacket and attendants. My son Stephen is intolerable again.

(STEVE rips the telephone cord out of the wall, wraps it around ESTELLE's throat and strangles her to death. Grinning mercilessly, he moves to center stage. He begins to sing "Everything is Hotsy Totsy Now" with the player-piano tape, his face and body twitching. He puts on a party hat and begins dancing madly as the tape segues into "Who's Sorry Now?" He alternates singing the song and screaming the title at the guests. RICHARD enters in-ertly, stares at his dead parents . . . at his brother . . . at the guests. STEVE continues to jerk obscenely, totally mad. As the tape sound explodes into static, the lights come up full and glaring in the whole theater, followed by a total and complete blackout.)

CURTAIN

William M. Hoffman *(left)* with Robert Patrick in *The Haunted Host* at the Caffe Cino, 1964

Photographer unknown, from the collection of Marshall W. Mason

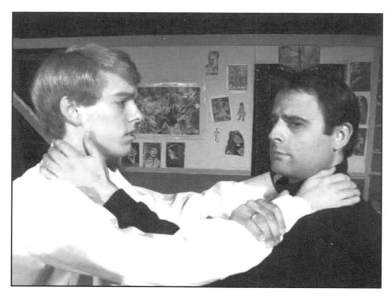

Richard Alexander Pomes *(left)* with Blake Balu in *The Haunted Host* in the Drama! production at the Cowpokes Space, New Orleans, 2004, directed by Daniel LaForce

Photo by Brian Kaz, provided through the courtesy of Robert Patrick

HOW "HOST" HAPPENED

I got the idea for *The Haunted Host* one morning in 1963, helping Lanford Wilson move a couch into the Caffe Cino to serve as a set-piece for his first play, *So Long at the Fair*. The couch had to unfold and fold with a corpse in it. Once it was placed, the director and stage manager tested it.

I was at the street door, about to leave. I turned back and saw them silhouetted by a worklight. Two abstract men unfolded a sofa, talked, then folded it back up.

A shiver went through me. I knew who the men were, I knew why they had opened the sofa, I knew why they closed it. I knew how they had come to that point, and I knew where they went from there. For the next few days (or weeks, I really don't remember), at work, at home, wherever I went, all I did was write *The Haunted Host*. (The title was part and parcel of the idea, a marquee under which I had only to walk to see the play in performance in my mind.)

There was but one obstacle. I had written comic books, short stories, and poems all my life, but never dialogue. I was like an alcoholic discovering alcohol. Somewhere in the archives of the Lincoln Center Library of the Performing Arts in New York are stacks of business forms, notebook pages, shirt cardboards, and god-knows-what-other pieces of scrap paper with dialogue for *The Haunted Host* typed and scrawled on them.

I sobered up, distilled *The Haunted Host* from all that dialogue, and took it in to Joe Cino. "Joe," I said, "I've written a play." Joe took it from me and threw it onto the top of a can of garbage. He explained that I was a nice person, and playwrights were terrible people, and that I would thank him one day. I took the play back and begged him. Lanford Wilson, Tom Eyen, and David Starkweather, three star Cino playwrights, happened to be standing by. They protested that I did a lot of work at the Cino and Joe should do my play. Lanford, with whom I lived and who knew the play intimately, even said he would do no more plays there unless mine was staged. Tom and David, who didn't know my play, nervously concurred. Joe shrugged, said, "You'll be sorry," and gave me a date.

Here I want to correct a lie of mine. I have often said that in 1964, we could find no actor willing to play gay, so I had to do the lead. The truth is that Neil Flanagan, the greatest of off-off actors, was dying to play Jay, the host, but I was so snobbish that, since Neil had starred in Lanford's *The Madness of Lady Bright*, I didn't want him starring in my gay play as well, fool that I was. Luckily, Neil held no grudge and played Jay superbly in a commercial production in 1969.

ROBERT PATRICK

THE HAUNTED HOST
Robert Patrick

a play in three scenes
for Joe Cino

The Haunted Host premièred December 6, 1964, at the Caffe Cino in New York. Jay was played by Bob O'Connor, Frank by William M. Hoffman. Marshall Mason directed.

SCENE 1

The setting is the living room of JAY's apartment. It is situated just above the main homosexual cruising crossroads, Christopher Street and Greenwich Avenue in Manhattan. There is a door to the hallway, another to the remainder of the apartment, and a window overlooking the intersection. The apartment itself is tacky as hell, littered, dirty, but not stagnant. It is apparent that whoever lives here is always on the go, although the appearance would suggest that he is going in a circle. There are clothes tossed around, magazines and books, dozens upon dozens of cigarette packages. On a desk is a huge, dirty, ragged stack of papers, tied into a bundle with cord. These are the writings of Ed, the ghost. A large photo of Ed hangs over the couch. He was a handsome young man, just short of classically beautiful. (NOTE: This script is written as if the hallway outside the host's apartment, and therefore the guest's comings and goings, are visible to the audience.)

At rise, JAY, the host, is kicking around the apartment looking very nervous indeed. NOTE: In some productions, JAY entered the apartment from outside, dressed as if for office work, and carrying packages which include the Kandinsky poster mentioned below. JAY is a few years older than Ed looks in the picture. JAY is energetic, flamboyant, dazzling in the personality department when he wants to be, and his gesture and expressions suggest intelligence. JAY is not very handsome, and his manner of dress — which suggests he has just walked through somebody's wet wash — is not designed to enhance whatever attractive features he might have. JAY holds a rolled-up poster in his hands, and keeps casting guilty looks at the photo of Ed, and at a spot in the air which contains Ed's ghost. Finally, in a mad burst of organized energy, JAY takes down the photo, props it up where it is clearly visible to the audience, and affixes to the wall the ugliest Kandinsky print ever remaindered at Marlboro Book Shops. (NOTE: Triple periods [. . .] indicate that JAY waits for a response from the ghost.)

JAY: *(To Ghost.)* There! *(Mock Bette Davis.)* Do you like it? *(Serious, thumbing through papers on desk.)* Did you like any abstract art at all? Well, it's NOT my favorite picture — *(Ironically.)* it's not even my favorite KIND of picture, but — *(Defensively.)* it interested me! *(Superior.)* Well, I know it bores YOU, but just possibly it might hold some kind of feeling or outlook, or whatever, that will come in valuable some time. Just BECAUSE it bores you, because it IS a strange way of feeling forced on you from outside — an emotion or attitude that you'd never feel, or never follow if you DID feel — a SHOCK! — just possibly it might help you get out of yourself for a minute. Because the things we like, even the people we like, are just ourselves, just — talking to ourselves. We have to get OUT . . . Because we need to, we have to. We live in such a crowd. *(Mocking his own melodramatics.)* We ARE such a crowd, every one of us; so much of us is other people that have come at us all our lives like — COOKIE CUTTERS! — that only some constant kind of openness, availability, can let in enough ideas to help us even begin to determine who in Hell we are. Who on EARTH we are. Who in HEAVEN we are! *(Smugly pleased with this phrase, but trying to conceal it.)* Oh, for Christ's sake, baby — don't admire my phrases — *(Mock-pedantic.)* check my premises! *(Ghost speaks.)* I will call you "baby" as long as you act like one. *(Ghost speaks, JAY interrupts.)* Yes, yes, of course our personalities are formed by our experience — and that idea, by the way, is not yours, but Sigmund Freud's, it came to you from outside, touché! — but all that means is that we ARE shaped, we CAN be shaped. I know it's no fun to change, or even to try to see what you're really like, to TRY to change, but we can . . . What? *(Ghost interrupts. JAY repeats his inquiry, mocking the Ghost's Southern accent.)* Do Ah buh-leeve that pee-pull evah really change? Of course, cookie! All we DO is change! Why, when you first started working for a living, when you first had sex — when you first started smoking, especially — didn't you change? Didn't your LIFE change, absolutely, every time? At least until you found a way to work the new prop, or the new character, into the same old inner drama! Or let some scientist come up with a new pill, or a new plastic, or a good oral contraceptive, or, please God, a psychology that works — or let some dumb damned politician pass a new law, and WATCH lives change! *(JAY fervently believes this, and is offended by the Ghost's quick reply.)* No, idiot, you can't change your feelings. I didn't say a word about feelings, get the spit out of your ears! *(He becomes intensely serious.)* Listen, you can't change what you feel — but you CAN change what you do. Look at us. *(Indicates messy room.)* You changed my life. I sure as hell changed yours. Only think — if we had known that we were going to. If we had decided to use each other for something good —

(The phone rings. JAY is puzzled; it never rings. JAY follows the phone cord and finds the phone deep in the wastebasket, under many papers, its cord wrapped around it. He unwinds the phone from its cord, blows dust from it, and answers, cautiously.)

Hello? *(JAY instantly snaps into a high-queenish character.)* Oh, HELLO, Jo Wanda . . . No, I don't answer the phone funny anymore, it encourages people to call . . . How are you? How's that man you're living with? . . . And the one he's living with? . . . You sound it . . . Oh, I'M fine, I'm good for another ten years unless I do something quick . . . Oh, nothing, I was just going through Ed's papers. Why? What do you need? . . . A favor? A favor? How dare you ask me for a favor, after all the favors you've done for me — and ruin my winning streak? What is it? . . . Huh? *(Looks around room, a little dazed.)* Uhh — sure! Sure he can stay here! I mean, if I can stay here, he can stay here. Just point him at my side of the Village and tell him to COME ACROSS! What's he like? . . . *(Laughs.)* No, you sex maniac, not what DOES he like; what IS he like? I don't care WHO he is, but WHAT is he? . . . Straight. Does he need a chaser? . . . No no no — I don't mind if he don't mind. Besides, I've already had your whole graduating class up here; I don't want to start on the underclassmen. I will put him in my living-bedroom. *(Tests softness of sofa with his foot.)* . . . I have my own sheets, thank you! You are not sending that child out on the streets of Greenwich Village on Saturday night with an armload of bedclothes — not here in the overkill area where I live! *(Peeks out window.)* Woo! Tell him to walk fast; the happy hunting grounds are infested tonight! You know, I live across from this little bakery — and all I can see are hot cross buns! Hurry the lamb over, I'll start some coffee. 'Bye. *(But Jo Wanda will not be put off without his usual sisterly farewell.)* And a good buh-buh-ba-bye to you, too *(Hangs up.)* Twit! *(Looks at room with new eyes, quickly and capably arranges during his next lines some modicum of order.)* La la la la — another little visitor from the future! *(To Ghost.)* Look, Jo Wanda is sending over some frat brother of yours and hers for me to entertain — so I would appreciate it if for once you would just behave like other people's ghosts and PLAY DEAD! *(JAY exits, toting laundry, before he can hear the Ghost's rejoinder. The phone begins to ring again. JAY re-enters with a pile of bedclothes, stares at phone, tosses bedclothes on couch and answers.)* Hello? . . . Look, I just talked to you, don't monopolize . . . Well, there's always the chance somebody will dial a wrong number . . . On his way? Already? How are you sending him, by stork? . . . So what now? . . . Secrets! . . . He is? . . . Oh, he is . . . Large bore or small bore? . . . *(Finishing Jo Wanda's sentence.)* And you want me to get him out of your hair . . . Oh, all the way out of New York, you've let your hair grow! . . . Well, consider it done! I will put the Dispose-All in gear. He will be back in Iowa for breakfast — which I will have on you, incidentally! . . . Ho-kay . . . Oh, by the way, let me know if you ever wanna get rid of Burt. *(Sexy.)* No charge.

(During this, the GUEST appears at the door, having w⟨ hallway checking numbers. GUEST is the living image o⟨ wears a grotesquely-colored collegiate letter-sweater, ca and an overnight bag, and has a conspicuous script rol⟨ pocket. GUEST rings. While waiting, he polishes his shoes in turn on the back of his trouser legs.)

Hold on, he's buzzing. *(JAY goes to downstairs-door speaker, buzzes it, shrieks into it.)*

"Hello! Hello! Hello!" *(JAY returns to phone.)*

(The GUEST hears him approach door and readies a big smile, is baffled when the door does not open, and momentarily eavesdrops on the phone conversation inside, which GUEST cannot make out, before ringing again. GUEST should comb his hair quickly and carefully in the interim.)

Now let me off the hook huh, I've got to mess the place up again before he climbs the stairs . . . A what? . . . A sur-what? . . . I don't want a surprise, sugar — I don't even want the inevitable! 'Bye! *(Hangs up.)* Twat!

(GUEST rings at the hall door again.)

Oh, Lord! *(Yells.)* Just a minute! *(Grabs some loose laundry and/or papers and litters the place again, runs over to a mirror and quickly ties his hair up in a ridiculous topknot or dons a mammoth string of beads. Surveys the effect. GUEST continues to ring, rather impatiently.)* Ring out the old, ring in the new! *(To Ghost.)* Would this get rid of you? One hopes! *(Instantly a little regretful, as he always is of unkindness to the Ghost.)* I'm sorry. *(Dances like Bambi to the door, puts on his queeniest air.)* Ready or not! *(Opens the door.)* Hell — *(Does an enormous take at GUEST'S resemblance to Ed, looks back and forth between Ed's photo and the GUEST. Slams door in GUEST's face.)* — Low! *(Runs to grab Ed's photo, hides it where GUEST cannot see it but audience CAN throughout the play, looks at the mess, says, "Oh, fuck it!", takes hair down or beads off and zooms back to fling door open; looks back and forth from GUEST to Ghost, checking resemblance.)*

GUEST: *(Who has been caught checking door number against a slip of paper.)* Uh — hello?

JAY: *(Whisks GUEST in.)* Well, hello, come in, I'm your host! *(Slams door and leans against it.)* And you're my parasite!

GUEST: *(Standing, holding his luggage.)* Uh, you were expecting me, weren't you? I mean, you looked at me funny.

JAY: Well, I'm funny-looking. *(These compulsive bad jokes usually cause JAY to be terribly polite afterwards.)* No no no, you look a great deal like someone. And I'm sure you are. Come on IN! *(HE ushers GUEST further into room. Phone rings, JAY picks it up, answers without waiting for a "Hello.")* Hello, Jo Wanda. I was expecting you to phone about now, don't start anything you can't finish in Hell! *(Hangs up three or four times noisily.)* Here, give me those!

(Grabs GUEST's bags and stows them behind desk. GUEST follows right behind and extends his hand, so that JAY turns around to find it in his face.)

GUEST: *(Winning friends, influencing people.)* I'm Frank!

JAY: Ha! And don't I wish that everybody was! *(Shakes hand.)* I'm Jay. Give coat. *(Whips coat from GUEST, making a face at its ugliness.)* Sit down. *(FRANK sits on couch. All this very quick.)* This is your bed. It unfolds into a nightmare! *(JAY is already exiting with FRANK's coat, which he holds like an odoriferous dead animal.)*

FRANK: Ha! Is that out of your play?

JAY: *(Surprised FRANK knows JAY writes plays.)* Yes, completely out. Want some coffee? *(JAY exits.)*

FRANK: *(Shouting.)* Black, no sugar!

JAY: *(Off.)* I must jot that down!

FRANK: *(Shouting.)* I thought I heard — do you have somebody here?

JAY: *(Re-entering with complete ill-assorted coffee service on tray.)* Not so much anymore, just the house ghosts. Why, is there anyone in particular you'd like?

FRANK: Uh, no — I thought I heard you talking to someone.

JAY: *(Eyeing phone viciously. Coffee gets served somewhere in here.)* Yes, a former friend!

FRANK: *(Delighted.)* Who, a ghost? *(JAY drops spoon or something.)* You really believe in ghosts? John said you did.

JAY: I scarcely believe in anything else anymore. Do you?

FRANK: No, frankly, I don't.

JAY: How about reincarnation?

FRANK: No. I believe that every human being is unrepeatable.

JAY: Like a dirty story. Well, actually the existence of ghosts has been recently proved. *(A little groggy due to FRANK's resemblance to Ed.)* Very recently.

FRANK: No kidding. *(Gets up, examining apartment.)* Hey, whaddaya pay here?

JAY: Ya pays your dues. *(Apologizing for mess.)* I used to keep plants. Man-eating plants. They starved. *(JAY gets FRANK's coffee accidentally, makes a face, grabs his own.)*

FRANK: *(Who is getting none of JAY's jokes.)* No kidding. Hey, what are these, mystic books?

JAY: What are what?

FRANK: These with the Egyptian titles.

JAY: *(Baffled.)* Egyptian which?

FRANK: Aak-Abu, Aca-Bek, Bel-Cav . . .

JAY: *(Joins FRANK at bookcase.)* THOSE are an encyclopedia. What are you, anyway, hipped on the occult?

FRANK: *(Embarrassed.)* Uh, no — but John said that you were interested in ghosts and spirits and like that, and that I should discuss it with you.

JAY: Isn't that typical of Jo Wanda? You want to do in a generous friend; you send them a poisoned opportunist.

FRANK: But who was it you were talking to? That guy that died?

JAY: *(Visibly shaken.)* Jo Wanda does tell all, doesn't she? No, it was somebody trying to sell me something on the phone. *(Indicates script in FRANK's back pocket.)* What have you got there, her dossier on me?

FRANK: *(Shyly, handling it to JAY.)* No . . . that's MY play.

JAY: Plays. I love them. *(Flings it backwards over his shoulder, is about to say something really scathing to FRANK. Phone rings. Answers it as before.)*

What's the matter, Jo Wanda, didn't you have time to teach him the Southern accent? *(Hangs up, wraps phone in its own cord, jams it in wastebasket, turns back to the puzzled but charmed FRANK.)* So, you write too!

FRANK: Well, not really, not yet. That's what I came here for.

JAY: Here? Tonight?

FRANK: Ha. No, I mean here to New York.

JAY: *(Quickly, to Ghost, to FRANK's bewilderment.)* Listen, baby, they're playing our song. *(To FRANK.)* And how do you LIKE New York?

FRANK: *(Whenever attention is focused on him, FRANK automatically becomes shyly charming.)* Oh, well, all I've seen of it so far, really, is between John's house and here —

JAY: Gay Street.

FRANK: Right. Gee, it sure is busy for such a cold night. All those people walking up and down the street. Such a dark little street, too — *(His naïveté on the subject is slightly assumed.)*

JAY: Yeah, well, it's one of those nights.

FRANK: One of what nights?

JAY: Monday, Tuesday, Wednesday, Thursday, Friday —

FRANK: *(Quickly.)* Ha! *(Philosophical.)* What are they all looking for?

JAY: *(After deadly pause.)* Approval?

FRANK: Ha! *(Changing subject.)* John SAID you were a pretty good writer. *(Heads for Ed's papers.)* Is that your stuff on the desk?

JAY: *(Hopping between FRANK and desk.)* No, that's the literary leavings of that "dead guy" you mentioned.

FRANK: Oh. John said he was pretty good, too.

JAY: *(High-queen.)* Well, I don't think Jo Wanda could have meant his writing. *(FRANK makes a piqued face.)* You don't like my calling John "Jo Wanda?"

FRANK: Frankly, no.

JAY: Daring of you to fly in the face of convention like that. Okay. *(Mock butch.)* Woddidja call 'im at college?

FRANK: Mr. Lawrence.

JAY: Oh, Mary!

FRANK: Well, he was a senior when I was a freshman.

JAY: Wasn't everybody? I mean, you're awfully young, aren't you? As it were?

FRANK: Well, I'm almost twenty.

JAY: *(Beginning a snide inquisition.)* And out of college? My!

FRANK: Well, no — I — left school when I was a sophomore.

JAY: Oh? And ever since?

FRANK: Well, gee, that's only been six months. I wasn't much of a student, I guess. *(Laughs, JAY joins in. Serious.)* I wanted to see more of life than I saw at school. Hell, YOU know —

JAY: *(Understandingly.)* Mmm.

FRANK: So I — knocked around on the coast for a few months —

JAY: The West Coast.

FRANK: Yeah, San Francisco.

JAY: Ah. And —?

FRANK: *(Feeling uninteresting, for once.)* Well, that's all. Gee, I don't want to talk about myself. What do YOU do? Besides write, I mean? Say, I'd sure like to see your stuff.

JAY: Oh, I'm still knocking around on this coast — quietly. We don't want to start reading to each other — *(Picks up FRANK's play and places it under Ed's huge pile of papers.)* — DO we?

FRANK: I WOULD like you to have a look at my play. John thought maybe you could help me to —

JAY: *(Grabbing cup of coffee, cigarettes, anything.)* My hands are full right now.

(This is enough of an insult for even FRANK to see. They stand embarrass-edly facing one another for a minute.)

FRANK: Oh.

BOTH: *(Simultaneously.)* Well — *(They laugh, but the tension is not broken. Brief pause and they speak together again.)*

FRANK: *(Referring to the Kandinsky.)* Who did that?

JAY: *(Simultaneous.)* What time do you have? *(They laugh.)*

FRANK: Nine to five.

JAY: *(Simultaneous.)* Kandinsky. *(They laugh.)* Nine to five. Great odds. *(To FRANK, with Bette Davis imitation, exactly as at start of play.)* Do you like it?

FRANK: *(Studying picture intently.)* Well, I don't know; I never understand that stuff. *(Charmingly.)* Maybe you could explain it to me?
(JAY trembles, turns away. This has all happened before.)
Or did you have somewhere to go? Hey, am I putting you out?

JAY: No, I wasn't turned on. No no no, not at all. *(With sincere warmth and graciousness, an elaborate Oriental bow.)* You're welcome.

FRANK: *(Warmly.)* Thank you.

JAY: *(Repeats gesture sketchily.)* You're welcome. No, I never go out anymore, everything comes to ME. *(Trying to close everything off without rancor.)* Look, you're probably anxious to get some sleep —

GUEST: Oh, gee, no, not my first night here. I thought I'd go out — if I only knew where to go!

JAY: *(Remembering his original mission, to get rid of FRANK.)* Uh — you know, New York is really a terribly dull town — you can ask Jo — John! It's terribly overrated.

FRANK: *(Acres of charm.)* Aw, I bet it's not, not if you have the right kind of person to show you around.

JAY: *(Coldly.)* Look, if you really want to "see more of life," as you said, you should get yourself a traveling job. Like with the World Health Organization? W.H.O.? WHO needs you.

FRANK: *(Obviously hurt.)* Oh —

JAY: *(Embarrassed.)* Look, I'm being — overly rude. Do you want the bathroom or anything? The little boys' room is right through here — and mine is just beyond.

FRANK: No, not right now, thanks.

JAY: *(Trying to make him feel at ease.)* Have you eaten?

FRANK: Yeah, yeah, I did already, thanks.

JAY: Well, would you like to write something? I must have a pencil around here someplace — *(Mock scrabble through a drawer.)*

FRANK: *(Chuckles.)* Ha! No, thanks.

JAY: *(A little desperate.)* Well, I haven't any music —

FRANK: I'm surprised.

JAY: Why surprised?

FRANK: John kept saying you were the stereo type. *(Brightly, before JAY can blow up.)* Hey, I know what we could do!

JAY: What?

FRANK: I could tell you about my bus trip from Iowa!

JAY: *(Instantly, self-preservation.)* Would you like some drugs?

FRANK: Uh, gee — I don't know — what?

JAY: *(Mock of tense.)* My dear, I was joking! *(Whips open well-stocked drug cabinet.)* Would you?

FRANK: *(Terrified, trying to appear sophisticated.)* Uh — well — I don't know. What is it, Mary Jane?

JAY: *(Scathingly.)* Yes, "Mary Jane." This particular kind is called "boo." *(As one connoisseur to another.)* Do you know it?

FRANK: Uh, well — yeah — sure — I had it — a couple of times — once.

JAY: Ah! And how did you find it? Cool?

FRANK: Well, to tell you the truth, it made me — drowsy.

JAY: Oh, that's easy — *(Whips out pills.)* Have one of these!

FRANK: What are they?

JAY: *(Offers some.)* They're heaven. Try it. It's a mild stimulant — compared to some. *(Mock scientific.)* Counteracts the drowsiness.

FRANK: *(Reluctantly takes a couple in his palm.)* How can you take this stuff?

JAY: *(Flips FRANK's palm up so the pills go down FRANK's throat.)* Like this! *(As FRANK sputters and gulps coffee.)* Oh, come on, anything I can take, you can take!

FRANK: It's an up?

JAY: It's an out!

FRANK: It'll keep me awake?

JAY: Only for the first seventy-two hours. *(FRANK is terrified.)* I'm joking. No, you can sleep if you want to, after the first couple of hours. Give it, say, thirty minutes to hit. Here, we can make your bed while we wait. Up!

(They fold down the sofa and make it up as a bed, or rather FRANK does. As the last section folds out, a WELCOME mat attached to it flops down. FRANK blinks. Jay kicks the welcome mat back and directs FRANK in making the bed.)

FRANK: Did you ever —

JAY: *(Throws pillow at him.)* Wanna pillow?

FRANK: Did you ever —

JAY: *(Throws another pillow.)* Wanna fight?

FRANK: Did you ever try —

JAY: Wanna pillow fight?

FRANK: Did you ever try acid?

JAY: Yes — once. You don't want to try that. *(Enacts this story vividly as FRANK makes bed.)* It was fine at first. The walls turned all fluorescent paisley mauve, and then the ceiling opened and a flight of golden stairs descended, and angels with silver trumpets heralded the arrival of the Great God Jehovah — and here He came! All white, flowing beard, His arms held out to ME!

FRANK: *(Beginning to get off, awed.)* Wow!

JAY: *(High-queen.)* And there I was — on acid! *(JAY hops down from the back of the sofa, where he has ended up, and dances giddily about the room.)*

FRANK: Uh, this stuff won't make me dizzy, will it?

JAY: No, I'm like this all the time. I'm joking. No, it DOES have a couple of side effects. It tends to make one talk rather loosely and honestly — and of course, if anybody hits a tuning-fork, you disappear, and — oh! The first half hour or so after it hits, it tends — in certain isolated cases — to bring out the sex urge in one — *(Dives onto the sofa-bed, mock-sexy.)* — or more.

FRANK: Uh, look — there's something I really ought to tell you.

JAY: Whatever could it be? *(Having fun making FRANK uncomfortable.)*

FRANK: If you don't mind my asking —

JAY: *(Super-sultry.)* Honey, I never mind anybody asking.

FRANK: It's —

JAY: Yeeeeees?

FRANK: *(Frankly.)* Are you a homosexual?

JAY: *(Casually.)* Don't mention it.

FRANK: No, are you?

JAY: *(Grabbing an ostrich fan or fur piece from somewhere.)* Do I LOOK like a homosexual?

FRANK: Please don't be offended — there's just so much of it around.

JAY: *(Dispensing with prop.)* Well, it ain't contagious — relax.

FRANK: Please, let me tell you how I feel.

JAY: Honey, I don't want to feel you.

FRANK: You see, when I was in college I took psychology.

JAY: — and vice versa.

FRANK: Why are you so defensive?

JAY: Because you're so offensive!

FRANK: No, you're just taking offense.

JAY: Well, I'm not taking any more! Now relax, Mr. District Attorney, whatever you may think you've got on me, I have twice as much on you.

FRANK: Anything you think you have on me is strictly in your imagination!

JAY: Don't be ridiculous, in my imagination I have nothing on you. Now, wait, I'm only joking. You shouldn't assume that every homosexual wants to sleep with every attractive boy he meets — just because a few million of us are like that.

FRANK: Tell me, did you ever see a psychiatrist?

JAY: You mean one of those people who tell you society is sick and then offer to help you adjust to it?

FRANK: You don't have to be crazy to see a psychiatrist. I'd like to see one myself.

JAY: *(Holds out hand.)* You're pseudo-aggressive — That'll be five thousand dollars.

FRANK: What you have is a persecution complex.

JAY: What I have is a complex persecution.

FRANK: But did you ever think of seeing a psychiatrist?

JAY: *(As if hallucinating.)* I think I see a psychiatrist!

FRANK: For instance, do you know what psychiatrists say about people who wear unattractive clothes?

JAY: *(Stung.)* Do YOU know what they say about people who don't wear underwear?

FRANK: I wear underwear! Oh, you're just being hostile!

JAY: Yeah, youth hostel!

FRANK: I think people and homosexuals should try to understand one another!

JAY: Ho, boy! People on this side, homosexuals over here! Wanna play Red Rover?

FRANK: I think the homosexual —

JAY: THE homosexual? Who he?

FRANK: I think the homosexual should find his place in society!

JAY: Where? Off-Broadway?

FRANK: I should think the homosexual —

JAY: THE?

FRANK: — would be tired of being persecuted!

JAY: You noticed!

FRANK: You're evading my question!

JAY: No, I'm ignoring it!

FRANK: ARE you a homosexual?

JAY: *(Proudly, brazenly.)* I'm THE homosexual!

FRANK: Now, look —

JAY: You look! There's a question I've always wanted to ask someone.

FRANK: What is it?

JAY: I hope you won't be offended.

FRANK: Well, what? No, of course not, What?

JAY: Well — you're heterosexual, aren't you?

FRANK: Sure!

JAY: Now, don't get angry, I'm only satisfying my curiosity — or perhaps I
should say I'm satisfying only my curiosity —

FRANK: Oh, come on —

JAY: Tell me, Frank, how long have you BEEN heterosexual?

FRANK: What do you mean? I've ALWAYS been heterosexual!

JAY: Started as a kid, huh? Tsk-tsk. Tell me, do you think one of your teachers, or
possibly even one of your parents might have been heterosexual? Do you
think that might have been the reason you —

FRANK: *(Interrupting.)* All right, all right, just shut up, okay?

JAY: Okay, Frank. Gee, I didn't think you'd be so touchy about it. Wow. Whew.
(Brief pause.) Tell me, is your play heterosexual?

FRANK: *(Snappy.)* You mean does it sleep with plays of the opposite sex?

JAY: *(Delighted to have drawn wit.)* Oooo. Getting off, ain'tcha? Well, you
know, you people DO tend to let heterosexuality CREEP into all your work.

FRANK: We let heterosexuality — What are you talking about? You people are
flagrant!

JAY: Flagrant? Flagrant? Did you say "flagrant?" Homosexuals are flagrant? Have you ever seen a Puerto Rican wedding?

FRANK: I think you ought to see a psychiatrist — fast!

JAY: *(On a roll, off-guard with victory.)* Why are you so anxious to get me on a couch?

FRANK: *(Quite sincerely.)* Because you're a nice person and I'd like to see you happy.

JAY: *(Not expecting that. Briefly stalled. Then, does a hideous grin.)* There! Now you see it. *(Does a hideous leer.)* And now you don't! *(Before FRANK can reply.)* Look, will you fold up that obscene couch? Like the Playmate of the Month, dear. I've got to go and get some cigarette papers to wrap this baby bunting in. *(Starts off — stops.)* But first, there IS one more question I'd like to ask you —

FRANK: Jesus, what?

JAY: College, Coast, cross-country — haven't you HAD your homosexual experience?

FRANK: That's my business!

JAY: Funny. I would have sworn you were an amateur. *(JAY exits with grass.)*

FRANK: Look, I am trying to preserve my dignity —

JAY: *(Sticks his head back in.)* Yeah? What was it like? *(Quick exit.)*
    (FRANK, alone, angrily finishes folding up couch. Then FRANK stalks over to Ed's papers, extracts his play. In doing so, FRANK has to lift Ed's bundle. FRANK weighs Ed's enormous output against his own slim script, puts both down. Slowly he allows himself to look into a mirror cross-stage. He goes over, combs his hair thoroughly, tries unbuttoning a button or two, nods with approval at the effect, then saunters back to the desk. FRANK extracts one of Ed's poems, reads it, sneers. Reads another, says, "Oh, come on." Reads another, mocks its apparently mechanical meter: "De-dum, de-dum, de-dum." FRANK is feeling pretty self-satisfied right now. He draws out another poem, starts to sneer — but it is apparently good.)

FRANK: *(Yells.)* Hey! This guy's no good, huh?

JAY: *(Pops in.)* You have taste. He was a great reefer-roller, though.
    (FRANK quickly hides the poem behind him and follows JAY around the room.)

    I am out of cigarette papers. I would rather be out of toilet paper.

FRANK: But you kept all that stuff of his, huh?

JAY: *(Grimly.)* It was here. *(Lightly.)* Now, where is that hookah?
    (JAY is searching for hookah. FRANK follows him, being terribly "nice" and "interested.")

FRANK: Oh, were you and him —?

JAY: I never touched him! *(Menacingly.)* And THAT man is dead. *(Returns to search.)* Hookah, hookah, hookah.

FRANK: Well, what was he — good-looking?

JAY: *(Private joke.)* He was as handsome as the NEXT man. Ah, here it is! *(JAY takes lampshade off huge hookah, all its hoses and mouthpieces tumbling out like some kind of squid. Explaining.)* I get so paranoid sometimes! *(JAY sits on floor to arrange hookah. FRANK extends his script.)*

FRANK: I'd like you to look at my play. *(JAY takes it, literally "looks at it," front and back, lays it on floor and sets hookah on top of it.)* *(FRANK laughs faux-good-naturedly, sits on floor opposite JAY.)* Ha! Uh — how'd you meet him?

JAY: *(Preparing hookah.)* It was a very unique meeting. He was an old frat friend of Jo Wanda's — a very, very, VERY *(JAY sucks at hookah to make his point.)* good friend of Jo Wanda's — so BURT sent him over to spend the night with me.

FRANK: Oh, I see . . . How'd he die?

JAY: *(Shocked.)* Alone.

FRANK: Oh. Suicide?

JAY: *(This is really too much for him.)* No, thanks, I just had one.

FRANK: You know, you're really very funny.

JAY: *(Thrusting hookah mouthpiece at him.)* I take drugs.

FRANK: Uh, no thanks. You better start it. I like to watch.

JAY: Thanks, baby.
(JAY does the ritual of lighting hookah, making sure it draws, etc. FRANK watches, fascinated. JAY is struck by the similarity of this to scenes with Ed, repeats, "Thanks, baby," then after a drag, in Southern accent, affectionately.)
Ah wish you wouldn't call me "baby."

FRANK: *(Puzzled.)* I didn't call you —

JAY: *(Quickly.)* I know, I know. *(Covering up his gaffe.)* Jo Wanda did. I'm glad it cost her a unit, the eunuch!

FRANK: I thought John was your friend.

JAY: So she is. *(Takes drag.)*

FRANK: Then why do you knock him?

JAY: Because she's so flat — and wooden — and closed.

FRANK: That's awful!

JAY: No, it's just her way. Here, smoke.

FRANK: Uh — maybe I had better just watch.

JAY: *(Jams stem in FRANK's mouth.)* No, join me — because I am coming apart. Boy, those pills hit like bowling balls!

> *(FRANK coughs on smoke. JAY grins. FRANK tries again, determined to do it. He continues to smoke throughout the next sequence.)*

> Here, you need one of these. *(Gives FRANK 'popper' inhaler.)*

FRANK: What is it?

JAY: Oh, just a little something to filter the New York air.

FRANK: Is this stuff dangerous?

JAY: No more than mother's milk — if you know your Freud.

FRANK: Yeah, I'm getting a terrific — uh — *(snaps his fingers, trying to think of word, is delighted when he does)* rush!

JAY: Not from me, toots.

FRANK: Hey, is it getting hot in here *(Opens or removes his shirt revealing an impressive chest.)* or is it just me?

JAY: *(Not sure ANYONE could not have said THAT knowingly, retreating from FRANK's physical appeal.)* I don't know — let's open yon window and see.

FRANK: What's life like in Greenwich Village?

JAY: Nothing's very lifelike in Greenwich Village. *(JAY giggles, goes to window, takes a hammer, pulls out nails, which have kept window closed, and flings it open. JAY looks down on the crowded street below. FRANK continues to smoke.)*

> Ah, there they are. My people, my puppets, my pageant, my parade! Hello, everyone. I love you all, every one of you, little six pointed creatures like snowflakes, each slightly different — even if you are all alike. Up and down, down and down, round and round, over and out! *(JAY observes, and calls FRANK's attention to a pick-up between a "fem" and a "butch.")* Oooh, lookie! Mince-mince-mince. Lumber-lumber-lumber. Mince-mince. Lumber-lumber. *("Fem" slows down.)* Miiiiince. *("Butch" slows down.)* Luuuuum-ber. *("Fem" approaches "Butch.")* Mince-mince-mince. *("Butch" approaches "Fem.")* Lumber-lumber-lumber. *("Butch" and "Fem" walk off together.)* Mince-lumber, mince-lumber, mince-lumber! *(JAY claps his hands in joy.)*

FRANK: *(Looking out of the window.)* Can't we go out?

JAY: Not that way!

FRANK: All my life I wanted to get to New York.

JAY: And what was your second wish?

FRANK: To meet interesting people.

JAY: *(Indicating street.)* Drop a handkerchief.

FRANK: *(Trying to make up, softly stoned.)* Look, you don't think I hold it against you, your being homosexual.

JAY: Well, you can't be homosexual in a vacuum.

FRANK: You can't help being homosexual.

JAY: *(Retreating a bit from this puzzling intimacy.)* Sometimes I can.

FRANK: I can't help being heterosexual.

JAY: Is that final?

FRANK: I didn't come over here to judge you —

JAY: You'll notice I didn't get into my bathing suit.

FRANK: I'd like us to be friends.

JAY: Three wishes and out.

FRANK: Please don't be flip. *(FRANK is in a pot-benevolent mood.)*

JAY: Well, all right, Frank. Look, now that we're being buddies —

FRANK: Are you going to start again —?

JAY: There's one question I've really always wanted to ask —

FRANK: You're going to start needling me again.

JAY: What do straight boys DO together?

FRANK: You're needling me.

JAY: *(Mock pique.)* Golly, how can I be a writer when I grow up if no one will answer my questions?

FRANK: Oh, well, I guess — if I was with a friend — buddy — pal — on a Saturday night, we'd go — I don't know — bowling — beer-drinking — looking for girls.

JAY: I guess everybody I know is still looking for the friend.

FRANK: Or — *(Has begun to fan himself with Ed's poem.)*

JAY: Yeah?

FRANK: If it was a really good friend — *(FRANK is turning on the charm.)*

JAY: Yeah? Yeah?

FRANK: One that I liked and trusted

JAY: Mm-hm.

FRANK: — and who shared my interests —

JAY: Go on

FRANK: And if the mood was right —
    (JAY nods, fascinated.)

— we'd probably read our manuscripts to each other!

JAY: You can quit fanning yourself, Scarlett, you just blew it. *(Of Ed's poem.)* Hey, what IS that?

FRANK: Oh, I have to admit — I sort of liked this one.

JAY: *(Snatching it from him.)* Come on, nobody's THAT young. *(Glances at poem.)* Oh, well, no wonder. This is a note of mine. I have the whole poem here somewhere! *(JAY goes to a drawer in the desk and starts taking out huge, neat piles — his own manuscripts.)*

FRANK: *(Wandering over, fascinated.)* Wow, you must have liked that guy a lot!

JAY: *(Seeking a certain manuscript.)* Maybe I killed him to get his priceless manuscripts.

FRANK: Not with all those! . . . He killed HIMSELF, didn't he?

JAY: *("Are we back on that?")* I went down to the 9th Precinct to inquire on that very point. And for the next eleven hours I was group therapy for a gang of cops. *(Still searching.)*

FRANK: That must have been rough.

JAY: They'd like you to think so.

FRANK: I mean with your friend dead and all . . . Why did they question YOU?

JAY: *(Still searching.)* They thunk I done it.

FRANK: Ha! . . . You didn't, did you?

JAY: *(Not believing what he is hearing.)* Didn't WHAT?

FRANK: Kill him?

JAY: Not yet! *(Finds poem.)* Ah! Now, stick that thing in your mouth and listen! *(JAY hands hookah to FRANK, quickly drops FRANK's play into wastebasket without FRANK noticing, grabs a chair to stand on, and reads with considerable dramatic power and bravura.)*

THE READERS OF CAHIERS DU CINEMA
ALL LINED UP TO GET THEIR ENEMA!

FRANK: That's great!

JAY: That's the title.

FRANK: Great title!

JAY: *(Reads on.)*

Jimmy lived for films of terror,
After homework without error.
This Phi Beta Kappa member went
Mad for visions of dismemberment.
Disembodied living brains,

Dangling ganglia like chains,
Flew on naked girls to twist 'em
In their naked nervous system.
Virgin Jim watched showgirls' shadows
Being torn apart in grottoes
By robots who, though they adored 'em,
Had no other uses for 'em.
Citizenshipped, summa cum-lauded,
Jimmy only was rewarded
Watching boys robbed of their features
To endow unviable creatures!
Jimmy's parents read an article,
And accepted every particle.
They believed, with the majority,
Monsters really killed Authority.
At the horror show they found him,
Happy children all around him,
Extracted him, and set two strictures:
He must not WANT to see such pictures!
They locked Jim in with his studies,
Thinking him and all his buddies
Willful, free, seditious arrants,
Learning to destroy their parents.
They mis-studied freak creation,
And misread externalization;
Sublimation is its thesis:
Jimmy tore HIMSELF to pieces!

(JAY has acted out every line, leapt about on furniture, become monsters, Jimmy, showgirls, and parents. As a finale, JAY tears the poem to shreds and flings it in the air.)

FRANK: *(Sincerely.)* Great! Just great! Great! *(Applauds, stamps his feet, subsides.)* I can't write poetry.

JAY: How did we get back to YOU?

FRANK: But John says I'm pretty good.

JAY: Hmmm. Well, your profile's not bad, you could pose for coins.

FRANK: I mean writing.

JAY: Just as long as you don't mean reading.

FRANK: You mean you don't want to hear my play?

JAY: E.S.P.!

FRANK: *(Hurt.)* Hey!

JAY: E.S.P., baby: Everybody Smoke Pot!

FRANK: But my play! *(Looks about for it.)*

JAY: *(Memory.)* Play! *(Starts digging through manuscripts again.)*

FRANK: Everybody at school thought I was a good writer. My English teacher used to have me over to his house nights!

JAY: *(High-queen.)* Yeah, I heard about him from Jo Wanda!

FRANK: I am a good writer, goddamit! I'm the best fuckin' writer around!

JAY: How's your writing?

FRANK: You're queer!

JAY: You're high!

FRANK: I'm not!

JAY: I am.

FRANK: You are?

JAY: WE are. Sit down! *(Shoves him onto sofa.)*

FRANK: Hey, what the hell did you do to my play?

JAY: *(Finds what he is looking for.)* Play! *(Comes up with three huge bound manuscripts.)*

FRANK: Don't you really want to hear it? *(FRANK is looking everywhere.)*

JAY: Sure, baby, and you can hear it, too! What a Beautiful Planet, the People Who Live Here Must Be Very Happy. A Trilogy by Jay Astor!

(FRANK sees the enormous manuscript and redoubles his efforts to find his own. JAY reads on, changing his voice for each character, reading rapid-fire.)

"The setting is a dingy hotel room. A blonde lolls on the bed. A man enters, slams and locks the door. HE: I don't believe this neighborhood is safe; everyone I passed was in plain clothes. SHE: Our problem, Jake, is I want to commit adultery and you just want to dishonor your father and mother! HE: Oh, shut up, Elvira; I haven't had so much fun since incest became a motif!"

FRANK: *(Finds his manuscript in the wastebasket. In disbelief.)* Who ARE you?

JAY: *(Triumphantly.)* "SHE!"

SCENE 2

(Lights up almost immediately. JAY is still reading, from the last page of the last volume. FRANK lies on the couch, stoned, smoking, covered with sheets of manuscripts.)

JAY: "HE: Half the fun of sex is getting your clothes off. SHE: And most of the other half is having them off. HE: I'll hate myself the morning. SHE: It is morning. HE: And — I hate myself. Curtain." Applause. Acclaim. Irreparable immortality.

FRANK: *(Weakly, sincerely.)* Great. Great. Great. The greatest.

JAY: *(Picking up the litter.)* I presume you mean the greater.

FRANK: Great, really great. You are amazing.

JAY: Yeah, well, don't drool on my poems. *(Picking them off FRANK.)*

FRANK: THEY'RE great! Everything you showed me is great.

JAY: Everything you showed me is great too!

FRANK: Why haven't you DONE anything?

JAY: *(Mock pass.)* Why, honey, I thought you didn't want me to.

FRANK: I mean —

JAY: I know, I know — *(Continues picking up.)*

FRANK: You keep saying, "I know, I know."

JAY: Well, if there's one thing I do, it's know.

FRANK: Whadda you know?

JAY: I know I'm seven years older than you.

FRANK: So?

JAY: So, haven't you learned anything since you were thirteen?

FRANK: Yeah. Jesus, you always win, don't you?

JAY: Sure, you play fair.

FRANK: No kidding, I mean it. You're great. You're a great actor, too. I feel like I really saw your play. Did you ever want to act?

JAY: No. It just happens. They did offer me the comic lead in *Oh! Calcutta*. But I didn't want him.

FRANK: That lead part is fantastic. Burt would be right for it.

JAY: Honey, Burt would be right INSTEAD of it.

FRANK: Really, you have a future.

JAY: I've had enough of my future, thank you.

FRANK: Seriously, what are you wasting yourself for?

JAY: *(To put an end to this.)* Well, I came to New York to write and sing and dance and act and paint.

FRANK: And what happened?

JAY: I'm available for any parts for writing, singing, dancing, acting painters. Any new business?

FRANK: Can't you be serious?

JAY: I had it removed.

FRANK: You don't even seem to take my compliments seriously.

JAY: *(Mock pass.)* Well, they're all talk.

FRANK: Christ, if I had all your talents —

JAY: Judas, you've had most of them —

FRANK: I can't write nearly as well as you —

JAY: You keep saying that like it was a virtue.

FRANK: All I've got is this one play! *(Holds it up like a torch.)*

JAY: *(Makes FRANK take play in his arms and hold it to his breast.)* Then you must hold it and keep it and cherish and nurture it, and never show it to anyone — *(shoves him away)* — or else!

FRANK: *(Beyond insult.)* You're great at this flip talk, too — you know, I'm really glad John sent me over here — *(FRANK has followed JAY into a corner and now takes JAY's shoulders affectionately.)* No one has asked me to stay overnight for years.

JAY: *(Human, after all, in the arms of a stoned, admiring youth.)* Stay overnight for years. *(Mock-faints and crawls away.)*

FRANK: *(All concern.)* Gee, what happened?

JAY: *(Defending himself with a wooden chair, like a lion tamer.)* I recoil from affection.

FRANK: Are you all right?

JAY: *(Mimicking FRANK's inflection.)* I'm GREAT! *(Cornered again, FRANK advancing admiringly.)* Uh, look — what's that play of yours about?

FRANK: *(Crosses to get it from where it dropped when FRANK rushed to help JAY.)* Oh, it's about this guy and this girl — and she's very conventional and narrow-minded — and he pulls out —

JAY: *(To no one.)* Anticlimactic.

FRANK: It's based on actual experience . . . Do you really want to hear it?

JAY: Need you ask?

FRANK: Well, gosh — gee — wow — okay — here goes — *(FRANK unconsciously imitates JAY's reading posture.)* It doesn't have a title —

JAY: Mmm. I like that.

FRANK: Oh, really? Well, maybe. Here goes — "Act One, Scene One. SHE: Hello —"

JAY: No, I don't like that.

FRANK: Huh? What?

JAY: "Hello." No. Sorry.

FRANK: But it's just — it's just — it's just —

JAY: I don't care if it's just or not; I don't like it. Haven't you got any stage directions?

FRANK: Sure, later on —

JAY: No no no. Get into it right off. It should be something like — "Act One, Scene One. SHE: Parenthesis. Enters, tender as the morning star, her hair sprinkled with rain, in a tone which instantly tells us that she has left her duck-tailed boyfriend waiting out in a light spring rain in his two-tone 1963 Mercury coupe, so that she can come in and beg her stern, grey-haired stockbroker father to let her PLEASE go to the opening of the new Pizza Parlor because it is, after all, her birthday and she hasn't had any fun since Mama ran away to join the roller derby. Close parenthesis. "Hello." *(Pause.)* No, it's the "Hello" that's wrong.

FRANK: How can "Hello" be wrong? *(As JAY goes on FRANK slumps, realizing he's again being played with.)*

JAY: You'd be surprised. Let's see; it should be something dynamic, bracing, youthful, intoxicating, alive, all the things I know you want this girl to be. "Hi?" "How's tricks?" "This is a stickup." No, no, no! Let me think. Girl, girl, girl. What, what, what? Maybe, maybe, maybe. No, no, no. Wait, wait, wait! I've got it, I've got it, I've got it. *(Becomes "Girl.")* "Hello, hello, hello!" No, it just doesn't say "girl" to me! *(Sits in mock concentration.)*

FRANK: *(Bitterly.)* Do you KNOW any girls?

JAY: The moment I see one.

FRANK: I guess you don't like girls?

JAY: Well, I wouldn't want my sister to marry one.

FRANK: *(Trying to regain his composure.)* I mean, I guess you see them as rivals for —

JAY: Yes, go on, for whom?

FRANK: I have trouble expressing myself —

JAY: Is that your only recommendation as a writer?

FRANK: I have trouble talking to people.

JAY: Try telling the truth?

FRANK: Well, look, if you do know some girls, maybe you could introduce me to —

JAY: I beg your pardon! Haven't I introduced you to enough tonight?

FRANK: Christ! I don't know why you people are that way! I should think you'd want to help younger people!

JAY: Yeah, younger and younger!

FRANK: *(Extends play.)* Why won't you —?

JAY: *(Grabs anything.)* I told you, Mack, my hands are full!

FRANK: Of what? What have you got to do?

JAY: I've got a lot of nerves to break down and you're not helping! What are you doing here, anyway? Who told you that you could write?

FRANK: Well, who told YOU?

JAY: YOU did!

FRANK: You wanna know what I think?

JAY: I wanna know WHETHER you think!

FRANK: I think the reason you're being like this is because you want somethin' from me that you know you're not gonna get!

JAY: What have YOU been smoking?

FRANK: Come on; I got all those cracks you've been making, and I know about John, and Burt, and you.

JAY: Sugarplum, I want your tender white body about as much as I want anything in this world! And I presume by now you know how much THAT is.

FRANK: Oh, yeah? Then how come you're takin' all this time with me?

JAY: I like to look at you.

FRANK: How come you read me all your stuff?

JAY: I like to listen to MYSELF!

FRANK: Christ, trying to get you people to be serious is murder!

JAY: Or be killed.

FRANK: How can a guy get anything done? All I want is to write about the world as I see it!

JAY: The world will sue.

FRANK: To write honestly! Truthfully! Fearlessly! *(On each word FRANK bangs the rolled up script in the palm of his hand.)*

JAY: I'LL sue!

FRANK: *(Pacing.)* And you ask someone to give you just a little help . . . and they're all either tied up with their home life, like Jo Wanda, or else they're too beat and scared and shy like you. Christ! I just want to write. Honestly! *(Whack.)* Truthfully! *(Whack.)* Fearlessly *(Whack.)* And all I get is a lot of hurt sensitivities and wisecracks! And people waste their lives sitting around talking to themselves about how wasted their lives are, and you ask 'em to help you not waste yours and they tell you their hands are full! Christ! The world is dying for someone who writes honestly! *(Whack.)* And truthfully! *(Whack.)* And —

(JAY echoes the words and mimics the actions on the last "Honestly, Truthfully" bit, which so enrages FRANK that he flings the script at JAY, striking rather hard.)

JAY: Oho!

(JAY hops up as if to do battle. FRANK, appalled at his own rashness, stands terrified. JAY lets him quiver for an instant, then snaps into "high-queen.")

Is my semi-precious stoned?

(FRANK gives a moan and falls down on the sofa, buries his face, frustrated, enraged. JAY picks up FRANK's script and is about to throw it out the window but looks up at the Ghost and relents, satisfies himself with hiding it behind a shutter, stands looking at the nearly-weeping boy.)

(To Ghost.) I'm sorry. *(To FRANK, who slowly rises in anger, thinking the epithets are directed at him.)* What a rotten, miserable, lying, self-pitying son of a bitch — *(Smiles.)* — I am. *(Goes to FRANK.)* Hey, let's leave this place to the graveyard shift, huh? Wouldja like to see the Village?

FRANK: *(Pouty.)* I thought you never went out.

JAY: Honey, I talk so much it can't all be true. Don't you want to see the Village? I mean, it's just downstairs. We can even bring some of it up.

FRANK: Yeah. I'd like to see the Village. I guess that sounds corny to you.

JAY: Alice, you say one more sincere thing and I'll throw you out of Wonderland and stop up my hole! Come on, get that awful coat; I'll get us in backstage at Burt's theatre.

FRANK: *(Excited.)* Can you?

JAY: Sure, would you like that?

FRANK: Yeah, really, because I want to write, honestly I do. And so I want to see all the shows and meet all the people and get to writing right off, because I don't want to wind up like you and Jo Wanda, just sitting around moping . . . I'm sorry.

JAY: Forget it: I don't want to be like you, either. Get your things.

FRANK: Hey, I didn't mean that. I just meant you've gone to pot!

(They laugh. FRANK is again embracing JAY, who is again leery of it.)

JAY: I said this stuff makes you honest.

FRANK: I'm sorry. Because I like you, I really do —

JAY: Yeah, well, those things are said. Come on, let's go before I do something I'll regret the rest of the night! Go get that horrible coat!

(FRANK just stands laughing, loving every word JAY says.)

Come on, come on, the pot thickens!

FRANK: *(Stumbling off beaming.)* You are great!

JAY: *(Alone, goes to door, presses buzzer and shouts into mouthpiece.)* Help!

FRANK: *(Re-enters with coat, stumbling.)* Wow, I shouldn't have moved, I'm dizzy. How long will this last?

JAY: *(Mutters.)* Another ten years unless I do something quick!

FRANK: What?

JAY: *("Let us be gay!")* What? What? What? Don't try to catch every little word. Just watch the movement they make, round and round and round to confuse you, but really down into the depths! *(Swirls FRANK in a low tango dip.)*

FRANK: Can you really get me into the theatre?

JAY: Stick with me, kid, and I'll have your name up in lights — even if I have to change it to Annette Funicello. *(Or appropriate look-alike movie actress for FRANK.)*

FRANK: *(Runs to mirror, laughing.)* Annette Funicello? Annette Funicello?

JAY: *(Laughs, grabs his hand, leads him running around room.)* Come on, Alice, come on! You can't get to Wonderland through the Looking-Glass! Come on, Alice, we're late! Round and round and round and down the rabbit hole!

(They spin in a little dance and then fall in a pile on the floor, FRANK on top of JAY, giggling like a fool. Anything might happen. JAY suddenly stops laughing, shoves FRANK away, stands, runs to opposite side of room.)
My God. My dear God.

FRANK: Huh?

JAY: I wasn't talking to you.

FRANK: *(Staggers to his feet, dragging his coat.)* Come on, let's go out.

JAY: Yeah, you with a whimper and me without a bang.

FRANK: Huh? Aren't we going out?

JAY: That's what they say — and I know why!

FRANK: Why, what?

JAY: Who? Which? When? Where? I did it.

FRANK: Did what?

JAY: You didn't do it; I did it. I did it again just now.

FRANK: What?

JAY: Weren't you going somewhere?

FRANK: Where?

JAY: I don't know, where?

FRANK: Hey, what's wrong?

JAY: Technically, nothing. It's a superb reproduction.

FRANK: Of what? *(FRANK is dizzy with confusion now.)*

JAY: Do I have to let you kill me this time? That'll only mean your turn comes up again next time!

(FRANK looks blankly at JAY, then fumbles over to the sofa and passes out. JAY shamefacedly picks up FRANK's jacket and is about to cover the sleeping boy with it, when suddenly JAY begins talking aloud, sometimes to the Ghost, sometimes to the sleeping FRANK, sometimes to the jacket, sometimes to himself.)

The amazing thing is that anyone as smart as I supposedly am could have been stupid enough all this time to lay the blame on YOU! You, teasing and tantalizing me out of my peace of mind, without even offering a piece of — well, let that pass! *(To FRANK.)* I don't want your body, I've got one of my own! *(Glances in mirror.)* Well, let that pass, too! *(To Ghost, about FRANK, lecherously.)* I've got half a mind to — *(To FRANK.)* But then you've got half a mind, too. *(To jacket.)* You've got this body and I've got this mind and love will make us one. *(To Ghost.)* One what? Very funny! *(To FRANK.)* But what if it should have my body and your mind? Oh, shut up. *(To himself.)* My trouble is I'm of two minds — *(To jacket.)* — with but a single thought, yes, yes — *(Screams, throwing jacket across room.)* BUTT OUT! Butt out! I am trying to coordinate! *(To FRANK.)* How dare you come in here and pull me apart just when I'm about to pull myself together? *(To Ghost.)* I could be very happy together! *(JAY is by now talking to the air, focusing nowhere in particular.)* People CAN be happy together, you know! Yes they can! Yes they can! Didn't you ever see the Late Late Show? Of course it depends on which one you catch. You watch the wrong movies and wow! *(Becomes Bette Davis.)* I won't let you go. *(Paul Henreid.)* Try to be an adult, Madeleine; there's nothing you can do to stop me. *(Bette Davis.)* There is — one thing I can do. *(Henreid.)* Madeleine — put down that tiny, pearl-handled revolver. *(Davis.)* If I can't have you, nobody can!

(JAY has been hopping from position to position to play this scene. Now JAY shoots as Bette, then hops over to fall as Paul. "She" shoots "him" several times, bringing him lower each time — until JAY is hopping from side to side of the room, shooting and screaming. JAY finally screams at himself and gets under control.)

(To GHOST.) Well, people CAN be happy. We were, weren't we? Gadding about the Village to keep away from un-neutral territory — "Your place nor mine?" — or finally, when we'd seen every movie south of Fourteenth Street and none of them, not one of them, had helped, sitting here, with me talking for two. *(Bright, brittle.)* Yes, some people contribute to the conversation; I pick up the check. Yes, someone SHOULD follow me around with a tape recorder — or a parrot! *(To FRANK.)* And you, sitting there, smiling,

basking in my neon nihilism, keeping up your little scrapbook of MY insulting epigrams. *(To jacket, as JAY shakes it.)* I started to let you hang around! *(To no one in particular, wandering, dragging jacket.)* Let, hell, I knew what I was doing. I knew what it took to keep you around — *(To FRANK.)* And I put out. *(To no one.)* Turning everything you said into a joke, giving you a little help with your ideas. *(Southern accent.)* "Here, Jay; here's a little idea Ah had fo' a poem. Finish it in twenty-five words or less." *(Screams.)* COLLABORATOR! And I did it! I gave myself to you. I did it, not you. I gave myself to you, and you didn't give one damned — *(Takes jacket in his arms like a baby.)* . . . You gave your life, of course. *(Suddenly, like one accused, backing away from Ghost, from FRANK.)* But it wasn't worth anything to you without me — *(To FRANK.)* And that IS based on actual experience! *(To Ghost.)* So you loved me? So? How was I supposed to know it! You never said it! What was I supposed to do, go on producing indefinitely for you to keep on confiscating? *(To FRANK.)* You crummy little Red, I don't WANT you here! *(Spinning from Ghost to FRANK to jacket in his hands.)* You WANTED to give up your life, that's what you were here for, that's what you were DOING here, while I —

(JAY stops, as if he had never before considered this question, begins idly to pull on FRANK's jacket inside-out and backwards. It has a quilted silver lining. JAY resembles Frankenstein's monster.)

What WAS I doing? What was it? Day after night, pouring myself into — *(JAY looks down, rips the jacket off, throws it away. To jacket.)* Well, WHATEVER I was doing — *(To Ghost.)* — I used YOU to do it with — *(To FRANK.)* — And I am NOT doing it anymore!

(Goes to desk, opens drawer, takes out gun, walks immediately to FRANK, holds gun to FRANK's head.)

Get up.

(FRANK comes a little bit awake, looks into gun barrel, frowns, and goes back to sleep.)

Get up.

(JAY shoots him in the head. It is, of course, a water gun. JAY drinks from it. FRANK shows no response at all. JAY lays gun down, goes over and takes a sip from some cold coffee — it is awful; JAY gets an idea. He takes the bottle of pills, opens them, shakes three of them into the coffee, stirs it with his finger, takes the boy's bag and loads it with a heavy stone or bricks used as bookends, replaces it, backs away from sofa, looks up to Ghost.)

I'm sorry. *(JAY walks directly over to couch, gives it a resounding kick, and screams.)* GET UP! *(FRANK stirs; chattily.)* I wonder if I should paint this place or just stay high all the time? *(FRANK subsides, JAY repeats kick.)* GET UP!

FRANK: *(Half-awake.)* What time is it?

JAY: The curtain was lowered to denote a lapse of memory. *(As FRANK again subsides, aggressively.)* How'dja like my PLAY?

FRANK: *(Going to sleep.)* Great, great, great . . .

JAY: Great, great, grate on my nerves. *(Leaps into the air and hops up and down on the sofa, shrieking.)* Get up! Get up! Get up up up up up!

FRANK: *(Sits up.)* Hey!

JAY: *(Sits innocently on back of sofa.)* Yes? What do you want?

FRANK: I don't want anything.

JAY: Gosh, it took me twenty-seven years. *(Pert.)* What do you want to do today?

FRANK: Sleep.

JAY: Okay, you've done that. Now have some coffee. *(Offers it.)*

FRANK: I don't want any coffee.

JAY: Yes, you do; you said so when you came in. It's from last night. You'll never taste anything like it — till it comes up.

FRANK: I just want to sleep.

JAY: *(Mock concern.)* Fight it, kid. Don't get hooked on it. I know! Have some black coffee! *(Holds FRANK's nose, forces FRANK to drink.)* Do you want a blindfold? That's right, drink it down like a little soldier.

FRANK: *(Choking, sputtering.)* Okay, I drank it. Now I just want to sleep.

JAY: Not in about twenty minutes.

FRANK: Oh, my God. Why? Is somebody coming over?

JAY: *(Terribly innocent.)* No, I put some Benzedrine spansules in your coffee.

FRANK: You WHAT?

JAY: *(Speaking very clearly.)* I. Put. Benzedrine. Spansules. In. Your —

FRANK: My God!

JAY: No sugar.

FRANK: Benzedrine!

JAY: You looked so tired. I thought it would pep you up.

FRANK: That's a drug!

JAY: Like penicillin.

FRANK: People are allergic to drugs. I could die.

JAY: Don't be silly. There's not more than one chance in three.

FRANK: Christ, I need a shower.

JAY: No, silly, I get a shower. YOU get a stag party.

FRANK: Don't you every STOP?

JAY: No, if you stop, you think. *(FRANK shows signs of setting back to sleep, so JAY attacks, "high-queen.")* Well, of course I stop! For a full moon, or a really good TV commercial, or a glass of coconut champagne in Times Square, or breakfast. Oh, what do you WANT for breakfast?

FRANK: I don't want any breakfast.

JAY: I've got this groovy new cereal in the shape of a jigsaw puzzle —

FRANK: Hey, don't; I can't take it this early —

JAY: You put it together, see —

FRANK: Please stop, okay?

JAY: — and it's an ad for the cereal. Sort of self-perpetuating, like the Village — "Each one teach one." *(FRANK reaches for a cigarette; JAY snatches the pack.)* Isn't that terrible what they're making them put on cigarette packages? "CAUTION: Smoking can damage your health." Imagine if they made other products put on them what happens if you use too much, like — like — like Ajax, for instance. *(Jimmy Durante voice.)* "Caution: use too much o'dis stuff, and yer hands'll look like a turkey's neck!" Or Doublemint. *(Sings syrupy.)* "Chew double our gum and you'll bug out your eyes / And probably double your collar size!" Or — or — Vaseline! *(Marlene Dietrich.)* "Careful, dollings, you CAN get too much of a good thing" *(Reaching his point.)* Or they might hang a big sign at the entrance to Greenwich Village: "Beware: entering area of free expression; stagger around here too long and you're liable to get EXACTLY what you want!"

FRANK: *(Numb.)* I really need that shower — what are you ON?

JAY: Drugs? In the morning? How dare you? But I will take a few if it's necessary to make you feel better. *(Pops a few pills.)* I guess that is how people get started — taking drugs to keep their junkie friends company. Oh, Frank, you really do need someone to take care of you. *(Sudden succession of bright ideas.)* I need someone to take care of! I'll take care of you. You'll be taken care of by me! I'll be the one who takes care of you. You'll be the one care of whom I take! Oh, darling, you'll see, it'll be a lovely little life. All around the Village they'll say, "Here come Frank and Jay!" No, I don't like that billing. Make it, "Here come Jay and Frank." *(Coyly.)* Possibly, "Frank, care of Jay!" *(Katherine Hepburn.)* Other people's lives, what are they? Debris, debris, piles of debris behind them. We'll make our lives a string of perfect little disappearing days — starting with today. And I'll take you under my protecting thumb! I'll see that you get everything you want. What do you want, Frank? Tell me what you want and I'll give it to you.

FRANK: *(Harassed to hysteria.)* I want a shower!

JAY: *(Leaps into his arms.)* Darling! I'll give it to you!

FRANK: *(Fights him off.)* Hey, come on, cut it out!

JAY: *(Still doing "lost in a mist of romance.")* Listen — a shower sounds good. Think I'll go take one while there's still some hot water. And when I come back, we'll start our lovely new life with me reading you my novel! *(Whisks out huge box of manuscript.)* You'll love it! It's based on the life of Lee Harvey Oswald. It's very long, and very dull, but it perks up towards the end! Bye now — anything you need? *(JAY stands poised in the doorway.)*

FRANK: No! God! Yes! Can I use your phone?

JAY: *(Taking it out of wastebasket.)* Of course, silly. I can't use it in the shower, it's dangerous! Bye. *(Grimly.)* Oh, and TELL Jo Wanda I said she can pay me later. She'll know what I mean. *(Brightly.)* Ta-ta! See you real soon. *(Starts off, returns.)* Oh, and Frank — if you WILL gobble that many pills at all hours of the day, you've got to watch out for hallucinations — seeing things? You can't tell what's real and what's not. *(Starts walking out, but slows down like a dragging record.)* Whaat's reeal aand whaat's noot. Whaaaaat's reeeeeal aaaaand whaaaaat's nooooot. *(Starts to speed up, winds up sounding chipmunk.)* What's real and what's not What's r'l 'nd w't's n't. Whtsrlndwhtsnt! *(Skitters off, talking faster and faster till it is an electronic screech.)*

(FRANK, alone, does what any boy would do in the situation; he bangs his head with his fists and screams silently. Then he takes the phone and with mounting fury unwinds the cord from around it. He dials — it seems to take hours — and then has to endure what seems to be the loudest phone-ring in history. Someone answers.)

FRANK: Hello? John? . . . Oh, it's not John. What number have I . . . Okay, okay, I'm sorry. I mean, *Lo siento, Señora. Pardóname, por favor.*

(FRANK hangs up, gets a little slip of paper with John's phone number out of his pocket, drops it, has to scrabble among all the remnants of JAY's poem to find it, finds it, reseats himself, wearily dials again, waits, in the meantime examining the palm of his hand for hallucinations. You would think FRANK had never seen the palm of a hand before. John answers.)

Hello! Jo Wanda? I mean John? Sorry to wake you, but . . . You just got up? What time is it? . . . Seven o'clock? My God, that play of his must have lasted for . . . No, never mind, I'll explain later, look, can I come over there? . . . Frank . . . FRANK! . . . Yeah, still at his place, what did you think? . . . What do you mean, Old Faithful didn't blow last night? . . . Janice who?

(We hear JAY offstage in the shower singing something like "Love Is Where You Find It," and gargling.)

Oh, THAT Janice . . . Jesus. Look, can I come over there? . . . No, he's been swell . . . No, he hasn't ignored me . . . *(Irate.)* No, he hasn't done THAT, either! I'll be right over . . . I'd like to shower there . . . I don't want to shower here . . . No, I told you he didn't! . . . All right, all right, I'll see you in a few minutes . . . Tell her what? . . . All right, please don't explain, I'll tell her — I mean HIM! . . . Okay. *(Hangs up. FRANK now starts to get himself together, finding coat, dragging out bag, which is incredibly heavy, and putting it back, taking only his overnight bag. FRANK begins to hunt for his script, and in the process looks where Ed's picture is hidden and pulls out Ed's picture, which seems to him, of course, to be his own — the last straw.)*

Hey! *(This is a cry of involuntary terror as FRANK drops picture back into its hiding place.)*

JAY: *(Off.)* Yes?

FRANK: Uh — I'm leaving! *(Gets into coat, ties shoes.)*

JAY: *(Off.)* Can't hear you. Be right out!

FRANK: I said I'm leaving! And I don't believe you about the hallucinations!

JAY: Just a minute! *(JAY enters, a-billow in an absurd, mind-blowing Mardi Gras outfit — fluorescent spangles and feathers, a flamingo fan, all topped off with a flowing Indian Chief's headdress. JAY gets between FRANK and the door.)* Now, what was that about hallucinations?

FRANK: Um —

JAY: You're not hallucinating, Frank; I really am wearing this two-piece bathing suit.

F RANK: Uh — I'm — going out.

JAY: Getting independent. That's a good sign in these cases. Remember, you can ask a policeman ALMOST anything.

FRANK: *(Shocked, drugged.)* Um, yeah, Look — I can't handle my big bag right now. I'll — I'll come back for it.

JAY: Anytime. I work days.

FRANK: Um — yeah, okay. *(FRANK would love to get to the door.)* Oh, and Jo Wanda said to tell you she's going to — send something back with me?

JAY: *(Grim.)* I'll bet she will. *(Flirtatious, dredging key out of some deep pocket.)* Hey, look, I dug out my extra keys for you!

FRANK: *(Accepting keys from as great a distance as possible.)* Oh. Well, thanks.

JAY: *(Heavy wink.)* We'll skip the usual deposit. *(JAY steps aside to let FRANK go, but feels a pang of guilt and stops him at the door.)* Uh — look — do you need any money?

FRANK: *(Puzzled by the kindness.)* Oh. No. Thank you very much —

JAY: Look, have fun in New York — really.

FRANK: Thanks, I will — I'll — hey, what are you — Oh, shit — I'll see you — I guess —

(JAY blows him a kiss and FRANK leaves quickly. JAY is jubilant the moment the door closes.)

JAY: Hooray! Ah's delivered! No more ghosts! This happy hunting ground is hereby declared off limits! *(Locks the door.)* Ah's delivered! Ah's delivered! *(To mirror.)* How do I look delivered? Oooof! *(Takes off headdress.)* No more deliveries, please! *(Runs to window to watch FRANK walk away.)* Lumber, lumber, lumber! *(Finds FRANK's script in shutter.)* Oh, Lordy *(Drops it like a hot potato.)* A dance in honor of my delivery! *(Does a little Indian dance, suddenly stops.)* Oops! Better be careful. My magic is workin' so well today I might make it rain! Not bad for a first try. *(Picks up coffee to toast himself.)* To the celebrated ghost chaser! *(Drinks. It is the doped coffee.)* Oh. Dear! I wonder what's the antidote to counteract a Benzedrine? Oh, hell! Here's to greater consciousness! *(Drains cup.)* A benny for your thoughts! *(Looks at messy room.)* Look at this mess! I almost let that kid fuck up my whole — *(JAY is picking up poems when he notices a special one.)* Oh. I haven't even thought of this one for — *(JAY becomes sentimental, goes to window to recite poem by the morning sunlight.)* "The hateful morning sun / interrupts a nightmare / of my loved one." *(Smiles sadly, shakes his head.)* "Nightmare of my loved one." *(To Ghost.)* What I actually dreamed was that you were riding on a Ferris wheel with one of those battleship-class weightlifter boyfriends of yours, and I was having to turn the damned thing. *(Ghost objects.)* Oh, all right, truck drivers. I can't see that there's any great — *(Realizes he is talking to Ghost again.)* Hey, what is this! I thought I just got rid of you for good! God damn it! You keep comin' back like a song, don'tcha? *(Shoots water-gun at Ghost as if Ghost was circling above him.)*

SCENE 3

(The lights come up almost immediately. JAY, in black turtleneck and slacks, is preparing for FRANK's return. JAY brings out fresh coffee, not bothering to clear the debris from Scene 2, talks to Ghost while doing so.)

JAY: I am not talking to you. No, it will do you no good to moan, I am not listening. I'll talk to you later, when I talk to him. Of course he's coming back. You ALL come back! *(JAY holds up FRANK's script to silence Ghost's arguments, seats himself, holding the script.)*

(FRANK appears in the hallway. He is dressed in new Village clothes and looks rather stunning. FRANK starts to knock, then takes out his keys and opens the door. JAY, the moment he hears the keys rattle, tucks the script under a sofa cushion and assumes a bright, Loretta Young air. FRANK hesitates a moment more to run a comb through his hair, puffs up his chest, and enters.)

FRANK: Hello. *(Goes at once to his bag.)*

JAY: Hello. Coffee?

FRANK: *(Taking bricks out of his bag.)* No thanks. What's in this batch, Mescaline?

JAY: Novocain.

FRANK: You sure drink an awful lot of coffee.

JAY: It keeps me wide awake. Sure you don't want some first?

FRANK: First before what? *(FRANK begins to look around for his script.)*

JAY: Before we start fighting.

FRANK: What do you mean, "fighting?"

JAY: Well, you've been over to Jo Wanda's, and she gave you the real lowdown on me, and what a terrible phony I am, and you've come back here dressed to kill, so I naturally assumed it's me you're going to —

FRANK: *(Interrupting.)* You know, you're a real bore.

JAY: Okay, we can start anywhere. Why am I a bore?

FRANK: You know, you're not worth talkin' to.

JAY: So? I do all the talking.

FRANK: You know, you're in love with yourself.

JAY: Jealous?

FRANK: The only thing I'm jealous about of you is your talent. I hate to see talent wasted.

JAY: When you could have used it?

FRANK: I told you, I'm a good writer.

JAY: *(Runs to telephone.)* Sure, let's call your English teacher to prove it; I'm sure he'll accept the charges.

FRANK: *(Grabs phone from JAY.)* What are you trying to do?

JAY: *(Quick queen.)* How sweet. You noticed.

FRANK: You know, I feel sorry for you.

JAY: *(Parodying the boy's hand-whacking gesture, right in FRANK's face.)* Honestly?

FRANK: You make me furious!

JAY: It works!

FRANK: What works?

JAY: Jiu-jitsu; using the other fellow's weight against him.

FRANK: I don't know what you're talking about.

JAY: That's all right. As you keep saying, I keep saying, "I know."

FRANK: You know, I don't know which is worse; to know so little you can't be taught, or to know so much you can't learn any more!

JAY: Aha! You're falling into my style, I notice.

FRANK: Well, it's a good style; somebody ought to do something with it.

JAY: Like help the younger writers? Like get them in backstage? Like have them over to his house nights?

FRANK: Well, why not? If you won't help yourself, why not?

JAY: Not "Why not," baby, "Why?"

FRANK: Yeah, well, John told me that, too. Why you were so nice to me.

JAY: Well, come on, baby; bring in that surprise witness.

FRANK: *(Brings Ghost's photo out.)* I look like that guy that died!

JAY: True, baby, you do. You look so much alike that you could have looked at each other and combed your hair. And combed your hair. And —

FRANK: You weren't even interested in me. All you wanted was my body.

JAY: And all you wanted was my mind.

FRANK: What if I did? What do you do with it but sit around here feeling sorry for yourself?

JAY: Instead of feeling sorry for whom?

FRANK: For that poor guy that killed himself — when you dropped him!

JAY: And others like him?

FRANK: I don't think you're capable of feeling anything for anybody!

JAY: Ho, boy! That's what our theater needs, brutal realism! Depraved queers and simple country boys! *(Takes FRANK's script out, throws it at him.)* Come on, baby, read me THAT script!

FRANK: *(Clutching the script.)* It's your SCRIPT. You're the one that always wants to turn everything into some kind of play. All I wanted was a little advice.

JAY: A little ventriloquism!

FRANK: Listen, we're both very bright. I thought we could pull it off together!

JAY: You mean watch each other masturbate?

FRANK: You're just trying to pick a fight!

JAY: I'm the perfect host. You came back for a fight.

FRANK: I came back for my bag and my script. I didn't want to see you again.

JAY: You've got a key. How come you came back when you knew I'd be here?

FRANK: *(Caught. Pause.)* You always win.

JAY: Only because I know it's a game.

FRANK: I don't know that game.

JAY: Oh, you play it awfully well, baby. You come in here with a smile and a song and a little wet dream of a play, and look up to me like the ghost of your English teacher, and I'm supposed to take it from there and go into the shadow-play that haunts this house! Only not this time. The position is filled. I've got a ghost of my own that fills all my needs.

FRANK: Ha! All except one. *(FRANK slumps sexually.)*

JAY: Sorry. You can't afford me!

FRANK: You're disgusting.

JAY: All right, let's evade it. It's not the point, but let's evade it.

FRANK: How can you stand being —

JAY: *(Mimicking "Whack" gesture.)* But evade it honestly!

FRANK: I hate to see a guy —

JAY: Truthfully!

FRANK: I could help you —

JAY: Fearlessly!

FRANK: All right! All right! You could help me! Is that what you want to hear me say? That I need you? I need you!

JAY: *(Stunned, confused.)* You never go ahead and say the next thing. *(Shakes it off.)* But that's all right. I don't want to hear it anymore. Jesus, how can even THIS be worse than I thought?

FRANK: What next thing? What did you say?

JAY: I said, "I'm going out the window. Do you want anything?"

FRANK: Out the —

JAY: It's the only thing open this late!

(JAY makes a sudden move as if to jump. FRANK leaps across the room, grabs him, throws him down to the floor, slams the window.)

FRANK: You're crazy!

JAY: And you want me to stay that way! You want me to do it all over again! Jay, the mad scientist! You want me to praise you and pour myself into you and write your plays for you. You want me to take my brain out and put it into your body and make a ghost out of you and a corpse out of myself!

FRANK: That's insanity!

JAY: I call it death!

FRANK: Is this how you killed him?

JAY: He killed himself!

FRANK: Why?

JAY: From debt, baby, most suicides are from debt, and he owed me his soul!

FRANK: For what? Why? How come? What is this with you? What is this constant attitude that the world owes you something, that it's done you so wrong? What has it done to you? What has it done you out of? How did it do you in? What did it do to you? What did I do to you? What did he do to you that he owed you his soul? *(Pause. Same volume.)* Huh?

JAY: Huh? Because it was my soul, that I had pumped into him, all the soul he ever had! And he never gave it back, soul or body, nothing, nothing, nothing!

FRANK: Well, did you ever come right out and ask for it back?

JAY: Why should I? He never had to ask me!

FRANK: Well, great! Cool! Fabulous! He didn't ask you for anything. You didn't ask him for anything. You didn't even ask him if he wanted WHATEVER it was you gave him! Why should you expect anything back, body, soul, whatever?

JAY: Because — I didn't want to make him into a monster. I didn't want to make him into a thief. I didn't want to make him into a ghoul. But I didn't want him to make me into a grave-robber. I didn't want him to make me into a zombie. I didn't want him to make me into a comic-book devil, extracting souls from his helpless victims. I didn't want us to be Dr. Frankenstein and Charlie McCarthy. I wanted us to be — beautiful. And instead, all I made of my quote mind and his quote body was just the usual ever-popular, show-stopping, handsome, toothsome, winsome and then some All-American hustler, Dead Ed. Baby, take a bow! *("Baby, take a bow!" directed to Ghost.)*

FRANK: Don't call me "baby!"

JAY: Why not? You applied for the role!

FRANK: I didn't apply for any "role." *(Indicates scattered papers.)* I just helped you get rid of him.

JAY: Sure, that's what I created you for!

FRANK: It was YOU who wanted to audition me for some "role" or other — some kind of lover!

JAY: You want to be a paid substitute for a lover. What IS that word?

FRANK: You're out of your head!

JAY: YOU'RE out of my head!

FRANK: You just turn everything I say around!

JAY: Why? What have you been saying around?

FRANK: You just turn around everything I say!

JAY: Well, everything you say turns around me!

FRANK: You reverse everything I say!

JAY: Ya notice it makes just as much sense that way?

FRANK: Look, you don't want me!

JAY: You flatter me!

FRANK: You don't!

JAY: I never said I did.

FRANK: You don't want me and I don't want you. It's just some kind of crazy defense you throw up when you think you're being encroached upon. You come on and then you run away, again and again!

JAY: *(Simultaneously with FRANK's speech above.)* You keep digging up your dull damned, dim body and throwing it into the conversation just when we're about to get somewhere important. And I want you to STOP IT!

FRANK: You don't really want me and you know you don't. Hell, if I grabbed you, you'd run!

JAY: *(Outraged.)* Try it!

> *(FRANK hesitates for a moment and then grabs JAY in a clumsy embrace. JAY slaps him, hard.)*

(Waving his hand.) Ouch! *(To Ghost.)* Don't you people ever SHAVE?

FRANK: *(To Ghost, to JAY's great surprise.)* And YOU keep out of this! *(To JAY.)* You see? Neither of us wants this kind of relationship.

JAY: Not with you, we don't!

FRANK: You won't be serious!

JAY: All right, what do we want then? Tell us!

FRANK: I only wanted to be your friend!

JAY: My ghost!

FRANK: I didn't even know about the guy!

JAY: *(Crushed.)* Weren't you counting on my devotion to SOME ghost of hopeless love?

FRANK: *(Pause.)* Well, what if I was? What if you were to help me a little? What if I was to let you? Wouldn't we both be getting what we want?

JAY: No! The ghost of it! The appearance of it! The feeling — just the imitation of the feeling. And we'd both have to give up our lives to get it. I'd tell you your dream, and you'd tell me mine, just so you could have the illusion of being respected, and I the illusion of being —

FRANK: I DO respect you!

JAY: — desired. Oh, God, suicide for that. And it is suicide, it is. You don't have to go as far as Ed did. The moment you try to live someone else's life for him, or let him live yours — it's suicide. And that's what we both wanted — to give up our lives to each other so we wouldn't have to live them ourselves. Say it with me. Say it. If I have to say it, at least say it with me. Because it's the honest truth for both of us: "I never wanted to buy you; I wanted to BE you."

FRANK: *(Long pause, shakes his head.)* I better go. Jesus.

JAY: You might as well. We can't hurt each other anymore. Besides, we've got it all in our heads now — the last act, to play back at convenience. The un-original soundtrack.

FRANK: *(At door.)* No. NO! What you're saying, all this mad scientist stuff, that witch's brew of mythology and psychology and Movie Mirror magazine in your head; I'll never think like that. Not unless I go crazy, too. *(FRANK has meant this as an insult, but it brings a sudden realization.)* But then, that's true, isn't it? If I ever do start to go crazy, that way — I'll know it, won't I? Because I'll hear — your voice — in my head — saying all these things.

JAY: Like a ghost.

FRANK: No. Like a friend. Warning me. Thank you.

JAY: *(Shocked, but guarded.)* So. You got a little piece of my mind after all. Well, I guess it's customary to give you boys SOMETHING. Goodbye. Tell Jo Wanda I'm sending back her "dish."

FRANK: Goodbye — *(FRANK starts out, stops.)* Look —

JAY: Huh?

FRANK: You — gave me something that I needed very much.

JAY: Don't rub it in. *(JAY starts picking up Ed's papers, carefully.)*

FRANK: Look, you're living in the past.

JAY: *(Bitterly.)* Have you got a present for me?

FRANK: You're so damned hard! I'd like to see you break, I really would!

JAY: You and who else?

FRANK: I could break you!

JAY: Could you now?

FRANK: Yes, I could!

JAY: *(Quietly.)* Honestly, truthfully, fearlessly?

FRANK: Yes. *(FRANK thinks for a second. Triumphantly.)* I love you. *(FRANK smiles victoriously and exits.)*

(JAY stands staring at the door, then looks slowly around the room. The Ghost is gone. JAY cannot find Ed anywhere. The phone rings. Not answering, JAY has the conversation he knows he is going to have, in between phone rings.)

JAY: Hello, Jo Wanda. *(Ring.)* No, he's not. *(Ring.)* Yes, he was. *(Ring.)* Yes, he
has. *(Ring.)* No, he won't be. *(Answers phone.)* Hello? . . . Oh, hello, Jo
Wanda . . . No, he's not . . . Yes, he was . . . Yes, he has . . . No, he won't
be . . . Mad? Why should I be mad? . . . Oh, that. Forget it . . . How DO I feel?
. . . Oh, happy. Sleepy. Grumpy. Bashful. Sneezy. Dopey. And Doc!
*(JAY slams the phone down, throws Ed's papers into waste-basket, and ex-
its, dusting off his hands.)*

CURTAIN

THEATRE DEC 1 0 1964
THE HAUNTED HOST

A play by Roobert Patrick, presented by and at the Caffé Cino, 31 Cornelia Street (through Sunday). Directed by Marshall W. Mason. **VILLAGE VOICE**

"That's what our theatre needs, depraved queers and simple country boys!" The speaker is Jay, the Host, who has been acting very much like a depraved queer all evening, and his listener is a simple country boy. The line is spoken in heavy irony, as are about three-quarters of the lines in "The Haunted Host," and yet the play is oddly convincing. Author Robert Patrick's central character is so elaborately twisty and continually witty at the expense of his own self-image that the play has intensity and application far beyond the narrow, obsessive situation it describes. The plot is less clear than it might be, and occasionally the technical devices are self-conscious; but the play is obviously the work of a sophisticated and talented writer.

Bob O'Conner, who plays the title role, gives perfect line readings, but lacks a sure sense of pacing, with the result that the play proceeds in leaps and spurts and seems more shapeless than it is. William Hoffman is convincing in the thankless role of his foil. Director Marshall W. Mason and lighting designer Dennis Parichy move the play through its various moods and moments effectively, although Mason must share with O'Conner the blame for lack of rhythms. Mason should restrain himself from writing program notes.   M. S.

For years, Robert Patrick remembered this review by Michael Smith as a bad one, and submitted it for this anthology with the following comment:

"I blush now at my arrogance and stupidity. I am thrilled to have been called a 'sophisticated and talented writer.' Director Marshall W. Mason was in no way responsible for my innate bad timing, but was certainly responsible for any few moments that were good."

Norma Bigtree as Mona, "a menace," promoting the Caffe Cino's longest-running show

Photo provided through the courtesy of Robert Patrick

DAMES AT SEA
Lyricists: George Haimsohn & Robin Miller; Composer: Jim Wise

Dames at Sea had its world première at the Caffe Cino on May 17, 1966, directed by Robert Dahdah. The show jump-started the career of a fifteen-year-old singer and dancer named Bernadette Peters before it moved on to 575 performances at the Theatre de Lys (now the Lucille Lortel).

SCENE ONE

Backstage at a 42nd Street Theatre

Time: 1933

Overture, then —

PRODUCER'S VOICE: All right, girls. Snap into it! Everybody on stage for the opening number!

(The lights go up on MONA KENT, star of the show that is in rehearsal. MONA is a platinum blonde, dressed in halter-top pajamas, with a diamond clip in her marcelled hair. MONA sings:)

MONA:

Verse:

When your job has fallen through
When your rent is overdue
When the butcher's gonna sue
Don't despair

Get that rhythm in your toes
Doll up in your swellest clothes
Go down where that green stuff grows
It's there
All there

(JOAN, a tough chorus girl with a heart of gold, joins MONA for the rest of the number. JOAN is in a practice dress, white shorts, a polka-dot top with matching bows in her hair and on her tap-shoes.)

Chorus:

On
Wall Street
Come on down to Wall Street
Where those
Millionaires
Will give your troubles
A holiday

You can have your Broadway
With its tawdry wares
Just gimme that street
With its shares
(Bulls and bears!)

Wall Street
It's the rise and fall street
Where you'll find a rich tycoon
To croon
All your blues away

You can have your Texas
With its home on the range
Just gimme a seat
On the Stock Exchange

In the middle of
Wall Street
It's the all in all street
You will never find me livin' in London, Paris or Rome
'Cause a ticker tape is tickin' in my dome

Tellin' me that
Wall Street, Wall Street, Wall Street
Where the big spenders all meet
Wall Street, Wall Street, Wall Street's my home!

(MONA and JOAN do a tap routine, using huge silver dollars as props. Just before the number ends the PRODUCER enters, smoking a cigar. He is in an early 1930s business suit, double-breasted, open, with the suspenders showing.)

PRODUCER: *(Entering through audience.)* C'mon, Girls — pick 'em up! Now, you babies — give!!

(JOAN shoots the PRODUCER a dirty look. The number ends.)

PRODUCER: O.K. Take five.

(JOAN relaxes at the side of the stage, fixes her make-up, hair, etc.)

PRODUCER: Mona, you're gonna be great in the part, baby.

MONA: I am? Then what about my billing?

PRODUCER: But Mona! You're the leading lady! Can't you just see it — Mona Kent in "Dames at Sea." Your name's gonna be in lights!

MONA: Yeah — but how big? Listen, you know the Wrigley sign? Well — I want it *that* big. In color. And twinkling!

PRODUCER: Mona! Remember my nervous condition.

MONA: Oh, bananas!
      (MONA exits angrily.)

JOAN: There she goes. The Lady Macbeth of 42nd Street.
      (RUBY enters. She is dressed in an old raincoat and a tam and is timid and bewildered.)

RUBY: Oh — er — pardon me.

PRODUCER: Who are you, kid?

RUBY: I'm a dancer, and I just got off the bus and I want to be in a Broadway show.

PRODUCER: Where you from?

RUBY: Utah.

PRODUCER: Listen, Ruby, you think you can tap your way to stardom overnight, don't you?

RUBY: Well — back home they said . . .

PRODUCER: Well, they're wrong! It's a jungle out there. Dog eat dog. Broadway's paved with broken hopes and worn-out dreams . . .

JOAN: Yeah, and worn-out feet, too . . .

PRODUCER: So take a tip from a guy who knows — and go on home!

RUBY: But I can't! I spent all my savings . . .

JOAN: Have a heart, Hennessey! Can't you tell the kid's got class? Give her a break.
      (An idea strikes.) Say, why can't she take Glenda's place in the line?

PRODUCER: What happened to Glenda?

JOAN: Wake up, you dope! Haven't you read the funny papers? Glenda sailed on the "Berengaria" this morning. She hitched up with Corny Astor the Third, last night.

PRODUCER: Well — there goes another glorified American — gold digger.
      (Resigned to RUBY.) O.K., girlie, do you know the music?

RUBY: Why, I — er —

PRODUCER: Do you know the number?

RUBY: Well, I haven't heard . . .

PRODUCER: The routine?

RUBY: Well, no one has shown . . .

PRODUCER: CAN YOU DO IT????

RUBY: *(After a pause, gulping bravely.)* I'll try.

> *(The PRODUCER motions to JOAN to help RUBY. JOAN comes downstage with RUBY as the latter takes off her tam and raincoat. Underneath, she is wearing a practice-dress — just a little more glamorous than JOAN's.)*

RUBY: Say, Miss, do you happen to have a Graham cracker on you?

JOAN: No. Why? You hungry?

RUBY: I'll say. I haven't eaten in three days.

JOAN: Oh, you poor kid . . .

PRODUCER: *(Impatiently.)* C'mon. Go to it, kid.

> *(The pianist strikes up the "Wall Street" melody. RUBY does an impeccable version of the tap routine MONA and JOAN did. After a moment the PRODUCER nods, satisfied.)*

PRODUCER: O.K., O.K. You're hired. Joan, brush her up a little.

> *(The PRODUCER exits.)*

> *(RUBY suddenly sways and puts her hand to her head.)*

JOAN: Are you all right, kid? Say, what you need is a square meal. I just remembered — I got a Babe Ruth in my handbag.

> *(JOAN exits.)*

> *(Again RUBY staggers. This time she crumples, very slowly, as DICK enters. DICK is a sailor, and a leading man in the best Warner Brothers tradition. He is carrying a battered little cardboard suitcase. He is just in time to catch RUBY as she faints.)*

> *(There is a long pause as he looks lovingly at her. Then DICK sings.)*

DICK:
> It isn't Jean Harlow
> It isn't Greta Garbo
> It's you, it's you, it's you!

> *(RUBY comes round and sings back.)*

RUBY:
> It's not Leslie Howard
> Or even Noel Coward
> It's you, it's you, it's you!
> It isn't Bert Wheeler

DICK:

    It isn't Ruby Keeler

BOTH:

    No one of them, no none of them will do

DICK:

    Not Myrna

RUBY:

    Or Cary
    Or King George

DICK:

    Or Queen Mary

RUBY:

    It's you

DICK:

    It's you.

BOTH:

    It's you.

RUBY:

    It isn't Richard Arlen
    Or Spanky McFarland
    It's you, it's you, it's you!

DICK:

    It isn't Aimee Semple
    Or even Shirley Temple
    It's you, it's you, it's you!

RUBY:

    Not Amos or Andy

DICK:

    Or Orphan Annie or Sandy

BOTH:

    No one of them, no none of them will do.

RUBY:

    Not Boris or Bela

DICK:

    Nor Hedda or Louella

RUBY:

    It's you!

DICK:

It's you!

BOTH:

It's you.

(By the end of the number RUBY, hunger forgotten, joins DICK in a soft-shoe routine.)

(When the dance ends:)

DICK: *(Pointing to the case.)* This is yours, isn't it? I followed you all the way from the bus station. You left it in front of the water fountain.

RUBY: *(Taking case.)* Gee, thanks. It's all I have in the world.

(RUBY opens the case and pulls out the only thing in it — a pair of tap shoes.)

RUBY: I sure would hate to lose these. I've had them ever since I was at Madam Melba's Tap, Ballet and Ballroom Academy.

DICK: Madam Melba's . . . ? Say, where are you from?

RUBY: Utah.

DICK: You too? Centerville?

RUBY: Why, yes.

DICK: Gosh! So am I.

RUBY: Gee, back home they said these dancing feet of mine would take me a long way.

DICK: Guess they were right. You're on Broadway!

RUBY: Gee! So I am!

DICK: D'you know, when I look into those big blue eyes of yours, I want to do just one thing.

RUBY: *(Puckering up for a kiss.)* What?

DICK: I want to sing.

RUBY: *(Still waiting.)* Anything else?

DICK: Yes. And dance.

JOAN: Ruby . . . Oh! Am I interrupting?

(JOAN ogles DICK in a good-natured kind of way, then turns to RUBY.)

JOAN: They want you to try on Glenda's costume for the Wall Street number. *(As she leads RUBY off:)* I don't know why — it's only three pennies.

(JOAN and RUBY exit. DICK throws his hat in the air with joy.)

DICK: *(Sings.)*

Now I am riding high and feeling swell

'Cause in my heart of hearts I know darn well

A certain gal has rung the bell
— I gotta dance!

I can forget each morning's gloomy news
And I'll be saying so long to the Blues
I'll jump into my dancing shoes
— I gotta dance!

I can beat old man Depression
I'll just have a dancing session
Now I've found out what that ballroom floor
Is for

I'm gonna set a new and happy style
I'm gonna face the future with a smile
For now I even see prosperity
Is just around the corner, follow me
Brother! Take a chance
— And dance!
(DICK follows the song with a tap routine. As the dance ends, MONA enters, smoking through a long cigarette holder.)

MONA: Well! Hello!

DICK: Oh . . . Hello, Miss Kent.

MONA: You know me?

DICK: Gee whiz, everyone knows Mona Kent.

MONA: What's your name, sailor?

DICK: Richard. But my friends call me Dick.

MONA: Tell me, Dick, what was that song you were singing?

DICK: Oh — that was just something I wrote.

MONA: It's good. Have any more?

DICK: Well — er — yes, I do.

    (DICK pulls some sheet music from his middy and hands it to MONA. She looks at it for exactly one second.)

MONA: It's marvelous.

    (MONA hands the music to the pianist and sits on the piano.)

MONA: *(Sings.)*
    No king or tsar
    No Dempsey or Gene Tunney
    No movie star
    His face was kind of funny
    No Lochinvar
    But Lordie, he had money

That Mister man of mine

He loved me so
And oh how well he knew me
When I was low
When I was sad and gloomy
He'd always know
And bring home diamonds to me
That Mister man of mine

Once he was a big shot
Swimming in cash
Champagne and roses all around
Yeah! He was a big shot
Then came the crash
And Jack came tumbling down.

My life is black. He's gone!
Since he adored me
I've had no lack
Of men, but they all bored me
He wants me back
But now he can't afford me
Ours was a fire whose flame was too brief
Gone's my desire now he's on Relief
No! I can't live on kisses
So I'll never be Mrs.
To that Mister man of mine.

MONA: It's divine! It gets you right here. It'll be just right for my big spot in the first act. Come to my dressing room, Dick, and let me find out what *other* numbers you've got hidden up your middy.

(MONA leads DICK off.)

(JOAN dashes on.)

JOAN: Oh, Miss Kent! Something terrible's happened. It's just awful . . .

(Almost simultaneously FRANK, another sailor, runs on. He and JOAN collide. Both together:)

JOAN: Why you flat-footed ape! When did they let you out of the zoo, you clumsy bum!

FRANK: You dumb, silly, stupid broad! Why can't you look where you're going? You blind or something?

(Suddenly they recognize each other.)

JOAN: Frank, honey!!

FRANK: Joan, baby!!

(They embrace enthusiastically.)

JOAN: What are you doing in that monkey suit? Last time I saw you, you were wearing gold epaulettes — in the upper loge at the Roxy.

FRANK: You should talk. *(Looking her up and down.)* At least I have clothes on.

JOAN: The same old Frank! I see you haven't changed any.

FRANK: You haven't changed either — thank goodness. Remember the whoopee we had in Baltimore?

JOAN: Sure do. And Atlantic City . . .

FRANK: And Buffalo . . .

JOAN: *(Heavily.)* And Bangor . . .

JOAN: *(Sings.)*
>You said we would charter
>An airship to Spain
>Instead we wound up
>On a Greyhound to Maine
>I felt every mile
>As we sat in the aisle

BOTH:
>What a funny honeymoon!

FRANK:
>But don't you remember
>That sweet little room

JOAN:
>As big as a bathtub
>As dark as a tomb

FRANK:
>The breezes did blow

JOAN:
>From the kitchen below

BOTH:
>On our funny honeymoon.

FRANK:
>But wasn't the garden heaven
>Around our tiny hotel?

JOAN:
>Yes, dear, the Garden was heaven
>Until you fell
>In the wishing well.

>I borrowed your toothbrush

FRANK:

    I borrowed your comb.

BOTH:

    We both forgot to bring our pajamas from home

JOAN:

    So harried

FRANK:

    We tarried

BOTH:

    We forgot to get married
    What a funny honeymoon
    Honey what a funny

JOAN:

    No matrimony

BOTH:

    Funny honeymoon!

    (When the number ends they kiss.)

JOAN: *(Dreamily.)* With a hey nonny nonny . . .

FRANK: *(Ditto.)* And a hot cha-cha!

JOAN: Say, what are you doing here, anyway?

FRANK: Have you seen my buddy?

    (DICK enters, escaping from MONA. He is adjusting his middy and breathing heavily.)

FRANK: Hey, Dick, you son of a sea-cook. I want you to meet Joan.

DICK: Which Joan? Joan Blondell? Joan Crawford? Joan of Arc?

FRANK: Nah, you jerk. *The* Joan.

    (DICK and JOAN are shaking hands when RUBY enters and worms her way into the center of the group.)

RUBY: And I'm Ruby.

    (MONA enters.)

MONA: I am absolutely famished. Say, Dick — how about joining me for lunch — at the Ritz?

JOAN: Oh, Miss Kent, something terrible's happened. It's just awful . . .

MONA: Well what, for heaven's sake?

JOAN: Oh, Miss Kent, it's just awful, something terrible . . .

MONA: *(Taking DICK's arm.)* Listen, Miss Whatsit, we haven't the time . . .

JOAN: But Miss Kent! It's Mr. Hennessey, the producer of this show! He just had a complete nervous breakdown and they're taken him off to the sanatorium.

(General consternation.)

MONA: That *is* terrible. It means the show can't open.

JOAN: But tonight's the first night!

FRANK: We gotta open.

RUBY: And it's my first show, Dick, what are we going to do?

DICK: *(Masterful.)* What's the show called?

JOAN: "Dames at Sea."

DICK: *(Looking at Frank.)* Well . . . ?

FRANK: You mean . . . ?

DICK: Why not . . . ?

FRANK: On the battleship? You crazy? What would the Admiral say?

MONA: Which Admiral? Admiral Bulkhead? Admiral Mainbrace? Admiral Sextant?
    Admiral Van Gangplank?

DICK: Van Gangplank! That's the one.·

MONA: You don't mean "Cupie Doll" Van Gangplank is your commander?
    Well — just leave him to me. *(To DICK.)* But — er — I guess I'll need an es-
    cort through the Navy Yard.
    (MONA takes DICK's arm and begins to exit.)

RUBY: *(Desperately.)* Dick!!

MONA: Who are you? I don't believe we've been introduced?

RUBY: *(Angrily.)* My name is Ruby!

MONA: Ruby, are you? Well — all I can say is, you could use a little polishing!
    Come on, Dick.
    *(MONA leads DICK off. He gesticulates to RUBY but she is shocked and mor-
    tified and turns her back.)*

JOAN: And all I can say is — FOOEY!!

FRANK: Hey, Joan, C'mon!

JOAN: *(Crossing to Ruby.)* No, you go ahead. I'm needed here.
    *(FRANK exits. JOAN looks sympathetically at RUBY, who is struggling with
    her tears. She takes a handkerchief out of her shorts and hands it to RUBY.)*

RUBY: Thanks!

JOAN: That two-bit phony. Listen, I knew her when she was queen of the taxi-
    dancers. She had more corns on her feet than the whole state of Iowa. Don't
    let *her* get you down, honey.

RUBY: I never want to see either of them again. *(She grabs her suitcase.)*
    Mr. Hennessey was right. Broadway is a jungle. I'm going back to Center-
    ville — where people are nice. *(Moves center for solo number.)*

Pitter patter, what's the matter with me?
pitter patter, rain is all that I see

Where is my raincoat, it's here somewhere
Why wear a raincoat when the weather's fair?

But ever since I saw him depart
It's been raining, raining in my heart

Where are my rubbers to ford the storm?
Why good are rubbers? — outside it's warm

But ever since my dream fell apart
It's been raining, raining in my heart

Once I saw a cottage on a sunshine lane
A fairy palace in disguise

I don't see it now, it must be rain
that's getting in my eyes.

Where's my umbrella, and where's my guy?
I need that fella to keep me dry,

It won't help if the sunshine should start
'Cause it's raining, raining in my heart.

JOAN: All right, go back. Forget Broadway. Forget your talent — your great
talent — and go back to the button counter at the five and ten. You aren't
big enough for Broadway. It takes push and drive and guts. You have to
claw and scratch and fight every inch of the dirty way. How do you think the
others did it? — the great ones? Look at Eagels. Look at Brice. Look at Bern-
hardt. She lost a leg!! Come on, kid!

(JOAN marches RUBY out.)

BLACKOUT

SCENE TWO: ON THE BATTLESHIP

(A string of signal flags indicates the ship.)

(DICK enters.)

DICK: This way, Miss Kent. He's up here on the bridge.

(MONA enters in full evening dress.)

DICK: Oh, Admiral. Someone to see you, sir.

(The ADMIRAL enters.)

DICK: *(Saluting.)* Miss Mona Kent, sir.

(DICK exits.)

ADMIRAL: Not *the* Mona Kent? The one who's opening in "Dames at Sea,"
tonight, at the Hippodrome?

MONA: *(Slipping off her furs.)* Correct. Except that we're not opening at the
Hippodrome, Admiral — we're opening right here. *(She looks around.)* This
is perfection! Now — I'll descend on my moon from that gun turret . . . and
the chorus can slide down the yard arm . . . and my pink baby spot can hang
from the mizzen . . .

ADMIRAL: Im-*possible*!!

MONA: Impossible — Cupie Doll?

ADMIRAL: *(Recognizing her.)* Thundering torpedo tubes — it's Consuelo!

MONA: *(With a slight Spanish accent.)* Sí, sí, Cupie-Doll. Remember the night
we met?

ADMIRAL: You were the waitress who served me chili con carne!

MONA: And you were the sailor who broke my heart . . . Listen . . .

(The "Beguine" is heard softly.)

MONA: *(Sings:)*

> The Beguine
> I hear the Beguine
> Deep in my heart it's beating a wild tattoo

> The Beguine
> The fatal Beguine
> Recalling tropical gloom
> Orchids in bloom
> Pungent perfume
> — And you!

> Do you remember
> Pensacola?
> Sultry desire
> Passions on fire
> Under the moon

> Those nights of splendor
> In Pensacola
> Lost in your arms
> Under the palms
> Near the lagoon

> You were so tender
> In Pensacola
> While guitars played a haunting, taunting tune

> I surrendered

In Pensacola
Was I mad
Was I wrong
To be glad
You were strong
No! I long
For Pensacola
Again . . .
(During the number MONA vamps the ADMIRAL. By the time she has fin-
ished singing she has the ADMIRAL panting in her embrace.)

MONA: Do we get the ship?

ADMIRAL: *(Feebly.)* Sí, sí.

> *(MONA leads the ADMIRAL off.)*

> *(JOAN rushes on, meeting FRANK.)*

JOAN: Oh, Frank! What are we going to do? The Liberty boat just sank.

FRANK: So what?

JOAN: All the chorus boys were on it.

FRANK: Who needs 'em? You got 900 right here.

> *(They exit. RUBY and DICK rush on from opposite directions. They both*
> *freeze in their tracks. RUBY turns away.)*

DICK: Ruby, darling, you must understand . . .

RUBY: I'm very busy.

DICK: But don't you know? Can't you tell? You're the only girl for me?

RUBY: *(Coldly.)* Oh, really?

DICK: *(Sings:)*

There's something about you
You're like the first breath of spring
There's something about you
Like songs that angels would sing

A sketch by El Greco
The bubbles in vintage champagne
A Swiss mountain echo
An orchid in cellophane

There's something about you
The heavens rolled into one
So living without you
Just wouldn't be fun

Darling, don't tell me I'm dreaming
Why not just say yes and agree

That something about you
Is something for me
(As the song progresses DICK completely wins RUBY over, so that by the time he finishes singing she helplessly lets him kiss her. While they are kissing:)

MONA: *(Calling from offstage.)* Oh Dick, darling? Help me with this damn zipper!
(DICK immediately breaks off the kiss and exits. This time RUBY is really enraged. She stamps her foot and exits in a fury.)
(FRANK and DICK cross over.)

FRANK: How's the audience?

DICK: Swell! The bridge is all sold out, and it's standing room only in the lifeboats.
(FRANK exits. JOAN dashes on.)

JOAN: Something terrible's happened. It's just awful . . .

DICK: What?

JOAN: This really is terrible!
(The ADMIRAL strides on.)

ADMIRAL: It certainly is. Miss Kent cannot appear.
(FRANK enters.)

DICK: But she has to. She's the star. The show must —

FRANK: Yeah, just look. *(Pointing out into the audience.)* All Broadway's out there! Queen Marie of Romania, and everybody!

DICK: Waiting to hear my songs. *(To ADMIRAL.)* What's wrong with Miss Kent?

JOAN/FRANK: *(Ad lib.)* Yeah — what happened? What's the matter, etc.

ADMIRAL: She's seasick.

DICK: Seasick? But we're in drydock!

ADMIRAL: Miss Kent is a very sensitive woman.

JOAN: What are we going to do?
(RUBY enters. All eyes turn toward her.)

RUBY: Joan, should there be twenty-five sailors in my dressing room?

DICK: Ruby, I have something to ask you. A favor. A big favor.

RUBY: Not if you were the last man on Earth!
(RUBY turns to go. JOAN stops her.)

JOAN: Ruby, wait. Kent can't go on.

FRANK: And you're the only one who can go on in her place.

RUBY: But I can't! I don't know the routines, the songs, the part . . .

ADMIRAL: BUT CAN YOU DO IT?

(RUBY looks wildly around the group. They are all counting on her. She gulps and swallows.)

RUBY: I'll try.

BLACKOUT

(Music introduction to "NAVY NUMBER.")

(Lights up on RUBY appearing through back curtains. She is wearing an Admiral's hat, abbreviated jacket with epaulettes, velvet tap shorts, gunmetal stockings and tap shoes with bows.)

(She is radiantly confident and goes through the number perfectly. She is joined by DICK, FRANK, AND JOAN.)

RUBY: *(Sings.)*

> I'm the Star Tar of the Navy
> I'm the Hit Miss of the sea
> When the ocean's getting wavy
> What a pretty sailor I'll be
>
> I'm the Swell Swab on the Poop Deck
> I'm the Shipshape Shipmate in the Hold
> I'm the Star Tar
> I'm the Star Tar
> Of the Navy blue and gold
>
> (heave ho!)
>
> I'm the Top Gob in the Crow's Nest
> I'm the Big Bell sailors love to ring
> In the Foc'sle I get no rest
> In the Captain's Cabin I'm the thing
>
> I'm the Sweet Salt of the Mess Hall
> I'm a True Bluejacket to behold
> I'm the Swell Swab
> I'm the Top Gob
> Of the Navy blue and gold.

(As the number ends, deafening applause, cheers, etc. break out. RUBY takes several bows, receives a bouquet with tears in her eyes.)

BLACKOUT

(The lights come up immediately afterward as the two girls run on stage taking off their hats, etc. The applause continues in the background.)

RUBY: Was I all right?

JOAN: *(In crossover.)* Oh, Ruby! You were *swell!* *(She exits.)*

(RUBY checks her hair, makeup, etc.)

(DICK enters.)

DICK: *(Seizing her.)* Ruby, listen to that applause! All Manhattan is at your feet. You're a star!

RUBY: *(Coldly, as she frees herself.)* It's rather crowded in here. Would you mind leaving?

DICK: But let me explain . . .

(MONA walks across on the ADMIRAL's arm, laughing gaily and paying no attention to DICK.)

MONA: *How* many ships did you say you had, Admiral?

(They exit. RUBY bites her lip, turns back to DICK.)

RUBY: Oh, Dick, I've been such a fool.

(They go into a big clinch.)

VOICE: *(Off.)* Places for the finale! Places for the finale!

BLACKOUT

(The lights go up again on the traditional triple-wedding finale.)

MONA/ADMIRAL:
> Let's have a simple wedding
> A quiet wedding for two

JOAN/FRANK:
> No crowds, no fuss, no bother
> Just Mom and Father will do

DICK:
> After our little marriage
> A baby carriage will roll into view

RUBY: *(Coyly.)*
> But first, dear, let's have a wedding

ALL:
> A quiet wedding for two
> Just me, Mr. Preacher, and you

REPRISES:

DICK:
> It's not Nancy Carroll

RUBY:
> It isn't Charlie Farrell
> It's you

DICK:

It's you

BOTH:

It's YOU

MONA:

It isn't Rudy Vallee

ADMIRAL:

Or Marion Tallee

BOTH:

It's you. It's you...

JOAN:

I'll buy you a toothbrush

FRANK:

I'll buy you a comb

BOTH:

And who needs pajamas in our new little home

JOAN:

Through the door I'll be carried

FRANK:

We finally got married

BOTH:

For our sunny honeymoon

DICK/RUBY:

There's something about you
The heavens rolled into one
So living without you
Just wouldn't be fun

ALL:

Darling, don't tell me I'm dreaming
Why not just say yes and agree
That something about you
Is something for —

Wall Street
It's the rise-and-fall street
You will never find me living in London, Paris or Rome
'Cause a ticker tape is ticking in my dome
Telling me that
Wall Street, Wall Street, Wall Street
Where the big spenders all meet

Wall Street's
The good gold-digger's home!
(All couples embrace.)

FINAL CURTAIN

EXCERPT FROM FAG HAG:

An Annotation upon William M. Hoffman's
Good Night, I Love You
Lucy Silvay

Good Night, I Love You was Bill's first play. He originally wrote it as a short story until Lance [Lanford Wilson] read it and told him it was really a play. It was based on a phone conversation between us in which Billy told me he had a fantasy about getting pregnant by Lance and having his baby. We played out the fantasy together over the phone.

The play was about a phone conversation between a gay man and his fag-hag girlfriend in which the man has a fantasy of getting pregnant by his male lover. It ran at the Caffe Cino. The production took full advantage of the Cino's space, placing the male actor, talking on a phone, at one end of the Caffe. His girlfriend, also talking on a phone, was high up on a raised platform at the other end. The part of the girl was played by Linda Eskenas, a wonderful off-off-Broadway actress with long black hair. She was *an original* and as wacky as I.

Billy and I have stayed friends for 43 years. He'll always be "Billy" to me. In a recent exchange of email, I sent him the chapter from this book entitled "Billy," in which I recounted that I was "madly in love" with him.

He emailed me back saying: "I was madly in love with you, too."

I emailed him in turn: "Wow!!!!!!!!!!!! A gorgeous fortieth Anniversary present [this was three years ago], to find out you were in love with me too. I never knew."

The following emails followed:

BILL: "You were my only female lover, sweetie."

LUCY: "Why didn't you ever tell me you were madly in love with me?"

BILL: "I was scared too. I was also . . . infatuated with Lance and recovering from my relationship with John. It was all very confusing to me at the time. I was communicating with you best, I think, through my writing, which was more honest than the rest of me . . . There were a lot of poems, plus *Spring Play* (about an actress who seduces a bi-curious man, in which I starred opposite Harvey Keitel), not to mention *Good Night, I Love You*."

LUCY: "God, this is more romantic than all those silly crushes I've had this year — and for years past."

The play's title referred to the way Billy and I ended our nightly phone conversations: "Good night, I love you."

GOOD NIGHT, I LOVE YOU
William M. Hoffman

A Play in One Act

Good Night, I Love You was first performed at the Caffe Cino
on September 7, 1965.

Directed by Neil Flanagan
Produced by Joe Cino

Lisa .... Linda Eskenas
Alex............................ Michael Griswold

For Lucy Silvay

TIME: A summer night in the 1960s.
SET: The bedrooms of Alex and Lisa; they live in efficiency apartments in the
Village or Upper East Side, New York City. The rooms are set on stage side-by-side;
that is, separated by a flat, the head of Alex's bed (stage right area) is flush with the
head of Lisa's bed (stage left area). Upstage, in both areas, are windows. Alex's bare
window suggests a view from a high-rise apartment building. The lights from other
tall buildings can be seen. They serve (for the first part of the play) as dim illumination for Alex's otherwise dark room. There are half opened Venetian blinds on Lisa's
window and long light-colored drapes. The light shining through them suggests a
blinking neon sign.
   Also in Alex's room: a single bed sloppily covered with a dark bedspread,
blankets, white sheets; upstage next to the bed is a small night table with a lamp, a
standard black telephone, an alarm clock, and an ashtray. There is the suggestion of
an air conditioning unit under the window.
   Lisa's room: a single bed with a white bedspread and boldly patterned sheets;
a small night table with a lamp, a Princess phone, alarm clock, a brush and comb,
and an ashtray. Extreme stage left area suggests a kitchenette. There are slippers on
a small rug downstage of the bed.
   In general, Alex's room suggests "masculine" disorder, Lisa's an almost cloying
femininity. Both Alex's and Lisa's sides of the wall might have appropriate pictures
or posters.

   *(AT RISE: Alex and Lisa are in their respective beds talking to each other
on the telephone. They are both in their early twenties. Alex is in jockey*

shorts. Lisa is wearing a beautiful nightgown — it might have a sheer contemporary look or be chicly thirties-style. Her cat Lulu, which may be played by a well-trained live cat or may be suggested by a toy one, is at the foot of her bed. The stage is as dark as possible without making the actors invisible. The illumination should come from the cigarettes the actors are smoking and the light from the windows.)

LISA: Alex, we should be married. Damn it, it's like being married, we're on the telephone so much. *(Intimate.)* We should be living together so we could be talking to each other in bed right now.

ALEX: *(Yawning.)* Yeah.

LISA: I had a dream.

ALEX: Make it quick. *(Looks at clock.)* It's one-thirty already and I have to get up tomorrow.

LISA: *(Angry.)* I'll make it quick. You always say that. Make it quick. Okay, I'll speak to you tomorrow. Good night.

ALEX: For christsake, Lisa, can't you understand that I have to get up in the morning? *(A concession.)* I love you. Tell me your dream.

LISA: I had another of my lesbian dreams.

ALEX: It's very simple: you're deep down a dyke.

LISA: We're been through that. You know I'm not. *(Yelling at her cat.)* Lulu, if you don't stop ripping up the bed, I'm going to have you declawed. Honestly, you're a terrible pest sometimes. *(To ALEX.)* Now he's sulking.

ALEX: I wish you wouldn't scream at her like that. You scare her.

LISA: For godsakes, Alex, I know how to take care of my own pussycat. *(Playing with cat.)* Don't I, angel? Come here, my love. Come to Mommy. That's my little baby. Sit with Mommy on the bed. Mommy's going to give you a big hug. *(To ALEX.)* Oh, Alex, he's so sweet. He's curling right up in my lap.

ALEX: *(Almost baby talk.)* Give her a kiss for me right on her nose —

LISA: Right on his black little nose —

ALEX: And a big squeeze. And take her in your arms and squirl her . . . And rub her black little belly —

LISA: *(Abrupt change to serious tone.)* This is silly . . . Does Tom like me? *(She pauses.)* He doesn't, or you would've answered me right away.

ALEX: I didn't say he doesn't like you. I frankly don't know what he feels about you. He's very guarded about all his feelings. You know that.

LISA: I hope he doesn't still think of me as a rival. I'm perfectly happy letting him have you for the time being. In fact, it's very convenient right now, if you want to know the truth. *(Almost a sigh.)* I think I'm in love with Steve.

ALEX: *(Dreaming.)* Don't you think he's the sexiest man you've ever seen?

LISA: He was so sweet tonight. We necked for an hour and a half and he bit my
       neck —

ALEX: I mean Tom.

LISA: Yes, Tom. *(Matter of fact.)* Tom is the sexiest man I've ever seen. I mean
       that. You have great taste in men.

ALEX: *(Suddenly serious.)* Lisa, I'm worried.

LISA: *(Concerned.)* What is it, darling?

ALEX: I think I'm getting queerer.

LISA: *(Matter of fact.)* That's impossible.

ALEX: I mean it.

LISA: How're you getting queerer?

ALEX: D'you promise not to tell anyone?

LISA: Of course. I never break my word to you. You're the only person I'm loyal
       to. I can lie to anyone but you. You can tell me anything.

ALEX: *(Slowly, with difficulty.)* Well . . . recently . . . when Tom's been with
       me . . .

LISA: *(Encouraging.)* Go on.

ALEX: Sometimes when Tom is with me I feel like a woman in a way. Not that I
       have breasts and a vagina . . . but that between the two of us . . . that he is a
       man and I am a woman in a way. But I remain a boy. Isn't that sick? Does
       that just turn you off?

LISA: No.

ALEX: I can't explain it.

LISA: *(Matter of fact.)* I think a lot of homosexuals feel the way you do but
       they'd never say it in a million years. And a lot of straight men. It's the op-
       posite of penis envy. Sometimes I think I'd like to screw a man —

ALEX: That's not all of it —

LISA: Wait a minute, will you, hon'? I want to get some cookies. *(To cat.)* Lulu,
       please get off Mommy's chest so she can get some cookies. *(She places the
       cat on the floor upstage of the bed, puts on her slippers, and goes to the re-
       frigerator. Her room is seen clearly for a moment by the light of the refrig-
       erator. She returns to her bed with a box of cookies.)*

ALEX: *(If cigarette is finished, he lights a new one while he waits.)* Hello. Are
       you there?

LISA: *(Picks up receiver. Munches cookies.)* Hello.

ALEX: Hi.

LISA: Go on, sweetie pie.

ALEX: I had a fantasy the other night that I was going to have a baby.

LISA: That's very funny.

ALEX: Let me go on. I had a fantasy that, God knows how, Tom made me pregnant.

LISA: Did you tell your group?

ALEX: No. I didn't go to group this week. Oh, are they gonna have a ball. They'll just *come* —

LISA: Alex?

ALEX: Yes?

LISA: Why do we always end up talking about you?

ALEX: You know, that isn't true!

LISA: *(Playing a whining child.)* You don't love me as much as you used to . . .

ALEX: *(Trying to placate her.)* About this dyke business — I have an insight. Here, listen to this —

LISA: *(Liking the attention.)* I love you when you're being intuitive —

ALEX: I'm being intuitive. Dykes mean protection to you. You always dream of dykes when you're having trouble with men. I know you're not about to become a dyke, but dykes're a way out. They'll protect you, like your mother did, like no one else will.

LISA: But why do I always dream of red-headed lesbians? Wait, I'll free associate . . . *(Pause. Thinking.)* I had a Spanish teacher with red hair, and there was that girl in camp. We used to kiss and make out. And there was a woman on the subway the other day. But that still doesn't explain the symbol of the red hair.

ALEX: The case of the red-headed dyke.

LISA: *(Angry.)* Good night.

ALEX: No.

LISA: *(Playing hurt feelings.)* You were very helpful but you are awfully cold. Why're you so cold to me tonight?

ALEX: The same old crap. I get tired of telling you the same old crap over and over again.

LISA: Tom is being cold to you.

ALEX: How d'you guess. Let's not talk about it. I'll just have to learn how to play it cool. If I turn off . . .

ALEX and LISA: He'll turn on.

LISA: This is very boring. All we ever talk about these days is Tom.

ALEX: I really have to get some sleep. Let's hang up.

LISA: Wait a moment!

ALEX: Good night.

LISA: Wait a moment . . . Before you go to sleep, I'm going to make up a bedtime story for you . . . *(Slowly, thinking.)* About Tom . . . About . . . About
you having a baby and still staying a man. *(Almost gleeful.)* A story about
Tom making you pregnant and you having his child.

ALEX: That'll put me to sleep — I'll be up all night masturbating.

LISA: Be serious. Now turn off the light. *(Turns on her bedside lamp, which puts
a small pool of light on her bed.)*

ALEX: It's off.

LISA: Light a cigarette . . . Are you doing that? *(Lighting a cigarette.)*

ALEX: *(Lighting a cigarette.)* Yes.

LISA: Okay. Are you ready?

ALEX: I'm ready.

LISA: *(Long pause. Drags deeply on her cigarette.)* One day you feel odd pains
in your stomach. You notice that it's swollen slightly. And you've been feeling sick morning after morning. You come to my apartment and say, *(Imitating ALEX.)* "Lisa, I know you're going to think I'm crazy, but Lisa — this is
like one of my true predictions. Lisa, I think I'm pregnant." "You're crazy," I
say. "Lisa, now look. I'm not crazy and I'm going to walk right out of here
and never come back if you don't take me seriously. This is the most important thing I've ever told you . . . Are you going to take me seriously?"

ALEX: Wow!

LISA: "I have all the signs of pregnancy and what's more I'm *sure* I am. It's like
the time I told you that you had tonsillitis."

ALEX: *(The friendly critic. He lights his lamp. Breaks mood.)* Very good, Lisa.
I'm getting interested. No kidding. I have to confess, sometimes, especially
recently, I haven't been very interested in our psychoanalyses.

LISA: I'll let that pass for the time being. Let's get back to the story . . . *(Suddenly
furious.)* When haven't you been interested? When!

ALEX: *(Matching her anger and surpassing it.)* Like when you blither on about
your stupid affairs with those godawful people you seem to pick up so regularly. Like your dope addict dyke, or Michael Fag, or David Impotent, or
Larry Lech. Now really, even though you know I love you, I think this is the
most boring collection of lovers I've ever seen. I've had to live through putting your dyke on cold turkey, or whatever the expression is. I've had to ad-
vise you how to get that practically a drag queen to bed. I've tried to help
you bilk rich, straight, stupid Larry for all he's worth —

LISA: *(A challenge.)* Do you love me?

ALEX: *(Still angry.)* Yes, I love you. You know I love —

LISA: Do you have to say it like that?

ALEX: It burns me when I think about it.

LISA: Well, how the hell do you think I feel when you go on and on about how you're going to have to break up with Tom? And listen to you whine that he's unfaithful to you? Or how unfaithful you think he is? And listen to you talk about your stupid faggot relationship! *(Pause.)*

ALEX: Okay, we're even . . . *(Almost a threat.)* Do you love me?

LISA: Yes, I love you. *(Timidly.)* Are you in love with me?

ALEX: I don't know how to answer that simply . . . I know that I'm not passionately physically involved with you.

LISA: That's the funniest thing you've ever said.

ALEX: Come on, darling.

LISA: Listen, I'm sorry I asked you that question. It's really unfair of me to put you in a corner. What can a person say to a question like that?

ALEX: Wait a minute. Let me answer it a little better. I feel things for you that I can't feel for a man, that I don't feel for Tom . . . Like when you had tonsillitis I couldn't stand you because you reminded me of my mother when she was sick . . . That doesn't sound too good, does it?

LISA: No, it doesn't, but I know what you're trying to say. At least I hope I know. Let's get back to the story. I believe you about the baby. We decide to call up Jim.

ALEX: Yes, Jim! He's very sensible. Yes, Jim, that's great! He'd know what to do.

LISA: He's become a pediatrician at Bellevue. I call him up with you in the room. Jim's at home with Ron. "Jim, this is Lisa. Listen, I want you to come over right away. It's important . . . I can't explain over the phone. Okay? . . . You're a sweetheart." He comes over in fifteen minutes. He has a very serious look on his face. You're standing by the window with your back to the door when he comes in. "Jim, you have to promise to take what I'm about to say seriously. We're coming to you for professional advice, so please don't breathe a word to anybody. Do you promise?"

ALEX: *(Gravely.)* "Yes, Lisa. Please tell me what's wrong . . . Are you pregnant?"

LISA: "No, no. I know you're not going to believe this, but I beg you to believe that Alex is serious. Alex thinks that *he* is pregnant."

ALEX: *(Falls on his back.)* He'd faint. He faints dead away. I love Jim. He really would try to help.

LISA: We finally convince Jim that at least *you* believe that you're pregnant. He takes you over to his laboratory to give you a rabbit test and some blood tests.

ALEX: Yes, blood tests and Jim dressed in white like a doctor. Wait a minute. I'm freezing. Let me turn down the air conditioner. Hold on. *(He puts on his slippers, goes to the air conditioner, and returns to bed. He covers himself.)* Hello, Lisa, go on.

LISA: *(Has been brushing her hair as she is waiting.)* I call back in the afternoon and ask for the results of the tests for a Ms. Masters. The results are positive. Jim calls. This is medical history. We have to persuade him, we have to implore him, not to publish this in some medical journal. You'd be a freak. He comes over again and probes you and feels you. You are *pregnant*.

ALEX: He can't believe it but he has to. Let's have *him* deliver the baby. I'd love to have my child delivered by Jim. And then I'd fall in love with him and leave Tom. A gay soap opera.

LISA: No! Jim wants you to have an abortion.

ALEX: No!

LISA: He tells you that you might be carrying a monster. That you might be jeopardizing your own life. He has to give you an X-ray. The X-ray is further proof. You are carrying a baby and you have some sort of uterus in your abdomen.

ALEX: No, my prostate gland has turned into a uterus.

LISA: He wants to give you an abortion immediately. But you refuse. He wants to give you a caesarean.

ALEX: No, damn it, that's unnatural.

LISA: I wish you'd have a caesarean. The other way'd be like a bowel movement.

ALEX: No. I say to Jim, "Jim, I can't begin to understand any of this but that's all I know is that I'm going to have a child and I want a child. This child is Tom's child, too. I will not murder it! I *will* take the risk."

LISA: "But it might turn out to be a freak. And we don't know if a man can bear a child. It might kill you."

ALEX: "I don't care. I want to risk it."

LISA: Jim agrees to take care of you secretly. He's not going to tell anyone about it.

ALEX: I bet he'd be thrilled if I get knocked up. He'd love to have a baby with Ron.

LISA: Now you have to tell Tom. You call him up and tell him you have to see him immediately. It's very important. He says, *(Imitating Tom.)* "Baby, can you call me back in about two hours? I'm right in the middle of something and I'm waiting for about ten phone calls. Okay, sweetheart, two hours, I promise, huh?"

ALEX: No, no. Actually it's more like this. *(Out of his covers. Facing audience.)* I
call him and *no one's there*. No one's there for the next twelve hours. *(Frantic.)* I'm going crazy. I try him once every fifteen minutes for twelve hours
and no one's there. He promised to be home but he's probably out to a
movie or walking from Times Square to the George Washington Bridge. Finally, there's at least a busy signal. I get him. "Listen, Tom, this is an emergency." I'm practically screaming. "You have to come over right away."
"Sure, sweetheart. Take it easy. I'll be right over. Half an hour." And he gets
here two hours later.

LISA: You're right. But I got all the other details, didn't I?

ALEX: You're really fantastic, Lisa . . . Look, he comes to my apartment. I'm
stoned on grass, paranoid out of my mind.

LISA: You shouldn't smoke if you're pregnant.

ALEX: I'm drunk. Be serious. *(Slowly. Eyes closed. Intent.)* He's at my house. All
the lights are off except the one by the bed and I have the television on too
loud. My room is clean. There's no lint on the rug. All the pots are hanging
on the peg board in the kitchen. There's milk for coffee in the refrigerator
for Tom . . .

LISA: Go on.

ALEX: *(Deep into the fantasy.)* "Tom. I'm serious. Please listen to me. I'm not
joking . . . I don't know how, but I'm pregnant." And Tom says, *(ALEX is
imitating Tom, who is totally repulsed.)* "I really think you *are* serious . . .
Of all the sick things! This really takes the cake. I know we both have this
thing about you being a woman and all that deep down. I know it's sexy and
all that. But fun is fun. I've had it! You can fuck off, you sick fairy!" I start to
cry as he puts on his coat. He takes me in his arms. "Tom, please believe
me. I've been examined by Jim and he says I'm pregnant. You can call him.
Here's his number. Call him." I dial the number and hand the phone to
Tom. Jim tells him about the tests and the X-rays and Tom believes him.

LISA: *(Losing control of ALEX and the fantasy.)* Alex, I'm scared. I don't want to
go on.

ALEX: No, Lisa, this is the great part. He sits down beside me on the bed and
smiles weakly and looks at me directly as he's never looked at me before. He
doesn't look trapped and doesn't look through me. "What can I say? You're
pregnant."

LISA: "What can I say?" That's just right.

ALEX: *(Ignoring LISA.)* "What can I say? It's weird but you're going to have my
child."

(The following two speeches are said together.)

LISA: "I love you. We're going to stay together always. The child will keep us together always. I will always love you . . . " *(Almost in tears.)* I don't want to hear any more!
(Long pause.)

ALEX: *(Ecstatic.)* "I want you to stay at home and take care of the child and keep house for us. I want to protect you forever." Tom will be my husband and I will be his boy who had a baby without becoming a woman.

LISA: It's beautiful.

ALEX: I loved it . . . Do you realize that this is the most exciting thing we've ever done together? This is the wildest thing I've ever heard of. *(Deeply grateful.)* I love you for it, Lisa. I love you so much.

LISA: Just wait till tomorrow night. We're going to make up a fantasy about me and Steve . . . Do you think this is sick?

ALEX: Yes! But I don't care . . . *(Looks at clock.)* I really have to get some sleep now. It's way after two. *(Adjusts pillow. Fixes covers.)*

LISA: Just one more minute.

ALEX: It's late.

LISA: Okay, good night.

ALEX: *(Not to hurt her feelings.)* No.

LISA: Do you love me?

ALEX: *(Countering her.)* Do you love *me*?

LISA: *(Hiding exasperation.)* Yes, I love you.

ALEX: *(Friendly.)* You *know* I love you.

LISA: Good night, sweetheart.

ALEX: Good night. *(Hangs up. Turns off lamp. Covers himself. Turns his back to the audience. Pause. LISA slowly hangs up. She quickly turns off the lamp. She covers herself. With her face to the audience, she lays her head on the pillow. Brief pause.)*

CURTAIN

the village VOICE, *June 22, 1967*

On Arab-Israeli War

Richard Yaffe, UN correspondent and former foreign editor of P. M., will analyze the Middle East situation on Friday, June 23, at 8.30 p. m. sponsored by Young Americans for Progressive Israel. The event will be at the Park Sheraton Hotel, Seventh Avenue and 56th Street, mezzanine, Skyline Room, Admission is $1.

$$\frac{BOY + GIRL}{1 + 1} = \frac{X}{2}$$

Meet attractive, interesting,
young, professional singles
SEND FOR FORM One plus One, Inc.
580 W. 215 St. NYC 10034

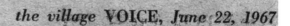

cafes & coffée houses

CAFFE CINO   31 CORNELIA ST. CH 3-9753

"The Off-Off B'way Theatre Shrine"—N.Y. Times
Winner of '65 Obie Award

George Birimisa's

DADDY VIOLET

with Dan Leach & Sylvia Strauss

George Birimisa's *Daddy Violet* confronted the horror of war, which has not changed in the years since the play's première. Certain other things, like violence in the Middle East and the pursuit of love through singles ads, have not changed, either.

DADDY VIOLET
George Birimisa[1]

As produced at the Caffe Cino in New York City in June of 1967
directed by George Birimisa with:

Sylvienne Strauss......................... ACTRESS
George Birimisa .... ACTOR ONE
Dan Leach................................... ACTOR TWO

The name of each actor is also the name of his or her character in the play. I am using the names of the actors in the Caffe Cino production, who created the roles. In order to personalize the play I will use the first names of the actors instead of Actor One or Actor Two. When Daddy Violet is performed it must be involved with the reality of where it is being performed to create the illusion that it is a total improvisation. The play will have pools of improvisations.

Where is the beginning of *Daddy Violet*? George Birimisa wanders onto the stage. He sips his can of beer and sweeps the stage as the audience is being seated at various tables. During the play the lights on the audience never go out because the actors have to see the audience and relate to them.

GEORGE: *(Shouting.)* Sylvienne! Pass out the programs. *(To a member of the audience.)* Lift your feet, please. *(He sweeps under their feet. Then he closes the front door.)* Go on talking, everybody. I haven't finished sweeping. *(Shouts.)* Dan?

DAN *(Offstage.)* George?

GEORGE: What?

DAN: How's the house?

GEORGE: *(Looks at audience.)* How are you?

AUDIENCE: Okay! Swell, etc.

GEORGE: They're fine.

DAN: How many?

GEORGE: Ah — thirty — maybe forty.

DAN: Not bad.

---

[1] Concerning rights to produce or reprint this play, contact the author at 627 Page St., Apt. 6, San Francisco, CA 94117, telephone 415.431.6254, email gbirimisa@sbcglobal.net.

GEORGE: Dan, Hurry up here. I can't think of anything to say. (*To a man in the audience.*) Did the Dodgers win today?

YOUNG MAN: I don't give a damn about them — ever since they moved to L.A.

GEORGE: You mean they're not at Ebbets Field?

YOUNG MAN: Where have you been?

GEORGE: That's a good question.

> (*When SYLVIENNE finishes passing out the programs she stands near exit smoking a cigarette.*)

GEORGE: (*To SYLVIENNE.*) Come on, honey.

SYLVIENNE: Just another drag. (*She takes a drag and steps on the cigarette. She walks on stage.*)

GEORGE: What are you going to work on?

SYLVIENNE: My relaxation and radiation.

GEORGE: Good girl.

> (*SYLVIENNE stands motionless. She is working on her radiation.*)

GEORGE: Dan, will you please —?

DAN: I'm coming, Mother.

> (*DAN enters.*)

GEORGE: What are you going to work on?

DAN: I don't know.

GEORGE: How are you feeling?

DAN: Okay, I guess.

GEORGE: How about some music?

DAN: A good idea. Maybe it will put me in the right mood.

> (*GEORGE runs to the back of the Caffe Cino. He puts on "Dedicated to the One I Love" by the Mamas and the Papas. DAN begins to dance by himself. He picks out a girl and asks her to dance. He escorts her to the stage and they dance. A man comes onstage and dances with SYLVIENNE. When the song is over GEORGE turns off the record player.*)

GEORGE: You in the right mood now, Dan? (*DAN nods.*) What are you going to work on?

> (*DAN shakes his body and then plops down on the stage.*)

GEORGE: He's working on his relaxation exercises. Let me see — what will I —? My radiation — yes!

> (*GEORGE runs out into the audience. He picks out a woman. He bends over, about six inches away from her face. He is radiating love. If the girl*

looks away he goes to another person — this time a man. If the person is wearing glasses, he tells them to take them off. GEORGE reacts to each person depending on what he sees or feels.)

GEORGE: *(Ad lib.)* You have soulful eyes. You are a dreamer, etc. *(GEORGE runs back to stage.)* My relaxation — yes. *(He puts his hands to his neck. Actor who plays this role must find the area where he is tense and utilize that area.)*

GEORGE: For me to fully radiate I must be completely relaxed and this is my area of tension. *(GEORGE has both hands to neck and he twists — sometimes it cracks.)* Ah — Dan?

DAN: What is it, Birimisa?

GEORGE: Help me with my neck.

> *(DAN stands up. GEORGE is kneeling on stage and he is bent forward. DAN gets behind him.)*

DAN: Relax your shoulders and back. Now let your head go — back and forth — back and forth. Now around and around — faster — faster. Now the other way. Keep going, Birimisa. *(GEORGE finally stops.)*

> *(DAN lies on the stage with his feet in the air. He isn't wearing any shoes.)*

DAN: Sorry about my dirty feet.

> *(GEORGE grabs his beer and wends his way among the small tables.)*

GEORGE: There's nothing symbolic about this beer. I get stage fright before my entrance and — *(He shrugs.)* I'm going outside to breathe in the freedom air of Greenwich Village and work on my psychological gesture.

DAN: Birimisa, how long do you want to go on with this improv?

GEORGE: Is that what this is? *(He exits.)*

> *(DAN gets to his feet and exits out the front door. SYLVIENNE runs to front door — peeks out to see them on the outside — then she runs back to the stage. She faces the audience. She feels her stomach. She pushes at it very hard.)*

SYLVIENNE: Will I ever break the armor? *(She puts her hands on her hips.)* Tighten my buttocks and ah — boom! *(She does a side bump, barely moving her hips.)* Golly! I've got to — *(Tries the bump to the other side and then to the front. It's a lousy bump and grind. She tries again — not very good. She runs offstage and talks to a man in the audience.)* I'm sure you have no idea how important it is for me to break through. Do you understand? Do you? *(She runs back on stage. She swivels her hips very slowly.)* One — two — three — four! Boom! Boom! Boom! *(She is very proud of herself. She runs into the audience and finds another man.)* Do you think if I sang a song it would help me to break through? *(She sings "Then He Kissed Me" and does a sexy dance and is very good at it. When she is finished with the song she runs up to another man and gets an inch away from him and puckers up her lips. Then she runs onstage, she crouches and becomes a seed and slowly blooms into a flower.)*

SYLVIENNE: Violet? *(She points to where she was a moment before. Bashful as she talks to audience.)*

SYLVIENNE: Hi, everybody! She says her name is Violet but her real name is Sylvienne. She quit Vassar and came to Greenwich Village six months ago. She is doing her Michael Chekhov exercises. *(Pause.)* The famous drama teacher? Does anyone here know who he is? I think he was the nephew of Anton Chekhov, the famous Russian playwright? *(Asking.)* Does anyone know who Anton Chekhov is? *(Many hands go up. She runs upstage. Again she tries to be a violet. Not very good.)* I better get to work on my Cheko — Chekhovian center! *(She stands ramrod straight with her hands at her sides and her eyes closed.)* Where — where is the center of my being? *(She feels different parts of her body. She touches each breast.)* I know where it's supposed to be but it just isn't there. George and Dan are so — so good at centers! *(Back to feeling her body.)* I know it's not in my abdominal cage. Maybe it's in my stomach. *(She feels her stomach. She crosses the stage with her stomach protruding. She shrugs her shoulders.)* Not too bad for a beginner.

SYLVIENNE: Now I'm going to work on my vaginal center. *(She closes her eyes.)* Con-cen-trate, vag-i-nal! *(She closes her eyes and smiles.)* Imagine a string is attached to my vag — *(She pantomimes a string attached to her vagina. She winks at a man in the audience who is wearing glasses. She is now playing a bad imitation of Marilyn. She sits on his lap. She takes off his glasses.)* You have sexy eyes.

(At one performance SYLVIENNE sat on a man's lap and said:)

SYLVIENNE: What are you doing after the show?

MAN: What's your vaginal center doing after the show?

(At yet another performance SYLVIENNE approaches a woman and says:)

SYLVIENNE: Would you like to pull my string?

WOMAN: *(Ad lib.)* I would love to.

MAN ONE: How 'bout pulling my ah — string?

MAN TWO: Let's pull them together

SYLVIENNE: *(Center stage.)* That's enough for warm-ups. I better get with it. *(She is back to being a violet.)* Me, Violet! Violet! Violet! *(She dances across the stage as a violet. She sings.)* Vi-o-let! Violet! Vi-i-ah-i-ah-o-let! I am blooming on the side of a mountain very high! I have broken through the rock-encrusted earth and I've pushed through the scraggly weeds. *(She pantomimes pushing out of the earth.)* Violet! Violet! Violet! I can feel the morning sun opening me up and below — below — below — *(She looks down in the abyss and pulls away. She is frightened. She goes back to previous line.)* I can feel the morning sun opening me up and below — below — the fog is a solid blanket hiding the Mekong Delta. Violet! Violet! Violet! The-sun-is-on-me. *(She looks at audience.)* Dan told me that Isadora Duncan did it much better fifty years ago *(Pause.)* and she did it stark nekkid.

(GEORGE comes striding down aisle from back of theater. He has left the broom onstage. He takes it backstage. Then he comes downstage. He looks at audience.)

GEORGE: I'm forty-three years old — *(He pulls down his lower lip and shows a missing tooth that is really missing.)* I'm losing my teeth — I've got a bum back and my center is in my crotch. *(He closes his eyes and clenches his fists.)* I've got to get it out of there! *(Pause and to himself.)* I am not an object! I am not an object! *(He stands straight, trying by will power to get his center out of his crotch.)*

GEORGE: My center is in my heart! My center is in my —

(GEORGE opens his eyes. He looks at individuals in the audience. He begins to moan softly and then he falls to the stage, his head over the edge. He is clutching his genitals. He is in terrible pain — he moans softly.)

SYLVIENNE: Me, Violet. *(Her hands frame her face.)* My name is Violet!

GEORGE: *(He sits up.)* You want to know something?

SYLVIENNE: What, George?

GEORGE: You can't be a violet!

SYLVIENNE: Why not?

GEORGE: Because you do not have the color of ah —

SYLVIENNE: You called me Violet!

(GEORGE's body begins to undulate. He is turning into a flower. He moves downstage, his body becoming graceful, a slow-motion dance that is a flower. He is feeling the beauty of his body.)

GEORGE: I lo — oooo — ve myself — yes I do.

SYLVIENNE: You really love yourself?

GEORGE: Yes — yes I do.

SYLVIENNE: *(She is fascinated.)* A scraggly weed turning into a beautiful flower.

GEORGE: I'm blue — a delicate blue — like a high cloud as dawn is breaking. Will you call me Violet?

SYLVIENNE: How are you, Violet?

GEORGE: *(His hands are feeling his ankles.)* My chlorophyll is cool — so cool — *(His hands move up his legs until he slowly pulls off his t-shirt and holds it over his head.)* — and oozing upward from the bounty of the good earth.

SYLVIENNE: So beautiful, Violet!

GEORGE: *(As he feels his body.)* Tell me of my beauty!

SYLVIENNE: You are radiant.

GEORGE: I am not an object?

SYLVIENNE: Your center is in your heart.

> *(GEORGE has undulated in front of her face. They are both radiant as they look at one each other. GEORGE does wild flower gyrations. Hypnotized, SYLVIENNE follows him. GEORGE begins to sing to SYLVIENNE.)*

GEORGE: *(Singing.)* Violet! Violet! Violet!

SYLVIENNE: *(Singing back to him.)* I am blooming on the side of a mountain very high —

GEORGE: *(Touching her hands, still singing.)* You have broken through the rock-encrusted earth and you've — *(he grabs her wrists and pulls her to a standing position.)* pushed through the scraggly weeds. *(GEORGE moves around her in a dance movement. He sings "Violet!" over and over. Then they rub petals and he pulls her down to the floor of the stage. They are kneeling on the stage, and he is feeling the softness of her petals.)* Violet!

SYLVIENNE: Yes, Violet?

GEORGE: *(As his hand moves up her arm.)* You are —

SYLVIENNE: Yes, Violet?

GEORGE: So — so beautiful.

SYLVIENNE: Yes? Yes?

GEORGE: *(His arms are around her now. He presses his body against hers in animal sexuality. He kisses her hands.)* Your petals are —

SYLVIENNE: Oh, Violet! You —

GEORGE: Softly smooth and so — so sensual. *(He is rubbing against her.)*

SYLVIENNE: Your — ah — your corolla ah — is — is —

GEORGE: Yes, Violet? *(He is kissing her neck.)*

SYLVIENNE: It's an exciting blue — purple and — a tinge of white.

GEORGE: *(Touches her breast.)* You've got a wild-looking stamen.

SYLVIENNE: And how — how is your calyx?

GEORGE: Early morning cool. You are so delicate! *(His hand is feeling her buttocks and moving toward her vagina.)*

SYLVIENNE: You are transcendent!

GEORGE: You are, dearest, lovelier than all the varieties of violets. *(His hand starts to feel her vagina.)* You are lovelier than —

(SYLVIENNE jumps up and punches him in the chest with all her might.)

SYLVIENNE: I am not like the others! I'm not like the others!

GEORGE: You stupid little apprentice! *(He runs offstage and addresses a man.)* That bitch doesn't know the first fucking thing about acting!

(DAN wends his way through the tables. His arms are outspread. He is flying. He runs to center stage and begins to do his flying exercise. Dan looks like a huge bird flying very, very high.)

GEORGE: *(Talking to a woman in the audience.)* He's flying now, really flying. *(DAN continues flying as GEORGE moves down aisle, talking to different people.)* There was a time when I thought I could be another Marlon Brando, but look at this kid —

(DAN is now doing a molding exercise. A molding exercise is defined as thinking of the air as a canvas and our body as the paintbrush and you are molding the air into an expressionist painting. DAN is moving gracefully across the stage, totally in his own world.)

GEORGE: This kid has only been studying the Chekhovian method for six years and I've been studying it for twenty. I could watch him forever. *(Pause.)* Ah — Dan?

DAN: What is it, Birimisa?

GEORGE: Do you feel up to your famous turkey?

(DAN faces audience. He starts with his chin and slowly works up to his eyes, then down to his arms, his back and his feet. DAN went to a turkey farm and spent hours studying the turkeys. After he fully becomes the turkey he picks out individuals in the audience. Then he jumps off the platform and hops about as the ungainly turkey and approaches an individual in the audience. He gets very close with the open-eyed stare of the turkey.)

DAN: Gobble — gobble — gobble! *(The gobble is very fierce and very angry.)* Gobble — gobble — gobble! *(To another person.)* Gobble — gobble — gobble! *(Then he jumps onstage and stares at the audience as the turkey.)*

GEORGE: That deserves a round of applause! *(The audience applauds at every performance. DAN goes back to his molding exercises, completely involved in his own world.)*

GEORGE: Dan, let's show these wonderful people what a really great actor can do. *(No answer.)* Mr. Leach?

DAN: What?

GEORGE: (*Looking at audience — then back to DAN.*) Let's put your center in your — ah — chest!

DAN: My chest?

GEORGE: Please!

(*DAN is motionless. Then he becomes very macho. He picks out a pretty girl in the audience. Very close to her.*)

DAN: What's your name, baby?

(*If she doesn't answer, he moves on to another girl. Responses are different at every performance.*)

DAN: What are you doing after the show?

GIRL: You better watch out. I'm with my boyfriend.

DAN: Ditch him! We'll turn on at the Electric Circus in the East Village and —

GEORGE: Hey, Dan, take it easy!

DAN: I'm havin a ball, fella!

GEORGE: Okay, Dan, back on stage! (*DAN comes onstage.*) Put your center in your mouth.

DAN: My mouth?

GEORGE: Correct!

(*DAN is thinking about it. He takes off his sunglasses and puts the handle in his mouth. His movement changes. He slowly turns into a screaming faggot. His eyes light up as he picks out a good-looking guy in the audience. He swishes over to the guy and runs his hand through his hair. Most of the guys go along with it but at a performance at the Firehouse Theater in Minneapolis a young man stood up and said:*)

YOUNG MAN: Get away from me, you fuckin faggot!

DAN: (*Ad lib.*) Oops! Wrong number.

DAN: (*Goes up to another man who smiles at him.*) Oooooooooooooooooh. Oooooooooooooh!

GEORGE: What is it, Dan?

DAN: I don't know. I've never had my center in my mouth before.

GEORGE: It's brilliant work!

DAN: I'm afraid that I —

GEORGE: Afraid of what?

DAN: (*Mesmerized by the smiling guy.*) I don't know. I've never experienced anything like this. It's like — heavens to Betsy — it's —

GEORGE: (*Hits DAN on shoulder the way a butch man might do.*) Are you freaking out?

DAN: *(Big grin. Looking for another man.)* It's fabulous! *(From one table to the other, flirting with all the men.)* Now I can understand the whole high-camp mystique. Susan Sontag and Andy Warhol. Why, it even makes Fire Island understandable. *(DAN moves to young lady whom he asked for a date.)* Do you have a cigarette, hon? *(After he gets the cigarette he moves to a guy.)*

DAN: Light me! *(Pause.)* Don't be nervous. I won't hurt you, hon! *(He sits in chair offstage and puffs madly on his cigarette à la Bette Davis.)*

GEORGE: Dan, onstage, please! *(DAN doesn't move.)* Put your center back in your chest. Think of Warren Beatty!

  (DAN turns his eyes up to the ceiling in ecstasy. GEORGE moves toward him. DAN moves away. GEORGE ends up chasing DAN among the tables.)

GEORGE: Tab Hunter! Rock Hudson!

DAN: *(Looks at GEORGE. Turned on.)* Together?

GEORGE: Get a grip, fella!

DAN: I love my new persona!

GEORGE: *(Makes his hand into a fist — very threatening.)* But you're the greatest actor with the biggest balls.

DAN: Please, Birimisa. I love my center right where it is. *(He runs around looking for another guy.)* I love it! I love it! I love it!

GEORGE: Think butch!

DAN: *(Stands in front of another guy.)* Ooooooh!

SYLVIENNE: *(Rushes over to him.)* Oh, Dan, dear, you look pale. Let me —

DAN: You don't fool me for a second, Miss Mini Monster! You'd love to have this gorgeous stage all to yourself.

SYLVIENNE: What on Earth did I do?

DAN: Germinate, bitch! Ughhh! Ughhhh! Girls! I can't stand them. *(He makes loud noise of vomiting.)*

SYLVIENNE: *(Looking for a sympathetic face in the audience.)* Of course you realize this is no accident.

DAN: Get her out of here! Get her out of here!

SYLVIENNE: Let me tell you about Dan Leach and how it all started! Originally he's from Dallas. His father was killed in a stampede in the Pecos Panhandle when Dan was just seven. However, it seems that Dan was riding his pinto pony that happened to start the stampede that killed his father and —

DAN: Oh, no you don't!

  (DAN is back to his masculine image. He grabs SYLVIENNE, lifts her up and shoves her out the front door.)

SYLVIENNE: (*Shouting.*) He thinks I'm his mother and he is full of shame about — (*Dan slams the front door on her.*)

GEORGE: Dan, your next line is Violet. You skipped a whole scene.

DAN: Shut up, Birimisa. I know what my next line is. (*To audience.*) You'll have to forgive me for breaking out of character, ladies and gentlemen, but that young lady is an apprentice with our group who just happens to be more interested in finding herself a man that she is in learning the Chekhovian method of acting. However, what is really bugging her is her last review. She was called "adequate" by a reviewer from *The Village Voice* — (*suddenly DAN is swishy fag.*) — who shall remain nameless!

(*GEORGE is seated on the edge of the stage. With one hand he is making the motion of a flower. His heart is not in it.*)

SYLVIENNE: (*She opens the front door and rushes up to the stage. Her petals are quivering.*) Dan, dear, I want you to —

DAN: I wasn't speaking to you, Vera Hruba Ralston! (*DAN turns to GEORGE.*) Violet?

GEORGE: You still Dan Leach?

DAN: I really don't know.

GEORGE: (*He is lying flat on the stage.*) Show me what your name is.

DAN: What a wonderful idea, Birimisa! (*DAN crouches on stage, his hands to his sides. Quickly he grows and flowers. DAN is six-feet-three and very high with his hands over his head.*) What's my name?

GEORGE: You're a flower, right?

DAN: You're so perceptive, Birimisa!

GEORGE: You red?

DAN: It may confuse you since I can't get my center out of my mouth.

GEORGE: You a lilac?

DAN: You're getting warm.

GEORGE: You begin with an L.

DAN: Part of me does.

GEORGE: You have more than one name, correct?

DAN: Ooooooh! You're so right, Birimisa

SYLVIENNE: I know! You're a pansy!

DAN: Wilt, weed!

GEORGE: You're a lily! (*Dan squeals in delight.*) You're a Madonna lily!

DAN: Honey, that was my persona ten years ago.

SYLVIENNE: Heavens to Betsy! You're — Easter lily!

DAN: Sizzle, bitch!

SYLVIENNE: *(Sneering.)* You want me to call you Easter?

DAN: Up your vinyl vagina, Miss Tessie Teeneybopper! *(Flirting with GEORGE.)* You can call me Easter, Birimisa!

GEORGE: *(Is a flower, undulating. His hands move sensually toward DAN.)* How are you, Easter baby?

DAN: My petals are quivering.

> *(GEORGE and DAN are almost touching. SYLVIENNE gets in between them. DAN gives her a dirty look.)*

DAN: *Ooooooh!* Such a putrid purple. Honey, you're not going to make out looking like that. Look at me! *(DAN is in all his glory as Easter Lily.)* I'm clear and cool and such an eggshell white!

SYLVIENNE: You're a screaming faggot hiding behind the arts.

DAN: Ooooooh! Do I detect a touch of sickly, jealous green in your stamen? You, my dear, are an artificial flower. Non-organic. You don't belong in the same ground with us. *(Looks at audience.)* There was a time when having a hot vulva was enough. Those days are gone forever.

SYLVIENNE: *(Losing control completely.)* You've always had the hots for George.

GEORGE and DAN: For Violet!

SYLVIENNE: Ah, fuck it! *(She exits to the back of the coffeehouse.)*

DAN: Dear me, such Anglo-Saxon smuttiness. *(He looks at GEORGE sexily.)* Violet?

GEORGE: *(Is undulating his body toward Dan — sexual — secretive.)* Yes, Easter baby?

DAN: You're a deep lustrous purple.

GEORGE: Thank you, baby! *(GEORGE is showing off as a flower.)*

DAN: Baby? Mmmmmmmmm. Do you mind if I call you Daddy, Violet? *(Pause.)*

GEORGE: No, baby, no! *(He is moving his pelvis faster and faster as the undulating Violet.)*

DAN: Oh, Daddy Violet, your fibrous stamen turns me on. It enflames me. It makes my chlorophyll boil. Your purple petals are like an ocean on a moonlit night.

GEORGE: Oh, babe!

DAN: May I, Daddy Violet?

GEORGE: *(Sexual frenzy.)* May you — what?

DAN: May I cultivate your root?

GEORGE: *(Grabs his crotch.)* The root of heaven.

   (SYLVIENNE is watching the scene.)

SYLVIENNE: *(Screaming.)* The root of heaven? How sick can you get?

GEORGE: *(Startled out of his fantasy. Pushes SYLVIENNE offstage.)* Get back in the soil.

SYLVIENNE: You're as sick as he is.

GEORGE: *(He pushes her offstage a second time.)* As you get older you'll realize how sick you really are.

SYLVIENNE: I'm tired of being a seed.

GEORGE: My advice. Stay nice and warm in the good earth. *(DAN smiles at her.)*

SYLVIENNE: *(Turning to DAN.)* But I thought that you — all those dreadful things you — is your center still in your mouth?

DAN: Yes, my center is still in my mouth.

SYLVIENNE: I wasn't blaming you. I was blaming your center — you know — calling me all those horrible names. Ah — Vera Hruba — ah — something or other.

DAN: Vera Hruba Ralston. An actress in the forties who just happened to be married to the owner of Republic Studios, Herbert J. Yates. She got all the starring roles in his B pictures.

SYLVIENNE: You are dreadfully confusing.

DAN: Nothing personal, Violet. As you grow you will learn to bypass the rocks and the scraggly weeds.

SYLVIENNE: Are you saying that your center is in your mouth — permanently?

DAN: Until I change it organically. I don't believe in chemical fertilizers.

SYLVIENNE: *(Flutters her petals.)* Am I really an artificial violet?

DAN: My dear Violet. *(He touches her leg.)* I must say that you do have a degree of organic life in your roots. I mean — wouldn't you say it would be rather difficult to grow on the side of a mountain overlooking the Mekong — *(He is looking over the edge of the stage.)* Mekong Delta! I can — oh — I can — Dear God — the Mekong Delta!

SYLVIENNE: What — what is it?

DAN: *(Utter terror, crawling across the stage, moaning and sobbing.)* I don't know, I —

SYLVIENNE: You don't know?

DAN: *(Clutching his body.)* I feel so — dear God. I —

SYLVIENNE: You've been working too hard. Doing your famous turkey must be a terrible emotional strain.

DAN: *(Screaming.)* My center is gone!

SYLVIENNE: It can't be! It can't be!

GEORGE: *(He grabs DAN. Holds him tightly.)* But — but that is impossible!

DAN: *(Trying to get away. They struggle.)* I don't have a center! Dear God, where is the center of my being?

GEORGE: *(Still trying to hold DAN.)* It's got to be somewhere. It's only logical according to the teachings of Michael Chekhov!

DAN: I know — I know — after all these years of studying the Chekhovian method. I'm a failure.

SYLVIENNE: Listen to me, Easter!

DAN: What?

SYLVIENNE: *(At the top of her lungs.)* Easter! Easter Lily!

DAN: What on earth are you talking about? *(DAN is still trying to get away from GEORGE, who is holding him.)*

SYLVIENNE: You're clear, cool and an eggshell white. You're Easter Lily!

DAN: I am?

SYLVIENNE: Yes! Yes! Yes!

GEORGE: Now don't panic. Let me think! *(He is still holding DAN.)* Dan?

DAN: Who?

GEORGE: Dan Leach! Dan Leach!

DAN: If only I can find my center. Dear God — where? Where?

(GEORGE lets go of DAN. He crawls upstage, away from DAN.)

SYLVIENNE: You've got to find it. Without you as a role model — a living example of the creative artist I —

DAN: I — I — *(He is pounding on the floor of the stage.)* I — I can't find it!

SYLVIENNE: Oh, my God! How could you — *(DAN is bent over. SYLVIENNE is beating him on the back with her fists.)* How could you do this to me? How could you? *(She jumps up.)* My center is in my heart! My name is Violet. I am blooming on the side of a mountain very high. I have broken through the rock-encrusted earth and I've pushed through the scraggly weeds and now I can feel the afternoon sun opening me up and below — below — *(She looks down into the Mekong Delta. She lets out a horrible scream.)*

GEORGE: *(He is looking down into the Mekong Delta.)* What — what is it?

SYLVIENNE: The fog has lifted — it is no longer a solid blanket hiding the — My God — I can see the Mekong Delta!

DAN: *(In pain and terror, his hands hiding his face from the horror.)* Great, baby great! Go with it! This can be an existential breakthrough!

(SYLVIENNE is staring into the Mekong Delta. She is hysterical. GEORGE is also hysterical. He is pulling his hair and moaning, staring down into the Mekong Delta. At the height of this scene all of them are moaning and screaming and ripping at their bodies — tearing their clothes.)

SYLVIENNE: The rice paddies — so close — so close — a baby in a basket — in the center of the flooded rice paddy — closer — closer — *(She screams and backs away from the horror below.)* — the baby is charred, burned, roasted. I — I can smell the flesh — I can smell the flesh — the eyeballs are dripping — boiling. I can — the mother — bloated — floating — purple green. *(She begins to beat her body — completely out of control.)*

(GEORGE is crying and screaming and pounding the stage with his fists. He drags SYLVIENNE to the edge of the stage. She fights him — clawing at him.)

GEORGE: Come out of your fantasy! This is not the Mekong Delta! This is not the Mekong Delta! *(He is screaming, trying to convince SYLVIENNE and himself. She has her hands over her face. He pulls her hands away from her face — he forces her to look over the edge of the stage.)* Salinas Valley! Salinas Valley! Salinas Valley! Salinas Valley! *(No response from SYLVIENNE.)* Salinas Valley! Salinas Valley!

SYLVIENNE: *(Whisper.)* Salinas Valley.

GEORGE: Salinas Valley! Salinas Valley!

GEORGE/ SYLVIENNE: Salinas Valley! Salinas Valley! Salinas Valley.

(GEORGE runs over to DAN who is bent over on his back in the position of a Vietnamese who is being tortured. GEORGE pulls DAN to a kneeling position.)

GEORGE: Salinas Valley! Salinas Valley! Salinas Valley!

DAN: Sal-in-uh —?

GEORGE: *(Twists his arm.)* Salinas Valley.

DAN: Uh — Salinas Valley.

GEORGE/DAN: Salinas Valley! Salinas Valley!

SYLVIENNE: *(Runs over to them — their heads are together.)* Salinas Valley — magic. I'm a fine actress — an organic actress!

DAN: My — my center has returned.

SYLVIENNE: Is it you-know-where?

DAN: It's in my heart.

SYLVIENNE: Life is wonderful!

GEORGE: *(They are hugging each other.)* We are really growing!

DAN: *(He is radiant.)* I will join the two of you on the side of the mountain very high. *(The three of them turn into Violets.)*

SYLVIENNE: *(To DAN.)* Such a deep purple! Such a masculine violet!

DAN: Thank you, Violet!

SYLVIENNE: My mind — that nightmare — looking down into the — *(She starts to look over the edge of the stage. DAN quickly pulls her back.)*

DAN: We are growing in organic fertilizer. And, remember, pain is always involved with growth. And, let us be honest, there is nothing worse than petal pain.

(DAN and SYLVIENNE hold hands and they begin to sing:)

SYLVIENNE/DAN: We are blooming on the side of a mountain very high. We have broken through the rock-encrusted earth and we've pushed through the scraggly weeds. *(They form a circle and start dancing. They go faster and faster in a hysteria of happiness, singing.)* Violet! Violet! Vi-o-let! We can feel the morning sun opening us up and below the fog is a solid blan-ket — *(they stop dead in their tracks — they are looking over the edge of the stage.)* hiding the —

GEORGE: Salinas Valley, goddamnit!

(For a moment they are motionless.)

ALL THREE: *(Singing.)* Violet! Violet! Vi-o-let!

DAN: The sun is on us!

SYLVIENNE: *(Looking down into the Mekong Delta.)* The Salinas Valley! Steinbeck country!

GEORGE: The fog has lifted — the mission bells are echoing across the verdant valley.

DAN: The morning dew is on the neat rows of lettuce stretching to the horizon — geometrically patterned.

SYLVIENNE: The acorns, silver-green and flecked with white on the tall, slender eucalyptus trees.

GEORGE: *(Gets between them. They have their arms around each other.)* A truck full of wetbacks — they're wearing brightly colored ponchos and singing of their homeland.

SYLVIENNE: Arcadia!

GEORGE: Paradise!

DAN: Eden!

SYLVIENNE: *(To George.)* Please, before anything else happens — that —

GEORGE: George Birimisa.

SYLVIENNE: Sylvienne Strauss!

DAN: Dan Leach!

(They hold hands and bow, taking their curtain call.)

CURTAIN

VINYL
Ronald Tavel[1]

In the mid-to-late sixties there would be some speculation that attempted to explain World War II. Specifically, people thought to ask, "How could the Japanese and Germans have committed those atrocities?" But before I was to become familiar with these treatises — the best as yet unpublished — it had occurred to me that the relentless record of human behavior in the Factory's film work argued the projects as a breathing canvas on which to possibly explore this big question and immediately notate the results. What would it take to get people to harm each other? Would you have to do more than ask them to inflict pain on someone else? An audience will look at real torture and believe they are watching something faked. Because, via commercial movies, we've been made to think torture and violent death are more dramatic than they are. But the torture in *Vinyl* is real, and it is leisurely.

That we had at our convenience the necessary means for dissecting torture was more than apparent in my access to professional sadists through Ondine's drug trafficking: some of his dealers happened to be, in a manner of speaking, moonlighting-wise, sexually so inclined. And then there was Tosh Carillo, whose instrumental, not to say coolly detached and business-like, dexterity in *Vinyl* brooks no argument. Though sexual topics were a priority for Andy Warhol, sado-masochism was not amongst his conscious concerns, and he later found it serviceable to disclaim any direct hand in the S-M metaphoring of both the film version of *Vinyl* and *Hanoi Hannah, Radio Star*. He let the inspiration and responsibility for the matter rest with me. And if I were to protest when questioned — by the medical, the morbidly curious, and the plainly salacious — but most notably by the highly regarded Japanese playwright, Suji Teriyama — about my personal interest in these practices, and claim them merely aesthetic, doth the playwright not appear to protest too much? This is somewhat akin to the irony of watching *Vinyl*'s torture and not believing that's what you are seeing. So I've always held it the better part of valour to let the matter rest where he did.

Like the audiences for the film version, the theatre audiences sat calmly by, confident that they couldn't possibly be watching people being really tortured inches from their very eyes at the Caffe Cino.

---

[1] For more background on this play, its colorful performers, and other film-related stage pieces, please visit www.ronald-tavel.com.

Harvey Tavel *(top)* directed *Vinyl* for his brother Ron *(below)* at the Caffe Cino, 1967

Photos by James D. Gossage

Cino première November 1967
Directed by Harvey Tavel
Choreography by Ron Pratt
Music by John Harrill

VICTOR........................... Mike Shaw
SCUM............................. Sterling Houston
PUB............................... John Harrill
COP .... Norman Thomas Marshall
DOCTOR .... Mary Woronov
DANCER .... Raymond Edwards

(VICTOR, lifting the barbells. VICTOR's head is bowed, he slowly, gracefully lifts the barbells with alternating gestures: head comes up slowly: careful profile: continue this for some moments.

DOCTOR's head three-quarter profile, looking evil, in left lower corner. VICTOR in exact center on wooden box with barbells. In back of VICTOR, left is COP in full profile, right is T.V. set with blank picture. Further back, facing full front between COP and VICTOR is SCUM. Farthest in background is PUB.

Everyone remains motionless.

VICTOR stands up slowly.)

SCUM: What are we going to do, Victor?

VICTOR: We'll do whatever comes along, Scum. We'll do whatever comes along, Scum, baby.

(VICTOR takes out a reefer, lights it, slowly inhales, looks about attentively, and turns just a bit, hands the reefer to SCUM, who smokes it piggishly.

PUB gets up, comes around to just right of VICTOR, with books in his hands, a pile of books in both hands.)

VICTOR: Pardon me, Sir. Excuse me, Sir.

PUB: Sorry, I'm in a hurry.

VICTOR: I see you have some books in your hands, Sir. May I look at them, Sir? It is uncommon to run into someone who still knows how to read, Sir. May I read your books, Sir?

SCUM: Read the Sir's books, Victor.

PUB: I'm sorry, boys, I'm in a hurry.

SCUM: I'll read the Sir's books.

(SCUM comes around to the right of PUB so that PUB is squeezed between him and VICTOR. SCUM takes the top book off the pile in PUB's hands and

VICTOR takes the second book. Both flip slowly through the pages, as if they were really interested in the books. Then VICTOR slowly rips out a page in his book, holds it up to PUB's face and crumples it up, lets it drop. SCUM does the same. PUB looks from one to the other in terror. They both rip out another page and do the same.)

VICTOR: I have always had the deepest respect for Sirs who can read. Haven't you always had the deep, deep respect for them as can read, Scum, baby?

SCUM: Yeah.

PUB: You two boys ought to be home in bed.

(VICTOR rips out another page and holds it up to PUB.)

VICTOR: What does this here page say, pray tell, Sir?

PUB: It — it — it says that man is a creature capable of individuality and multiple direction and that to try to mechanize him is to —

VICTOR: Ain't that nice? Ain't that nice, Scum?

SCUM: Yeah.

(VICTOR crumples up the page and lets it drop. Then he and SCUM proceed to tear up endless pages from the books while PUB stands squeezed between them in total panic. Then VICTOR and SCUM pull more books off the pile and hit PUB on the head with them and drop the books to the floor. PUB screams during all this, shitting green.)

VICTOR: Let's have a little of the old up-yours with this kind Sir, shall we Scum?

SCUM: Yeah, lets have a little of the old up-yours.

PUB: No! No! Not the old up-yours. Anything but the old up-yours!

(SCUM grabs PUB's hands and holds them out in front of PUB, clasped together. VICTOR proceeds to split down the backside of PUB's trousers. Then VICTOR makes standing up fucking gestures against PUB's back, panting and groaning with violent delight. PUB shrieks in terror. SCUM giggles and laughs piggishly during the procedure.)

VICTOR: How is it, Sir? Feel it, Sir? Had enough, Sir? Had enough, Sir?

PUB: You two boys ought to be home in bed.

(VICTOR finally finishes pleasuring his victim, groans in orgasm and pulls away.)

VICTOR: OK, Scum, it's your pleasure now.

SCUM: Thank you, Victor.

(SCUM attempts to mount PUB. VICTOR pulls him away.)

VICTOR: Hey, what do you say first?!!

SCUM: Oh. Can I, Victor?

VICTOR: Can?!

SCUM: I mean, may I, Victor?

VICTOR: May you what??!!

SCUM: May I please give the old up-yours to this here kind and obliging Sir, Victor baby?

VICTOR: Yes, you may, Scum. Yes, you may.

(SCUM proceeds to the fucking gestures on the shrieking PUB. VICTOR stands a bit aside and relights his reefer. He takes a few puffs while the ravishment proceeds.)

VICTOR: Look, Scum, will you take the good Sir in the back with you? I do not feel like looking at this old up-yours sight anymore.

SCUM: What do you mean? I can't stop in the middle.

VICTOR: *(Furious.)* Get the hell out of here, I said, or I'll open your bottom myself.

(VICTOR shoves the two fuckers back around the right of the set. At the same moment, DOCTOR stands up and goes around to the left so that he reaches the back of the set at the same time that SCUM and PUB do.

Now VICTOR stands alone, smokes his reefer and slowly begins his speech. During the speech SCUM finishes fucking PUB and SCUM resumes his original position. PUB resumes his original sitting position. Then DOCTOR slowly puts the leather mask on PUB's head. He also drips the candle wax on him. He tortures PUB with the straps and other s-m equipment. All this between DOCTOR and PUB goes on very, very slowly, very stylized, and in complete silence. It continues going on without a word until the end of the scene.

SCUM stands stupidly, very apeish during VICTOR's speech. COP continues to hold his unmoving profile.)

VICTOR: OK, OK, I am a J.D. So what? I like to bust things up and carve people up and I dig the old up-yours with plenty of violence so it's real tasty. And then if I get busted by the cops, so what, so what the hell, I say, you can not have J.D.'s like me running loose all over the city. Then it's me that loses if I get busted, so what the hell do you care? But, babies, while I am still free, it is me that's having the fun, you dig, with breaking up china shops and carving up cuties and the old up-yours with lots of real smooth violence to give it some juice.

And like I do not give a hot damn about what is the reason for all the bad I do. Nobody wants to know what is the reason for the good that the squares do. The squares do good because they dig it. And so I do bad because I dig doing bad. And I do not tell anyone to follow me or not follow me, they can damn well do as they please.

Like I think badness is being yourself, it is being me, just me, Victor, The Victor, like God in Heaven made me for his shrieking happiness. But goodness is following the cops because the cops can not permit the just me, this city can not permit Victor. So ain't I really good because I am against the cops who are against what God in his Heaven made me?

Maybe I do not know what I am talking about. But I know I do what I like because I like it.

(SCUM farts or belches or both as VICTOR nears the end of his speech. COP throws back his head, still in profile and laughs like Satan. The rock 'n roll disc starts to play. VICTOR goes into his dance. It is innocent, frenzied, savage, etc. When the dance ends, SCUM farts again.)

VICTOR: What did you fart for, Scum?

SCUM: I farted for the music, baby.

VICTOR: It was beautiful music, Scum.

SCUM: Yeah. You was real pretty dancing, baby.

(SCUM lets out a series of cat calls, hubba hubba whistles, and generally makes fun of VICTOR and the music.)

VICTOR: The music was beautiful.

SCUM: Yeah. So are you, baby.

VICTOR: I said the music was beautiful, Scum.

SCUM: Yeah, I heard you, baby. The music was beautiful baby, and you are beautiful, baby.

VICTOR: Come here, Scum!!

(SCUM walks brazenly forward, like a cheap hussy, and plants himself to the left of VICTOR. VICTOR takes out his razor blade very slowly and pulls the neckline of SCUM's shirt forward. Then he razors down the entire shirt. SCUM stands still in dumb bewilderment and humiliation.)

SCUM: Why-for did you do that, Victor baby?

VICTOR: Because you are a pig and an ape and a shitty slob who never learned how to be a social being and who never can learn, no how, Scum.

SCUM: Why-for did you do that, Victor baby?

VICTOR: I did it because you can never love music, Scum!!

(SCUM hits into VICTOR and a struggle ensues. During the fight SCUM mercilessly pounds on VICTOR's head while VICTOR fights fair. VICTOR finally succumbs to the blows on his head and passes out on the floor.)

SCUM: Officer, Officer!! Help! Help!!

(COP stands up.)

SCUM: Officer, Officer, arrest this evil juvenile delinquent.

COP: What are the charges?

SCUM: He tried to cut my throat with his nasty razor, Officer.

COP: That ain't enough.

SCUM: Well, he loves music, Officer.

COP: Ah, why didn't you tell me that before? Excellent, I'll take over from here.
(*COP lifts up VICTOR and carries him a bit back and places him in the chair at left looking right. COP smacks VICTOR's face a few times to revive him.*)

COP: Wake up, boy, wake up! Wake up, I said.

VICTOR: *(Waking.)* Oooooo. Where am I?

COP: You are in the arms of the law, boy. In the tender bosom of the law.

VICTOR: Go to hell, Cop!

COP: Did you try to kill Scum, boy?

VICTOR: No, I did not try to kill Scum. I did not try to kill Scum because he can not be killed because he is already dead. Scum was born dead.

COP: Shut your damn face up, boy!
(*COP spits full into VICTOR's face. The saliva runs down his cheeks. VICTOR does not move.*)

VICTOR: Thank you, Sir, thank you very much, Sir. That was very kind of you, Sir.

COP: Shut your damn face up boy. Do you want to stay in prison forever?

VICTOR: No, Sir, I do not. I will do anything to get out of prison.

COP: Only good boys can get out of prison. Bad boys must stay in prison.

VICTOR: I will be a good boy.

COP: You can't be good. You are bad. But we can make you good. Will you let us make you good?

COP: Yes, yes, anything.

COP: Good. Then sign here.
(*VICTOR signs the paper.*)

VICTOR: Is that OK, Sir?

COP: Yes. Still, I am bothered. Bothered about this process of making boys good. Goodness is a thing inside of a person. It must be chosen.

VICTOR: I'm not sure I understand you, Sir.

COP: *(Talking really to himself.)* I should like you to know that this process, boy, has nothing to do with me. I mean, I never wanted it, I never wanted it to be used. I mean, I would protest it, protest it really if it would do any good. But then I am only a small peg in a big machine and I have my career to worry after. This is an ethical problem. We are going to convert you into a boy who never wants to do bad.

VICTOR: Oh, I would love to be a good boy, Sir!

COP: *(Still talking really to himself.)* Oh, I shall not be able to sleep nights because of this. I wonder what God in Heaven desires. What good are good people to him? Doesn't he need them to make a choice in order for goodness to be meaningful for him? Listen, boy, in years to come, when you think back to this moment, I want you to remember that I really had nothing to do with it. I would go now and pray for you, except that for what is going to happen to you now prayers won't do any good. But, I think, in choosing to have choice taken away from you, you are choosing the good. It makes me more peaceful to think that. Yes, putting it that way makes me more powerful.

VICTOR: Thank you, Sir. You are very good to me, Sir.

COP: Doctor, we are ready for you now!

(DOCTOR pushes VICTOR closer to the TV set and prepares to do his work. DOCTOR begins the "cure." He moves very, very slowly, as if in slow motion. DOCTOR ties VICTOR's arms to the arms of the chair with the trunk straps. Then DOCTOR flips on the TV set. Silence for a few moments.)

DOCTOR: Now, you must trust us, Victor. We are doing this for your own good.

VICTOR: I trust you, Doctor.

DOCTOR: What do you see on the screen, Victor?

VICTOR: I see a quiet street. It is late at night . . . An old man is walking up the street, real old . . .

DOCTOR: And now, what do you see?

VICTOR: I see some J.D.'s jumping out at him . . . They are carving him up . . . They are pulling him apart . . . It is all very realistic . . . I never saw a flicker like this . . . It is terrible, terrible to look at. Where did they make a flicker like this? I did not know such films existed.

DOCTOR: Do you like it, Victor? Do you want to see this flicker again?

VICTOR: No, no, please take it off!! No more.

DOCTOR: All right, here is the next film.

(DOCTOR turns knobs on the TV again.)

VICTOR: But this is another bad film.

DOCTOR: It is no different from your life. What do you see?

VICTOR: I see some J.D.'s grabbing a young chick and giving her the old up-yours . . . one after another . . . I can hear her screaming . . . it is awful . . . why don't they stop? . . . Why don't they let her go?

(DOCTOR lights a candle while VICTOR is speaking and lets a few wax drippings fall on VICTOR's arms. VICTOR cries out in pain but as if the pain were from watching the film and not from the wax drippings.)

DOCTOR: Not very pretty to look at, is it, Victor?

VICTOR: Please stop these flickers. Please stop these flickers, Doctor.

DOCTOR: No, Victor, it is not time yet.

> *(DOCTOR turns knobs on the TV again. Then he picks up the leather mask and fixes it on VICTOR's head, slowly, very slowly. Both the eye and mouth patches are not on the mask.)*

DOCTOR: Tell me what you are looking at now, Victor.

VICTOR: I see a J.D. carving a cross on an old lady's face . . . Now he is cutting out one of her eyes . . . Ahhhhhhhhh . . .

DOCTOR: Yes, go on.

VICTOR: I can't, I can't go on. Please stop this . . .

DOCTOR: Why, we have hardly begun your cure.

VICTOR: But I can not stand what I am looking at!!!

DOCTOR: Why not? It is all the things that you love to do and always have done, Victor.

VICTOR: Yes, but I do not understand . . . When I used to do these things it made me feel very good. When I carved up someone or ran some poor bastard down with my car I felt free . . . free . . . but . . . now . . .

DOCTOR: But now what?

VICTOR: But it is different looking at it. I mean, sitting here and seeing all those things makes me feel sick.

DOCTOR: Ah, God moves in mysterious ways His wonders to perform. No man really understands these miracles. Your reactions now are the reactions of a normal organism facing the Devil's work. You are being cured, Victor! You are being made sane, Victor!

VICTOR: But how can that be? How can I be made sane if I feel so much pain now? . . . Do you?

DOCTOR: Do you really feel pain now? . . . Do you?

VICTOR: Why, no, I feel much better now. I feel peaceful now.

> *(DOCTOR slowly clips the eye patches onto the mask. DOCTOR has very demoniacal expression on his face.)*

VICTOR: What are you doing now, Doctor?

DOCTOR: You are going to see some more movies, Victor!

VICTOR: No, no more, no more now, please!!! I beg you! I beg you, Doctor!

> *(DOCTOR turns knobs on TV set once again.)*

DOCTOR: Now what do you see, Victor?

VICTOR: I see little children having their teeth pulled out by yellow dwarves . . . I see virgins with long white gowns . . . and gladiators are setting fire to their gowns . . . I see virgins trying to crawl out of the flames . . . I see the gladiators pushing them back into the flames . . . I hear their screams!! Oh, please, stop this, stop this!

(DOCTOR puts the funnel into VICTOR's mouth and straps it around the mask. DOCTOR proceeds to speak into the mouth of the funnel. At this point, the rock 'n roll music begins to play very softly in the background. It must not interfere with the speaking of the characters.)

DOCTOR: You see Japanese soldiers hanging victims to trees by their thumbs . . .

VICTOR: Ohhhhhhhh!!!!!!!!!!

DOCTOR: You see victims' nails being torn off their fingers! You see their heads being sliced off with swords!!!!!!

VICTOR: I beg you to stop! I feel sick! I feel pain!

DOCTOR: You see the victims' balls being twisted off!

VICTOR: ACHHHHHH!!!!!!!!!!

DOCTOR: You see the cut-off heads with the eyes rolling round in the heads as if they were still alive!!!

VICTOR: I feel pain! I feel pain! I feel pain!! Pain!!!!!

DOCTOR: You see the blood spurting like a fountain out of the headless necks!!! And the soldiers are laughing! Like you laugh, Victor.

VICTOR: I don't laugh. I am not laughing! I am sick, sick!

(DOCTOR unstraps VICTOR's arms from the chair.)

DOCTOR: Would you like to sock me now, Victor? Would you like to crack me one for making you watch all this?

VICTOR: YES!

(VICTOR raises his clenched fist to hit DOCTOR, but his force slackens, his fingers open pitifully, and his arm finally drops.)

VICTOR: No, no, I do not want to hit you, Doctor. I do not want to hit anyone, anymore, Doctor.

(DOCTOR speaks again into the funnel fixed on the mask.)

DOCTOR: We shall watch some more movies, Victor . . . You see the people being herded into the gas chambers now . . .

VICTOR: Let the poor people free! Please free them . . .

DOCTOR: You see the bombed buildings and the starving urchins!!!

VICTOR: Feed the starving urchins . . . Please, feed them, Doctor.

DOCTOR: You see thousands lined up against the walls . . . The firing squad is getting ready . . .

VICTOR: Yes, I see the firing squad getting ready . . . and . . . and . . . and . . . I hear . . . I hear my beautiful music! Why are you playing my music??!!

DOCTOR: What is wrong with the music?

VICTOR: I can not bear to hear it! It is as terrible as the tortures!

DOCTOR: Every man must kill the thing he loves most, Victor. I am sorry. It is the price to be paid for goodness.

VICTOR: But it is not fair to the beautiful music. The beautiful music . . .

DOCTOR: Nothing will be beautiful to you anymore, little pig!! Little good pig gone to market, gone to butcher!!

VICTOR: Yes, I am a little good pig gone to market.

(DOCTOR smiles with great satisfaction. DOCTOR turns off the knobs of the TV set. DOCTOR slowly undoes the funnel straps and removes the funnel from VICTOR's mouth. DOCTOR then takes the mouth patch and snaps it onto the mask so that VICTOR is completely imprisoned.)

DOCTOR: All right, Cop! My work is finished. You can come and get your little angel now.

(COP comes forward, rubbing his hands with great satisfaction.)

COP: Thank you, Doctor, thank you very much. And now, Ladies and Gentlemen, may I present the new model of a new brighter civilization? Here he is, without drugs or hypnotism. An earth angel! Please remove the mask, Doctor.

(DOCTOR slowly takes the mask off VICTOR's head. VICTOR rubs his face, brushes his hair, and stands.)

COP: Tomorrow morning we will send little Victor out into society, docile as a lamb. A model citizen in a model city. No more the J.D. or the great affront to his elders. The demonstration, please, Doctor.

DOCTOR: Hello, Victor, filthy piglet. Boy, you stink! You are a heap of crap, all told, aren't you?

(VICTOR remains motionless, staring at the DOCTOR. The DOCTOR smacks his face).

VICTOR: Why do you do this, Doctor, I have never harmed you.

(DOCTOR twists VICTOR's ear very hard and then pulls out on both his ears. VICTOR does not move. DOCTOR pushes VICTOR's nose up on his face. VICTOR appears to be crying.)

VICTOR: Why are you doing this, dear Doctor?

DOCTOR: Filthy coward! Why don't you hit me? Piglet! Fruit!

(VICTOR attempts to punch DOCTOR, but his arms fail him again and they drop useless to his side. DOCTOR laughs like Satan. COP, PUB, and SCUM all applaud loudly, jeer and hiss and spit. VICTOR addresses DOCTOR when the hissing stops.)

VICTOR: May I shake your hand, please, Doctor?

(VICTOR extends his hand and DOCTOR takes it as if to shake it but he twists it in back of VICTOR. VICTOR begins to cry.)

DOCTOR: Cry-baby! Fag!

COP: Fag!

SCUM: Fag!

PUB: Fairy.

(PUB comes forward and stamps on VICTOR's feet, one after the other.)

PUB: Young thug, you! Miserable hooligan! Rough! Take that and that! I'll scratch your eyes out.

(PUB scratches along VICTOR's face. PUB jumps up and down.

VICTOR reaches in his pocket and takes out his razor blade and offers it to PUB.)

PUB: Keep your crummy bribes, little monster! You should be home in bed.

(PUB bows deeply, as if this were a performance.)

COP: You see, Ladies and Gentlemen, little Victor is made to do good by being drawn naturally evil, as he is. His desire to do bad now is accompanied by dreadful feelings of pain. To stop this pain, Victor must resort to opposite activity, namely, doing good. Does everyone understand?

PUB: But he has no choice! Fear of terrible pain drives him to do good. He is debased. It is all insincere.

COP: Shut up your damn face, Sir! Shut it up! We have cut down on the crime rate.

DOCTOR: Victor made his choice when he chose to take the cure. All this proceeds from that choice.

PUB: But perfect love can destroy fear and make good too.

COP: I am glad you brought that up. I shall now show you love such as has not been seen since the days of chivalry! Regard our good Doctor here. Is he not as tempting a morsel as was ever presented to a practiced bugger? Turn around, Doctor and Present your charms to Victor.

(DOCTOR turns around and extends his buttocks toward VICTOR. VICTOR looks at them deliriously and makes as if to attack, but at the last moment, he slips down, kissing those buttocks, as it were, instead of buggering them, and finally slips all the way down to the floor, and ends by kissing the DOCTOR's feet.)

VICTOR: O, most beautiful of all humans, most beautiful of all God's creatures, more beautiful than the angels in His Heaven, allow me to place my heart at your boots, under your boots for you to trample and crush. I give you all the rain drops and all the flowers in the world; I divest myself to make the carpets for your boots . . .

(VICTOR continues to grovel and lick DOCTOR's boots while the others all look on laughing and hissing and applauding and enjoying themselves to the hilt).

CURTAIN

THE CLOWN
A FANTASY
Claris Nelson

CHARACTERS:

>   The PRINCE
>   The DUKE
>   The PHILOSOPHER
>   The SUPERINTENDENT OF THEATERS
>   The CIRCUS MANAGER
>   CECIL
>   The BOY
>   The HEADSMAN

SCENE: A Gothic castle. The arch UC leads to the gardens; the arch UR leads to the great hall and the Prince's chambers; the arch DL leads to the HEADSMAN. A throne is UL. An arras is DR. The PRINCE and CECIL are discovered as lights come up.

PRINCE: Ridiculous! Nonsense! Seven days in the week, and the Royal Entertainers come down with the measles on Sunday!

CECIL: They send their apologies, Your Majesty.

PRINCE: Their apologies! I spend the entire week organizing the castle for a really fine entertainment, and when everyone is finally prepared, some careless idiot infects the Entertainers with the measles! All my creative energy gone to waste for an entertainment that won't take place! And they have the audacity to send their apologies! Just thinking about it exhausts me. *(He sinks to the throne.)*

CECIL: The audience is due in half an hour, Your Majesty. We must provide an entertainment. If we cannot have the usual dancers and singers, perhaps the Superintendent of Theaters could provide a play.

PRINCE: Perhaps he could, but the theater is so vulgar these days. Revenge, revenge, revenge, nothing but revenge, and the forces of good either win, or die heroically. Sometimes they even do both. The theater is declining, my good man, and soon we shall live in uninterrupted *ennui*.

Jayne Anne Harris at age 11, in Claris Nelson's *The Clown*, 1967.
When the editors reviewed this photo among stacks of other material, they thought it had
been mis-filed, and asked the playwright, "There's no role for a young girl in *The Clown*.
What play was this?" Claris Nelson replied:

"*The Clown*, and Jayne played the Boy. This was no deliberate gender obfuscation. She
happened to be the best person for the part. She was a Harris — always a plus for talent,
skill, and unfailing professional behavior."

Photo by James D. Gossage, provided through the courtesy of Ann Harris

CECIL: I have heard rumors of a traveling circus in the neighborhood, Your Majesty. Perhaps they might provide an entertainment.

PRINCE: A circus! A herd of rascals and vagabonds cluttering up my castle with their filth and their children! They expect us to pay for the privilege of being revolted by their clumsiness! Have you no taste, no delicacy? A circus, indeed!

CECIL: But we must have an entertainment, your majesty. All week the court has been entertaining itself, and as a result, the wine cellars have been depleted, the court ladies look extraordinarily haggard, and in the whole countryside there isn't one bear left to be baited.

PRINCE: Very well. Bring me the Superintendent of Theaters, and the Circus Manager — only the manager, mind you — and the Royal Philosopher. He may be able to think of a whole new way to entertain the people. And bring the Duke. I haven't seen him all week, and one can only trust the Duke when he is constantly in sight. Wait — I soiled my glove a few moments ago in the wine cellar. Bring me a new pair.

CECIL: *(He takes a pair of lavender gloves from his pocket.)* Here you are, Your Majesty — lavender for Sunday. *(He gives the gloves to the Prince.)*

PRINCE: Thank you, Cecil, you're an angel of organization. *Au revoir. (CECIL exits UR. The PRINCE speaks as he puts on the fresh gloves.)* I love lavender. It's worth a whole week of eggshell, and saffron, and robin's egg blue, for just one day of lavender. Every morning I'm tempted to pretend it's Sunday. Of course, Cecil won't allow it. It would ruin his schedule and I don't insist. After all, if I wore it every day, even lavender would become mundane! Ah! But the entertainment! Surely we won't be reduced to an orgy? An orgy is a weekday entertainment; one needs something special for Sunday. *(Enter CECIL and the DUKE.)*

CECIL: Your majesty, the Superintendent of Theaters was found in consultation with the Circus Manager concerning the loan of some costumes. They will be here presently.

DUKE: Your majesty wished to consult me?

PRINCE: I wished your opinion on a matter of grave importance. The Royal Entertainers have been attacked by disease. We must find another form of entertainment. I thought you might have an inspiration on the subject.

DUKE: I? An inspiration? Most humble thanks, Your Majesty, but I am a simple man, not given to the delicate intricacies of cogitation, and inspiration is a phenomenon quite beyond my modest sphere.

PRINCE: Very well, but please, in your own humble way, listen to the ideas already presented, and offer some simple judgment from your modest point of view.

DUKE: Oh, most assuredly, your majesty. My inspiration may falter, but you may rely upon my unwavering integrity.

PRINCE: Cecil, what have you done with the Royal Philosopher?

CECIL: He should arrive within the minute. Ever since he read the latest treatise, he made it a rule never to walk over fifteen paces per minute. He says that a faster pace would upset his contemplative frame of mind. Ah! Here he comes! *(The PHILOSOPHER enters.)*

PRINCE: See here, sir, what is the meaning of this delay? The matter at hand is of dire importance. You must discover a new form of entertainment immediately.

PHILOSOPHER: Entertainment? With the world in such a state of filthiness, with everyone's soul diseased, you can think of entertainment?

PRINCE: Ah! You've seen the circus!

PHILOSOPHER: The circus! A diversion for those who cannot endure the consciousness of their own misery! No, Your Majesty, not I. Only two days ago, I, too, might have actually attended the circus, but today — ah, today! I can face the horror of my own existence. I can even contemplate it! Do you realize, your majesty, that you are occupying space?

PRINCE: My good man, I realize that you are occupying time, which is something we have precious little of at present.

PHILOSOPHER: Time! Now there is a concept! If only one understood its true nature.

PRINCE: Its nature is to pass much too rapidly. We must find an entertainment within this half hour, or my entire week's work will go to waste!

PHILOSOPHER: My soul is ill. How can I think of entertainment?

PRINCE: Please. It is spring. The sun caresses me in the morning, the stars tickle me in the evening, and the moon washes me in its soft blue light. It is a Sunday in spring, and I am wearing lavender gloves. And you stalk about at fifteen paces a minute announcing that your soul is ill! Forgive me, my friend, but I cannot believe it, and if I could, I am afraid I could not become concerned. Be so good as to pace off a bit, and contemplate the illness of the Royal Entertainers, and the necessity of devising a new entertainment, else I shall be forced to allow the Royal Headsman to release your sick little soul from its earthly torment.

DUKE: Well spoken, your majesty. It is the duty of the Supreme Ruler of our land to insist upon the happiness of his subjects.

PRINCE: Thank you. Cecil, where are the — ah! Here they come! *(Enter the SUPERINTENDENT OF THEATERS and the CIRCUS MANAGER.)*

SUPER: Your Majesty! *(He bows with a flourish.)*

MANAGER: Your Majesty. *(He bows without a flourish.)*

PRINCE: Superintendent, you have no doubt heard of the tragedy which has occurred. The Royal Entertainers have been felled by the dread hand of disease. It is your duty to produce a play for the entertainment today.

SUPER: My actors, as replacements for mere entertainers? Really, Your Majesty, I beg you to consider, we are artists, we do not cater to the public's taste. We would very likely bore an undiscriminating audience, used to enjoying the Entertainers. Besides, our plays must rehearse for months before we perform. No, it is out of the question. We cannot possibly perform.

PRINCE: You are the Circus Manager?

MANAGER: Yes, Your Majesty.

PRINCE: Could you perform for us this evening?

MANAGER: Of course, Your Majesty.

PRINCE: Very well, Superintendent, you may go.

SUPER: Your Majesty! You wouldn't let this ragamuffin destroy the whole atmosphere of the Royal Palace?

PRINCE: We must have an entertainment. Your actors will not perform; his circus will.

SUPER: Ah! To think that you would numb your sensitive taste by watching such drivel! I am truly appalled.

PRINCE: That's your privilege. *(To the CIRCUS MANAGER.)* The Circus Performers can be here within half an hour?

MANAGER: Of course, your majesty. Would you care to pay us now, or must we wait until after we perform?

PRINCE: Pay?

MANAGER: Naturally. You don't expect us to perform miraculous feats of skill and daring for nothing, do you?

PRINCE: But it is a privilege to perform in the Royal Palace!

MANAGER: For those who are well fed, yes. But we eat only when we are paid, and we are paid only when we perform. Now, we can only perform when we are inspired by the thought of food, which means that we must be paid.

PRINCE: How much pay will your company require?

MANAGER: The more we are paid, the more inspired our performance will be.

PRINCE: I am afraid that at present our Royal coffers can inspire very little, Cecil?

CECIL: At present the Royal coffers are on a strict budget. We can't afford anything.

MANAGER: In that case, forgive me, gentlemen, but I cannot waste my performers' time, nor yours.

PRINCE: But this is impossible! I must have an entertainment! I insist on an entertainment! Cecil, I shall return in twenty minutes. You will present an entertainment. *(Exit the PRINCE.)*

CECIL: Gentlemen, in view of this development, may I request that you wait in the gardens? I require a moment of silence in which to reach a decision.

SUPER: If you wish.

MANAGER: As you like. *(They exit. The DUKE whisks behind the arras.)*

CECIL: *(To the PHILOSOPHER.)* You may go into the gardens, too.

PHILOSOPHER: I? Into the gardens? With birds, and trees, and flowers? Certainly not! I shall retire to my cell. *(He exits.)*

CECIL: Oh, my Heavens, what am I to do? I'm all unsettled! As if an entertainment could be arranged in half an hour! All week I've been following the Prince around, re-organizing his entertainment, and now he leaves it in my hands twenty minutes before the guests are to arrive! *(We hear the sound of a lute from the gardens.)* Oh help! I must think — what's that noise? Every time I try to think around this Palace, something interrupts! *(Enter a BOY from the gardens, playing a lute. He is dressed like a peasant.)*

CECIL: What do you want?

BOY: I want to see the Palace of the Prince.

CECIL: You're in the Palace.

BOY: I know.

CECIL: Well get out of it!

BOY: But I want to see it.

CECIL: Aren't you seeing it?

BOY: I have seen the gardens. They are filled with fountains that spray crystal showers into the sunlight, and each shower has its own rainbow. Oh, the trees, each new leaf reaches out to catch the warm wind, and the wind smells of a thousand flowers. I have heard that the Palace of the Prince is the most perfect in the world, and I want to see all of it, every window, every statue, every stone.

CECIL: Do you play that?

BOY: Yes.

CECIL: Do you play well?

BOY: My father is a ballad singer, and he taught me to play and sing as he does.

CECIL: Hmmm. Would you be so good as to play something?

BOY: Here? Oh, but wouldn't I disturb someone?

CECIL: No, no, not at all. Please play something, I beg you to.

BOY: I'd be glad to. If you're sure no one would mind.

CECIL: No one will mind. Please go ahead.

BOY: All right. *(He plays the tune to the little song on the last page.)*

CECIL: You said you could sing, too.

BOY: I can but you asked me to play.

CECIL: Can't you do both?

BOY: Of course. In fact it's very hard not to do both.

CECIL: Please do both.

BOY: If you're sure . . .

CECIL: It won't disturb anyone.

BOY: *(Singing, to same tune.)*

> Long, long ago,
> The world was a young thing,
> Young as the new spring,
> New as the morning,
> Fresh as the dew.

> Long, long ago,
> The world was a child's toy,
> Made for a small boy,
> Full of a child's joy,
> Shining and new.

CECIL: Is that all?

BOY: My father only taught me two verses.

CECIL: Can't you make up more verses?

BOY: I've never tried. I don't know how.

CECIL: Do you know other songs?

BOY: Yes.

CECIL: Tell me, would you like to play and sing for the Prince?

BOY: I? But I only sing for the pleasure of it.

CECIL: But wouldn't you like to sing before the Prince? It would give him pleasure, too.

BOY: Of course, I would love to play for the Prince, if you think he would like me to. But I've never played when people were watching, except just now for you.

CECIL: Never?

BOY: I've played for the animals in the forest where I live, but there are no people in the forest except for my father and I. The animals seem to like our songs.

CECIL: Then the Prince would like them, too. How many songs do you know?

BOY: If I sang them all, it would take from now until dawn.

CECIL: That's plenty. You wait here now, and don't move. I'm going to get the Prince. I'll be right back. Don't go away!

(Exit CECIL. The boy plays a few bars of the same song. The DUKE enters from behind the arras.)

DUKE: Hello, my fine young musician.

BOY: You startled me.

DUKE: So you are going to perform for the Prince?

BOY: Yes.

DUKE: Good luck, my lad. The Prince is the most discerning judge of music.

BOY: Oh, but he mustn't expect me to sing the songs of the court. I know only the songs my father taught me.

DUKE: Of course, the song itself must be beautiful. But the performance must be exquisite. The Prince has highly sensitive ears. And when someone sings poorly — well! Only yesterday a singer came to the Palace from Venice. To my ears his voice sounded like an angel singing of the joys of heaven. But to the Prince — well, the Prince's ears were so offended that he ordered the singer's head to be cut off.

BOY: Cut off! But I cannot sing like an angel! What will happen to me?

DUKE: Oh, I suppose your head will be cut off a little quicker.

BOY: But I don't want my head to be cut off! I only came to see the Palace of the Prince! I never asked to sing! I must run away, before the Prince comes! *(He runs toward the door UR.)*

DUKE: Not that way. The Prince is coming that way. *(The BOY runs toward the gardens.)* Not that way. The garden wall is surrounded by his Majesty's Royal Guards. *(The BOY runs toward the door DL.)* Not that way. That passage leads to the headsman.

BOY: But I must run! At once!

DUKE: You can't escape. But there is another way to save your neck. The headsman carries a huge ax. You might tip-toe up behind him, snatch it from him, and fight your way to freedom.

BOY: But I've never learned to fight!

DUKE: Fighting is the only way to escape with your head attached. *(The BOY hesitates.)* And, when you have the ax, be careful not to let the Prince see you. For if he does — well, one angry glance from the Prince and you will be frozen like a marble statue. It's a gift he has from a wizard. And once you are frozen — no more head.

BOY: But he's coming right away!

DUKE: Well, if you should see him first, you'd better hit him quickly before he sees you.

BOY: With the ax?

DUKE: Of course. Remember, your life depends upon it. The headsman and his ax are at the end of the passage, behind the vermillion door.

BOY: Might you get the ax for me?

DUKE: I? Of course not. He would recognize my footsteps. Remember — your head. *(The BOY exits down the passage.)* Just fancy, if the Prince should come in, he might be in danger. He might even be killed. Well, well, well. I've always wanted a kingdom. *(He sees the PRINCE coming.)* Ah-ha! The mouse approaches the cheese, and the trap — *(He goes to look down the passage for the BOY, but is stopped by the sound of a scuffle. The HEADSMAN and the BOY enter.)*

HEADSMAN: Young man, being a headsman is a serious business. I beg you, in the future, try not to interrupt. *(Exit the HEADSMAN.)*

BOY: I tried to tickle him to make him drop his ax, but he wasn't ticklish. What should I do?

DUKE: It's too late. You've bungled it. Just try not to anger the Prince. *(As the PRINCE and CECIL enter, the DUKE slips behind the arras and the boy hides behind the throne.)*

PRINCE: Cecil, where is the child?

CECIL: *(He finds the BOY behind the throne and pulls him out.)* Here, Your Majesty.

PRINCE: Well, sing something.

BOY: Oh, really, I'd rather not, your majesty. I don't sing very well at all.

CECIL: Nonsense! He just has stage fright, Your Majesty. He's never performed in public before.

PRINCE: Go ahead, child.

BOY: No, really, if Your Royal Majesty doesn't mind . . .

PRINCE: My Royal Majesty does mind. Sing something, or I shall become very angry.

BOY: Oh dear no. Don't do that. I'll sing. *(He tries to play, but the notes are wrong. He tries to sing, but his voice is just a screech.)*

PRINCE: Cecil, for heaven's sake, do you call that singing? His vocal cords sound as if someone had hacked them in half.

BOY: Oh, no, Your Majesty! Please!

PRINCE: Quiet, child. My, Cecil, he is a strange type. Very interesting. Obviously he can't sing. But perhaps, if we gave him to the Circus Manager, he would be enough payment!

CECIL: But they can't eat the boy, Your Majesty.

BOY: Please, no!

PRINCE: No, of course not. But he's a very rare type. They might use him in the sideshow. Bring me the Circus Manager. *(Exit CECIL. Enter the PHILOSOPHER.)*

PHILOSOPHER: Your Majesty. A few moments ago I heard a screech which left my impenetrable calm absolutely shattered. It is my duty to remain in a contemplative frame of mind. I beg you, Your Majesty, not to allow this little annoyance to recur!

PRINCE: I'll do my best. Run along, now. *(The PHILOSOPHER starts to go, but stops when CECIL, the CIRCUS MANAGER, and the SUPERINTENDENT OF THEATERS enter.)*

CECIL: Here they are, Your Majesty.

PRINCE: They? I only asked for one.

SUPER: I heard a peculiar sound emit from this direction a few moments ago. I'm investigating the source. One might use it as a sound effect when a head is removed off stage.

BOY: Oh no!

SUPER: That's it! Where is that sound?

PRINCE: It was that boy, there. He's a rare type. Boy, come here. *(To the CIRCUS MANAGER.)* Sir, could you use the boy in your side show? You must admit he's unusual.

MANAGER: He's unusual, but will he draw crowds?

SUPER: Draw crowds! He'll draw the whole kingdom! Say something, boy.

BOY: What should I say?

SUPER: Tell me why you are afraid.

BOY: Oh, I can't sir.

SUPER: Of course you can.

BOY: But the headsman will cut off my head!

SUPER: Nonsense, boy. I won't let the headsman hurt you.

BOY: Oh, thank you sir. But mightn't the Prince still be able to harm me?

SUPER: Stuff, boy! Why should the Prince harm you?

BOY: Because I sang badly. I wouldn't have sung at all, except that he would have been just as angry if I hadn't sung.

SUPER: But the Prince won't harm you. Who told you he would?

BOY: A man. He was here a moment ago.

SUPER: Well, never mind. You see gentlemen? He is completely innocent! He's perfect, he's divine, he's delicious! I must have him, Your Majesty. For years I have tried to find a living example of innocence. My actors don't believe that such a thing exists, and they refuse to play anything that doesn't exist. I've found examples of witches, and ghosts, and evil incarnate, but innocence seemed impossible. Now, at last, I have found it! My actors will be able to play the forces of innocence which are destroyed in the revenge tragedies. Your Majesty, if I can have this boy, we will perform a tragedy for today's entertainment.

MANAGER: It's true. He's very rare. Give him to me, Your Majesty, and we'll exhibit him in the cage right next to the white cockatoo. For a gift like this, my circus will perform free!

PHILOSOPHER: Nonsense! Innocence? In this day and age? Impossible! Innocence is the inability to perceive forces of darkness at work. How can anyone fail to perceive them? Allow me, gentlemen, to point out your error. Young man. Where is your home?

BOY: In the great forest.

PHILOSOPHER: The forest! The forest is dark, is it not?

BOY: In the morning, streams of light come through the branches of the trees, and each drop of sun warms a leaf, or a bird, or a seed in the earth.

PHILOSOPHER: And in the streams of sunlight you see specks of dirt, do you not?

BOY: I see specks of gold.

PHILOSOPHER: The ground is covered with dead, decaying leaves, is it not?

BOY: The leaves that fall to make room for the new leaves cover the ground and keep the earth warm in the winter.

PHILOSOPHER: Winter is cold.

BOY: Winter is soft and white, like the breast of a dove.

PHILOSOPHER: This is ridiculous! Is there nothing ugly in your forest?

BOY: What is "ugly"?

PHILOSOPHER: Good Heavens, boy, look about you! The world is a foul and evil place! If it is good and beautiful, why were you afraid?

BOY: Because the headsman might have cut off my head.

PHILOSOPHER: Do you know why he would have cut off your head?

BOY: Because I sang badly.

PHILOSOPHER: Is that enough reason to cut off a person's head?

BOY: No.

PHILOSOPHER: Then why might he have cut off yours?

BOY: I don't know.

PHILOSOPHER: I'll tell you. Because the world is evil, my lad. Because it's vicious. Because it's ugly.

SUPER: Enough of this drivel. The boy is obviously innocent, and I want him kept that way. I want the child, and I'm willing to pay for him by performing the latest tragedy immediately.

PRINCE: But I'm tired of tragedy. Can't you perform a comedy?

PHILOSOPHER: A comedy! Unheard of!

PRINCE: You stay out of this.

SUPER: A comedy is out of the question, Your Majesty. The child will inspire my actors to perform a tragedy on short notice. But innocence cannot inspire comedy. We will perform comedy when the child runs out of innocence, not a moment before.

MANAGER: My circus will perform, Your Majesty, if you give me the child. We never perform tragedy.

PRINCE: Marvelous! I adore comedy! Do you have dancing bears and cycle riders and clowns?

MANAGER: We have dancing bears and cycle riders, Your Majesty. But clowns? No. You see, to be a clown, one must be capable of genuine happiness, or sadness. Otherwise, the clown is dull. Well, the last person capable of genuine emotion died before I was born. Clowns today pretend to be happy, or sad. But they can't pretend very well, because they have neither felt real happiness nor seen it. Therefore they are dull. I refuse to have bad clowns in my circus. And so, I have none at all.

PRINCE: But I must have a clown. I insist upon a clown! Unless you have a clown, I will not give you the boy.

MANAGER: I cannot show you a clown unless you give me the boy.

PRINCE: I beg your pardon?

MANAGER: The child is innocent. Since he is innocent, he feels real emotion, because he doesn't know enough of the world to feel anything else. He will be the clown!

PRINCE: Wonderful! Superintendent, find him a costume.

SUPER: Your Majesty, you're making a grave error. The circus manager can give you only cheap spectacle in return for the child. I can give you the noblest heights of tragedy.

PRINCE: Fiddle! I don't care a fig for your tragedy! Go, find a costume.

SUPER: Since you insist.

CECIL: Your Majesty, the guests arrive in three minutes.

PRINCE: Very well. Circus Manager, you will bring the rest of your troupe.

MANAGER: But Your Majesty, we are camped some distance from the Palace, and we cannot perform without some preparation. It will be at least half an hour before we can return.

CECIL: Your Majesty, the guests are beginning to arrive in the great hall.

PRINCE: What am I to do?

CECIL: Why not have the boy entertain the guests until the rest of the circus arrives?

PRINCE: Marvelous! You heard me, go! And hurry back.

MANAGER: Yes, Your Majesty. *(Exit CIRCUS MANAGER.)*

PRINCE: Now then, quickly, the costume!

CECIL: Here it comes.

SUPER: *(He enters.)* Here.

PRINCE: Thank you. *(To the BOY.)* Put it on.

BOY: But I don't know how to be a clown.

PRINCE: Nonsense! Just act like you always do. You'll be a clown.

BOY: I don't understand.

PRINCE: It's not your place to understand. Hurry up!

BOY: Yes, Your Majesty. *(He begins to put on the costume.)*

PRINCE: Cecil, announce the clown to our guests.

CECIL: Yes, Your Majesty.

PRINCE: Hurry, child!

BOY: I'm afraid.

PRINCE: Ridiculous!

BOY: What should I do?

PRINCE: Do? Don't do anything! Talk to them.

BOY: What should I say?

PRINCE: Tell them about yourself.

BOY: Myself? But do they want to hear about me?

PRINCE: Of course! You're fascinating!

BOY: I? But what shall I tell them about myself?

PRINCE: What do you know?

BOY: I know where I live, and who my father is, and what I have seen today.

PRINCE: Good! Tell them that! Run along now, Cecil is waiting.

BOY: I'm afraid.

PRINCE: I don't care! The guests have come to be entertained! I've spent all
week organizing this affair. Now, entertain them! Off with you!

BOY: Goodbye.

PRINCE: I'll be watching. *(Exit BOY.)* Now then. Clean, fresh lavender gloves,
everything in order — I shall watch the entertainment! *(Exit PRINCE.)*

PHILOSOPHER: God.

DUKE: *(Entering from behind the arras.)* What seems to be the matter, your
lordship?

PHILOSOPHER: Oh, you. The matter is that the world is unbelievably rotten.
You heard what is about to happen?

DUKE: The child is about to entertain the populace. *(Laughter comes from off
stage.)*

PHILOSOPHER: Exactly. The innocent one is about to be destroyed. Can anyone
doubt that the world is evil?

DUKE: Evil? The world? Who is evil? Surely not you and I.

PHILOSOPHER: You will never admit your evilness because you cannot admit it
to yourself. But I am evil. I am standing by while innocence is destroyed.

DUKE: I cannot comprehend this concept of evil. As you have observed, I do not
admit that I am evil. But neither do I deny it. I cannot do either one, because I cannot understand the meaning of your term. Evil? Evil compared to
whom? To the child? No. I know more, it is true, and I act upon that knowledge. But I always act as any person of knowledge would. I am no less evil
than anyone else, but I am no more. If I threaten a man's life, it is with the
knowledge that, were he in my position, he would do the same. As for the
child, he simply does not know enough to behave like a normal well informed person should act. I am not more evil than he, for evil has nothing
to do with the question. I am simply better informed.

PHILOSOPHER: If you refuse to give a moral judgment on the question, that is your privilege. None-the-less, innocence is being given knowledge of the world. It is being destroyed. *(Great laughter from off stage.)* Wait here three minutes and see what has happened to the child.

DUKE: Three minutes? And how do you know that he will return in three minutes?

PHILOSOPHER: Because he won't be able to stand their questions, their jeers, their laughter. He will hear in their laughter no love, but only mockery. He will see in their eyes no kindness, but only contempt.

DUKE: Very well, if you insist, let us wait. But in the interval, allow me to inform you that the child, no matter how changed, will be no more changed than you were when you first realized that the world was looking at you and laughing.

PHILOSOPHER: No, it was not that that changed me. It was seeing the world laugh at others, whose souls were more tender than mine. *(Another tremendous laugh.)*

DUKE: Laughter has no effect on you?

PHILOSOPHER: No. I laugh at me, myself.

DUKE: To return to the point. The child may be depressed for a few days. He may begin to behave more normally. But he will not be greatly changed. *(Enter the BOY.)*

PHILOSOPHER: Well?

DUKE: Well, my lad, how was the performance? Were you successful? Answer!

BOY: What? Oh, I beg your pardon, sir. I was thinking.

PHILOSOPHER: About what?

BOY: About the guests. About myself.

PHILOSOPHER: There. You see? Can't you see it in his eyes? He has been destroyed!

BOY: I?

DUKE: Nonsense! He has simply become one of us.

PHILOSOPHER: It's the same thing.

DUKE: Very well, boy. Tell us what has occurred.

BOY: I began to tell them of my home in the forest. I told them of the birds and the sunlight, the flowers, the trees. But they laughed. Then I told them of my father. I told them how he traveled through the forest, singing his songs to the wind that whispers through the fir trees. But they laughed again. Then I told them of all the things I had seen today, of the spring, of the Palace, of the vermillion door. But they laughed more. So then I didn't tell them anything. But they still laughed, they laughed until their voices shrieked and their eyes ran. So I came away.

PHILOSOPHER: And is the world ugly, now?

BOY: Ugly? No. It is confusing.

DUKE: You see? And do you want to stay here in the Palace and be one of us?

BOY: One of you? No. The Palace of the Prince is a beautiful place. I shall stay until I have seen every inch of it, the cracks in every window, the chips in every statue, the crevices in every stone. But when I have seen them all, I shall return to the great forest, and sing of what I have seen to the wind in the fir trees.

PHILOSOPHER: Give him time, he'll learn.

DUKE: You don't care to remain with us?

BOY: No. I can watch you and your Palace, but I cannot be one of you. I have other things to do.

DUKE: Other things?

BOY: I must sing my songs.

PHILOSOPHER: The child is hopeless.

DUKE: Shall we observe the presentation of the circus?

PHILOSOPHER: Never! I must return to my cell! Good day! *(Exit PHILOSOPHER.)*

DUKE: *Au revoir.* Will you accompany me?

BOY: No, thank you. I have seen the circus.

DUKE: Well then, goodbye. *(Exit DUKE.)*

BOY: *(He sits on the ground and plays several notes on his lute. Then he sings to the same tune as before. He sings the last two verses slowly, because he is composing the words.)*

Long, long ago,
The world was a young thing,
Young as the new spring,
New as the morning,
Fresh as the dew.

Long, long ago,
The world was a child's toy,
Made for a small boy,
Full of a child's joy,
Shining and new.

Now, now,
My heart is an old thing,

Lonely and cold thing,
Better than nothing,
Nothing would do.

Now, now,
My heart is a child's toy,
Made for a small boy,
Full of a child's joy,
Broken in two.

CURTAIN

Connie Clark in *The Singing Lesson,* by her brother, Daniel Haben Clark, 1964

Photo by James D. Gossage, provided through the courtesy of Daniel Haben Clark

THE SINGING LESSON
Daniel Haben Clark

Copyright ©1964

First Produced at La Mama E.T.C. and The Caffe Cino

CHARACTERS:
  BRUCE
  MARA
  HARRY
TIME: 1961
PLACE: A loft in New York City

(The loft is equipped with a standing mike and spotlight, a stereo and tape recorder, a bar and several chairs. Also a blown-up photo of the "Dragon-ess." BRUCE comes on, flicks on lights and straightens ashtrays, empty glasses, etc. Enter MARA.)

MARA: Brucie-boy! How are you tonight?

BRUCE: Fine. Where's Harry?

MARA: *(Throws coat and bag on chair.)* He's having a fight with the bartender downstairs. Kerrigan, that is, our landlord.

BRUCE: Aren't they closed yet?

MARA: Just. Kerrigan's threatening to evict us.

BRUCE: He's full of it! We're only here between four and seven. Neighborhood's deserted, except for a few bums. That's why we took this dump. So we could make all the noise we wanted.

MARA: *(Goes to bar, fixes herself a drink.)* You want a drink?

BRUCE: I'll fix it myself. Oh, by the way, did you get the check?

MARA: What check?

BRUCE: The check from the beer people, for the calendars.

MARA: *(Pats bosom.)* Yes.

BRUCE: . . . Are you going to give it to Harry? . . . Sign it over to him?

MARA: I'm thinking about it.

BRUCE: But his tooth? The front one!

MARA: I said I was thinking about it.

BRUCE: *(Continues straightening.)* . . . Well, Harry'll be up in a couple of minutes.

MARA: Christ, what a night! . . . And last night! You and Harry leaving me here like that, passed out!

BRUCE: Harry was sick, I had to get him home.

MARA: Yes, that's your job. But what about me? Taking me home when he can't . . . that's one of your jobs too isn't it? I didn't wake up till almost nine! Half an hour to get to unemployment and me still in an evening gown. I ran downstairs to hail a cab . . . All those people on their way to work, the men leering at me. The taxi driver leering at me . . . I figure prominently in the fantasy life of New York's taxi drivers.

BRUCE: Look, I'm sorry about last night, or rather this morning.

MARA: It's not just last night. It's every night, every morning. It's Harry! He's not good for me, that boy. No, he isn't good for me at all.

BRUCE: Break it off with him then.

MARA: That's what you'd like, isn't it?

BRUCE: Yes, actually.

MARA: All it would mean to you if I did is that you'd have a rough time with him for a week or so . . . Then he'd find someone else. Somebody else with nothing better to do than sit here all night listening to him. He always finds someone. It never takes him long. Before me there was Terrence and before Terrence . . . God! I almost forgot.
(Gets folded telegram from her bag.)

BRUCE: What's that?

MARA: A wire from Terry, I got it this evening just as I was dressing to go out.

BRUCE: From Yucatan?

MARA: Terry's not in Yucatan . . . He's in Costa Rica.

BRUCE: What's he say?

MARA: *(Ignores him.)* Sweet Terry, Love of my life, if only . . . Oh, well . . .
(Kisses telegram, tucks it in bodice.)

BRUCE: What does Terry say in the wire?

MARA: It's to me. He sent it to me, thank you —

BRUCE: Just asking.

MARA: It's funny, Terrence probably thought Harry would help me as an actress.

BRUCE: He's a singer.

MARA: But through the Dragoness he knows everyone in the theatre. He could take me around, introduce me.

BRUCE: What about that party he took you to tonight?

MARA: Typical! . . . Merrick was there, Kazan, Williams . . . And what does our boy Harry do? Starts a fight with the host . . . Ah, yes, tonight was a three star occasion . . . Three fights, count 'em, three. First the host, then that agent at Sardi's, slugged him . . . Then the lady columnist at El Morocco.

BRUCE: Who?

MARA: Kilgallen! . . . Bit her in the ankle!

BRUCE: But his tooth!

MARA: I know, the front one . . . Three stars, no four Kerrigan makes four.

BRUCE: (Goes to door, listens.) I wonder if he's having any trouble down there?

MARA: Don't you get in to it. They're just talking. Besides, he knows better than to start anything with Kerrigan.

BRUCE: I guess so.

(Goes to bar, fixes self a drink.)

Maybe Harry ought to cool it awhile. The Dragoness is threatening to cut off his charges all over town if he gets into anymore trouble.

MARA: It's a wonder they still serve him. I suppose they just do it for her sake. She's been such a good customer all these years. They're used to her boys by now. Who knows, they may have put up with worse than Harry.

BRUCE: Listen, take it easy on him tonight: He's been very worried lately. He hasn't been able to sing. His concern about his front tooth has rendered him incapable of song. He hasn't sung for nearly a week now. He's got to practice tonight. They put off his audition today but . . .

MARA: Again?

BRUCE: He was sick! He'll have to show up tomorrow. He knows that but it bothers him that his tooth isn't right.

MARA: But with his temporary on it looks all right.

BRUCE: He can get by with the temporary tomorrow, but he must get his permanent soon, for under the temporary, his tooth is rotting! And if he does not get his permanent soon, he will lose his front tooth! . . . It would be wonderful if you could put his mind at ease.

MARA: Oh? . . . How could I do that?

BRUCE: . . . By reassuring him of your intentions.

MARA: My intentions in regard to what?

BRUCE: In regard to the check!

MARA: What check?

BRUCE: The beer check from the calendar people —

MARA: Oh, that one. I'm not quite sure what my intentions are in regard to that one, in regard to the calendar check from the beer people. No, I'm not at all sure.

BRUCE: But you had led us to believe . . .

MARA: What?

BRUCE: That you would sign it over to him.

MARA: I had led you to believe that?

BRUCE: You said you would.

MARA: Must have been drunk.

BRUCE: No, you weren't, not then, I remember.

MARA: I don't . . . Anyway, why should I pay for Harry's tooth? I thought the Dragoness was paying for it, for all his teeth. I thought that was her birthday present to him.

BRUCE: Now, Mara, don't be cute. You know all about that.

MARA: Do I? . . . Do I know all about that?

BRUCE: The Dragoness has paid the dentist forty five hundred dollars, but she refuses to make the final payment, the final five hundred, unless . . .

MARA: Yes? . . . Unless?

BRUCE: . . . Unless he meets her conditions.

MARA: Yes, I know the old girl is making conditions these days. She's tired of getting him out of scrapes, tired of apologizing for him, tired of cleaning up his messes after him. Just in general, she's tired.

BRUCE: Yes, but she's been getting very specific lately, very particular. Particularly where you are concerned.

MARA: Go on! I'm all ears! Tell me just how specific, how particular has she gotten where I am concerned?

BRUCE: Can't you guess?

MARA: The Dragoness might be willing to pay the dentist his final five hundred if Harry would be willing to meet a very specific, very particular condition of hers, where I am concerned? . . . Isn't that it? She will pay the dentist if he will give me up?

BRUCE: That's it.

MARA: And when, when did this happen? When did the Dragoness clarify her position? When, after weeks of vague threats and mumblings, did she finally make herself so beautifully clear?

BRUCE: Last night, or rather this morning, when I got him home.

MARA: This is marvelous! Marvelous! Harry wants to have his cake and eat it, with his new tooth. He wants his new tooth and me too. He wants me to give him the five hundred so he can defy the Dragoness, force her to accept me.

BRUCE: Yes.

MARA: Not because he wants me that much. He just wants his own way. He wants to show her he can get his own way with or without her . . . And this is my big chance. I'm expected to jump at it, my big chance to prove my usefulness, my love . . . They're the same thing to Harry, usefulness and love.

BRUCE: I should think you would jump at a chance like that.

MARA: What's it to you?

BRUCE: What do you mean?

MARA: What difference does it make to you who pays for the teeth as long as they're paid for?

BRUCE: It doesn't make any difference.

MARA: And you'd just as soon he broke it off with me in fact that's what you want.

BRUCE: He'd just find someone else . . . Harry doesn't want to break it off with you. Harry very much wants you to pay for the tooth . . . I want what Harry wants.

MARA: Of course . . . Well, as I told you, I'm thinking it over . . . Besides, something else has come up.

BRUCE: What?

MARA: Something else . . . I want to have a little talk with him.

BRUCE: All right, have your little talk, but don't say anything to upset him!

MARA: I'll say anything I Goddamn please to him!

(HARRY is heard on the stairs, MARA and BRUCE turn to door. HARRY lurches into room. He is draped with dusty Christmas decorations.)

HARRY: Merry Christmas! Everybody! Merry Christmas! *(Drops a tinsel rope around MARA, puts a "Santa" hat on BRUCE.)* There you are, my pretty young people, Merry Christmas! I found all these goodies in the bar below. They still had them up. I thought that a bit inappropriate seeing as how it's April. I pointed this out to our friend, Kerrigan, the proprietor. He agreed with me, and when I told him I would be only too happy to take them off his hands, he was so grateful he served me an after-hours drinkie. Wasn't that just sporting of him to do that?

BRUCE: Mara said he was threatening to evict us.

HARRY: No, he wouldn't do that! Kerrigan's too much of a sport to do that! Not after the way we fixed this place up. Remember what a dump this place was until we fixed it up? Why, we've improved his property for him. Besides, he can't evict us. The lease isn't in my name, it's in the Dragoness's name and there isn't a landlord living capable of evicting her. The only way to evict a dragoness, is to find a knight in shining armor to come riding up on a white horse. And, as you undoubtedly know, the age of chivalry is dead. So, sweeties, worry not. We're staying put.

(MARA has fixed him a drink, hands it to him.)

HARRY: Thank you, sweetie! . . . Oh, I meant to ask you before . . . Did you get the check?

MARA: What check?

HARRY: The beer check from the calendar people.

MARA: Yes, I got the calendar check from the beer people.

BRUCE: She wants to have a little talk with you, Harry.

MARA: Yes, I want to have a little talk.

HARRY: About that, about the check?

MARA: About that and about one or two other things . . . But later and preferably alone.

HARRY: But, of course, sweetie!

MARA: Just now I think it would be very nice if you would be a good boy, at last, and sing real pretty for us.

HARRY: Let's dance first! Feel like dancing! Haven't danced in years! *(Sings.)* GOTTA DANCE! GOTTA DANCE! GOTTA DANCE!

(BRUCE turns on music, MARA dances with HARRY, slowly, seductively. BRUCE watches a while, then tries to cut in. MARA pulls away from him.) Whatsa matter, Bruce? You mad cause she won't dance with you? I'll dance with you!

(He does.)

MARA: I must say, you dance much better with him than you do with me.

HARRY: Of course, I do. But you mustn't let that upset you, my pretty, it is only natural. After all, you are only five two and I am six feet tall. Bruce is six-two, therefore I dance better with him than I do with you. Besides, Bruce and I have known each other longer.

MARA: Ever since you were children together in the North Woods.

BRUCE: It was not in the North Woods that we were children together. It was in the California wine country, south of Fresno.

HARRY: Why wouldn't you dance with Bruce?

MARA: I don't know. I didn't feel like it.

HARRY: He's a better dancer than I am.

MARA: True . . . He's also bigger and better looking, stronger. But I've never been able to figure it out. He's the seemingly steady one, the one who does all the managing, the one who keeps you going . . . And even after nights like this he gets up and goes off to work, to that place where he works with those big strong hands of his, works with his hands, even though he lives with you and the Dragoness and doesn't really need the money. He's self sufficient, he's the stronger . . . I've never been able to figure it out . . . There you are, Bruce, an attractive, intelligent young man, yet you have no life of your own at all. No people, no person of your own. Why don't you have your own life, your own person? Why are you always hanging around his people? You don't make it with Harry . . . We know that. He doesn't make it with you, he doesn't make it with the Dragoness, he hardly ever makes it with me! . . . I'm not complaining. I don't really care that much about that part of it. But I bet if some night I did care, did complain, if some night I did want Harry to make it with me and he didn't feel up to it . . . Too drunk or whatever . . . I bet you'd offer to do it for him . . . I bet you would and you'd probably be better at it than he is . . . No, Bruce, I can't figure you at all. There you are with Harry and you've always been with Harry ever since you were children together in the swamps of Florida.

BRUCE: It was not in the swamps of Florida that we were children together! It was in the hills of old Virginny!

MARA: And your beard . . . How long have you worn that beard? Ever since you discovered you were bigger and better looking than him? . . . Did you decide to hide your handsomeness behind that beard out of deference to Harry? So as not to embarrass him by being bigger and better looking?

BRUCE: Watch it, Mara!

HARRY: Now come on, what's all this strife? All this gloom? I feel good! I want my pretty people to have fun! . . . Let's do something . . . Let's go bowling. Come on, let's go bowling!

MARA: In this dress?

BRUCE: All the alleys are closed.

MARA: I thought you wanted to sing.

HARRY: I do, but I'm not ready yet. Bruce, play one of last night's tapes.

BRUCE: You mean one of last week's tapes?

HARRY: All right, one of last week's tapes.

(BRUCE turns on tape. HARRY's voice comes out of the speaker, backed by a "practice record.")

"YOU LEAVE ME BREATHLESS, YOU BEAUTIFUL THING
YOU ARE SO WONDERFUL, YOU'RE LIKE A BREATH OF SPRING
YOU LEAVE ME SPEECHLESS, I'M JUST LIKE THE BIRDS
I'M FULL OF MELODY, BUT AT A LOSS FOR WORDS
THAT DAINTY CHIN OF YOURS — THAT LITTLE GRIN OF YOURS
THAT DO SO MUCH TO MY HEART
PLEASE SAY YOU'LL COME TO ME
OR WHAT IS LEFT OF ME
WILL FALL APART
YOU LEAVE ME SPEECHLESS, FOR WHAT CAN I SAY?
I CAN'T SAY ANYTHING, YOU TAKE MY BREATH AWAY!"

(Own voice.)

Cut it.

(BRUCE turns it off.)

MARA: Play the rest of it. I love that song. I love it when you sing it to me. It's beautiful.

HARRY: So are you beautiful, that's why I sing that song to you.

MARA: You used to sing it to Terrence too, didn't you? He asked you to sing it for me the first time he brought me here.

HARRY: Terrence used to like that song and I'd sing it for him. Terrence was beautiful too . . . But he wasn't a good listener. He'd listen to that song, but when I sang my other songs his mind would wander. His mind would be occupied elsewhere, I could tell.

MARA: I have a mind too.

BRUCE: Yes, she has a mind too.

HARRY: I know she does. She has a very pretty mind. What's on your mind sweetie? What's on your pretty little mind?

MARA: Nothing.

HARRY: Whatsa matter — doll baybee? Aren't you happy? Don't you have what you want? I want my baybee doll to be happy, want my doll baybee to have what she wants. What do you want, baybee doll?

MARA: You.

HARRY: You have me. You do have me. Hasn't she me, Bruce?

MARA: "All To Myself Alone" like in that other song you sing.

HARRY: She wants me all to herself alone, Bruce.

BRUCE: I know she wants you all to herself alone, but I also know she can't have you all to herself alone, and that even if she did, she wouldn't know what to do with you all to herself alone.

MARA: I resent Bruce.

HARRY: She resents you, Bruce.

BRUCE: I know she resents me. I resent her but I am willing to put up with her. And I also know that, though she won't admit it, she is willing to put up with me.

MARA: No longer . . . I am no longer willing to put up with him, and I am no longer willing to put up with the Dragoness, I resent the Dragoness!

HARRY: She resents you.

MARA: Yes, and she is no longer willing to put up with me . . . would do anything to be rid of me . . . Bruce informed me of her latest ploy before you came in, her refusal to make the final payment on your teeth unless you break with me . . . Bruce explained to me what a splendid chance this was to prove my love, my usefulness to you . . . By simply signing over my beer check from my calendar people, I could enable you to defy the Dragoness, to have your teeth and me and her . . . Well, I'm not so sure I think it a splendid opportunity . . . I don't know that I am quite that eager to prove my usefulness, my love . . . The Dragoness can refuse . . . I can refuse too!

HARRY: What's bothering you tonight? You weren't like this last night and last week you said you'd . . . What's with tonight?
     (Turns her back on him, goes to bar, fixes drink.)

BRUCE: . . . She said before that something else had come up.

HARRY: What?

BRUCE: I don't know, she wouldn't tell me . . . But before that she was saying you never do anything for her as an actress.

HARRY: Is that what's bothering you, Mara?

MARA: . . . That's one of the things that bother me.

HARRY: What would you like me to do for you in that respect?

MARA: Everything . . . Anything . . . Rack your brain! See what you come up with!

BRUCE: She thinks Terrence imagined you would help her as an actress.

HARRY: *(To MARA.)* How is Terry anyway? Have you heard from him?

BRUCE: Maybe that's what's bugging her! Terry! She got a wire from him today, from Guatemala.

MARA: Terrence is not in Guatemala . . . He's in Honduras!

HARRY: What's he say in the wire? . . . Is that it? . . . Is that the something else that's come up?

BRUCE: A wire? Maybe Terry's in some kind of trouble.

HARRY: Is he in some kind of trouble down there?

MARA: *(Takes telegram from bosom, reads it.)* "In Hell down here . . . Stop . . . Must get out . . . Stop . . . Can you send money for flight . . . Stop . . . Will repay . . . Stop . . . Please . . . Stop . . . Love . . . Stop . . . Terry."

HARRY: So that's it . . . Terry . . . Your old sweetie . . . The past.

MARA: Yes, Terry . . . Whom I loved. *(Tucks wire back in dress.)*

HARRY: In the past. Do you still love him? As you did in the past? So long ago when you were so young and he was so different? So different than he is now, at present? Do you love him at present? As you loved him before? Do you contemplate loving him again in the future? Despite the way he has changed? Terry's a different boy than the one you loved so long ago. We all know the circumstances under which he went down there.

MARA: You're a fine one to talk!

HARRY: Do you love him?

MARA: He needs me.

HARRY: I need you.

MARA: He can't need the whole check, the whole five hundred . . . How much can the fare be? The fare back up from down there? The money for "flight"? He probably only needs half, two hundred, two hundred fifty.

HARRY: He may only need half, two hundred, two fifty, but my dentist will not settle for half. I need the whole five hundred now, at present. I whom you say you love now, at present, need the whole five hundred. I need it for my future, your future, ours . . .

MARA: Hah!

HARRY: For I am a singer and what is a singer without his front tooth?

MARA: Do you think I imagine I have a future with you?

HARRY: I don't know what you think about that. But what kind of a future could you have with Terry, with Terry as he is now.

MARA: One thing I'm sure of.

HARRY: What?

MARA: He would repay me.

HARRY: But I will repay you. I will give Bruce a hundred a week to give to you and you will be repaid in a mere five weeks.

MARA: No, you won't. You may the first week but the second week you will see something, something you want, something you must have. I've seen you before with the others.

HARRY: When before, what others?

MARA: The other times you "Borrowed" . . . From Bruce, the money he earned with those big hands of his . . . Even from poor Terry . . . And the Dragon-ess, despite the huge allowance she regularly gives you unasked, I have seen you "borrow" from her . . . And you never paid any of them back, never! You saw things, things you wanted, things you had to have.

HARRY: What things?

MARA: The vicuna bathmat, the solid gold garters set with Lapis-Lazuli, the chinchilla underpants.

HARRY: You will be repaid in five weeks.

MARA: Why don't you pay the dentist that way?

HARRY: That's not my style.

MARA: That's your style with me.

HARRY: You're family.

MARA: Hah! . . . So, I'm family now.

(HARRY tries to kiss her, she eludes it, sits down. He bends over, kisses her forehead, half kneels before her.)

HARRY: Mara . . . How would you like me to help you as an actress?

MARA: You're changing the subject.

HARRY: But I want to help you.

MARA: You want to butter me up.

HARRY: No . . . I sincerely want to help you . . . Don't I, Bruce?

BRUCE: Of course,

HARRY: How can I help you, as an actress? What can I do for you in that respect?

MARA: I want you to think of a way . . . I want it to be your idea . . . Think about it!

HARRY: Okay, I will . . . I'll think about it right now . . . You think about it too, Bruce.

MARA: No: I want it to come from you!

HARRY: All right. *(Goes to bar, refills his glass.)* I know, I'll give you singing lessons!

MARA: Singing lessons?

HARRY: Yes, let's start right now!

MARA: I don't know . . . I've never sung before.

HARRY: What does that matter?

MARA: But I've always had a thing about my voice, my singing voice.

HARRY: So what? You can learn to sing. I can teach you. I will teach you. The idea appeals to me very much: I'm getting excited about it.

MARA: Wonderful! . . . But not tonight. I'm tired. I'm drunk.

HARRY: Nonsense! Bruce, adjust the mike! Stand there, Mara.

(He does. She does.)

Let's see . . . We'll start with something simple, something you know . . . "You Leave Me Breathless." You must know that by now. Have we still got the lyrics, Bruce?

BRUCE: In the album with the practice record.

(Hands him album. HARRY takes out "Practice record" and hands it back to Bruce, then gives album with lyrics to MARA. BRUCE puts record on stereo, turns up volume.)

HARRY: We'll just take it through once to get the quality of your voice. All right now. Here you go. Start!

MARA: *(Sings.)*

"YOU LEAVE ME BREATHLESS, YOU BEAUTIFUL THING
YOU ARE SO WONDERFUL, YOU'RE LIKE A BREATH OF SPRING
YOU LEAVE ME SPEECHLESS . . .

(She loses time with the music, the lyrics don't fit.)

I'M JUST LIKE THE BIRDS . . ." Let's start over again, please!

HARRY: No! Pick it up! Pick it up!

MARA: "THAT DAINTY CHIN OF YOURS, THAT LITTLE GRIN OF YOURS
THAT DO SO MUCH TO MY HEART" . . . Harry! let me start again.

HARRY: Continue!

MARA: "WILL FALL APART
YOU LEAVE ME SPEECHLESS, FOR WHAT CAN I SAY
I CAN'T SAY ANYTHING, YOU TAKE MY BREATH." . . .

(Her voice cracks, she collapses on chair.)

HARRY: But that wasn't bad at all. Was it, Bruce?

BRUCE: No, not at all. *(Winks.)*

MARA: It was terrible! I can't sing! I never could!

HARRY: Not true! You have a nice little soprano, if you could ever manage to get that tiny little mouth of yours open.

MARA: It's true. My mouth is too small. It's always been too small . . . Well, not always.

HARRY: Just a question of getting it opened up for you.

MARA: Yes, opening it up, expanding, stretching, enlargening this little mouth of mine for the purpose of song, for the purposes of stage and screen, for all sorts of purposes. I am constantly told that my mouth is too diminutive and that therefore I lack sex appeal. Or at least sex appeal of the contemporary type. The commercial, marketable type. I have been told this by every agent, producer or director who has ever granted me an interview. They sit there and, visibly aroused, tell me I have no sex appeal. They get up and chase me around their desks telling me I have no sex appeal. It is all I can do to avoid being thrown on top of those desks and raped while they shout at the top of their lungs that I have no sex appeal! . . . My mouth, it seems, is too small. Too small for today. Today a woman's mouth is supposed to resemble two red rowboats, one piled on top of the other. And yet it wasn't always that way. A small mouth used to be considered an asset. A rosebud, that's what I have. A rosebud, that's what I am. Soft and fragrant, arousing the protective instincts of the male. But today's male either has no protective instincts or doesn't care to have them aroused. Today's male does not admire the rosebud. No, the tomato: The tomato, not the old fashioned kind, small and tasty, but the large chemically grown variety. Grown for the market, today's market. Not sweetness, vulnerability . . . Size, capability! A mouth that is capable . . . Of song . . . of anything! Capable and ravenous! . . . Where did it start? Was it the wars? Men sent all over the world. Exposed to a world full of women with ravenous mouths? . . . And where does all this leave me? Stuck with my rosebud . . . Oh, I do my best with lipstick — but underneath it all lies the face of a saint . . . Do you know how I earned the money that first brought me to New York and paid for my acting lessons?

HARRY: No, how did you earn the money that first brought you to New York and paid for your acting lessons?

MARA: By posing for religious calendars for the Arch-Diocese of Chicago. My face was quite famous there. It hung on half the kitchen walls of the Arch-Diocese of Chicago. I was St. Bridget, St. Agnes, the Madonna herself! Even the Cardinal wanted to know who was the girl with the saintly face . . . if they want a saintly face nowadays in New York or Hollywood they import it from Italy, but it had better have a damn good bozoom beneath it . . . My bozoom's very good. That's undeniable.

HARRY: That is undeniable.

MARA: And bazooms go a long way. A saintly face however . . . Well, the saintliness of a face doesn't last long in New York or Hollywood . . . Hollywood! . . . All those men, staring at you, wondering . . . Will she? Will she go . . . Will she go down? . . . How far down will she go? . . . Yes — I did the bit, the whole bit and goofed it up pretty consistently, I was easy to get and I was had! Had and left! Easy, therefore, had . . . Easy, consequently left. Ah, yes, five years ago in the Arch-Diocese of Chicago . . . I still pose for calendars. A different kind. I have done my best to make myself over, from a rosebud to a tomato . . . I have done my best in order to oblige, in order to please. Please who? Anyone . . . You I suppose . . . Do I please you?

HARRY: Of course you please me. You delight and thrill me!

MARA: Then why can't I have you all to myself alone? Why do I have to share you, with the Dragoness, with Bruce?

HARRY: But . . .

MARA: They are necessary to you, more than I . . . They come first. Why? Why do you need them? Why do you need her? Why can't you just get up one afternoon, all by yourself and actually go to one of these auditions she keeps arranging for you. Go and sing! Sing and get a job. In a night club, a real night club. Instead of coming here to your own private cabaret, the Chez Harry! You perform from four till seven every morning . . . Bruce is your accompanist, I'm your audience, the Dragoness pays the rent . . . God! How I hate that woman! It isn't really her, the woman, I hate . . . It's what she represents!

HARRY: Why? What does she represent that you hate her so? . . . What made you christen her the "Dragoness"? Bruce and I simply called her "The Old Bitch" . . . Why do you hate her? What does she represent to you?

MARA: Success! . . . The Dragoness is a successful actress, which is what I want to be and can't be . . . And she has you, whom I want and can't get . . . Yes, she's a success and I hate her for it! . . . She killed her husband forty years ago for his insurance. She used the money to finance her first play. It just happened that she was a good actress. Now she is famous, retired but still famous . . . I just happen to be a good actress, but I haven't got a husband. If I had a husband, I would love him, not kill him. But I haven't got one, I haven't even got you . . . You aren't much. But I'm willing to settle for it, for what you are. I'm willing to stoop so low as to settle for it . . . And when one is willing to stoop so low as to settle for it, for what you are, and still, still isn't able to get it . . . Why can't you be a man for me? . . . Why can't anyone be a man for me? A man for me to be a woman to?

BRUCE: Mara! Shut up! I'm warning you!

MARA: And there is Bruce — Bruce, who comes even before the Dragoness, who is even more necessary to you than she is . . . Bruce who has been with you ever since you were children together in the bayous of Louisiana.

BRUCE: We were not children together in the bayous of Louisiana! We were children together in the Canadian Rockies!

MARA: Where are you from anyway? I know where I'm from . . . I'm from the Arch-Diocese of Chicago and I'm fed up! . . . Fed up with being told I have no sex appeal, with being had and left. Fed up with being asked to pay for your front tooth instead of helping poor sweet Terry, who may be in trouble down there, real trouble . . . Why can't you be a man for me?

HARRY: Because I don't have to. You don't make me. Because I know very well that, though you won't admit it, you will continue to put up with the Dragoness and with Bruce rather than lose me . . . Won't you? . . . You will and you will pay, won't you? You will pay rather than lose me.

BRUCE: I will pay . . . I will get the money somehow . . . I will pay!

HARRY: That isn't what I want.

BRUCE: I want what you want.

MARA: What have you got? I would like to know just what you have got?

HARRY: I have size and capability . . . You said it yourself. Size and capability are what is required in today's market and I possess both these attributes.

MARA: You may have them. You may possess both these attributes, but you rarely use them, at least not as far as I can make out.

HARRY: I don't have to. I have them. They are mine . . . But then there is a bit more to it than that.

MARA: Oh? What? Tell me.

HARRY: . . . You are a very lonely, very frustrated, very unhappy young woman, Mara . . . The Dragoness, Bruce and Terry too. All frustrated, unhappy, lonely people . . . And strangely but strongly drawn to me . . . Why? . . . I do nothing to relieve your frustrations, your loneliness . . . I do nothing to make you happy . . . I do nothing to make you unhappy.

MARA: What?

HARRY: I don't. I, myself, do nothing to make you unhappy, any of you. I do nothing to you and I demand nothing of you . . . I may ask, and I usually get what I ask, but I demand nothing. And I do nothing.

MARA: Except stand there and let us all make fools of ourselves over you.

HARRY: You're a very determined group. You ask me what have I got? That's irrelevant. It is not what I have, it is what you people do not have . . . No, it is not what I have got, it is what you lack.

MARA: You prey on it.

HARRY: What?

MARA: This lack of ours . . . This loneliness, this frustration of ours. You prey on it!

HARRY: No.

MARA: You take advantage of it!

HARRY: A boy has to get along somehow . . . And, after all, you invite me to take advantage of it . . . To prey on it, if you will . . . You are a very determined group. You and the Dragoness and Bruce and even Terry.

MARA: No, not Terry. He went away. Away from you.

HARRY: From you too. He went away from you, too. And he is better off away from both of us. And you are better off away from him.

MARA: How?

HARRY: Could Terry be a man for you? Was he ever and could he be now? Mara . . . Why don't you find a fellow who is able and willing to be a man for you and be a woman to him? There are such men. I'm not one, Terry's not. But there still are many such men. A girl like you shouldn't have any trouble finding them.

MARA: I don't. They find me.

HARRY: Then why don't you take one? Why don't you take such a man and be a woman to him?

MARA: They bore me.

HARRY: Nice guys bore you? You only like fags like Terry or heels like me? . . . That's all you feel up to, or down to, right?
    (She throws her drink in his face, BRUCE grabs her shoulders.)

MARA: Get your hands off me! Get those big, hard working hands of yours off me!

HARRY: Bruce! Get your big, hard working hands off her!

BRUCE: I told you to take it easy, didn't I?

MARA: Don't worry, Bruce. I'm not going to do anything more. I'm not going to say anymore either . . . I'm going to shut up now. It's Harry's turn to talk. Keep talkin', Harry . . . No! Don't talk . . . Sing! Sing!

HARRY: All right.
    (HARRY to mike, BRUCE to recorder, turns on music. HARRY suddenly becomes sick to his stomach, dashes offstage to bathroom. BRUCE and MARA start after him. BRUCE stops MARA at the door, grabs her again.)

BRUCE: No! It's me he needs in there: It's me that's going to help him!

MARA: No! It's me! It's me that he needs! It is I that can help him.

BRUCE: No! You bitch! You upset him! You upset Harry!

MARA: I've a perfect right to upset him! He should be upset! I shall continue to upset him until I get what I want from him!

BRUCE: I'll kill you first!
    (His hands on her throat.)

MARA: You can't kill me! You won't! . . . Look at my face! Look at it! . . . You can't kill St. Bridget, St. Agnes, the Madonna herself! . . . You can't!
    (He is paralyzed but does not release his grip on her throat.)
    (HARRY reenters, pulls him off MARA and throws him to the floor.)

HARRY: Now cut it out! Both of you! This is silly!

MARA: He was going to kill me! But he couldn't! Could you? He couldn't kill me, he couldn't kill them . . . No, Bruce . . . you couldn't kill me, for not only am I St. Bridget, St. Agnes . . . I am also Juliet, Ophelia . . . Especially Ophelia, for Ophelia was mad! . . . No one can kill me! Only I can kill me! For I am all those things . . . And what are you? You are nothing: You are nobody! You're nothing! You're nobody!

HARRY: Enough now, Mara, enough — leave him alone! . . . He is necessary to me!

MARA: Are you all right?

HARRY: Yes. I'm fine now . . . I shall sing now . . . Bruce!

   (HARRY goes to mike, BRUCE to recorder. MARA takes check, then the telegram from her bosom.)

MARA: Oh, Terry . . . Where are you?

BRUCE: Terrence is in Nicaragua.

MARA: He is not in Nicaragua, he is in El Salvador.

   (She kisses telegram, then drops it. She gets a pen from her bag, takes check, puts it on bar and endorses it, then sticks it in HARRY's breast pocket. She falls into one of the chairs, closes her eyes.)

   Sing for me, Baby! Sing for me!

HARRY: *(Sings.)*

   "YOU LEAVE ME BREATHLESS, YOU BEAUTIFUL THING
   YOU ARE SO WONDERFUL, YOU'RE LIKE A BREATH OF SPRING
   YOU LEAVE ME SPEECHLESS, I'M JUST LIKE THE BIRDS
   I'M FULL OF MELODY, BUT AT A LOSS FOR WORDS"

CURTAIN

WHO KILLED MY BALD SISTER SOPHIE? OR: THANK GOD FOR SMALL FAVORS!
Tom Eyen

To Neil Flanagan and the memory of Caffe Cino

Who Killed My Bald Sister Sophie? was first presented by and with the Theatre of the Eye Repertory Company at the Caffe Cino, New York, on February 20, 1968. It was directed by Neil Flanagan, with a set by Josef Bush, costumes by Lamston's 5 & Dime, lighting by John P. Dodd, and the following cast:

Hanna	Helen Hanft
Arizona	Steven Davis
Sophie	Connie Clark
Voice of Barker	Neil Flanagan
Stage Manager	John Hartnett

The play was revived for a series of midnight performances at the Astor Place Theatre beginning February 6, 1971. This production was again directed by Neil Flanagan, with the same cast excepting Jean David as Sophie.

TIME: Five minutes to seven, the moment after the curtain falls on *Why Hanna's Skirt Won't Stay Down.*

PLACE: A Fun-Wax House, Coney Island, U.S.A.

SETTING: As for *Why Hanna's Skirt Won't Stay Down*, with the addition of one poster at far left: SOPHIE (complete with Avon sample kit) holding a small replica of Michelangelo's "David" between her legs, with blood oozing from that area. This poster may be modified for community theater reproductions to show SOPHIE simply holding the statue in her hand (one in the hand is worth two in the bush).

A clock is again set at five minutes to seven. As in *Hanna*, the barker may be visible on stage or, as in the original production, only heard.

MUSIC: Quick-changing, as in *Hanna*. The soundtrack of the Burton-Taylor *Cleopatra* may be used for scenes occurring in Egypt, etc.

LIGHTING: Like music, should change with and as quickly as the emotional moods. A flickering rainbow for the carnival, sun-baked sand for Egypt, and a gentle baby-pink wind to carry the memories.

Connie Clark as Sophie, Stephen Davis (Van Vost) as Arizona, and Helen Hanft as Hanna in *Who Killed My Bald Sister Sophie?*, 1968

Photos by James D. Gossage

FIRST IMAGE: Darkness. The eternal music of the carnival begins, joined by the canned laughter, building in volume and erupting into hundreds of blinking lights of the midway. The music, laughter, and dancing lights together await their new victims.

VOICE OF BARKER: Step right up! Step right in, folks! Admission only ten cents! See "How Rome Burned while Nero Played!" See "Lovely Marie Antoinette at the Guillotine!"

(HANNA appears, dressed as in Part I. She looks knowingly at her own poster, lovingly at ARIZONA's, then, seeing the breeze-hole, puts her hand over it to test the air pressure.)

BARKER: See — "Why Hanna's Skirt Won't Stay Down!"

(HANNA now jumps over the breeze-hole with gay abandon, her arms and skirt rising together to the sky. She gives a loud sigh of relief.)

HANNA: AHHHHHHHHHHH! *(Becoming aware of audience, she stops.)* I come here every payday and stand over the breeze-hole. It keeps me calm, if not cool. There's something about air — the pressure. The sensation of something trying to penetrate your body. Now don't you put no Freudian connotation on that one! I can't stand assumptions! I just happen to like a little cool breeze. It's my only outlet in life! *(Air returns.)* Ahhhhhh. Air, cool. Air, cool.

(Continues ad lib as ARIZONA enters, in denim shirt and Levi's. He ignores HANNA and closely admires his own poster. Flexing his muscles, he smiles approvingly to himself and begins undressing.)

BARKER: See — Smiley, the smiling narcissistic wonder, trapped in the mirror maze!

(ARIZONA turns, seeing HANNA in high ecstasy. He is now naked except for his American Flag bikini briefs.)

ARIZONA: What some people won't do for a little attention! *(Flexes muscles.)* That dizzy yenta is always here. Me? I come, I go. I come, I go. I come, I go. *(Continues ad lib.)*

SOPHIE: *(Off.)* Here's my dime, sir!

(SOPHIE is now seen in the carnival arena in a white tailored suit, circa 1940, a large white picture hat with a false hairpiece coming through a hole in its center. In her delicate hand, which has never washed a pan, she holds a large Avon sample kit, containing all her worldly possessions — cosmetic samples, several much-fingered letters, the replica of "David," and a very large blood-stained bread knife.)

SOPHIE: I've paid my dime. Now I want it my way — the truth!

ARIZONA: *(Still flexing muscles, not seeing SOPHIE.)* Now, take me! I'm different.

SOPHIE: *(Checking him over like an expensive steak.)* You certainly are, young man. All right, I'll take you. You're available. Your type always is — and besides, I pay well.

(ARIZONA finally acknowledges her existence.)

NOW, BOY! — get the palm tree out, my white deck chair, turn off that damn breeze-hole, bring all the lights up red-hot, put some sand on the floor, play some of that soft near-Eastern music, get out that broken table fan — *and don't forget the pyramid!*

(All in the manner of an Army drill sergeant. ARIZONA does her bidding quickly. While he is doing this, HANNA begins feeling the oncoming terror of her past and the lack of air. She begins to sweat, gradually falling to the ground. When she lands, she pulls a small fan out of her bosom and begins fanning herself frantically for revival or survival, as the case may be. As the new music comes on, blending with the heat of the red lights, a new mood and locale penetrate the arena. We begin again, but now through the eyes of SOPHIE.)

SOPHIE: *(Sitting in her deck chair, looking the picture of coolness.)* There is something about Egypt in the summer!

HANNA: *(Rising up on one elbow, fanning.)* It's fucking hot — oy vey, Maria, that's what it is! It's so fucking hot a person could die of suffocation!

SOPHIE: There is something about the way the sun protects the pyramids with its guarding rays.

HANNA: It protects those old pyramids, all right, but what about my sensitive skin? The last person who passed by alive thought I was a fried gefilte fish casserole!

SOPHIE: God began here. History has kept it as He made it. Just the sand and the sky. Man's civilization has not destroyed God's desert paradise with its deceiving progress!

HANNA: Is sanitation a crime? In Cairo they still have little holes out in back of their homes — and the last one I used, I fell in! And let me tell you, folks, it ain't Wonderland down there!

SOPHIE: What could be a more ideal vacation? And such a bargain! Why, only $499.99 round-trip air fare from New York —

HANNA: The plane had only two engines.

SOPHIE: — including meals —

HANNA: The meals were White Tower rejects.

SOPHIE: — a first run movie —

HANNA: The movie was the life story of Sonja Henie, *The Red Ice Skates.*

SOPHIE: — hotel accommodations —

HANNA: Our hotel is an ancient landmark, but a modern fleabag —

SOPHIE: — All for less than five hundred dollars. Such a bargain — even including fabulous scheduled sightseeing tours.

HANNA: Ahh, the tours! Let me tell you about the fabulous tours! The kind where a guide, who probably had to fake his way through the second grade, takes you out into the desert, points to the ground, and says in a phony English accent — which he probably picked up with a good case of syph from the last British cuntess he slept with — he says —

ARIZONA: *(As guide.)* "Here, on this ancient sand, Nefertiti got screwed!"

HANNA: So it all goes to prove — you always get fucked in a bargain! *(To SOPHIE again.)* When is the guide coming back, Sophie? This is not exactly my idea of happiness!

SOPHIE: Patience, dear, we've only been waiting here a few — minutes.

HANNA: Minutes? *Minutes!* It's been a few days!

SOPHIE: Oh, well — whatever. It hasn't been very long. Relax, dear!

HANNA: *(Fanning.)* You've got something cooking in the fire, Sophie, and I got a suspicious feeling it's my ass!

SOPHIE: *(Taking a deep breath.)* My heart! . . . ahh-h-h, my heart cannot hold malice in this sanctifying tropic climate!

HANNA: My hair . . . ah-h-h, my hair cannot hold a tease either!

SOPHIE: *(As Columbus must have said to his crew.)* So I said to my sister, Hanna, "To Egypt, sister! We have not yet *bean* to Egypt."

HANNA: Egypt! We haven't even *bean* to Miami Beach yet!

SOPHIE: But Egypt is Romance, History, Mystery, Adventure!

HANNA: It's fuckin' hot, Sophie! It's so fuckin' hot a person could die of affected sapphocation! *(Fanning.)*

SOPHIE: *(Smiling quietly.)* So to Egypt we came — I have always made the final decisions!!

HANNA: But not the last word! God may not have given me a brain, but he gave me a mouth . . .

SOPHIE: Hanna and I arrived in Egypt yesterday.

HANNA: Maybe, if we start walking, we can find the way back to the hotel!

SOPHIE: The guide said he would come back. He will come back. We've spent too much time waiting to ruin it all by leaving now. Activities must be planned. Life must be put on a schedule. Thanks to me, we accomplish things!

HANNA: I have never known anyone who accomplished more things and gained so little in life as my *older* sister, Sophie.

SOPHIE: *(To audience.)* I think it is time to tell you — we are not alone in Egypt!

HANNA: Thank God we are not alone in Egypt!

SOPHIE: Our little son is with us.

HANNA: It is *my* son! Not *our* son! My son! She cannot deprive me of my, my, my, my son! And he's not little! He is tall like the mountains — his smile could shame the sun! He is even more handsome and stronger than his father!

SOPHIE: Whoever the unfortunate man was! All right, it is Hanna's son for now.

HANNA: She always says that! "For now!" *He is always my son!*

SOPHIE: Either case, he is not here.

HANNA: Thank God he's not! He would be dying like his mother. Like Hanna, he likes air — he needs air!

SOPHIE: He is back in our hotel room in Cairo.

HANNA: Wherever that is — the one kind Sophie found without air conditioning — probably the only one of all the modern hotels there without it! Sophie has a genius for always finding exactly what she wants — not that she gets it, but she finds it.

SOPHIE: He is a sweet, shy boy.

HANNA: He is too ashamed to come out now.

SOPHIE: He is reserved. He is polite. He does not offend with verbal rudeness.

HANNA: He does not talk now. Before we came . . .

SOPHIE: *Stop!*

HANNA: Two days before we came, my vulturous sister . . .

SOPHIE: *Stop!! (Hanna does.)* You agreed to stop when I asked you. I have agreed to do likewise. We have agreed not to become overly personal. That was Mother's worst quality. She would become overly personal with the first person she met. Why, the whole town we were raised in knew our innermost thoughts and actions! Now, you don't want to become like Mother whom you hated so much? *(Looking at man whom HANNA was talking to.)* And besides, that man doesn't understand a word you're saying. He's only a camel herder! He wouldn't even understand intelligent English!

(Glaring at HANNA, she returns to deck chair and reads the Bible.)

HANNA: *(Continuing, to the same man, nervously and slowly, knowing that her life may end momentarily.)* My vulturous sister cut out his tongue! His tongue! Like a pig! Oh, she said it was just an accident . . . a simple kitchen accident . . . that happened *in his bedroom when he was sleeping!* My son woke to the pain of his tongue being sliced from his mouth! And now . . . my son is no longer tall; he stoops from shame. Now my son cannot smile, he cannot shame the sun. He is no longer strong. He can't be strong if he can't smile. *(To the man, more personal now, as SOPHIE begins hearing.)* And all because he said the wrong thing! It was the truth, but still the wrong thing to say! He told her . . . he didn't love her! Love her? He didn't even like her! He liked, loved Hanna! He loved Hanna!! *(With the controlled insanity one would expect of a sinner at the Last Judgment.)* You see, you must never tell her you don't love her. And in particular, never, *never*, tell her you love me . . .

SOPHIE: *(Using the same man, apologizing.)* Please excuse my sister, she suffers. Her boy was recently wounded in the war. The Viet crisis. Shot in the — wounded in the face. She's never been able to accept war, and since I've always been her — scapegoat. *(Realization of her attempt to justify.)* I don't have to tell you all this! He was wounded in the Viet war! *That is all!*

HANNA: She tells everyone that. Always simplifying the truth — even if she has to lie to do it!

SOPHIE: My sister has always been on the border of schizophrenia, so her previous and future comments are all illusory. She admits only her illusions, ignoring the reality. Therefore, Hanna is never to be believed. *(Quite pleased.)* My sister, regrettably, is a confirmed pathological liar.

HANNA: She's saying it again. She tells everyone that. How I hate that! And she's so definite about it. So calm, so cool. *(With fury.)* You don't believe her??? *(Break, calm.)* Of course you do; everyone always has. *(Back to play.)* Please, Sophie! It's too hot. Maybe we can find another hotel room with air conditioning.

SOPHIE: It's already been arranged. Our hotel accommodations were included in our package deal. *(To audience.)* Hanna is always trying to change things, confuse patterns, screw up formulas.

HANNA: Hanna has screwed many things in her life, but never formulas.

SOPHIE: We must accept, Hanna. Accept!

HANNA: Sophie has always accepted what was given her in life. In other words, my sister has always been cheap.

SOPHIE: It's not that I mind spending the extra money, but we could put it to more practical use. Like buying crying Madonna souvenirs on the special Holy Land excursion tomorrow.

HANNA: Sophie has never missed a Mass on Sunday — which is quite odd for a Jewess. She's always accepted everything — everything, except that he is *my son!!*

SOPHIE: He is Hanna's son for now.

HANNA: There she goes again! "For now!" "For now!" Always! Always — he is always my son! You better accept that, Sophie. Accept that — and that that guide is not coming back! *(Pulling her up from chair with care, as one would help an invalid.)* Let's walk. *I'm not waiting here any longer!* *(HANNA becomes faint.)*

SOPHIE: *(Helps carry HANNA as though they are walking a long road.)* Hanna has been prone to violent screaming — compulsive, some people say. Emotionally uncontrolled, mentally unstable, socially insecure, others say. And, in moments of crisis, quite vulgar.

HANNA: *(Dropped by her sister, on whom she was leaning for support.)* That bald cunt! She's always thinking behind my back. How I hate that! I never hear her — never out loud — but I can hear!

(ARIZONA appears in Arab garb.)

SOPHIE: Here . . . we are, dear. Rooms, please.

ARIZONA: Reservations? Do you have any reservations?

SOPHIE: Of course I do, young man — about everything! Everyone should. Selectivity is the key. I am Sophie O'Brien and her sister from Boston, Massachusetts.

HANNA: Springfield, Illinois, Sophie. I've already told them. Everyone knows that.

SOPHIE: You know everyone, don't you, dear? But, of course, in your profession, I suppose, one meets a great many people.

ARIZONA: *(Back to play.)* Oh, yes, here it is. Room 304, and here is your selectivity key.

SOPHIE: I hope it's a decent room. There mustn't be a draft. I catch colds easily.

HANNA: Draft??? There's not even air!!

ARIZONA: Yes, Room 304 has no windows, as you ordered. One table fan.

HANNA: There is a fan?

ARIZONA: *(Staring at SOPHIE as if they were planning something.)* However, it hasn't worked in years.

HANNA: I really needed this today. I need all this foreign intrigue after that flying freighter ride over here, and then being stuck in the desert two days?

SOPHIE: That will be fine, young man. You may take our bags up. We're going to have a look around.

(ARIZONA exits with bags.)

HANNA: Around where? There's nothing but sand around here!

SOPHIE: But there is a pool! Look, dear! You can't say the hotel doesn't have a lovely pool.

(ARIZONA comes back as a lifeguard, and blows whistle just as HANNA is about to jump in.)

HANNA: *(Looking down into pool.)* Where's the water, Sophie?

SOPHIE: *(Watching ARIZONA as lifeguard.)* What did you say, dear?

HANNA: The water! There's no water in the pool!

SOPHIE: *(Feeling ARIZONA as one would touch a fine statue.)* Don't be so demanding, dear. It's a new hotel. They probably haven't gotten to the details yet!

HANNA: *(To ARIZONA.)* Could you help me, please?
     (ARIZONA begins to respond to her physically.)

SOPHIE: *(Continues casually to the audience, ignoring her sister's momentary victory.)* As you all must have gathered by now, my name is Sophie O'Brien and to my direct rear is my sister Hanna. We're from Springfield, Illinois. Except for an illegitimate daughter, Gilda, whom we have never met, our mother conceived nine children, of which only two survived — myself and, to my direct rear, the whore of Babylon.

HANNA: *(Coming up for air.)* Of all the odds, I had to get stuck with that loser!

SOPHIE: Mother and Father were first cousins, and the blood similarity causes weak children — you know, hemophilia. We were lucky to survive. You see, marriages of this sort create children who are subject to great losses of blood, upon being punctured.

HANNA: *(Coming up for air again.)* Every chance I got I would quickly stick pins in my sister!

SOPHIE: Even as a child, Hanna was subject to physical violence. How many nights I would find myself being awakened by the sting of a needle!

HANNA: She wouldn't bleed! The bald bitch just wouldn't bleed an ounce!

SOPHIE: I was the first child and she was the ninth.

HANNA: Sophie is nine years older.

SOPHIE: Five!

HANNA: Nine!

SOPHIE: Five!!

HANNA: Nine!!

SOPHIE: *Five!!*

HANNA: *Nine!!*

SOPHIE: Seven?

HANNA: *(Resigning from battle.)* All right. Seven.

SOPHIE: I have always been the one to make compromises.

HANNA: Hanna has concentrated on making other things. That's how she got a son. Hanna has had four sons! *(Pushing ARIZONA away.)* That's all, Buster Brown.

SOPHIE: All of whom she quickly put in adoption agencies.

HANNA: I was one of the great mothers of our country. You ask Melinda, that little bitch. I've already confessed about the agencies. I was young. A person changes, mellows. It's not that I've become old . . . I'm just not young any more . . . *(HANNA sits in chair.)*

SOPHIE: Hanna was never punished in her youth, which accounts for her uncontrolled life — a life which I shall straighten on this journey. I love my sister. I want to help her. You see, I lost track of my sister during her formative years. I went to college, the University of Chicago, Liberal Arts. I was home, however, for Easter vacation during my senior year, and Hanna and I decided to spend our brief reunion shopping in town. *(She moves next to HANNA.)* All I can remember about that meeting, oddly enough, was the bus ride to town.

(SOPHIE and HANNA may mime bus ride, standing or sitting.)

ARIZONA: *(As bus driver, sitting in chair in front of them.)* Come on, folks! Move to the back! Come, come, move it back!

HANNA: Look! Sophie, he's doing it again!

SOPHIE: I was a senior at C.U. and Hanna was a high school sophomore. That was the first time I discovered my sister's sexual delusions.

HANNA: Look! He's exhibiting his privates again! He always does that. How I hate that! Private exhibition in public!

SOPHIE: Don't be ridiculous, dear. No such thing is happening. *(Reading paper or Bible.)* Besides, whoever it is, he will be leaving soon.

HANNA: Always have to make it simpler. "He'll be leaving soon!" As though you really knew!

SOPHIE: It's only logical. He has to. One stop will be his, and he'll leave.

HANNA: Well, this one ain't leaving! It's the bus driver! Every time I get this bus I have to get a free show. *(Yelling.)* Ahh! I've seen it already!!

SOPHIE: *(Looks quickly.)* Where? *(Disappointed.)* He's doing no such thing.

HANNA: Oh, that was fast! *(Yelling.)* Ahh! Next time, I hope you get stuck in the zipper!

SOPHIE: Hanna, please . . . Oh, hello, Mrs. Bronson. Yes, it's a lovely day. Oh, Hanna's just upset, she has a . . . a . . . headache.

HANNA: There he goes again! He's Jewish!

SOPHIE: *(Anxiously.)* Where?

HANNA: Boy, is he a sneak! He's playing prick-a-boo behind the coin box. *(Confidentially to SOPHIE.)* Want to know his name?

SOPHIE: Hanna, please! Oh, Mrs. Katz, yes, father's feeling much better now. *(Looks at HANNA for answer.)*

HANNA: His name is Percy. He's in love with me. How I hate that! Being loved by a public exhibitionist! For four months he's been doing that. Of all the girls who get on this bus, I have to get the attention! *(Turning fast.)* I saw you, sneak!! *(To SOPHIE.)* Isn't he cute?

SOPHIE: Hanna, please! All the other passengers are staring at us!

HANNA: Of course. They always do. They all look at me screaming and think I'm insane, and meanwhile, that idiot up there is going crazy with himself. *(Sees it again, falls on her knees.)* Ahh-h-h! *Mercy, Percy, Mercy!!*

SOPHIE: Get up here, Hanna! Maybe if I would speak to him politely about the situation, he would stop.

HANNA: *No!* I mean, you try! I hardly make it back here alive when I put my ten-cent fare in the box. And then . . . then that ape says to me, with a southern accent yet, "Since you put ten in my box, honey, I'd like to repay you by putting ten in yours." Now, I don't know what he means by that remark, but it don't sound too gracious to me! Ahhhhhh, there it is again! *(Yelling to him.)* You're a public servant, not a public exhibitionist!

SOPHIE: *(Checking ARIZONA as the bus driver more closely now.)* There is no such thing happening! He has both hands on the wheel! Fantasy!

ARIZONA: Spring Street!

HANNA: He's tired, that's all. By the time we get to Spring Street, he always gives a sigh, rolls his eyes, puts it away and goes back to his business of shouting . . .

ARIZONA: Come on, folks! Move to the back! Come, come, move it back!

HANNA: Yeah, now he's finished, the schmuck! Now I have nothing to do but look out the window at the boring scenery.

SOPHIE: *(Sits in DRIVER's lap.)* That was the last time I saw my sister. That Easter I eloped and moved to Jersey City.
    (ARIZONA as bus driver carries her to another area.)

HANNA: I was sixteen and she was twenty-five . . .

SOPHIE: Twenty-three!

HANNA: And she had this boyfriend from next door. I can't remember his name, but he had a smile that would shame the sun. Ever since then, all I've ever wanted from life was one smile to shame the sun. I used to watch him on the sofa with her, and even in the dark the room would glow. Of course, part of this was due to Sophie's shining bald spot on the crown of her head. Poor thing was born that way.

SOPHIE: Why must you continually tell the neighbors that lie? Whatever leads you to believe such a thing?

HANNA: You always wear a hat.

SOPHIE: I like hats. A lady should always wear a hat.

HANNA: To bed? Why do you wear it to bed, Sophie?

SOPHIE: My sister's life has been a series of stupid questions. No answers or reasons, just stupid little questions filling in the void, sucking up time. Not that I don't love my sister dearly. True, we have never been close. We have led separate lives — I choosing one of occupational fulfillment, she one of sexual saturation and moral abandon. Not that my sister's private affairs are any of my business. But really! I mean, a lady of culture and breeding does not just lay down on the sidewalks of Boston, Massachusetts, and publicly offer herself to young boys passing!

HANNA: She's lying again! That was in Springfield I did that! Springfield, Illinois! Lincoln's birthplace!

SOPHIE: Nevertheless, I fell madly in love with Smiley, the boy next door, and the only one who ever really looked at me twice. On the third look we were married and moved to Jersey City, he having a wonderful job opportunity waiting there. I've never seen Hanna or Springfield since.

HANNA: Well, thank God we never heard from her again! Of course, we have never been a family to write! After a very quick puberty affair with a certain bus driver named Percy, he was transferred to another route — the Springfield State Hospital area. But I stayed attracted to older men. When I was sixteen, I liked men twenty-five; when I was twenty-five, I liked them thirty. When I became thirty, it reversed. I began liking them twenty-five; and now that I'm thirty — thirty! I like them sixteen! I'm back where I should have started . . . You see, I'm still a child at heart!

SOPHIE: Her and Peter Pan!

HANNA: *(Ignoring comment.)* Father and I never heard from Sophie again, although an item in the *Springfield Herald* caught our eye —
(Gunshot in the darkness behind HANNA. Lights come up to find ARIZONA as Smiley, dead on the floor.)
"Local Boy Killed in Action . . ."

SOPHIE: A new city, a loving wife, a wonderful job opportunity . . . and then the fool had to go and die in the war!

HANNA: Sophie never even came to the mock funeral.

SOPHIE: My husband died in '43, in a small village outside of Munich. Oh, yes, he died a hero. Citations — "Died in the line of duty," "Preservation of the

American cause," "Freedom for all!" Many citations! I have them all here in my sample kit. Even a President's condolences — "He died to make men free!" No, no! He died *to make Sophie lonely!* To destroy every ambition or dream I ever had! To make my life a series of door-to-door excursions, numbing my fingers pushing in little buzzers, hoping some day to be electrocuted by one. Oh, he hated me! My husband hated me! What else was he trying to prove by risking his neck? *Those other men didn't try to leave that foxhole! I would hate his memory if I had one! But all I have now are these! (Pulling pieces of paper from her kit, she squeezes them.)* These! All I have to show for my life are pieces of paper! A president writes and say she's sorry. *He's* sorry!! *This is all I'm stuck with now! (Looking at paper, fondly.)* You know, Franklin Delano Roosevelt had such lovely handwriting! *(Puts it back in bag.)* This is worth a hell of a lot of money, you know!

HANNA: Father died when I was seventeen, and I decided it was about time to get out of Springfield.

SOPHIE: Having three illegitimate children in that small community, I'm sure, had nothing to do with that decision.

HANNA: How I hate that! Repeating things people know! So I took my total inheritance of $24.36, after the debts were settled, and moved to the nearest big city, Chicago.

(Sounds of Chicago, lights go red, ARIZONA becomes a bartender, SOPHIE becomes a singer, singing: "Chicago.")

ARIZONA: Come on, girls, come on! Let's move those ass muscles! Hey, Wanda, get these drinks over to Table Ten!

HANNA: Due to Father's overgenerous will, I had to get a job immediately . . . and I got one in a speakeasy on State Street. There I met my first legal husband, a bartender. After a short prenuptial affair . . .

(Both bump into each other and grunt.)

. . . we were married.

(SOPHIE sings a few bars of "Oh, Promise Me.")

HANNA: I do!

ARIZONA: I do!

HANNA: A beautiful June wedding. The club gave us a lovely reception. Oh, I loved him all right — but the marriage only lasted four months. That's when our first child, my fourth, came . . .

ARIZONA: *(Sees SOPHIE, who winks at him. He goes to her.)* On second thought, I don't. *(He leaves.)*

HANNA: But, nevertheless, for the first time I loved — and my love became contagious. I had to love the world. I also had to find another adoption agency for the new kid. But I had learned to love, and more important, I had learned how to make people love me. At last I'd discovered what I'd always wanted to know. But then, that discovery, like all great assets, has always been my main problem. I learned that to love, or be loved, one must at all times be honest, protective, and, whatever, hold on tightly. Only, somehow I destroyed what I wanted, or whoever wanted me, by strangulation, suffocation. Not that I didn't keep on trying. No one can give up something good when you've gotten it once. But I only ended up loving too often, having too much — yet only keeping small souvenirs, like two ticket stubs to Ice Capades. So now? Now, every time that I meet someone I'd like to love, I turn my back. I find that which I dislike, which I hate. It doesn't hurt so much when I strangle, kill that. So therefore, I am now unfortunately surrounded by what I hate, and what hates me. *(Breaking.)* Chicago and I never did make it and, discovering after my fifth month there that a Greyhound bus leaves every fifteen minutes, I decided it was time to move. And, like everyone else who has to move and is not quite sure of where to run, I came to New York.

(ARIZONA walks across stage and is shot from some unknown height.)

SOPHIE: After my husband deserted me — I mean, died — that day, I picked up the morning paper and found work immediately as a friendly Avon representative. I began a new life. Yes, a new life . . . *(Smiling with pain.)* of waiting. *(Almost proudly.)* I have waited patiently in doctors' offices, employment agencies, ticket lines, crowded restaurants, in Bohemian cafes for lovers who somehow managed never to appear. But I was always taught, anything good must be worth waiting for! . . . Something good takes time! But still, there's a terrible helplessness in valuable time passing while you're just sitting there, when the thought comes that your greatest expectations might never be realized, merely because of *one* unkept appointment or one meeting that chance never gave you. So you begin rationalizing, "Well, perhaps I've confused the time, I've only been waiting here *(Checks large clock overhead.)* a — ten minutes! Perhaps he's confused the time! I've only been waiting here — barely an hour. You know he could have lost the address! Anyway, I've only been waiting here a few hours. Well, perhaps he's had a slight accident — *(ARIZONA is shot again)* — and was killed in a war, and won't be able to come after all. But then I haven't wasted that much time! Why, I've only been waiting here a — *(Sees clock clearly now.)* a — lifetime!"

HANNA: We can't wait any longer, Sophie! That guide is never coming back.

SOPHIE: Luckily, I was given employment as an Avon representative in Jersey City. Not that I had had any previous selling experience, but on the application one must fill out for Avon, the most important asset one must possess is the ability to wait — wait patiently in front of closed doors, that is. Thanks to my past record in life, I was given the job immediately.

HANNA: After my unnoticed arrival in New York City — oh, maybe except for a few horny Puerto Ricans who hang out in Port Authority — I found work on

42nd Street. No, no, you! (*Pointing to a meek man in the audience.*) I
didn't say I *work* 42nd Street! How I hate assumptions! Where are your
manners? Where the fuck did you leave them, at home? (*Seeing someone a
little more sympathetic.*) I work in a movie house. I'm a ticket dispenser on
42nd Street, remember? Okay, you! So it's not a great career, but there are
benefits! In that job I found humility. Lousy jobs always give you that. I even
took to praying, again. Hanna had found God again. How many times I
would watch the sweet old matinee ladies passing and mentally say to myself, "There, but for the grace of God, goes my fat, old, retarded, bald bitch
sister Sophie. Thank you, God, that she's not one of them! Thank you, God,
for the Hudson River guarding New York from Jersey City! And forgive me,
God, for my own sins — for I know what I do, but I just can't help it!" Sitting there alone in a glass cage you can see life clearly — you could, if only
the cheap management would clean the goddamned glass once in a while!

SOPHIE: Hanna, it's time to tell about the boy! (*Getting nervous and checking
watch.*)

HANNA: It's not even . . . (*Checking large overhead clock — always set at five
minutes to seven.*)

SOPHIE: It's past time, dear. Don't be afraid; they'll understand. And besides,
you tell the story so well. It's really one of your best stories.

HANNA: She's patronizing — how I hate that! All right! The boy! One of my sons
has been returned to me; I have found one of my sons.
    (*ARIZONA begins combing his hair in mirror-maze.*)

SOPHIE: So she says! Her "son" she calls him — but then, how else can a lady of
maturity explain a nineteen-year-old boy?

HANNA: Being a good mother, I have always kept close track of the whereabouts
of my children.

SOPHIE: She ran into him in a Coney Island fun house on a rainy day, she says!

HANNA: (*Seeing ARIZONA.*) Sonny!

ARIZONA: Mammy!!!
    (*They embrace madly.*)

SOPHIE: Mother and son reunited! He has been her husband, her lover, and
now her crutch!

HANNA: Yeah, a son was returned to me! This was my lucky year — that is, until
I also ran into my sister, whom I hadn't seen for twenty . . . too-short . . .
years!

SOPHIE: Ring! I said — "Ring!"

HANNA: I had an omen that day. My astrological charts told me, "Hanna, this is
the day the evil finger of fate is going to stick up your destiny!"

SOPHIE: For the third time — "Ring!"

HANNA: I sensed something disastrous around ten in the morning. My cold-water flat's door was ringing — which was strange, since I didn't have a doorbell. "Who is it? Who is ringing out there?"

SOPHIE: Avon calling! "Ring!" Avon calling! "Ring!"

HANNA: *(To ARIZONA.)* Get dressed, son! *(Opening door.)* Avon who?

SOPHIE: *(Rushing in quickly.)* Hello! I'm Constance Withers, your friendly Avon representative. May I show you our new spring line?

HANNA: Honey, it's the middle of the night! *(Sees SOPHIE's portable doorbell ringer.)* A portable doorbell! My, aren't you a pusher!

SOPHIE: *(Seeing ARIZONA.)* My, what a lovely apartment! *(Placing bag on table, she slaps roach crawling on table.)* That wasn't a pet, I hope?

HANNA: Look, precious, if you don't mind, I'm not entertaining this morning.

SOPHIE: Now, my dear, we received your card asking for cosmetic aid. Now the wonderful world of beauty can be yours for only pennies a day! Please don't worry about money; our time plan allows all to share in the lovely world of glamour!

HANNA: If you're from the Health Board, I don't know who it was!

SOPHIE: *(Not to be stopped.)* Now . . . here is a base guaranteed to eliminate all unsightly blemishes! Hides while it medicates those sagging eyebags, tightens the skin and can also be used as a bust enlarger with the proper exercises outlined in this easy-to-read pamphlet! *(Shoving it into HANNA'S hand.)*

HANNA: *(Reading.)* "So You Have Tired Tits!"

SOPHIE: *(Shocked.)* It says, "Bust Exercises!" Bust Exercises!

HANNA: Oops, sorry! Look, gorgeous, I'd just love to chat, have tea and all, but I don't allow women in my apartment. You can sort of call this the Y.M.C.A. Annex!

SOPHIE: You don't —

HANNA: Been my rule ever since I can remember. It's all because of Sophie, my older sister — sibling rivalry, but then I don't suppose you're interested in my confused childhood. I'm not. *(Pulling her out the door by the hair — hairpiece falls off.)* Say, Pushy, ever do anything for that bald spot?

SOPHIE: Uhhhhh . . . bald spot?? *(Puts hairpiece back on quickly.)*

HANNA: Now, Baldy, don't get vague on me! The bald spot on the crown of your head! Right here — the one you cover up with this little bird-nest coiffure! *(Pulls it off again — SOPHIE screams.)* Bad circulation, that's what it is! One thing about me, I've always had good circulation — from here to L.A.!

SOPHIE: *(Grabs her hair from HANNA, throws it on top of her head, and goes on.)* Now here is Avon's answer to cracked fingernails — "Vampira Fingers!"

HANNA: My sister Sophie had a bald spot like that! I'm almost blind in one eye, you know!

SOPHIE: By merely applying this polish, which medicates — I beg your pardon?

HANNA: Don't look at me like that! I'm half-blind in one eye. My sister's bald spot . . .

SOPHIE: I see . . . It medicates while it is drying into a lovely protecting —

HANNA: Don't shut me off, sister! Not here! Nobody shuts me off in my own house! I used to go to the beach with her and the reflection from the sun that that little bald spot would pick up almost blinded me completely — my left! You got that strange body, too! Sophie had one — no one was quite positive which side was the front and which was back!

SOPHIE: Perfume is our specialty. For morning wear — "Oh, What A Beautiful Sunrise!" Isn't this lovely? *(Pushing it up HANNA's nose.)*

HANNA: And those feet! Just like hers — wider than they were long! Everyone swore she had ten toes per foot!

SOPHIE: *(Faster.)* Spray deodorant, spray talcum, brushes — perhaps you need a brush? You do! Here are several of our biggest sellers: The Guinevere for long tresses, The Pickford for curly hair, and The Joan of Arc if you happen to have a crewcut.

HANNA: She never stopped! What she lacked in hair she made up in words! What some people could say in a minute, Sophie could take two weeks! She was a . . .

SOPHIE: Manic neurotic? *(She continues her sales pitch under HANNA's speech.)*

HANNA: Yes! She could talk if you were listening or not! She never seemed to pay any attention to you! . . . She'd talk about the weather, the neighbors, the cost of meats . . .

SOPHIE: *(Simultaneously.)* Eye makeup has always been of great importance in glamorizing the American female! A lovely mascara for night wear — "Oh Those Tropical Nights" — or for daytime loveliness, "Oh Those Tropical Days."
(She and HANNA end simultaneously.)

HANNA: Sophie! You are my older sister Sophie from Jersey City!

SOPHIE: Withers! Constance Withers from Boston, Massachusetts, your friendly Avon representative.

HANNA: You are my sister Sophie.

SOPHIE: *(Nervously.)* I . . . I have a sister. She's either dead or somewhere in Chicago. She was small, unsure, afraid. You . . . you are Frances Jean Kessler, 309 West 46th Street, Apartment 3, Rear West.

HANNA: Fran*cis Gene* is the fag across the hall! I'm Hanna O'Brien, Apartment 3, Rear *East!*

SOPHIE: Well, then I'm afraid I've made an awful mistake. You are my sister.
(The two women size each other up silently. ARIZONA, as the boy, runs in and grabs HANNA with much enthusiasm.)

HANNA: Son . . .

ARIZONA: Mom, you won't believe!

HANNA: What are you doing home so early?

ARIZONA: I made it!

HANNA: Cutting classes again?

ARIZONA: They took me!

HANNA: Oh, son, meet your Aunt Sophie.

ARIZONA: I'm in the Army now, Mom.

SOPHIE: I'll say one thing for you, dear. You certainly have an attractive son.

SOPHIE and HANNA: Oh, memory is a strange force. How many unpleasant ones I've tried to throw away, discard, shut out — only for them to be caught somehow in my subconscious, to return and remind me of everything I chose to forget. Namely, my — *(Simultaneously with:)*

HANNA:	SOPHIE:
older sister, Sophie!	younger sister, Hanna!

(They both fall in adoration of ARIZONA as the boy, making the sign of the cross.)

ARIZONA: My parents always wanted me to go into the priesthood.

SOPHIE: *(Kneeling.) Gloria in Excelsis Deo. Et in terra pax hominibus bonae voluntatis.*

HANNA: *(Kneeling.)* Glory to God in the highest, and on earth, peace, to men of good will!

ARIZONA: So I started at the bottom — as an altar boy — back in the womb of my birth, Salome, Arizona.

SOPHIE: *Dominus Vobiscum. Et cum spiritu tuo.*

HANNA: The Lord be with you, and with thy spirit!

ARIZONA: Altar boy for eleven years, first grade to junior — but in my senior year — in my senior year — *I was blown!*

SOPHIE: *(Screaming.) Hosanna in Excelsis!*

HANNA: Shhh, keep this clean. There are four nuns on this excursion. *(To woman in audience.)* Hey, Sister, you dropped your beads!

ARIZONA: I was blown, my mind. I couldn't take the ritual any longer — the rehearsed ritual of the candles, the incense, the solemn choir, the petrified gods. So I left Salome, Arizona, in my senior year. I can still remember my father standing there asking, "Why, son, why?" *Why?* There is no answer to that question except, "Why not? Why should I stay in Arizona, Pa? I don't have asthma."

SOPHIE: *Sursum Corda!*

HANNA: Lift up your skirts!

SOPHIE: *"Sursum Corda"* means lift up your hearts!

HANNA: Listen, sister, you say your mass and I'll say mine!

ARIZONA: That asinine comment was the only answer I could give him and I left Salome and ran to where I am now, only to find the same rehearsed ritual —
(Both women hold tightly to his legs.)
— but now I cannot move!

SOPHIE: *Deus, tu converus vivicabis nos.*

HANNA: Thou wilt turn, O God, and bring us back to life.

ARIZONA: It's not that I'm young —
(The women, still kneeling, pull him in opposite directions.)
— it's just that I'm not old enough to know which way to go.

HANNA: Let's cut this mass short — my knees ache! So you met me, your real mother, at Coney Island, right?

SOPHIE: Real mother, really! Reality would kill you, dear.

HANNA: You better watch it, Sophie, or I'm going to hang your picture hat in the check room with the rest of your dreams.

ARIZONA: And I met this woman — I mean, my real mother — and came to live with her. She's putting me through college. Columbia. I'm a science major — numbers, theories.

HANNA: They know that, dear. That guy may be a schlemiel, but he's not retarded.

ARIZONA: But the truth is *(Confidentially.)* — I go to N.Y.U. I couldn't get into Columbia. But Mother finds a need to tell her friends that I go there. Not that there's anything low-class about N.Y.U. It costs the same, if not more. But, well — Mother's already gone and told everyone I go to the more prestige-sounding Columbia. So I have to tell everyone I go there, too. I mean, I can't make a liar out of my own mother, right?

SOPHIE: *(Still staring at HANNA.)* I'll say one thing for you, dear, you certainly have an attractive son.

HANNA: No, Sophie! Please, no. Not the boy!

ARIZONA: *(Trying to break tension.)* Life almost had a pattern to it for a while, my going to school and Mother's work, and then . . . our life sort of cracked open at the seams! Life lost its moment of security! Confusion — I got drafted! Oh, sure, Mother told me to go down there and tell them that I was . . . was . . . like that guy across the hall. But I couldn't! I'm a red-blooded all-American guy! Someone has to preserve freedom! Right? What if everyone did that? What if everyone got exempt that way? Right? — Oh, sure I tried, but they didn't believe me! Mom! It didn't work! They didn't believe me!!! They're going to take me, *Mom! It's not right!!* Right? *(Sees SOPHIE.)* Oh, I'm sorry. I didn't know we had company.

SOPHIE: Constance Withers from Boston, Mass, young man. Your friendly Avon representative. *(Nearing him.)*

HANNA: Your Aunt Sophie, dear — your mother's long lost . . . *older* sister.

ARIZONA: And on top of that, this lady moved into our pattern.
     (SOPHIE advances on ARIZONA and they freeze embracing, he reluctantly. Spot hits HANNA.)

HANNA: And then my son's accident —
     (ARIZONA as the boy screams in darkness.)
     and after the accident —
     (Gunshot in darkness.)
     — my son could no longer smile — he was ashamed to smile — he could no longer shame the sun!
     (Lights come up on ARIZONA as the boy, facing the audience, his mouth bleeding. SOPHIE seems guilty, being found with him, a bread knife in her hand.)

SOPHIE: It was in the Viet War! He was shot in the — wounded in the face! That's all! That is all there was to it!

HANNA: Wars have always been Sophie's out! It was her! Didn't you see? She did it. She always uses war for an excuse. My son came back from Viet Nam in perfect health. It was the night after he came back, while he was sleeping, she did that to him — to his smile. *(HANNA is again alone in spot.)* It was the only way she could get the one thing I had — his smile. She's always thought I stole it from her. "You lost yours, Sophie!" — And her husband?

He wasn't killed in the Second World War! He wanted a divorce to marry a German girl. Sophie refused it, but he still never returned. Oh, they found a bullet-filled body with his tag on it in a foxhole outside of Munich, but it wasn't him. Her husband put his tag on a dead man's body to escape her. And she knew! She would never believe his death — and she was right. She found him after the war, traced him all the way to Germany, to a small town only twenty miles from that foxhole he was supposed to have died in. Her husband, living without his identity with a German girl, preferred that to having one and living with Sophie! And she —

(HANNA laughs with the fear of God. Sound of a gunshot in the darkness. ARIZONA falls. As the lights come up:)

She killed him all over again . . .

SOPHIE: Stop!! I am being unjustly represented in this case! They want the truth! They've paid their dimes!

HANNA: And no one knew anything except his illegal German wife, and she couldn't tell too much. When she found her American lover's dead body on the floor of their small apartment, she ran into the center of the village and killed herself with a bread knife in front of a hundred German villagers whose eyes were too tired from the recent war to even notice. So, please, make her stop bothering my son! She has done enough. He no longer shames the sun —

SOPHIE: *Stop!! (Laughing it off.)* I told you, that man doesn't understand a word of English. *(She goes to same man, however.)* She's upset. She gets raving mad when she's jealous — and now that he's no longer perfect, she being an immature child who tires of a good thing too easily, he bores her. The only time she shows any interest in him is when I'm nice to him — but I cannot help it. He is the image of my first husband. Hanna has always sought that image. Something about their smiles. And now . . . after so many years, we're back where we started! So, as a last great gesture, I invited my sister and — my nephew to Egypt.

HANNA: Egypt! We haven't even been to Miami Beach yet!

SOPHIE: You see, I had won the Avon "Name That Perfume" contest for its employees. I named the winning entry for the exotic new perfume line — "La Très Hotte Femme."

HANNA: That's French . . . for "Bitch in Heat!"

SOPHIE: The prize was a Mediterranean cruise with two weeks in your favorite country. I've always been intrigued by this ancient masterpiece. The sand, the sun —

HANNA: Son-of-a-bitch! Who could imagine how much sand and sun could be in one place? Hell must be down the block!

SOPHIE: So I said to my sister, "To Egypt, sister! Come with me to Egypt!" It was the least I could do! Besides, I hate to travel alone, and I've always wanted to come.

HANNA: There are easier ways!

SOPHIE: And all things that Sophie plans, they come true. Why, here we are — Hurry, Hanna. Run. *(SOPHIE laughs, blending into the canned laughter of the carnival.)*

HANNA: It seems I have been running my whole life for other people's amusement. So I stopped. Stopped trying to please. Stopped expecting. Stopped wanting — wanting that small weapon so few get — security. *I just couldn't find it, Papa!!* Find it? How could I? I wouldn't recognize it if I bumped into it. *You never showed me what it looked like!* So I retired. I stopped running. It was much easier not wanting any more. And then — when you think life has stopped bothering you, it throws you that one last great punch in the stomach. It sticks its evil middle finger up your peace of mind — namely, my older sister Sophie — and I finally came to that day, that moment, when I knew — beyond a question of a doubt — "Hanna, baby, *finis.*"

SOPHIE: She just doesn't stop, does she? *Finis*, indeed! Why does she try to be so clever? Why doesn't she just admit what she is? A lying whore with a dumb son, with whom she is currently having an incestuous affair! Remember who you are, dear!

(SOPHIE takes her place in her deck chair as HANNA seeks the nonexistent air of the breeze-hole.)

We must never forget who we are.

HANNA: *(Now in her original position on floor above breeze-hole.)* My name is Hanna O'Brien and I am dying in a strange desert — and the sad thing about it is, there is no one I love around me.

SOPHIE: *(Laughing victoriously.)* There is something about Egypt in the summer!

HANNA: It's fuckin' hot, that's what it is. It's so fuckin' hot a person could die of suffocation!

SOPHIE: And now, as a great climax to a worthless life of physical insanity, my sister has found a new toy. Her life has been a collection of toys — some live, some bronze, some made out of sea shells. And now she has found a new one in Greece. *(Taking statue of "David" out of her Avon kit.)* We were in Greece before we came here.

HANNA: Please, Sophie, it's too hot here! I'm dying!

SOPHIE: It's your age, dear, not the heat. It's a statue, not an unusual one by any means. You could buy it in any souvenir shop catering to the perverted tourist. It's of a boy, of course. It's a very common boy — muscular, tall, well — I presume, in scale, if he were alive, he would be tall — proportionately, that is —

HANNA: *(Fanning.)* She's clarifying! She's patronizing! Don't you just hate her for that!

SOPHIE: — and the sad thing is, Hanna has forgotten that it is a stone reproduction. She has taken to having long afternoon chats with her new-found toy. Now, I have been able to accept all the disturbed qualities of my sister — her basic cheapness, her insensitivity, her God-given stupidity, her selfishness, her constant vulgarity — but I cannot accept a sister of mine talking to a goddamned plaster-of-Paris stud!!!
(HANNA grabs statue from her.)
Give it to me, Hanna!

HANNA: It's mine, Sophie! Mine!

SOPHIE: Give it to me, dear! It's not good for you.
(Lights fade on SOPHIE as they tug at statue.)

HANNA: I can't fight any more. It's too hot to fight. Please, Sophie! Mine!

SOPHIE: *(From darkness.)* I love you. Give it to me.
(SOPHIE wins and statue disappears into the darkness with her. Spot hits HANNA. She turns to it, lost for words. She has been fighting for her life, and has now lost what was left of it.)

HANNA: I'm always losing things. Most things I don't mind losing. They're just excessive memories that clutter up your life. But some things are irreplaceable. Some things you can't go on without. I — I just lost this little statue I picked up in Greece. It was very reasonable — only six drachmas. That's only $1.98 in the States. But this is a particular statue. *It is irreplaceable!*

SOPHIE: *(In darkness, or light, if area permits nudity.)* You look pale, dear. You should lie down and take advantage of the sun. I think it's about time I lay down and took advantage of yours.
(ARIZONA is seen mounting her.)

HANNA: I love toys, always have — but I always break them, ruin them. How I hate broken toys! So I'm always having to buy new ones. But I could never replace that statue because I'll never get to Greece again and they don't sell this particular kind in the States. It is irreplaceable! So, would you make my sister give it back to me! Please make her stop taking my things!
(ARIZONA and SOPHIE are clearly seen now, he on top of her without his bathing suit.)
Stop taking my things, Sophie! Stop! Sophie, please! Stop!!!

SOPHIE: No, Hanna, please not yet!
(Lights fade on the two.)

HANNA: *(In spot alone.)* Make her stop! Please stop it, Sophie! *STOP!!!*
(Lights come up on SOPHIE, motionless on floor, ARIZONA gone. Her skirt is ripped off and her slip is covered with blood.)

HANNA: My sister died in Egypt. Her death was a great mystery, but then few of her old customers will remember or really care. I wasn't there at the time.

I'd returned four days before with my son. I mean, I have to work for a living, and two weeks is all they'd give me. She was found on the desert near Cairo with a statue I'd bought for her for only $1.98 in Greece. It was found jabbed between her — oh, that's not important. Nothing is — now. She was just dead — that's all there was to it. *Finis.* And Hanna? Nobody — nobody now. *(Desperately trying, but failing to restrain tears.)* Not that we were that close or anything. We never even wrote. But I always liked saying, "We — my sister Sophie and I. She's older!" I always liked saying that. "We — my sister Sophie and I. She's — older!" I guess I won't be able to say that anymore. "We — my sister Sophie and I. She's — dead!" *(One last plea.)* Take the boy, Sophie! Don't leave me by myself! You don't have to die. Take him, it's a present! I owe you that. Take him, just don't leave me here by myself! I can't find my way out alone. Take him! I'll give him to you. Just don't die, Sophie! Please! Don't destroy the *"We."*

(The carousel music returns.)

BARKER: Step right up, step right in, folks! Admission only ten cents!

HANNA: Oh, damn! Those cheap bastards and their grubby dimes! Okay, Arizona, get in position and make it look good! Don't give them the satisfaction of seeing this — not for what they're paying! *(To SOPHIE on floor.)* Okay, bald bitch, get up! *Get up!!* Rest period is over. *Over!!*

(SOPHIE rises in confused daze.)

Get off your tired ass! If you're going to stick around here you gotta work for your supper! *Stand up!* They can't see you layin' down. They want it clear, sister — right in their eyes!

(SOPHIE stands near her own poster, statue of "David" in hand.)

BARKER: See "Why Hanna's Skirt Won't Stay Down!" See "Smiley, The Smiling Narcissistic Wonder Trapped in the Mirror-maze!" And our latest attraction — the bleeding wax replica of Constance Withers, a Friendly Avon Representative from Boston, Mass — raped by a statue!!

HANNA: Now remember, Baldy, when that gate out there opens and they pay their grubby fee, they want what they were told they'd see! They want Hanna's skirt up at all times, they want him to smile nakedly, and they want you to bleed, sister! They don't give a damn about your stupid war stories, your cheap excuses, your worthless president's sympathy letters! No sympathy here. *Bleed, sister!*

ARIZONA: *(Beginning to freeze in mirror-maze.)* You might as well do what Hanna says. You're here for good now.

SOPHIE: But I'm not part of this place! I've got to travel — that's part of my profession!

(All begin freezing in position.)

ARIZONA: Be a good kid — and — you'll go far! Like — me. I — just got — an — offer from the big time — the fun house over in — London. Hanna says you — get — as much as fif-fifty cents over there — and all you have to do is your — ja-job. It's sim simple. I smile — Ha-Hanna — screams and you — b-l-e-e-d.

HANNA: (Freezing over breeze-hole.) Ahhhhh! You tell — her — Smiley. Ahhhhh!

SOPHIE: (One last attempt to escape.) But I'm not part of this place! I come, I go.

(SOPHIE begins to freeze as HANNA and ARIZONA smile at her through their own terror. Lights begin to flicker anxiously, awaiting the arrival of newcomers to the magical trap.)

HANNA: Now — when — that — gate — out — there — opens, you — mustn't say — say — a word. Ahhhhhhhhh!

SOPHIE: I'm not ——— par ——— part ——— of —— this —— pla ——— place! I ——— come. I ——— go. I ——— come ——— I ———

(She freezes into standing death.)

CURTAIN

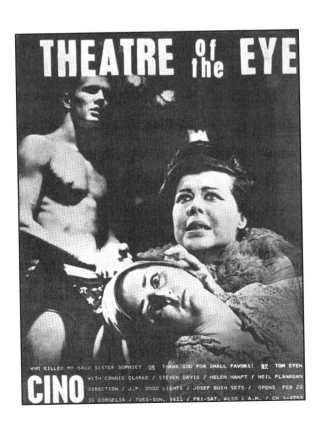

Tom Eyen's Theatre of the Eye performed at any off- or off-off-Broadway venue available, but many of Eyen's plays, including *Who Killed My Bald Sister Sophie?*, premièred at the Cino

Stephen Davis (Van Vost), Helen Hanft and Connie Clark in a poster advertising *Sophie*'s opening in February of 1968

SEX IS BETWEEN TWO PEOPLE
Lanford Wilson

Sex Is Between Two People opened at the Caffe Cino in New York on December 30, 1965, on a double bill with Mr. Wilson's *Days Ahead*.

CHARACTERS:

ROGER and MARVIN: Two boys in their early twenties, very ordinary and very much alike in appearance.

SCENE: *Center stage is erected the three white, low walls of a room at a public steam bath. There is a bed upstage against back and both side walls. A light hangs center stage. A bedtable sits beside the head of the bed, it has on it an ashtray. Roger's clothes are on a hook on the opposite wall. The light is on, the room empty.*

ROGER: *(Just outside the door.)* This is my room here.

MARVIN: You're on the corner?

ROGER: What?

(Enters right behind MARVIN. They are both in the typical steam room robes. Each has a room and locker keys on a rubber band around one wrist. MARVIN is carrying a pack of cigarettes and matches.)

MARVIN: Is someone here?

ROGER: Huh?

MARVIN: The light's on.

ROGER: No, I left it on, I guess.

MARVIN: You're on the corner.

ROGER: Yeah.

(Not looking at each other. ROGER stretches, his arm behind him, to touch MARVIN. MARVIN sits, missing the touch, and looks around under the table.)

MARVIN: It's not a bad room.

ROGER: Yeah, it's not a bad room, really. It's an alright bed. *(MARVIN is standing at the foot of the bed rather uncomfortable.)*

MARVIN: Yeah.

ROGER: I mean it's nothing special.

MARVIN: Well, no.

ROGER: But it's alright.

MARVIN: Better than you'd expect.

ROGER: Yeah. Sit down.

MARVIN: Well, sure. *(He sits, facing the audience at the foot of the bed.)*

ROGER: What'd you say about the light?

MARVIN: What?

ROGER: You said something about the light.

MARVIN: No, nothing. I just said it's on. I guess I hadn't expected it to be on.

ROGER: Would you like me to turn it off?

MARVIN: Oh, no, I don't mind. I didn't mean anything. I like it on.

ROGER: You're sure, cause it could go off.

MARVIN: On's fine.

ROGER: That's fine by me then.

MARVIN: I mean, either way.

ROGER: It doesn't matter to me either, either way.

MARVIN: Unless you want it off.

ROGER: No, on's fine.

MARVIN: It was just that for a moment with the light on I thought there was someone else in the room — that's stupid, because it doesn't mean anything. I mean like when you leave a room you usually turn the light off and when you come in you turn it on again, so with it on, I thought for a minute maybe someone had come in, you know. Before us.

ROGER: *(ROGER, who hasn't quite listened, but has laughed a little anyway, is thinking of something else.)* You mind if I have a cigarette? *(This said immediately on top of the other speech.)*

MARVIN: *(Who is carrying a package of cigarettes and matches.)* You want one of mine?

ROGER: I have one here.

MARVIN: I'm carrying mine around with me.

(They both take a cigarette from their own packs, rather hurry to light a match. Both light matches at the same time. They had each had in mind to light the other's cigarette, but they don't show it. Both blow matches out at

the same time. This they laugh at. ROGER, who is near the ashtray, puts his match into it, but neglects to allow MARVIN to.)

MARVIN: What'd you say your name is? *(His hand with the match drops down.)*

ROGER: Roger.

MARVIN: Oh, yeah, I remember — I never remember a name, it's absolutely my worst fault. At least, I hope it is. I mean, I'm always running into people who come up to me in the street with a big smile and say "Marvin!" and I just look at them like I don't know them from Adam. *(He flicks his match back under the bed with a deft movement.)* I mean I remember their faces, but I kinda slur over their names, you know, but I mean, I . . . remember.

ROGER: *(Joining.)* Remember their faces . . .

MARVIN: Right.

ROGER: *(Awkwardly.)* But . . . you forget their . . .

MARVIN: Names. Right.

ROGER: It's impolite, really, I guess, or just plain egotistical. I have the same thing. That's funny. I don't think — no, you didn't tell me your name at all, did you? No, you didn't, I don't think.

MARVIN: *(Slightest pause.)* Marvin.

ROGER: Oh, yeah, yeah, you did tell me, too, didn't you.

MARVIN: Yeah, I thought I . . .

ROGER: I remember. I'm as bad as you are. You'd think they'd have memory courses or something, like to remember names or something.

MARVIN: Yeah, they probably do.

ROGER: Yeah, they probably do. I mean you'd think a fellow'd have sense to go to one.

MARVIN: Yeah. If he knows he has that problem. You'd think. *(He starts across for the ashtray, it could bring him very close to ROGER. He thinks better of it and gets up.)*

ROGER: Here . . .

MARVIN: *(Flicking his ashes in the ashtray.)* No thanks, got it; that's OK. *(He sits again exactly where he was.)*

ROGER: *(Sets the ashtray between them.)* Here you go.

MARVIN: Fine. That's swell.

ROGER: Do — uh, have you been here before?

MARVIN: You haven't seen me here, have you?

ROGER: No, but that doesn't necessarily prove anything.

MARVIN: Do you come here a lot?

ROGER: Uh, no; actually I don't. I don't really know the procedures, actually. I mean this is my first time here.

MARVIN: I haven't been here before either. I thought you probably hadn't.

ROGER: How come?

MARVIN: You just don't look like the type, you know, to uh, come here, you don't, look like, you know, the type that comes here. Or that you'd think comes here.

ROGER: See that's what I thought about you; you come here by yourself?

MARVIN: Yeah.

ROGER: Me too.

MARVIN: Really?

ROGER: Oh, yeah. You been down in the steam room yet?

MARVIN: Uh, no. Not yet.

ROGER: Me either.

MARVIN: Yeah.

ROGER: I'll probably run down there after a bit, see what it's like.

MARVIN: Yeah.

ROGER: It's weird.

MARVIN: You're telling me. You see that guy with the toupee?

ROGER: The thin one? With the black toupee? Yeah.

MARVIN: God. I mean, what a phony toupee.

ROGER: You see the guy with the — in his room — the tattoo?

MARVIN: That writing? Was that a tattoo?

ROGER: Sure.

MARVIN: I thought it was, but I couldn't tell for sure.

ROGER: Couldn't *tell?* It must have been six inch high letters.

MARVIN: Well, I wear glasses usually.

ROGER: Oh, it's very clear, though —

MARVIN: I could read it alright, I just thought it was ink. Like maybe someone had written it on him when he was asleep and he didn't know it was there.

ROGER: Sure he knew it was there.

MARVIN: It's a stupid place for a tattoo. I thought it might be a tattoo; either that or someone had written it there as a joke; but I couldn't tell. I'm not that vain, really. I wouldn't want you to think that.

ROGER: About what?

MARVIN: About glasses. Well, of course, you wouldn't think that, because if I were, I wouldn't have mentioned that I wear them so I couldn't be. I left them in my room because I thought I might be, you know, if I was going down to the steam room . . .

ROGER: Sure.

MARVIN: Actually I don't carry them with me much; I only need them for movies and things. That's where I'd been, to a movie.

ROGER: Oh. What'd you see?

MARVIN: Oh, it was awful. Some costume thing, with Sophia Loren.

ROGER: Don't you like her?

MARVIN: Oh, yes, I love her, she's marvelous.

ROGER: I think so too.

MARVIN: That's the only reason I went, she's lovely.

ROGER: She's one of my favorites.

MARVIN: She was lousy in this one though.

ROGER: Which one?

MARVIN: I can't remember. I walked out. They were dragging some big Spanish cannon all over the countryside.

ROGER: I don't know it, I guess. And you just came here after the movies?

MARVIN: Yeah.

ROGER: I wonder about that guy with the tattoo, he must just *live* here.

MARVIN: What've you done, you just been wandering around?

ROGER: Yeah. Kinda. I got dressed and just walked around. I've not been here long actually.

MARVIN: Me, either. Well, about an hour.

ROGER: An hour?

MARVIN: Well, it took a little nerve to go outside.

ROGER: Oh. I guess. I probably been here that long, I guess.

MARVIN: Especially, for me, I mean my room is right next to this room where about fifteen people were — you know — did you go by there? There's this wild orgy. Did you see that one?

ROGER: Oh, yeah.

MARVIN: Well the room right next to that one is mine.

ROGER: On the right or the left?

MARVIN: Let's see. On . . . the right.

ROGER: Oh, yeah. Next to the corner.

MARVIN: Is it? Yeah, that's it.

ROGER: I don't know, I guess it'd be easy enough to just fling off your robe and jump in there with them, I mean with that many people it doesn't matter what they look like, you wouldn't know who had a hold of you anyway. But, I don't know. I've heard about orgies.

MARVIN: Yeah, but I hadn't actually seen one before. Not a real one. I didn't believe my eyes.

ROGER: That's what I mean. I suppose it's alright.

MARVIN: If you like that sort of thing, but it's just not for me.

ROGER: Me either. I just don't think I'm that promiscuous or something.

MARVIN: No, I'm not either; that wouldn't be any good for me.

ROGER: I know, I mean, sex is between two people; for me anyway.

MARVIN: Right. It's alright if you like that sort of gang bang.

ROGER: Right. I've got nothing really against it. Did you come from a party?

MARVIN: Huh? Oh, no, I just decided to come in.

ROGER: I was at a party. Got pretty high. I mean I had to — it was the God-awfullest party anyone had ever seen. People just sitting around talking. Endlessly.

MARVIN: Yeah. God I hate those.

ROGER: Me too. I kept thinking if someone would just start dancing or something. You know — *instigate* something.

MARVIN: Yeah.

ROGER: But they wouldn't, of course. If someone would just *initiate* something.

MARVIN: Yeah. I hate parties like that.

ROGER: Me too. So I thought at least I've heard the baths are wild.

MARVIN: Well, it is, god knows — they weren't lying. They're wild as hell, at least in that room next to mine.

ROGER: Well everywhere. Did you see the guy with the two wristwatches?

MARVIN: I don't think so.

ROGER: I don't know how you could miss him. A real mess, tall guy.

MARVIN: I didn't notice.

ROGER: You know what — I think I got pretty drunk — at the party. Do you think steam would be good or bad?

MARVIN: For what?

ROGER: I mean I've heard it'd kill a hangover.

MARVIN: You got a hangover?

ROGER: No, I mean prevent a hangover.

MARVIN: It might.

ROGER: It probably wouldn't hurt.

MARVIN: I don't see how it could. It's good for a cold. I know that.

ROGER: Why don't we go down to the steam room — how's that?

MARVIN: *(Too big.)* Say! That's fine.

ROGER: Swell.

MARVIN: I tell you what, why don't I meet you down there?

ROGER: OK, fine.

MARVIN: I have to go by my room — I left my shorts on, I can't wear them . . .

ROGER: Oh. OK.

MARVIN: Fine then, I'll meet you inside or by the pool?

ROGER: Make it by the pool and we can go in together. And we can talk, you know, we can come back here, and talk.

MARVIN: Good, I'd like that. I'll see you later then.
    (MARVIN exits. They are both up, but somehow managed not to touch. ROGER thinks a moment. Looks nervous and almost panic-stricken, then very quickly he dresses, throwing his coat over his shoulder, getting his keys from the table. He opens the door.)

ROGER: Oh, hi, Marvin. There I remembered.

MARVIN: *(Off.)* Yeah. And you're Roger. We're not as bad as we thought, see?

ROGER: *(Still in the doorway.)* How come you're dressed?

MARVIN: Oh, I had to go down and ask the desk something and I thought I'd catch cold.

ROGER: Oh, well I'll see you.

MARVIN: You going out?

ROGER: Oh, yeah — I'll probably be right back — I guess I drank too much at the party. I thought I'd go out for some fresh air. I'll be right back.

MARVIN: Fine. I'll see you then.

ROGER: Right. *(He steps back into the room and closes the door. He jumps up on the bed and looks over the wall into the hall. Then around the corner upstage.)* What's he doing, damn him? Following me around, anyway?
    (He goes to the other wall and looks over, quickly ducks his head away so he won't be seen and quickly sits down quietly. He undresses just a little

hesitantly and puts on the robe. He starts to go out, hesitates, gets the keys off the table, looks nervously about, checks the room, opens the door, looks out, both ways, looks back in, then comes in and gets the cigarettes off the table. He goes to the door and leaves, closing the door very softly behind him. In a split-second he re-enters, casually but determinately walks to the light and turns it off. The room is lit with the dimmest possible red light. He turns and leaves, shutting the door quietly. We see only the very dim room, lit as if by an exit sign somewhere. A long pause.)

CURTAIN

Paul Boesing as Rover

Judith L'Heureux, as Ruby, floats
resplendently past Rover

Edward Ladner, Scott Micancin, Keith Carsey and David Spielberg
as the vandals Eeny, Meeny, Meiny and Mo

*Photos by Conrad Ward from the 1965 Caffe Cino production,
provided through the courtesy of Robert Patrick*

HURRAH FOR THE BRIDGE (QUE VIVA EL PUENTE)
Paul Foster

Hurrah For The Bridge was first produced on September 15, 1963 at the Caffe Cino, directed by Sydney Schubert Walter and with the following cast:

ROVER	Paul Boesing
RUBY	Judith L'Heureux
EENY	Edward Ladner
MEENY	Scott Micancin
MEINY	Keith Carsey
MO	David Spielberg

CHARACTERS:

ROVER: An old man, about sixty, strong and firm in all his movements. He wears an old coat and pants.

EENY, MEENY, MEINY, MO: All in their early twenties. All dressed in blue jeans and leather jackets

RUBY: A tall, gaunt woman, about forty.

(The set: A junk cart. It is piled enormously, precariously high with rags; rich colors, black, purple silks, gold tassels, velvet remnants. To the back is a long pole with a pulley and a cord attached to it. The cord disappears into the hollowed-out rag pile. The rest of the stage is bare.

Twilight.

In the dark it begins. The sound of a pile driver, wheezing, steamy, rheumatic and sluggish. Now twilight.

Shouts, cries, exuberant whistles. Suddenly MEENY runs on, terrified. He runs to one side, to the other, back again, unable to find a direction to flee. Shouts:)

MEENY: Git! Git! Git that mother!

Where?!

Hey! Hey! Over there!

(Refuse cans overturn, bang, rattle, thrown down. Running feet.)
Son of a bitch.

There! There!

There he goes!

(Yells. EENY, MEINY and MO run on panting, then stop dead. MEENY braces himself, waiting tensely. They circle slowly, confidently about him. EENY and MEINY point umbrella sticks to force him into the center as he darts and retreats, seeking an escape. Giggles of anticipation. Tense pause.)

EENY: Squirm . . . baby.

(Giggles. MEENY rushes. Sticks stop him repeatedly.)
Ah, ah! Move it . . . move it easy . . . that's it . . . bump a little. *Ah, ah!* Grind it . . . slow and easy.

MO: She's got the jitters.

(Giggles.)

MEINY: Shut up!

(Pause. Now softly.)
You wasn't invited.

EENY: Dance . . . come on . . . that's it, baby . . . strut your stuff.

(MEENY rushes to break out again. EENY jumps loudly in front of him. He retreats, terrified. Giggles.)
There you go . . . bump a little . . . you see . . . it's not so hard. Now . . . tease it . . . tease a little. Toss out a keepsake.

MEINY: *Shoes!*

EENY: Listen, honey. The man is talking. He said . . . shooooooes.

(EENY advances with his stick. MEENY kicks off his shoe. EENY picks it up with the point of his stick, giggling, and hands the prize to MO.)
The other one . . . got to have a pair.

(MEENY rushes. MO stretches out his arms and throws him back. He falls and quickly jumps into a kneeling position, ready to defend himself.)
Try that again, and you won't make it. Oh nooo. You know . . . lay out your wares. Inspection time.

MEINY: *Shirt!*

MO: You hear!?

EENY: That's a girl . . . slip it . . . eeeeeasy . . . slow and easy.

(MEENY unbuttons slowly, still kneeling.)
Put some style into it, honey. Come on . . . you ain't trying . . . Ah! Ah! Ah! Don't stop . . . few more buttons and . . . upsidaisy!

(Noise of the machinery a bit louder. Pause. They listen.)

MO: Hear that? Third shift, just beginning.

MEINY: They're not waiting for you. Mixing trucks lined up, churning up the cream. They're ready to pour.

MO: Shut-up-I-said.

EENY: Hurry it up, sugar. Slip it off.

> *(MEENY rips off his shirt and throws it. He dashes. MEINY throws him down and stands over him.)*

MEINY: *Pants!*

MO: Come on! Git the hell out of them! Third shift is ready for you.

EENY: Strip 'em . . . tease 'em off . . . skin 'em down. Got to do it sometime. We're going to show you the water and the moonlight.

MEINY: Everybody's going. Everybody that's anybody.

> *(Giggles. Suddenly, MEENY bolts from under him. He is thrown down, struggling. The umbrella handles are hooked under his arms and he is dragged off screaming. Machinery wheezes very loud.)*

MO: The trucks are unloading! *The third shift is starting to pour! Here we come!*

EENY: *Smile, baby! It's got to last you a thousand years!*

> *(They exit. Lights and noises fade. Long pause. Lights up. The creaking of a cart nears. ROVER enters. He laboriously pushes a junk cart. He pushes as though numbed by the continuous hard effort. The bell rings once, smartly. He stops and sits on the handles of the cart, exhausted.)*

ROVER: Aye. I hear ye, Ruby. We air almost there. Thank God it rang . . . at last. Wheels, air wobblin'. Wearin' out, they air. Me too, fer all thet. Wobblin' an' wearin' out.

> *(He pulls off his ragged gloves and flexes his fingers.)*

Lookit them. They air goin' too. Bent, twisted. Roots they air.

> *(Smacks his fist gently into his palm.)*

Hands. Used to be good an' strong. Hard! Used to be tight an' strong an' . . . Oh, stop now afore ye git started all over agin.

> *(Impatiently, he tries to pull on the gloves again.)*

Joints. Swollen together so's the glove won't fit over the joints. Gloves. Hard, crusted. But it's me glove what holds me joints together, so pull 'em on. Git 'em on!

> *(They go on at last. Then with renewed gusto.)*

There she goes! I'll keep at it, Ruby me love. Ye know I will, don't ye? Let these here hands fall off, an' I'll push ye with me raw nubs. Aye, let the nubs fall off, an' by God, I'll push ye with me shoulders.

> *(Pause. Suddenly wearier than ever.)*

Sure . . . sure, I'll push ye over every street an' stone by me raw nubs, an' if they wear out . . . if they wear out? Why, I'll tie a cord on me neck, an' by God, I'll pull ye! I will thet, Ruby. Pull ye by me neck.

(Pause.)

By . . . me neck? I will! I've pushed ye, hain't I? Well, I kin pull ye in this cart too.

(Pause. Softly, almost a whisper.)

Cart, ye say? If't it breaks, ye say? Why . . . I'll tie it back agin. Tie it with wire!

(Pause. A whisper, fearful of the possibility.)

No wire? Always wire about . . . no?

(Angry determination.)

I'll nail it up! Pound it back agin!

(He jumps up and shakes his fist at the cart.)

I'll bolt it! *Pound the bolts! Bolted bolts!*

(Pause.)

Aye . . . she'll hold then.

(Pause.)

If't breaks? I'll put ye on me shoulders an' carry ye.

(Pause. Compellingly insistent.)

But . . . fall down with the load? Aye, thet's possible. Me shoulders air old, thet they air. No use denyin' thet. They air old an' bent down, broken down, sprung, loose. They air rottin'.

(Pause. Quietly.)

Fall down? Then I'll set ye down, Ruby. I'll set ye down gently on the road an' set a watch over ye till I find some way to git us to the river. Because that is where we air aimin' to go, an' thet is were we shall go. Hain't thet so, Ruby?

(He cannot stop his thoughts. In spite of his efforts, he blurts it out.)

I told 'em to be ready an' waitin', waitin' at the ready for ye when ye come on by. An' I promised 'em then. I promised 'em because ye told me to promise, an' so *I did*, by God! *I did!*

(He shouts to the cart.)

I will git ye there! Hain't no power on earth kin stop me from't!

(He circles about, uncertain. Now quietly.)

Nor earth . . . nor heaven. Aye. An' when the Inspection Party comes on . . . why . . . I'll parade ye by as pretty as ye please to be paradin', an' not a man kin say I didn't do me best by ye. I do me best by ye, don't I? Sure I do. Ye'll tell them thet, won't ye? They'll see. They'll know. They'll see I do what I promised I'd do.

(Pause. He strikes a rigid, pathetically comic military stance.)

An' they'll clap me on the back, they will when we git there. An' they'll say, *"Good old Rover! Ye did what ye said ye'd do."* An', an' I'll be standin' at attention, ye see, like this, straight as an arrow, an', an' I'll answer up smart an' proud, "Yes sir, right on time!" An' the Inspection Party'll walk up an' down afore me, jest lookin' me up an' down, jest to make sure it's me. Oh, they got to be sure. They don't make mistakes. Never, about nothin'. Well, they'll look me up an' down, an' I'll say, "Yes sir, right on time. Not a minute too soon, an' not a minute late. On time, sir. Jest like I promised, sir." An' they'll be as pleased as puddin' with thet. They know how to 'preciate a job done to satisfaction, they do.

(Pause. He relaxes.)

An' . . . well, we'll git on fine. Oh . . . they might ask how was the trip. They jest might! Or . . . or anythin', ye never know what an Inspection Party is apt to come out with, but ye got to be ready with the answers. Answer up! Good an' clear. Thet's how they like answers. Oh, well . . . we'll git it on right.

(Pause. His mood changes.)

An' then . . . *They* will come out to *ye*. As usual. An' *they* will fawn an' paw over *ye*. Jest like I wasn't there. Jest like afore! Jest like I left 'em standin' there all hunched up, all bunched up, all ganged up together on the brick pile wavin' goodbye to *ye! Ye! Ye! All the everlastin' time! Ye an' more of ye till their bellies was full of it!*

(Pause.)

Never forgit it neither. They never cared what happened to old Rover, but it was old Rover who lifted ye off the bench where ye bedded down. Lifted ye, as tender as ye pleased to be. And it was a long time *afore* they came.

(His voice trails away as he gathers his memories. This progression should build slowly and solidly so that the collapse at the end is crushing.)

Aye, they came . . . an' they came . . . an' came, an' kept on comin'. No end of 'em. Treaded on the grass an' ganged against the iron fences an' the numbers of 'em mauled it so hard it buckled an' went down. It fell on the rest of 'em, an' ye never heard a sound . . . not a word.

(Pause.)

'Cept fer the squoshin' of 'em it fell on, ye'd never know it went down. But it went down, an' so did the trees by the weight of 'em, an' so did the water they drank up, an' the ones what got stuck underfoot in the tramplin', treaded under the ground by the weight of 'em.

(Pause.)

A great disaster.

(Pause. Very tenderly.)

Ye remember, me sweet, dear Ruby . . . lifted ye an' . . .

(He begins again. He is stuck, unable to break out of this one track.)

. . . they went down, the lot of 'em . . . down on the ground. Eyes down an' head down too . . . an' I promised . . . by the lovin' . . . Holy God, I will take ye to the bridge over the river.

(He sighs heavily, lifting the weight of his memories. He tries to start afresh.)

Thet was . . . when was thet? Before all the hammerin' an' poundin'? After the stanchions went up anyway, wasn't it? Maybe it was, maybe it wasn't. Keeps comin' down . . . an' they put 'er right up agin, so it's tough to figger it all from thet. *Ah!* Who'd tell me anyway? Who'd tell old Rover? Who tells an old dog? Dogs air good to bark an' snarl an' show their teeth. Thet's when they air good for somethin'.

(Pause. He sits wearily on the cart handles.)

But what good's an old dog who's lost his teeth? Lost his eyes almost, who's bent down an' his legs air wobblin'? An' when they air done with him . . . the old dog disappears, an' soon not even the children kin remember his name or if he had a spot on one eye. They cain't even remember if he cocked his leg by a tree or squatted down.

(Pause.)

They scratched me on the ear, but jest the same old dogs jest don't git answered. Oh, no complaint. Not me. But they never answered me jest the same.

(The bell rings smartly. He sighs heavily and picks up the handles and begins to push.)

Ah, well. Time to git on. Giddap, Rover. Pick up. Move it on.

(At once, the bell rings again. He stops.)

Stop it, Rover. Set it down.

(He sits again. Bell rings as soon as he does. Picks up and begins to push again.)

Giddap, Rover. Pick it up. Move it on.

(Bell rings at once, harder than before.)

Stop it. Set it down.

(Sets it down. Starts to sit and bell rings immediately, harder than before. He is slowing down with the effort. He picks up now with great effort.)

Giddap. Pick it up . . . git 'er up.

(Bell rings furiously hard. He barely has time to set it down, when it rings again. He tries very hard to lift it, but this time he cannot. He strains, then buckles under the weight. He tries again. Bell rings insistently and long. Tries to lift again, but cannot.)

I hear ye! I hear ye!

(Tenderly.)

Any minute now, me rose. We'll be gittin' along.

(The bell barely lets him finish, when it rings again.)

I hear ye! I'm tryin' . . . I'm tryin' . . . lift up . . . *Lift up!*

(With a great effort, he finally lifts it.)

She's comin' along! I did it, Ruby!

(He tries with great effort to push. It moves a tiny bit.)

Push it, push, move it . . . on . . . it's goin' now . . . push . . . harder . . .

(Bell rings. He is confused, desperate to understand.)

I . . . I jest got it goin'. She's movin' . . . feel it movin'?

(Bell rings insistently. He holds on. He does not set it down.)

I cain't stop now! Not when she's movin' agin'!

(Waiting.)

Ye hear! Please . . . please?

(Bell rings angrily by way of reply. He drops it suddenly and rushes to the rag heap, pleading.)

I am tryin'! Put me best into it! The nubs air bleedin', honey . . . they air bent. Don't ye understand? They-air-bucklin'-down. Ye hear me? *I am tryin'!*

(Pause. Waiting.)

Ruby . . . ye listenin' in there?

(Pause. Suddenly, he paws the rag heap angrily, desperate to address her face to face.)

Ye air not listenin' to me! Ye air not payin' attention! *Listen to me!* They're bleedin' an' swellin' an' they *won't hold up!*

(EENY, MEINY and MO run on quietly. They stand panting. They discover ROVER and stare ominously as he shouts. ROVER pauses, hears their heavy breathing behind him. He turns slowly, surprised to see them. He smiles. It fades under their stare. He is uncertain whether to come forward or not. Pause as they stare, waiting. Finally, ROVER moves forward a bit, cautiously. EENY jump-shouts loudly; ROVER runs back to the cart awkwardly. They laugh, not loud, more a snicker of menace. Long strained pause as they survey each other to see who acts next. Slowly, confidently they close in on him.)

EENY: Eeny . . .

MEINY: Meeny . . .

EENY: Meiny . . .

(They wait for MO, who alone remains in the same place, more sullen than the others.)

Mo, baby?

MEINY: Catch this mother by the toe.

EENY: If he hollers, let him go.

(Softly.)

MO: Your ass I will.

(Snickers.)

MEINY: He ain't got one.

EENY: Shut your face!

(MEINY reacts angrily. He starts to attack EENY then stops dead as EENY quickly braces for defense. MO stands back, ready to accept either one as victim, whoever is the loser. Pause. MO smiles at MEINY.)

MO: So . . . what are you waiting for? Afraid?

(Pause. He laughs. MEINY loses his courage.)

Third shift is ready for the next one. Go on . . . they'll take anyone. They ain't particular. *Papa* wouldn't mind a substitute . . . for the time being. Would you, *Papa?*

ROVER: Git! The lot of ye! Git on! Git on!

(The tenseness is broken. They all focus on ROVER, who cautiously backs off to the cart. MO's tone drips sarcasm.)

MO: *Papa* . . . is getting all hot and bothered . . . ain't you, *Papa?*

ROVER: Wha . . . now . . . ye best git on . . .

(They advance on him as he continues to retreat cautiously, all except MEINY, who does not take part.)

MO: You don't like the kiddies to enjoy themselves? Just nice clean fun, *Papa.*

ROVER: Wha . . . ye got no cause to . . . to . . .

(ROVER detaches one of the handles and stands ready to defend himself. They stop, then giggle delightedly at his helplessness. Now calmly:)

MO: Would you look at him? Now, would you?

(Giggle in their anticipation.)

EENY: You're in trouble now, baby. You don't want to play with that . . . *Papa.* You might fall and hurt yourself, give . . . you can do it . . . just reach out your hand . . . oh, come on, *Papa.*

ROVER: I . . . I'm tellin' ye . . . fer the last time . . . the lot of ye . . .

MO: You're going to hurt yourself with that big thing.

(ROVER stiffens.)

ROVER: I'm warnin' ye . . . git on!

EENY: *(Coaxing soothingly, maliciously.)* Give . . . be nice . . . see . . . he's getting ready . . . there he goes . . .

(ROVER begins to weaken as though against his will. They snicker.)

That's it . . . reach out . . . his arm is bending . . .

(ROVER stiffens again, then almost without effort he extends his arm a bit.)

There he goes . . . come on, *Papa* . . . just a little more . . . *Papa* . . . *Give!*

(At once they shout and jump at him and wrestle away the pole.)

ROVER: *Ruby! Ruby! Ruby!*

MO: *Toss him in the river!*

(They lift him by the hands and feet and swing him back and forth, bouncing him in the air. He shouts, terrified.)

ROVER: *Ruby!*

EENY: *Heave him down the bank!*

(They release him, pull his coat over his head so that he cannot see nor maneuver and drag him in a circle by his feet.)

ROVER: *Ruby! Ruby!*

EENY: *Drop him in the cream! They'll bury him in it!*

(To MEINY, who has remained on one side, sullen.)

If you have no objections. Do you have any objections . . . sweetlips?

(MEINY snaps his arm in the crook of his other arm.)

MEINY: *Rotate!*

(EENY advances.)

EENY: Ohhh, now ain't he cute? He wants to be a pile driver.

(EENY jumps at MEINY. They fall struggling. MEINY is pinned. MO drops ROVER as they both take hold of MEINY.)

MO: You lose, loudmouth! It's your turn. They're waiting for you.

(They carry MEINY off screaming.)

EENY: Sssh! Quiet, baby. You're going to have nice cold mush.

MO: *In the mouth!*

(They exit. Long silent pause. ROVER's head is still entangled in his coat. He flops about awkwardly.)

ROVER: Jump on 'em! Take 'em by surprise! Spring on 'em, Rover!

(He sits, painfully disentangles himself. A long sigh.)

Phantoms . . . that is what they air. Phantoms agoin' to a phantom bridge. Jump on 'em? No. To hell with 'em.

(Pause. Now furious.)

Let 'em sink down . . . deep in the mud with the stanchions, the big ones. Ton on ton. Push 'em in the black suck of the black suckin' mud. Tons of tons. Ah! It all washes away. Tons of tons. They build 'er up agin. Ton on ton. The second wasn't done when the first washed away. *Tons!* They had to go on with it, so they sunk 'er down agin, but then . . . they set a watchman on it, an' covered him over. Tons on tons. She stayed put then!

(Pause.)

They watched the stanchion from the bank to see if the watch was watchin'. It stayed put! He was watchin'! So they all said, least ways. So in the next one they set in some more to watch the watchman watchin' an' they all watched the watch's watchers In they went, an' over 'em tons of tons. Swarmin' in the water. Ye had 'em all singin' an' smilin' an' wavin', holdin' onto the babies' hands. In they went, an' ye smiling an' waving to 'em as they went in deeper. Ye didn't know, Ruby . . . ye didn't.

(He becomes more animated. His thoughts flicker and burst into reality before his eyes. He must convince us of what he is seeing.)

Smilin' an' wavin' 'em on . . . but ye didn't know. Down the bank they went! Smilin' back. Arms locked together, tight and taut! The roar closer . . . the sloshin' nearer . . . the lambs waded in . . . almost there . . . all in? All ready? *Here it comes! Floodin'! Pushin'! Roarin'!*

(He jumps up, rushing about, directing the operation.)

Over here! Move it! The mush! Settin' up fast! Don't move down there! She won't flow even.

(Whispers anxiously.)

Think she'll hold? Think she will? Ye didn't know. Ye keep on smilin'. Keep on wavin'. Settin' up fast now . . . maybe . . . she'll hold.

(Pause.)

She'll hold!

(A low humming, sad-sweet and melodious. Really a hymn of adulation.)

Look . . . on the banks. Listen to 'em! *Hurrah! Hurrah! Hurrah, for the power of them what holds 'em there!*

(His attention moves to one side as he peoples his stage and arranges it.)

There. The foreman . . . the foreman. He's standin', arms on hips. Feet planted on the big rock. Up there. The sweat apourin' from him with the strainin' . . . *Round 'em up! Gang 'em up! Stop the damn singin'! Stop 'em!*

(The humming becomes increasingly dissonant, evolving into a continuous moan. The pile driver, wheezing, steamy, begins sluggishly loud, drowning out the humming. ROVER, softly:)

Stop 'em . . . he said. The singin' of 'em . . . it slowed everythin' down . . . slower . . . slower . . . almost a whisper . . . quiet . . . silent . . . kin still hear 'em, though . . . A hummin' almost . . . soft . . . listen . . . listen . . .

(An hysterical laughter from inside the cart rips the air. Everything stops at once, only the laugh in the long silent pause. It stops. ROVER sighs heavily, clearing his memory.)

Ye didn't know, Ruby.

(He begins again, spirited, rousing himself.)

Thet was some time ago. Ye were young an' fair. Thet's how I first saw ye, young an' fair with the flocks of 'em thick about ye like birds feedin' out of yer hand. They was everywhere ye moved. I had to fight me way through 'em jest to look on ye. They knelt down to ye, in those days, an' they told their younguns about ye an' the younguns come with flowers made in a wreath fer yer hair, like gold it was . . . in those days.

(Pause.)

An' now . . . they're gone. They've left ye, an' I'm all ye have got.

(Determined.)

Oh, don't ye fret. They'll come back. Thet much is fer sure, sure as the sun is risin', an' the bridge an' the stanchions'll rise agin too. The Inspection Party'll see to thet. Oh, they air good men, they air. Honest an' good. Ye cain't take thet away from 'em when all's said an' done. Always good to me. Always took the time to smile an' tip their hats to me, they did. Mind ye, tip their hats! Now thet's more'n the rest of 'em did. An' there ain't no two ways 'bout it neither.

(Pause.)

Why . . . why they even answered me when I asked 'em questions. They never come right out with, "Yes, sir" or "No, sir." Cain't expect 'em to go thet far, but they . . . well, they *smiled* . . . sometimes anyway . . . when they happened to see me. *They smiled!* Thet's more'n the rest of 'em did.

(Pause. Softly.)

More'n ye did . . . Ruby.

(The cart shakes and a cardboard flag is run up the mast abruptly. In big letters it reads: "Shut up and push!" He does not see it.)

Ye wouldn't care to tell me . . .

(Bell rings to focus his attention to the sign.)

I know! I know! I promised! Don't need to pour it on me head ever' blessed minute!

(The sign is hauled down. Bell rings irritatingly. He picks up and pushes.)

Aye . . . I know . . . me promise. *Now . . . Now thet's the part! Right there! Stop!*

(Drops the cart down.)

Don't sluff on by it agin! Stop right there. Ye tell me . . . if anybody has a right to know it's me. Ye air alone, no one but old Rover to watch over ye. Yer askin' days air done an' I got to answer fer ye, so tell me . . . in . . . in the first place . . . an, an, *Oh!* It's been so long since anybody paid attention to me, I forgit the right questions, but . . . but ye go on now, an' tell me, in . . . in the second place . . . they . . . they . . . *ah, well!* Ye answer thet one!

(Pause.)

I'm a'waitin'! I asked ye afore, an' afore, an' afore. Ye had time to pound thet one around. Now I'm askin' ye *why*, or so help me if'n ye don't answer up, I'll . . . I'll let ye rot. *Rot-right-here!*

(He kicks the cart violently, shakes it, enraged.)

Answer me! Answer me!

(Another flag is run up quickly, a hastily printed one. It reads in big letters, "You." He stands back, waiting.)

Git on with it! I what?

("You" is hauled down the pole. Then a large "P" is run up.)

"You P"? What kind of talk . . .

("P" is hauled down, and a large "R" is run up, then an "O" and an "M." Pause.)

Aye . . .

("M" is hauled down and "Mized" is run up.)

"Mized"? Not true, not a word of it. I was there ever' blessed minute. Never missed a thing. Ye jest recollect some more.

("Mized" is hauled down. Pause. "Mozed" is run up, upside down. Hauled down, then run up and down triumphantly, right side up.)

Not true neither. I-was-there-*all*-the-time! No "most" of the time at all.

(Angrily, "Mozed" is jerked down. Cart bounces and "Muzd" is run up with a question mark next to it.)

No . . . hain't correct neither. Try 'er agin.

(Cart bounces violently. "Muzd" is hauled down and the first flag is run up as before, "Shut up and push!")

Oh.

(Pause.)

Thet I promised. Gave me word, gave 'em all me word when they stood there, bendin' there, worshippin' ye, hundreds of 'em, far as me eye could see. Ground covered with 'em . . . an' they went down.

(Pause.)

Oh, God, Ruby! I cain't git it out of me mind!

(He buries his head in his hands. Humming blows up softly. He looks up, involved again.)

Ye hear 'em, Ruby? Ye hear 'em? Sing out. Sing out!

(Louder the sounds. He jumps up and begins to direct the scene.)

Oh, they air singin'! Sound yer bell, Ruby. Sound yer little tinkle bell, honey. Let 'em hear it to the last one of 'em, out to the far ends where they're still comin' in!

(He shouts, trying to push his voice to a great distance.)

Sing! Sing out! I'll play an' we'll all sing out!

(He begins to play his harmonica. The humming grows louder and more dissonant, menacing. He stops, frightened at what he has done. The noises blast at him. He runs to the cart in fear and crawls under it, hiding his head in his coat. Mocking laughter from the cart. All sounds recede and all is quiet. Pause. He peeps out timidly, then crawls out cautiously.)

We'd better go . . .

(Dumbly, he picks up the cart and begins to push.)

. . . if we're goin' to git there. Push it on, Rover. Push it! Not far now.

(Pause.)

Ye know they'll come on agin . . . an' ye cain't stop 'em. They'll keep comin'. They kept comin' till they had to stop comin'. When there wasn't room fer no more of 'em. Ye didn't care. Ye smiled! Ye waved 'em on in.

(Pause. He stops still holding the cart, staring blankly ahead.)

They went all down.

(Sets down the cart.)

An I took ye up, tender as ye please to be took up, an' I put ye in the cart . . . an' thet's when . . . *Oh, God, I cain't git it out of me mind!*

(Starts again, falteringly, determined to rid himself of his thoughts.)

An . . . an' I promised 'em all, I'd push ye on by. *Ye didn't deserve it! Not ye! Sloshed 'em down! Led 'em down! Smilin' to git 'em down!* Promised . . . gave me word on it . . . all of 'em what could hear me, an', an' fer them what couldn't hear me no more, I put me mouth to the ground, right in the mud . . .

(He loses his composure. He pounds his fists repeatedly on the floor. Pause. Finally, he looks up dazed, following the flaw. He smiles. A whisper, barely audible.)

Smile . . . smile, remember? Do you? It's me . . . old Rover . . . remember? Ye air supposed to. *Ye air supposed to! Smile! Smile! Wave 'em on, Ruby! Wave an' smile at 'em! Come on! Plenty of room! Move in closer! Here they come! Run 'em down! Trample 'em down!*

(A conspiratorial whisper to RUBY. Humming begins and increases in volume.)

Git ready fer 'em. Turn up yer sweet smilin' face, me Ruby, me rose. *Smile, ye black hearted devil! Git yerself up on the bank an' wave 'em in!*

(Pause. A breathlessly anxious whisper.)

Gangin' up . . . gangin' up . . . hurry on, little uns first . . . gang up . . . bunch up . . .*Jam up!*

(The humming competes loudly.)

They're comin' agin! The fields air full of 'em! Far as the eye kin see! Sing out! Ye licy beggars! Oh, Oh, Rover . . . Ye arrived on time! Ye kin stop! It is over!

(In the distance, running feet, loud police whistles. Sounds stop at once. Silence. EENY and MO run on stage, panting as though they have been running a great distance. There is a desperate look about them as they back on, facing the sounds of the whistles off stage.)

I . . . I brung her on by, jest like I said. See? She . . . she fought me . . . she, aye, she fought me. Fought me hard! But I brung her on.

(They stare at him, uncomprehending.)

I did! Brung 'er on jest like I said, with her crown of gold fer yer inspection.

(They are deadly serious. MO jerks his head, motioning EENY to the cart. He rushes to it and hinges down the front. MO pushes ROVER to the floor to one side. Pause. EENY holds up a tattered veil attached to a wreath of dry flowers.)

EENY: It's empty! Nothing but junk! Bastard!

(He throws them back inside. Goes to ROVER and pounds him. Police whistles and running feet approach loudly. ROVER holds onto MO's sleeve and will not be brushed off. EENY waits for him, then runs off.)

MO: Let go! *Let go!*

(He pushes ROVER down, but he holds on, dragged along to the extreme edge of the stage.)

ROVER: They all come back. See them? See? They air all waitin' here, all of 'em. *Tell him! Answer up!* He's come to inspect ye all! *Sing out! Wave him on!*

MO: *Let go, you damned fool!*

(MO flicks out a large, gleaming knife. ROVER exhorts his hoards on, unaware.)

ROVER: Sing out everybody! *They air here! Rise up, Ruby! Parade yerself!*

(To MO:)

Dragged 'em by me nubs! Bleedin' an' raw! An' . . . An' . . .

(MO sticks the knife in. ROVER smiles strangely and groans softly, really a sigh. Lights flicker dimly and the chorus of dirgelike, distorted voices begins. MO is confused. A fear comes over him.)

Ru . . . by . . . me . . . love . . .

MO: *The damned fool. Hey . . . Hey! What the hell . . .*

(MO is terrified. He tries to push ROVER from his sleeve roughly, then re-moves his hand slowly yet forcefully, as though fearing contagion. He backs away dreadfully.)

The . . . damned . . . fool . . .

(He runs off. The inside of the cart lights up bluely. Stage lights are dimmed to a dark blue. RUBY descends from the cart slowly. She is dressed in a long, white, gauzy peignoir, overhung with tattered, ragged net. Her light hair hangs loose and unbrushed on her shoulders, and on her head a wreath of dry, brittle flowers. Her face is impassive and chalk white. She walks straight, head held high. A strange elegance attaches to her. She is, after all, amorphous as a puff of smoke. A breeze billows out her hair and costume. A deep blue light follows her as she moves toward ROVER, like an apparition.)

ROVER: *Ohhh . . . ye air . . . young an' fair . . . me Ruby . . . me rose.*

(RUBY floats resplendently beside him, and pauses. Like an angel, she looks at him for the merest second. A laugh, more amused than involved.)

Ruby . . .

(RUBY steps off stage. ROVER falls. The humming evaporates. Lights fade to black. Silence.)

CURTAIN

"... I had no idea what to expect and I must tell you that I would not have left before the last line even if my seat had caught fire. Because an essential something was taking place, and that something was an aliveness, a theatricality, a way of using theatre to say what cannot be said any other way. And in using theatre in this fashion, the playwright also used the audience, committing us against our will and against ourselves, threatening everyone on stage and in the seats. Life was giving ground before some greater, other thing."

Arthur Sainer of *The Village Voice*,
reviewing *Hurrah for the Bridge*

Charles Stanley as Medea (background and, in foreground, holding infant Shawn Livingston as the young Prince of Colchis), and Pat Holland as the Nurse in H. M. Koutoukas's *Medea of the Laundromat*, 1965

Photomontage by James D. Gossage

MEDEA OF THE LAUNDROMAT
OR
THE STARS MAY UNDERSTAND
H. M. Koutoukas

A Tragical Camp
Dedicated to Mary Frances Robel and Charles James[1]

Medea is traditionally played by a young man resembling
Clint Eastwood, with the sensitivity of Montgomery Clift.

SCENE: A self-service laundromat. As the overture ends, the curtains rise, and this play *must* be done in a theatre with curtains. It is dawn and the NURSE, kneeling, rises with a baby in her arms.

NURSE: *(Demented.)*
WOMEN OF CORINTH, LAY DOWN YOUR LAUNDRY:
The great-grandson of the SUN sleeps —
The son of a demi-goddess dreams,
Of glories he will never see,
Honors he will never be paid.
(Rocks the child in her arms, then lays it in a clothes basket.)

(Viper-like. Hissing.)
Must you always gather like maggots
At tragedy's door —
Or do you free yourself from guilt
By coming here to bleach your clothes.

Would you erase King Creon's guilt
Disconnect yourself by cleanliness
From the unholy lights you've chosen
To guide your lives.

---

[1] Property of: H. M. Koutoukas, 87 Christopher Street, New York, NY 10014. Originally produced at the Caffe Cino under the title, *Medea or Maybe the Stars Will Understand or Veiled Strangers.*

Your whole land — has brought about this day,
Creon is but the voice you chose
To represent the filth that no soap
Nor bleach can remove from
Corinth the evil of these days
Or show more to all time than
The evil *you* call *Greece!*

(Pointing at child.)

Each of you share in what has happened here
Each of you are sums of the total horror
And responsible for what HAS *(Pause.)*
And what WILL happen!

(Softly.)

Prepare for night
For you have insulted
None other than . . . MEDEA —
MEDEA the Sun's granddaughter
MEDEA the Crown Princess of Colchis
MEDEA daughter to a thousand Kings
MEDEA — the opposite of all your logic
MEDEA — priestess to the Code you've forgotten
MEDEA — who's been named "terror" and witch.

(Sneers.)

By your DEAD, King Creon,
Your mighty King *(a bit of a sneer here)*
who could not even save his daughter
From Medea's wrath.
She comes soon to this place —
Brings history to this dreary land;
Do you think she will stop in her fury,
Without the notices of your sins too —
ALL will suffer as do their chosen Kings.

(Sound: Drums of funeral procession. Wailing voices. General terror.)

(Leans against machine.)

No wedding will take place today —
Instead the burial and result
Of dignity outraged, of love defiled . . .
Courage turned to HATE is honored here in Corinth.

(With fury and fire.)

Medea has avenged
All the blasphemies Jason has hurled at her.

She is the ocean's rage,
The fire's pangs.

WOMEN OF CORINTH,
Expect only the impossible today
For Medea has been outraged!

(Pause. She looks at the child.)

Her son will know no honor,
Sans throne and glory
He will follow unknowing
A Queen's wake, that has been destroyed by its going,
All that might have been
Or what was dreamt of.

(Huskiness.)

Go to your home and weep
For Medea has no home or land
Go to your home and pound your breasts
For this is your sin,
All Corinth shall fulfill
Medea's fury!

(Picks up child.)

(Sound and lights: Crash of many cymbals. Single spot up on NURSE.)

(Lullaby to child and make circle.)

Sleep . . . sleep . . . dear Prince without a land.
Dream of all that might have been
Had your mother *not* loved a vile Greek!
Hush — hush — Nanny sings — no worries
Still — Still — there's little silence
Know it well before your mother comes.

The deck has been stacked — stacked deck of pestered passions
By slow shufflings of the cards in Destiny's hands —
Yet LOVE was chosen over duty by Medea
And fulfilled with action — by Medea!
All that the Gods would have . . . has turned opposite.

(Huskily.)

All odds have faced Medea now.
Homeless, free from all discretion,
In her fury affirming the most dreadful accusations
Hurled against . . . her and her father's house.

Sleep fill your night — sleep, sleep . . .
No sleep for Nanny for she stands over
Revealing you to the stars alone.

Sleep, sweet infant Prince —
That you could sleep forever!
But no — there is more to come —
And I am weary from just watching
What has happened — yet made sleepless all these nights —
At what MAY come!

(Kneels.)

(MEDEA enters, silently. Her arm covers her whole face except for her eyes. The drape of her sleeve veils her whole body and facial features.)
(Sound and lights: MEDEA's theme up. Intense violet light upon MEDEA. Spot on NURSE begins to fade.)

NURSE: *(Masks the child.)*
Who are you, strange woman —
Why have you not left with the others
To mourn your wretched King and his dreary daughter?
Go from this place —
Medea comes to this place this night . . .
(Darkly.)
Preceded by her myth!

MEDEA: *(Groans.)*
Oh, wretched
Wretching — wrecking myth —!

NURSE:
Strange woman — you do not intrigue *us!*
Go from here — do not wake Medea's child
(Focus on MEDEA.)
For he is all she now possesses.
She will not tolerate your veiled ways!

MEDEA: *(Revealing herself.)*
Medea's myth precedes and terrifies even MEDEA!

NURSE: *(Throwing herself at MEDEA's feet.)*
Oh, Mistress — the full night was wretched from your absence.

MEDEA: *(Paying no attention.)*
(Screams.) Where is *MY* son. What fate has —

NURSE:
No fate — he lies safe in my scarf. Sleeping as all babes should.
(NURSE clears MEDEA's scarf. MEDEA comes to crib. NURSE picks up veil.)

MEDEA: *(Tender.)*
He knows no difference
In his tiny rest
Then golden castles

Near green-held rests
With clouds and amber depth he sleeps
A touch can clear his terror
And a tit can solve his pain.

(Bitter.)
Only to grow to unheralded manhood
Only to know life as a gypsy waif
Here is a prince — never to know kingdom
Here is the blood of a God and a Greek!

Never to know the glamour of kingdom
Never the brilliance of power and wealth

(Softly.)
Warrior unshielded, dusk without dawn,
Unwritten music by poets long dead.

Sleep, sleep son of Medea —
Mother protects you . . . FROM KNOWING YOUR FATHER.

(NURSE comes down.)

NURSE: *(Takes her arm.)* Come, come let him rest and you rest also.

MEDEA:
Rest — Medea rest? — Without home,
Empty of power and wealth — you would have Medea rest . . .
Never — NEVER — the circle must be completed or I curse the Gods
Who have drawn it! No rest for Medea until her name and heart
And HATE are cleansed. Cleansed with the horror of these vile Greeks!
BEFORE THIS NIGHT IS THROUGH THE SCREAMS OF ALL GREECE WILL
INTERRUPT THE GODS THEMSELVES IN THEIR ETERNAL DIALOGUE.

NURSE:
What, Medea?

MEDEA:
Yes — you heard. Perhaps your ears closed at the fear of it.
Medea and Medea alone revenges all nature and will send
Greece screaming from its vile logic, from its agoras, from
Its chattering imitations of its cheap clever Gods.

(Softly.)
MEDEA WILL REMIND THE GODS OF WHAT FURY MEANS.

(Smiles.)
She will shake the foundations of their laws, rape open
The fears of their young, quake up a thousand fears and
Force them down Corinth's throat.

(Softly, as if pronouncing a judgement — Cobra gesture.)

All Greece will remember Medea and shriek out
At the memory of her glamour.

NURSE:

Rest — I pray — our journey will be long —

MEDEA:

Yes —
Our whole life will be journey
Without land or joy in sight —
Preceded constantly by our myth
We shall wander damned unsleeping
Wandering our life away . . .

NURSE:

Don't think of it!

MEDEA: *(Wailing.)*

I had lost my style

(Come down; lose style for a minute.)

I could not find my way.

(Come back up.)

Then fury married hate
Making the road clear
And mauve remembrance
Grew furious at present thoughts.

NURSE:

You did only what you had to do.

MEDEA:

NO! No force molded my actions save my own choice of hate
To armor up and save my wrecked grace. The deeds I did
Were deeds the Gods should have done. So then as always
The end is never near enough, the moment in between is
Always the reminder that no dream is full till it finds its form.

NURSE:

Dreams come true and nightmares too!

MEDEA: *(Threat.)*

Before the sun rises on this morning . . .
MEDEA will be whole again.

(Rebirth. Touch of joy.)

No longer will her features be confused with Jason's. No longer
Will her desires have an open space. The splinters
Of love will be full removed, turned to daggers
With which to scorch Jason's eyes.

NURSE:

    Medea — the child is present.

MEDEA:

    Then let him too know — for he will grow to manhood . . .
    That his mother taught all men a lesson that they can
    Never fully learn!

    I am the rage
    I am the scourge
    The heart and tenderness and hurt
    Of all things that have been left to die —
    Wasted on the shores of useless love.
    Features lost and confused in another image —
    Medea draws her portrait anew . . .
    Medea draws her features strong, alone,
    In fire, madness and with bloody soil.
    No one, no thing, no God
    Dare deny Medea the rightness
    Of her insanity . . .

NURSE:

    You are not mad, Medea — just foreign to this country!

MEDEA: *(Smile.)*

    Not mad — watch this day closely Nurse — and you will
    Learn again what the full moon is all about.

NURSE:

    Ancient Greece protect us from our seldom truths —

MEDEA:

    Truth be damned! *(Turn from her.)* What's Truth — a food for pigs and
    cowards. A reason for dreary bacchanals — *(Over shoulder.)* Do they have
    you believing in truth now, old woman . . .

NURSE:

    In Colchis we believed in Truth —
    (Hand on machine.)
    As we did in honor and in courage.

MEDEA: *(Sadly.)*

    Truth of Colchis is another thing! It was the truth of autumn and the har-
    vest, truth of spring and fountains that never had gone dry from lack of rain.
    Truth in Colchis was of a nobler kind, of earth and lust and passion woven
    in a warm lovers' embrace by the seaside on the sandy shore. Not like this
    Greek truth that confuses everything to nothing, not like this vile beauty
    that the people of Corinth confuse with their Gods. In their temples, even
    lies abound in symmetry, not one thing out of place — not one muscle lost.

In Colchis the Parthenon would have been a urinal — and beauty would never have been made servant to truth.

(Sound: Child crying.)

NURSE:

The infant prince!

MEDEA:

I will go to him, I am STILL his mother, in fact little else than his mother . . . leave us. *(Smiles.)* Go watch Creon's funeral, go see Corinth honor the mighty monarch of their land, go see if tears may prevent skin from rot!

NURSE:

Should we not leave —

MEDEA:

Trailing our curses behind us? No — soon enough. Medea will not be stabbed in the back as she cowers to some hideous mountain cave — my heritage is ancient, my glamour undeniable, I have many stunning land-scapes to paint across Greece before I leave. I would be alone. My child calls for me!

(Wait until NURSE exits.)

(Sound: Child crying.)

(NURSE hesitates, then leaves.)

MEDEA: *(Lifts infant.)*

Do you weep at dreams or morning sweet young becoming
That knows nothing but the first of things.

(Rocks child in her arms.)

Weep not, weep not — your Mother still has strength
Enough to protect her sweetest jewel. If that were all —
If loving and caring were all that the Gods demanded,
What a soft, tender mother, Medea would be.

(Bitterness.)

But no, Medea must be the panther mother,
    doing all the things for her cub but
Unable to be always gentle — rage has scorched out my breasts.

(Rises.)

There is no longer sustenance for love. Sweet child a-meshing
So many moments when everything was good.

Everything was so good *(Steel-edged.)* once — or was it being young
With an overflow of giving that made it seem so? Would
Any arms have brought me to my powers and needs and
Lusts so quickly. *(Pause.)*

(Noticing child's smallness.)

Medea was so young once,
And innocent of men as stars are innocent of men.
Then she was touched and brought to flower — her
Lacks were made evident in one night and burned a space
Within her that only *(Work for erotic tone.)* lust encased in love could fill.
Lust comes so quickly and love is so tender — nights
Once so empty find too soon their reason, which passion
Burns, leaving nothing of all reason save burnt embers
Of what might have been.

(Almost histrionically.)

I have wept till my eyes no longer see the reason. I have
Screamed out with pain that made music seem inconsequential —
Yet always there . . . deep within me like some gnawing thing
There always remained the remembrances of dreams and of
What might have been — had Medea loved not so wantonly,
Had Medea not needed so desperately.

Then all was given — nothing left but Medea's hollow screams
Upon the echo of her own desires — clawing, screaming, sobbing,
Then in silence realizing that something had been taken that
Could never be returned — something resembling the haunting
Dreams of childhood summers by the sea.

(Sobbing, holding child close.)

Dreams can never be.

(Falls to knees.)

Dreams can never be. Dreams can never be.
Weep for the lost hopes of innocence — spring shall not come
Again nor childish fancies of rainbows and moonbeams. Sooner
Or later it becomes either gold or mud and everything boils
Into scorching generality.

Yet passion chose to come to this land of logic — a priestess
Of the ancient cult and princess descended from the sun chose
Through her lover to deny all that gave root to her and sustenance.
So valuable — so valuable a young girl's dreams — that whole
Futures have been wretched to protect hope from despair.

(Kisses baby, puts it in basket.)

I would be tender,
I would be so soft,
I would you have more
Than all the things of earth
But look even though you cannot know,
The man who took all from your Mother
And traced his features through me upon your countenance

(Slowly, tenderness turns to rejection.)
Denies all that was sacred.
Shattering dreams for lies
Turning love to hate for its own posterity.

(Pause.)

(Single spot on MEDEA as she goes center for invocation.)

Gods of the ancients
Dark deities of old
Why have you allowed Medea
Descendant of the sun
Herself a demi-goddess
To find herself betrayed
In this cruel place where logic
Runs haywire and is revered afore the heart?

Have all the Heavens denied Medea life and love
Do they join Jason in betrayal of a young girl's dream?

Gods of cobra
Gods of the dark
Gods of the ocean
Gods long forgotten
For painted tinseled marbled perfection.
Of distorted Athenian Grace
Listen — Medea speaks.

(Two beat pauses.)

Princess,
Demi-Goddess
Witch and enchantress too
Invokes pre-cosmic forces
Residuals of the most ancient sands
To rise up and defend her grace
Save dignity and wreak vengeance on this vile race!

(Screaming.)

If any God or force or creature
Dare deny Medea
They will meet the volcano force
Of love turned to hate and vengeance
They will feel fire itself and cold cold winter
If they dare stand between her *(Beat pause . . .)* and what she must do.
None shall deny Medea
Her right to grace
No force in Heaven or Hades
Will destroy her dream of what might have been.

Had she not come to this wretched place
Had she not loved a cursed prince from a cursed land.

With or without
In terror or in plenty
Medea WILL do what needs to be done
To close the circle her dreams once opened!

(Sound: MEDEA's theme up.)

Medea has become deadly
So beware all men and elements
Havoc is my last friend
Tragedy mine only firmament!

I'll rip open the heavens
Rather than deny my pride
I'll rage up the sea
Rather than do injury to my honor.

I have begged on my knees
Only to drop my enemies to theirs
Alone — hopeless — in a foreign land
With no attention paid my tears
I returned to the ancient knowledge
That these Greek fools put themselves
In disdain toward and wove disaster
With bitterness and mine own hands.

One more deed must be done
Before the sun rises
Before I leave this wretched land.

I will cause mountains to tremble
And waters to be still.
Medea who was so young once
Now sacrifices her full illusion
To her ancient Gods.
God of the cobra
God of the night
She begs forgiveness
And will with her own hands
Tear her name into the horror of this place.
To prove that she has not left the ancient cult of passion
To show her return to all that she once loathed
Destroyed, and fled from.

The Gods have not shown Medea justice
So Medea must BECOME justice

Raging these moments through
Till all that has been done
Will find itself undone.

(Sound: Infant crying.)

Yes, you too will be cast upon the scale
For justice has been forced into Medea's hands
Your mother wears no blindfold and sees
The faint hint of Jason on your tiny features.

(Her eyes become inflamed.)

All that was Jason's by and from Medea
Must be erased as Medea's love was itself destroyed.
Yet it was not remembered that love does not die —
It merely waits, turning sour upon the heart, into hate.

No more — no more the willow walks
With windswept forgiveness 'neath mountain pine
Jason has turned my flesh to stone my fires to pitch,
And as such, they return to him.

(Picks up child.)

You would be cursed
If you grew into manhood
Exiled you would never
Have had the dreams of life.
What more can a mother give
Than new hope, refurbished faith —
And when unable, what greater gift
Than protection from the tortures
Of life without meaning.

(With tenderness.)

Sleep — sleep — son of Jason,
In your new bed — your last bed —
No silk sheets, no tiny shoes, no tutors.

(With hate.)

Just sleep — you will not spread Jason's seeds
Into another.

(Places child in washing machine.)

Jason — Medea's final gift —
More horrid than Crayola's golden gown
Which destroyed Creon too.

(Laughs.)

I remove you from history
As you stole me from my maiden dreams and hopes.
I kill that young becoming

That was both of us combined.
Removing all traces
Of our being for now and all eternity!

(Pause.)

If you would hurt a man —
Then hurt his only son.

(Warmly.)

Son, Son, the gods know well your mother's horror,
They will make you prince in a land that no one knows of.
This is far better than starving on a gypsy road —
Your Mother's last kind act to you —
And last revenge.

(She closes the door.)

(Slowly, she puts a coin in.)

(Sound: chaotic music up.)

(Screams.)

Oh wretched fate — damned destiny
That such love should turn to THIS.
Medea is no longer human
No longer woman
No longer or evermore will she be loved.
Weep for the deeds
That needed doing
Weep for the love
That turned upon itself.
MEDEA IS DEADLY YET STILL SHE WEEPS FOR LIFE.

(NURSE enters.)

NURSE:

Medea —

MEDEA: *(Demented.)*

Remove these vile robes of Greece from Medea —
No longer will she remain trapped
And victim to a cowardly race —
Quick — quick — woman —
My jewels and all the worn ritual
Of the ancient cults of dear Colchis
Land of my youth that I betrayed
And whose honor I now do justice to.

(She tears off her clothes and dresses in the golden temple gowns of Colchis.)

(Music up full: MEDEA begins a temple dance.)

NURSE:

> The child, Madam —
>
> *(Pause. She looks in crib.)*
>
> The beautiful prince, fruit of your womb?
>
> *(She sees the child in washing machine.)*
>
> Strange woman —
> Fury and hate have done this —
> Strange woman —
> Only the Gods now may understand
> The result of your deadly passions.
>
> *(MEDEA pays no attention, keeps dancing in a frenzy.)*
>
> *(Looking out door.)*
>
> Madam, Jason approaches —
>
> *(MEDEA pays no attention. she dances for the gods and in her ecstasy grows strong.)*
>
> *(JASON enters.)*

JASON: *(Screams.)*

> MEDEA —
> Witch —
> Hear me or you will DIE!
>
> *(Brings out knife slowly.)*

MEDEA:

> Medea has known a thousand deaths
> And still lives — cowards cannot kill.
> Remember Jason — I saved your life several times —
> But never once could you or did you try to save mine.
> I have no fear — you've taught me the strength
> Of my own power — I am more armored than you.

JASON:

> Why Medea — why —

MEDEA: *(Still dancing.)*

> Because love couldn't, Jason —
> Because the gods couldn't, Jason —

JASON:

> Wretched woman destroyer of all you cannot have!

MEDEA:

> You FORGET, Jason, I brought you HONOR,
> With the fleece — I made you immortal
> With my own name — killing all I loved

For your love — which in turn tried to
Slay me —

JASON:
Witch!

MEDEA:
Thank all the Gods for that, with double thanks.

JASON:
Where is my son —

MEDEA:
He has joined our love, Jason.

*(JASON screams, upon seeing the child in the washer. He goes toward it.
But MEDEA steps in his way. He lifts his sword but she throws Clorox in his
eyes. He screams, backs up, draws his sword — which MEDEA picks up. He
gropes in wrong direction for washer with child.)*

MEDEA:
Your son is lost to you, Jason, as your love for
Medea was lost —

JASON:
The horror of your deeds breaks out beyond all belief.

MEDEA: *(Gently.)*
The stars may understand.

(Pause.)

As we once thought
We understood the beauty of our yearnings. The sea
May recognize in rage, the wind in fury —

JASON: *(Starts to rise.)*
You are not human —

MEDEA:
I was once TOO human, but you destroyed that, Jason.

(He grabs in her direction.)

I have your sword . . . beware *(Laughs.)* husband.
Beware — Beware — Beware . . .

JASON:
Let me touch my son — just once — or a lock
Of his hair before his memory is lost forever.

MEDEA:
Nothing Jason. Nothing of your son, or Medea . . .
You sought to destroy me in this vile land and
Now you learn that your hate returns — did you

324   *Return to the Caffe Cino*

Believe that Medea would really like some feathered
Creature — did you really think she would?

JASON:

Wretched woman — you have destroyed everything,
Everything —

MEDEA:

No Jason, not everything, just all the traces of
My love.
Now Jason, the circle turns complete — except for the
Fires that will soon envelop this place —

JASON:

Fire —

MEDEA:

You would not have me leave your son —

JASON:

You will not bury the child —

MEDEA:

Neither the child

(Pause.)

Nor you, Jason —
Your taste of Hell comes now — Medea's kind
She gives her real fire — a kinder Hell than
You gave her.

NURSE:

Medea, this must all end — the Gods!

MEDEA:

The Gods know exactly what I'm doing.
They are the only ones. Nurse, torch up this place —

(Tosses gasoline on JASON.)

Set fires that the dead may meet the dying. Weep not,
For things are as they should be, Medea knows.

(NURSE lights torch.)

JASON:

Medea — please — remember — forgive —

MEDEA:

You taught me the lies in all those words, Jason. You taught too well and
    now learn your own lessons.

JASON:

You are forever damned —

MEDEA:

Perhaps among mortals who love
And who are loved back *(Sigh.)*
Perhaps among the innocent and undemented
Perhaps where joy is the common meter —
But you, Jason, led me from those places —
To somewhere near the Gods and stars.
Perhaps the Gods will forgive
Perhaps the stars will understand . . .
I hesitate Jason,
I will not put words
Into the mouth of omnipotence
Yet I will defend honor
Where omnipotence fails.

(JASON blindly tries to find way out.)

(NURSE hurls torch at JASON.)

JASON: *(Shrieking.)*

Medea, forgive me — forgive me . . .

MEDEA:

Jason, there's no such thing —
Crawl down to the cracked mirrors in your unused wedding chamber
And make love to your pretensions

(Pause.)

Caress your preconceptions.
Touch your sail's rotting mask and remember
The miracles my love performed —
Then weep, Jason, for having known
What love was, and at having destroyed it.

JASON:

Aahhh —

NURSE:

Madam, hurry, the flames —

(The set slides back into the distance. MEDEA and NURSE are in a wooded place. We see the flames in the distance with JASON burning alive. We hear his screams.)

(Sound: MEDEA's theme up.)

NURSE:

Now, Madam — what now?

JASON:

Medea —

(MEDEA winces briefly.)

MEDEA: *(Fury.)*

My shade will meet you at the final crossing, Jason. Beware Jason —
For death is not too far from life
And no matter where you are tortures wait.
My shade will meet you at my crossing.
Exile — punishment — terrors of the homeless
Of the ever-constant legion of living dead
Await us —

NURSE:

No, Medea —
For it is written that only the stars can understand —
(Magical lights as MEDEA ascends to the constellation Virgo.)
So you join the godly bodies
In eternal transcendence
As symbol of Justice's terror
And Honor's sweet revenge.
No man or God may judge a deed like this
It is as infinite as space itself and yearning.
Farewell, descendent of the sun —
Princess of Colchis journey well through eternity
You've marked God's eternal conversations with your screams —
All ages and all men will be in awe of you.
(Drums, rolling with trumpets in salute.)
Constant reminder of all past passions
And misspent desires — veiled strangeness
Will forever remind men of their duty
In welcoming strangers
And doing fulfillment to their vows.

Maidens will weep,
For what young men have taken —
You are reflected in each love gone bitter.
Medea! The Gods now do you the honor
That all of Greece could not learn!

TRIUMPHANT MUSIC
CURTAIN

H. M. Koutoukas in 1965

Photo by Néstor Almendros, from the collection of Jean Ann Davidson

Jim Jennings and Walter McGinn in Robert Heide's *The Bed*, 1965
Photo by Conrad Ward

THE BED
Robert Heide[1]

First Cino run, June-July 1965:
Starring Jim Jennings and Larry Burns

Second Cino run, September 1965:
Starring Jim Jennings and Walter McGinn

CHARACTERS:

JIM: A young man

JACK: A young man

The play The Bed, *in its essence, is dealing with the problem of inverted time-that-is-timelessness. The two characters have what might be called in technical circles a time-space problem — closely identifiable with schizophrenic time, non-time or irrational time. Any director or reader should bear in mind that, while the play reads quickly, time is being dealt with in an acausal manner; that is, the performance time is slowed down by dramatic time intervals.*

In no way is the time element in The Bed *pushed forward-into-activity or into measured time; rather, time is paradoxical, neither here, nor there. Many gaps. Actor-movement should occur only when indicated — and at other times should be physically constricted . . . as opposed to explosive-outer-directed-emotion that is implosive (inner directed) and, almost, catatonic-waiting-to-break through. (It never does in this instance.)*

Actual playing time may be anywhere between 30 and 45 minutes to one hour. The play should appear to be happening in space. We might think of a space capsule. (In performance, the bed was almost the entire stage. As a symbol it could represent gravity-pull-limitation, a death slab in a morgue, a padded cell, a coffin, sleep, sexuality, whatever problem the bed might

---

[1] Rights to *The Bed* are under U.S. copyright protection. Permission to perform or reprint this work must be obtained in writing through: Robert Heide, 84 Christopher St., # 3-R, New York NY 10014-4253.

represent itself to be to an audience.) Like the mime who is walking for-
ward in visual time but who is actually physically walking backward,
time, herewith, has become non-conceptual. In this non-conceptual time,
movement and emotional intention-actions must be emphasized and
strained to an exaggerated point. For instance, while in conceptual time it
may take two minutes to cross a street, in non-conceptual time it could
take 2-4-6-8-9 and so forth.

EXAMPLE: JACK: Do whatever you like. Get up if you want to.
Go. Leave me alone.

JIM: I have lost time. How long have we been in . . . this time?

Verbal delivery can be normal. Duration points between lines are op-
tional, so that reactive periods in terms of their own experience of mean-
inglessness and emptiness would be quite long.

SCENE: *A medium-sized apartment in a large American city.*

The suggestion of a lavatory (down right), sink, etc.
The suggestion of a phonograph machine.
Scattered clothing.
Liquor bottles.
A clock.
Books.
Sunlight.
A great white double bed on a raised-tilted-slightly-forward-toward-the-
audience-platform.

JACK (on one side of the bed) and JIM (on the other) are asleep.

Silence.
JIM's left hand moves slightly.

(Pause.)

(JIM breaks suddenly out of a nightmare. Sits up. Moans. Twitches.
Scratches his head. Looks slowly about the room as if trying to connect one
object with another: Attempting, perhaps, to make the pieces merge into
one whole.

Anguish.

Stares for a long moment at figure of JACK, who is curled up into the posi-
tion of the womb.

Alienation.
JIM pokes JACK.
JACK groans.

Long silence.)

JIM: *(Groggy.)* Think we should get up?

JACK: *(Not moving.)* Drop dead!
(Pause.)

JIM: What time do you think it is?

JACK: *(Slowly.)* Look at the clock . . .
(Pause.)

JIM: I think it stopped . . . working.

JACK: Throw it out the window.
(Pause.)

JIM: How long have we been lying in this bed? When was it that we were last
seen . . . for instance . . . out . . . on the street?

JACK: You're getting me into one of those conversations.

JIM: What conversations?
(Pause.)
Sun seems to be out.
(Pause.)
I . . . I've been having difficulty with my breathing again. My lungs. During
the night I almost suffocated. I . . .
(Pause.)
. . . I had a nightmare.
(Pause.)

JACK: What about?

JIM: I don't remember.

JACK: That's good. Ha. Ha.
(Pause.)

JIM: Do you think we should . . . both of us . . . make an attempt to get out of
this bed?

JACK: *(Tossing slightly. Clutching pillow.)* I want to sleep.

JIM: For how long?

JACK: Do whatever you like. Get up if you want to. Go. Leave me alone.

JIM: I've lost time. How long have we been in . . . this time?

JACK: Two days . . . about. Have a drink or something. Go to the refrigerator-
box. Get something to eat if it pleases you. Live it up. Then . . .

JIM: I feel hung over.
(Pause.)
I'm tired of sleep, fed up with eating, of drowning myself in drink into a
coma.

JACK: Quit intellectualizing.

JIM: Where . . . where . . . are we getting this way?

JACK: What difference could it possibly make. Get this through your thick skull. I'm tired. Bored.
(Slight pause.)
I don't know. Try reading again . . . or maybe you could take up Yoga or something. Didn't you used to study Yoga?

JIM: I'm getting up. Are you?

JACK: Eventually I'll have to . . . I guess.

JIM: Do you want to go out . . . .

JACK: No.

JIM: For a walk?

JACK: Where?

JIM: Anywhere.

JACK: *(As he delivers the following lines he counts his fingers over and over again, almost as if to reassure himself of their existence.)* Uh . . . this week one of us will probably have to go to the bank. Draw money out of the account. Pay the rent. Get in some booze. Some food.
(Pause.)
Food.

JIM: When?

JACK: Later this week. Ha ha! I guess. Ha ha!

JIM: What're you laughing about?

JACK: *(Happily.)* Filthy-God-damn-money. A silver slab of a spoon stuck in my mouth since the day I was born . . . blasted out of my mother's bloody womb. Thinking of the old-man-dead-rotting-a-grinning-skeleton-dead-rotting in black earth six feet underground. Pappa no longer with us. What does any of it mean to the old bastard now? What does it mean to the old lady guzzling booze uptown? What does it mean to me? Money . . . deposited for me in the Bank of America . . . so that I can go on living . . . or some such thing. Did you hear me? *Go on living* . . . this beauteous tawdry torturous existence . . . and so that you can go on living-guzzling with me. Very feasible arrangement. You. Me. In the morning. In the evening. One day we'll be under earth too, just like the old man. I wonder which one of us will go first? Ha ha! Hey, you listening to this story of my life? Think it's amusing?

JIM: Stinks.
(Pause.)
Ah . . . there's just something wrong . . . wrong . . . with this . . . this entire set-up.

(Pause.)

With you. With me. With both of us together. Something's *not* working. I can't go on. I've just about passed the point of endurance. I am not up to this. I'm thinking of maybe pushing off. Out.

JACK: What?

(Jim buries his head in his hands.)

Take a walk, and come back later.

JIM: We don't do anything. We . . . we're like two objects frozen in time, in space, not even on earth, really — suspended. Weightless being. Occasionally we go to the john to pee or to take a crap. We shove food down our throats . . . pizza pie, hamburgers . . . sent up from the corner; chocolate puff pastries, ice cream. Basic functionalism. Eating.

(Short pause.)

I feel nauseated. This process going on like some great senseless flux. On and on and on. You. Me. Sex is dead. No, it's God. God is dead. No, it's Nietzsche, Nietzsche is dead. No, I am alive, here, and yet . . .

JACK: Why don't you just drop dead?

JIM: Maybe we're already dead and don't know it . . . haven't become fully aware of it. Dead. Non-existent. Living-dying. Maybe . . .

JACK: Why in the hell don't you stop trying to figure the whole thing out? What's to explain?

JIM: Nothing . . . I guess.

(Pause.)
(Shakes Jack.)

Get up already . . . slob!

JACK: No. Leave me alone. I just want to lie here . . . lie here and . . .

JIM: . . . and?

JACK: . . . stare into space . . . until something happens in my head . . . inside my lunatic head . . . maybe an idea . . .

JIM: What idea?

JACK: I don't know yet what idea . . . or if there will even be any. But I'm going to lie here. Maybe an idea will turn up . . . maybe . . . something from the past. Lie still. Somehow even if I wanted to now . . . I couldn't move . . . couldn't budge . . . out of this bed. I have to just lie still here. Still.

JIM: I can't anymore. I'm getting up. I am . . . going to get up . . .

(Gets up quickly.)

. . . up and out!

(Begins to move his arms wildly and to pace around the floor in a circle.)
(PAUSE.)

Mind if I play a record?

JACK: Do whatever you like.

> *(Almost an offstage aside.)*

You're lucky you have a sucker like me who lets you do whatever you like, who supports your miserable existence. You're lucky.

JIM: *(Having heard perhaps only the word "support.")*

I'm not about to argue about your filthy lucre . . . to discuss economic problems with you. Your poor-little-rich-boy-guilt-problem act makes me sick. It's getting to be a drag.

JACK: Cut it! Cut it!

JIM: Your wealthy-overbearing-father-complex-complexities . . .

JACK: All right. Cut the . . . bull. Psychology today. Cut the role you're playing down to half. I don't like these blanket judgment-assumptions, of yours. It just ain't that easy.

> *(Short pause.)*

Play some music. Brush your teeth. Wash your armpits. Go out. Bring me back . . .

JIM: What?

JACK: I don't know.

> *(Pause.)*
>
> *(JIM goes over to the window ledge area. Gets up onto ledge on all fours.)*

What are yah doing now?

JIM: Thinking of jumping out.

> *(Pause.)*

Playing a game. Think it would make any difference . . . to . . . any . . .

JACK: *(Objectively speaking — reciting factual data.)* You might not make it. I mean, finish yourself off all the way. We're only four floors up off the ground. Maybe you'd just break a leg or something. You know. If you're gonna make the Big Blackout there are ways that aren't quite as messy. Pills for instance. A good way.

JIM: How would you know?

> *(Gets down.)*

Hmmmm. Yeah.

(Walks to phonograph machine. Turns it on. Song: Anyway You Want It. Dave Clark Five — Epic Records. Very loud. Blasting, as in a discotheque. This is the monotonous drone of the "outer" world bombarding the situation.)

(Neither JIM nor JACK moves throughout the length of the recording. They wear blank expressions on their faces and appear not to be listening to the sound. At record's end, Jim makes it to the bathroom area.

Brushes teeth.

Washes armpits.

Puts on trousers.

Puts on shirt,

      socks,

      shoes.

Gazes at himself for a long moment in mirror (front.)

Not quite sure that the apparition he sees in the glass is actually himself.

Walks slowly toward bed.

Sits on bed.

Arms drooped, between legs.

Head down.

Head up.

Stares vacantly at fixed point (front.)

Silence.)

JACK: *(Hand over face.)*

    What are you thinking about?

JIM: *(As if relieved of an intolerable burden.)*

    Nothing.

    (Pause.)

    Are you coming out with me or . . . staying?

    (No answer.)

    (JIM proceeds to leave.

    Stop. Halt at doorway.
    A long, tense staring at figure of JACK.)

    (JACK pulls himself into a ball and refrains from eye contact or gesture.)

JACK: *(Soft.)* Where are you going?

JIM: I don't know. *(Slight pause.)* Out . . . maybe . . . for a . . . cup of coffee.
    To . . . uh . . . get some cigarettes. I just don't . . . I wish that . . .

    (Hold moment.)

    (Slow exit — JIM.)

    (Door slam.

JACK up quickly out of bed. Wanders around the room looking at objects — at anything — with no specific intention.

Finally picks up clock.

Shakes clock.

Indicates throwing of object-clock out of window —

Image = shortstop hurling a baseball.

Looks at object clock. Studies it for a moment.

Laughs.

Puts clock back in its place.

Goes to phonograph. Plays "Anyway You Want It."

Sits on bed. Stares out front with a blank, bewildered expression on his face. Looks at audience faces. Toward the middle of the record he slowly places his hands over his face.

Record end: reject.)

CURTAIN

John Gilman and Robert Frink in the 1968 revival of
Robert Heide's *Moon*

*Photo by James D. Gossage, provided through the
courtesy of Robert Patrick*

MOON
Robert Heide[1]

Caffe Cino Première: February 1967
Caffe Cino Revival: February 1968

ENVIRONMENT: The set should be a maximum of simplicity and symmetry meant only to "represent" symbolically an apartment in the Village.

The room and the objects in it are of a dark bilious color.

In contrast blazing white light like the high-power-intensity lighting that might be used inside of a microscope.

On the wall: A square of multi-colored plastic with two transistor knobs which represent dials used in the play to turn sound "on" and "off."

The usual areas and objects: windows *(4th wall)* shelves, tables, seating arrangements, kitchen facilities — a range, coffee pot, cups, etc., the outer hallway and door into the apartment.

CHARACTERS:

SALLY:	A young woman in a loose-fitted black sweater and skirt. An unmade-up appearance. Ballet slippers.
SAM:	A young man. A turtle-neck sweater. Baggy pants. Sandals or slippers. He does not bother combing his hair.
INGRID:	A girl dressed in the latest and most exaggerated of the newest fashion, with emphasis on breasts, legs and shoulders. Flat shoes. She enters and leaves wearing a black fur coat. Her dress is silver. She carries a large handbag filled with pill boxes, make-up, poppers, anything imaginable.
HAROLD:	A tall young man. Dungarees. A leather jacket. Heavy workman's shoes that are coated with mud.
CHRISTOPHER:	The young man upstairs. White pants. White shirt. A clean, scrubbed appearance. A look of innocence.

The characters, with the exception of CHRISTOPHER and INGRID, wear black.

---

[1] Rights to *Moon* are under U.S. copyright protection. Permission to perform or reprint this work must be obtained in writing from: Robert Heide, 84 Christopher St., # 3-R, New York NY 10014-4253.

AT RISE: SAM is reclining on the daybed, back to audience. SALLY sits closely on a low stool. SALLY breathes heavily, twitching and playing restlessly with her hands. She stares full force at SAM as if she expected some movement on his part. She makes a quiet, gurgling sound in an attempt to attract attention. SAM remains tight-faced, his head buried deeply into an open book. It is not discernible whether or not he is actually reading. He seems tense, withdrawn. Abruptly, SALLY jumps up as though she were about to let out a scream. She paces wildly like a confined beast. Her body seems to heave as if she even felt 'trapped' in it. Quickly, she switches 'on' the phonograph. Over the speaker system we hear "2,000 Light Years" by the Rolling Stones. SALLY dances wildly attempting to distract SAM. She soon becomes caught in a free-form dance. Perhaps she is rehearsing for a dance class. The record begins to repeat itself. About one-quarter of the way through the second playing, SAM rushes up and shuts off the machine with forceful intent and anger as if he might begin to let loose a rage at any given moment.

SAM: *(Loud, nervous.)* There are times I'd like some . . . silence . . . around here . . . peace of mind . . . quiet! *(Pause.)*

SALLY: *(Pacing back and forth.)* I . . . ha . . . ha . . . feel nervous . . . fidgety myself. There's somehow a tenseness . . . a heaviness in the air. I don't know. I mean . . . *(Slight pause.)* . . . I'm not sure what . . . Oh nothing . . . I guess I'm just a little on edge . . . *(She sits down. Pause.)*

SAM: *(Sitting.)* What happened last night . . . to us? I don't seem . . . I'm not able to remember . . . anything.

SALLY: *(Getting up, confronting him.)* You became violent . . . you had consumed a great deal of liquor . . . it was strange . . . I mean — I had never known you to become so violent before. You came at me and . . .

SAM: Let's not talk about it. Let's go into something else . . . some other subject . . . something less . . . strenuous.

SALLY: *(Moving further into him.)* Maybe you're feeling guilty.

SAM: I don't want to talk about it . . . whatever it is . . . you want to go into it . . . I don't! That's final . . . whatever it is — I say!

SALLY: Whatever what is? *(Pause.)* Look! Will you just talk to me? Talk? *(Pause.)* Well, I can't take it.

SAM: Take what?

SALLY: Your silence. Your withdrawals. Your . . . non-communication. I'm fed up. *(Pause.)*

SAM: I'm sick . . . I feel sick. I have a hangover. My head is bad. All day I . . . oh, what's the . . .

SALLY: Does that mean we can't talk . . . say anything? *(Pause.)* Maybe you'd rather be alone. Have your withdrawal . . . alone. It feels stuffy in here. Hot.

Close. I can't breathe. Maybe I'd better go out. Get some air . . . (*Beginning to go out, moves frenetically.*)

SAM: (*Gets up. Pulls her down. Slaps her.*) Sit down! Relax your complicated little anxieties. Have some coffee. Later we will discuss whatever it is that needs discussing between . . . ourselves . . . between us. For now, let us discuss only everyday things. My mind . . . (*Slight pause.*) . . . Later I will be . . . prepared to face . . . to look at the ugliness . . . the abstractions . . . the truth of things. Here, smoke a cigarette.

SALLY: (*Putting cigarette to her mouth and lighting it nervously. Quickly, she extinguishes it. Gets up, moves downstage.*) Today is not such a good day for me. I feel . . . nervous . . . ha . . . ha. Sometimes I don't know what is happening to me, either . . . what is the matter with me. Something stirs up inside of me . . . like some blind instinct I can't control . . . inside of me. I feel I could burst open . . . explode. I get to feeling desperate. I want to run somewhere . . . away . . . I just don't know . . . where . . . out to the store . . . to a movie.

SAM: (*Behind her.*) Just try to remain calm . . . try . . . (*Slight pause.*)

SALLY: (*More composed.*) Let's begin again . . . a new conversation . . . not relating to yesterday at all . . . uh . . . tell me . . . I mean . . . Let us forget those few moments of anxiety we just had . . . begin again. Calmly. Can we? Can we begin again calmly? Yes. (*Pause. SALLY puts her head into SAM's lap as she sits on the floor.*) What kind of day . . . tell . . . what it was like . . . earlier . . . what you did . . . what went on?

SAM: (*Reserved.*) Just a day. The usual happenings. Statistical reports. Office rituals. Making additions and additions and pushing buttons . . . then . . . (*Pause.*)

SALLY: What?

SAM: (*Half to himself.*) Oh, nothing . . . I was thinking about things not really adding up . . . anywhere . . . in my head . . . I mean . . . my life.

SALLY: (*Jumping up.*) Is that some personal inference to me? Are you meaning to imply . . . ?

SAM: (*In a rage, grabbing her.*) Look, will you shut up before I break your arm? Shut up, I said!

SALLY: (*A pause. A transition.*) Did you see today's paper? Did you see the paper . . . read the news today?

SAM: I didn't feel like looking at it . . . my head and all. I had two Bromo Seltzers. What an idiotic party! Stupid people! "Hello, and what do you do with your life, young man? How are you justifying your existence?" Blah! Social events! (*A slight pause. SAM moves onto the floor.*) Anything in it?

SALLY: What?

SAM: In the paper . . . anything in it . . . today's paper . . . of interest . . . that I should know . . . be informed about?

SALLY: *(Circling around him.)* Only the usual everyday chaos . . . problems. Someone slashed open five people . . . with a knife. He tied them up, gagged them and . . . in Texas . . . I think it was. A young man. Eighteen. In a beauty parlor it was. Five women. He said he did it for the publicity, to get his name in the paper. He wanted to be a celebrity . . . become recognized . . . I guess. Something about high food prices having something to do with the high cost of war . . . or something. Some paintings . . . old masterpieces . . . were stolen. *(Coughing and gagging.)* Air pollution. *(Slight pause. She gets onto the floor with SAM. Lights go down.)* The moon. There was a feature article on the moon. *(Laughing to herself.)* It's strange . . . funny . . . I mean.

SAM: What's funny?

SALLY: *(Playful.)* I mean . . . I was just thinking . . . you can't really talk about the moon the same old way anymore like people used to in Shakespeare's plays and all. You can't say . . . with poetic emphasis . . . "O Moon!" like in "Romeo and Juliet" or *(Singing now, somewhat flatly.)* "It's only a paper moon . . . hanging over a cardboard sea" or *(More throaty. Matronly, like Kate Smith.)* "When the moon comes over the mountain." I'm really crazy about Kate Smith aren't you? God Bless America. *(Low.)* Moo . . . Moooooooooon. *(Dramatically — staring forward.)* "The cow jumped over the moon . . . hey diddle diddle the cat and his fiddle . . ." or something. The whole idea struck me as just 'funny' . . . somehow . . . I guess . . . ridiculous Moon. Blah! I mean there it is . . . really just there . . . if yah wanna look at it. No longer just some romantic 1920's sing-song abstraction . . . something to aspire to . . . to look at from a great distance through a telescope. Wait. Here's a picture. I'll show you. *(Goes to handbag and brings out a newspaper; sits back down.)* Here. *(Pointing.)* I mean doesn't it look odd and bumpy and all? See . . . here! Right here is this diagram . . . the first moon city. Moon city. They plan to build it . . . to live there . . . a whole lot of people . . . on the moon — eventually . . . soon . . . in the not-too-distant-future. And Later, Mars . . . Venus. Whole communities under a huge air-conditioned-oxygenized plastic bubble! It's kinduv fantastic . . . I think . . . I mean living up there in space and all . . . I mean not that we're not in space too . . . right here . . . already, now . . . I mean . . . well . . . people . . . the idea of it . . . real people . . . you and I maybe . . . and everybody . . . living on the moon. It would be like being a real pioneer . . . up there. The first experimental community . . . mmm.

SAM: *(Bursting her dream bubble, he gets up. Brighter light.)* So when do we make reservations?

SALLY: Huh?

SAM: *(Going back to his novel.)* Reservations . . . numbskull. Plans? Don't we have to make plane or rocket reservations . . . or something?

SALLY: *(Deflated. Sad. Bewildered by her own enthusiasms.)* Yeah . . . yes . . . I guess so. *(Pause. Angrily.)* Probably it won't happen for some time though . . . even . . . in our lifetime, I mean. A moon community. Maybe it will.

SAM: *(Taking over the room like an actor.)* Probably it will turn out to be just another Levittown, U.S.A. . . . the U.S.A. starring Richard M. Nixon and Spiro Agnew . . . with shopping centers, five and ten cent stores, Grand Unions, Bowling Alleys . . . Super highways, movie houses *(Slightly deflated.)* . . . beauty parlors. *(Finally SAM brings things back to some notion of reality. There is a prolonged silence in which the two characters do not utter a sound.)* My book . . . the book I was reading . . . did you see it?

SALLY: *(Looking.)* What? Oh. Book. Uh . . . no . . . let me see . . .

SAM: *(Looking around the room.)* I don't know where it is. *(Finding it.)* Ah, here it is! I found it. *(He sits down. He begins to read.)*

SALLY: Can we hear the radio?

SAM: No! I'd rather it remain 'off' if you don't mind. I'd rather listen to just . . . silence.

SALLY: Okay. Okay. Don't yell! *(Slight pause, nervous.)* Would you like some coffee?

SAM: If you're gonna make some . . . if you're having some . . .

SALLY: *(In the kitchen area.)* Is the book good?

SAM: What?

SALLY: *(Looking for a confrontation.)* Damn you. Will you listen! I said — is the book you are reading any good?

SAM: It's okay.

SALLY: *(Angry.)* Well. Why are you reading it if it's just okay? Haven't you any better way to live out your existence?

SAM: How?

SALLY: Hmmmm. I don't know. You said once you wanted to paint a picture or something.

SAM: *(Ignoring her last statement.)* No. I mean it's good . . . I guess. *(Slight pause.)* Anyhow, I know how it ends.

SALLY: *(Curious.)* How?

SAM: *(Perturbed.)* How?

SALLY: *(Demanding.)* How?

SAM: *(Scratching his head.)* Hmmmm. Well . . . you really wanna hear? Well . . . this couple have been making it, see. I mean both of them are married . . . I mean each one to someone else like, but they are having this affair see . . . with one another, that is. Get it?

SALLY: Yeah. Dope!

SAM: So they are driving back from this weekend on the French Riviera, St. Tropez, I think. It's French . . . the book . . . I mean it takes place, see, in France. Well, the whole book is about how they can't . . . either one of them . . . have an affair . . . even . . . anymore.

SALLY: What?

SAM: Anyhow, they are suffering from a kind of modern metaphysical bore-dom . . . and all . . . living in an increasingly mechanized and alienated world. They feel alienated from one another . . . alienated even to them-selves . . . see . . . each individual self. They can't get together . . . yet they can't really be apart either. He . . . the man, is married to this famous chan-teuse named Cleo who is never at home 'cause she has this . . . her ca-reer . . . and so he feels, existentially speaking, that he is in her eyes — like an object, like an old table or chair — very Sartrean — I mean, they talk a lot about life being one big nothing and all . . . in the book. *(Slight pause.)* Or was it Heidegger?

SALLY: *(Under her breath.)* Heidegger.

SAM: See, he, the main character, is a philosophy student. So, anyhow, he doesn't feel related to this wife who is so obsessed . . . uptight . . . having this "overneed" for her career. She sings these very sorrowful songs — *(SALLY jumps up making a screeching sound. Looks stage front. Looks into fourth wall mirror.)* and, when she's not doing that, she is looking in the mirror — checking out her image and all. Well, she doesn't like sex either.

SALLY: *(Loudly.)* Who? Who?

SAM: Cleo . . . even though she's supposed to be some sex image to her fans. They write her dirty suggestive letters which she, in turn, answers. *(SALLY mimics letter writing.)* See. It makes Henri, that's our hero's name, feel dis-gusted . . . even though he never brings the subject forth . . . out into the open. So Henri takes up with Francois . . . see. She's married . . . kinduv . . . to this uncle of hers who's this novelist . . . older. Anyhow, he knows about the affair. In fact, he encourages it. See, he's bored, too . . . with everything.

SALLY: *(Worried.)* Then what happens?

SAM: Well, it gets complicated 'cause everywhere they go . . . well . . . it gets more and more frenetic . . . the tension . . . the plot . . . hysterical . . . and Francoise thinks she is pregnant by some Oriental houseboy, too. *(He grabs SALLY. They play out the "game" of the novel fully. They mimic driving a car together.)* Well, being bored and all she drives off on this highway into this Mack Truck. *(SALLY screams.)* In a red Porsche — sort of like James Dean. It ends with a double funeral where Cleo sings "Chanson de Morte," "The Song of Death." *(Lights down. At this point we hear the voice of Cleo singing in French over the loud speaker with full orchestra. This goes on for one full minute. Lights up.)* But everyone is bored even there, too. I mean, what does death mean if you're really hip and all? Anyhow, to make a long story short . . . Cleo meets the uncle . . . at the funeral, which the uncle paid for . . . heh . . . heh . . . and they grab hands . . . *(SALLY and SAM grab hands. Hollywood music ensues loudly. They act out a Hollywood ending.)* . . . touch one another. They feel . . . well . . . through the death of Francoise and Henri they have a reawakening . . . a kinduv catharsis into . . . being able to "really" feel and all. You know, like maybe things are not so bad after all? So anyway, they go off and make it or something. I mean it ends on a kinduv positive note . . . y'know. *(Music off.)* But not too positive . . . heh . . . heh. Hey, are you listening?

SALLY: I thought you said you just read the end?

SAM: *(In a fury.)* Yeh, I did, but I read this review of it in *The Village Voice*. I mean, they gave the whole story and all. That's what made me wanna read it. They said it was . . . well . . . subtle in its exploration of character relationship . . . that's what made me wanna read it. I mean . . . *(Intense, angry.)* . . . people feel alienated. They don't know how to get together. Oh, Christ . . . I don't know! Don't ask me questions about what I'm reading. I lost my goddamn place!

SALLY: *(Dreamy.)* Maybe they'll make a movie out of it.

SAM: Yeah . . . they are already with Jean Seberg and Marcello . . . no . . . it's not him . . . somebody like him . . . Belmondo . . . no. It's . . . what the hell is his name? Trig . . . Trig . . . Trigonet . . . Jean Louis Trintignant. I wish I had a name like that. Yeah. *(Movie soundtrack music pours forth. The lighting goes kaleidoscopic.)* Brigitte Bardot will be Cleo and maybe Charles Boyer for the uncle. Ha ha. A super-Technicolor, panavistic . . . spectacle . . . in pornovision! *(On the word "pornovision" SAM and SALLY roll around on the floor together in mock copulation. They breath heavily, remaining on the floor. They make sounds, then separate exhausted, still on the floor.)*

SALLY: *(Entering movieland.)* Jean-Louis Trintignant. Wasn't he in *The Sleeping Car Murders?* Didn't we see that at the Eighth Street . . . or was it the Garrick?

SAM: Did we see that? Did we see that one?

SALLY: Yeah . . . I remember . . . you fell asleep in it.

SAM: Oh, was it good?

SALLY: Okay, I guess. It's not my type of thing.

SAM: Who got murdered?

SALLY: Murdered?

SAM: Yeah. "Sleeping Car Murder." Murder mystery. Who got murdered?

SALLY: *(Getting up.)* Six people . . . I think . . . two homosexual lovers plot the whole thing to get this lottery check from this actress . . . Simone Signoret. She is in love with one of them . . . not knowing he's gay . . . or knowing . . . and thinking she can change his direction . . . I don't remember which. Ha.

SAM: *(Moving restlessly.)* Oh, yeah . . . and one of them works for the cops or something . . . as a detective . . . and he's working to try to solve the case.

SALLY: Then, you weren't sleeping?

SAM: Well, partly.

SALLY: *(Running after him, tickling him.)* How does it end? I'll *murder* you, you ass. How does it end? Tell me.

SAM: *(Rolling on to the floor.)* Stop it! Cut it out! Stop!

SALLY: *(Straddling him.)* They don't make it. They're gonna live happily ever after on some South Sea Island in a rose-covered cottage on Simone Signoret's money . . . but they don't make it. They get caught and they don't make it. Ha! Ha!

SAM: *(Half sarcasm, half humor — getting up.)* Tough! Nobody makes it, bitch.

SALLY: *(Serious now. Angry.)* They don't? Why not?

SAM: *(Flying into fantasy.)* Cause I say so and I'm the President and I have the power and I'm gonna blow up the whole world anyway. Blow it up. *(Throwing imaginary hand grenades.)* Boom. BOOM! Boom.

SALLY: *(Confronting.)* You're a paranoid-schizophrenic living in Greenwich Village with delusions of grandeur and an inclination toward anticipating disaster out of every situation. Ha. How's that for a penny analysis?

SALLY: *(Furious.)* I could be Jesus Christ and you wouldn't know the difference.

SALLY: *(In a full-fledged argument.)* He was another paranoid, too.

SAM: Says who?

SALLY: *(Moving in circles around SAM.)* Albert Schweitzer, baby . . . in this book I read, "A Psychiatric Study of Jesus." He said there is a lot of evidence to support that old J.C. may have been another psychotic with another Christ complex out to save the whole world just like you, or maybe destroy it.

SAM: *(Throwing his arms around her as if they were about to ascend into space.)* Boom. Boom. Boom. Then we could go live . . . pioneer on the old green cheese moon.

SALLY: *(Breaking off. Sitting.)* Ah, who cares. I'm sick of the whole world anyhow. Why pretend anything else? *(Pause.)*

SAM: You sure you read that book correctly?

SALLY: Whadahyamean?

SAM: I mean you're always reading things into things. Your fantasy projection transferences. *(No reply. Pause.)* How about lighting a joint? *(Goes to kitchen where he gets joint.)*

SALLY: *(After him in the kitchen.)* Go ahead! You light it! Transcend existence. Catatonize yourself. What do I care!

SAM: *(Grabbing her, pulling her down.)* What!?

SALLY: Go ahead! Break my arm too.

SAM: Nobody's breaking your arm. *(Slight pause. SALLY waves her arm at SAM in jest and anger.)* Let's sit down and keep quiet . . . shut up . . . for a while.

SALLY: *(A last stand.)* You'd like to avoid all communications with me . . . just blow pot all day long . . . reach Nirvana or something . . . who knows what or where you want to get to. The moon. Dreams. Movies. I'm sick of it all. It's all just *lies* anyway. *(Hysterical.)* Lies! *(Screaming.)* Lies!

SAM: Now, calm down. You're having one of your free floating anxiety attacks again. Just calm down, sweets . . . love . . . valentine.

SALLY: *(Biting.)* At least it's not free-floating paranoia or simple-schizophrenia or some swimming-in-a-sea-of-ambiguity . . . like you.

SAM: Your terminology is really flying. You sound like some coffee-klatch in the dorm after Psych 1 at N.Y.U. The girl who's always waving her hand in the last row who knows all the answers but none of the . . . now, just calm yourself. Here. *(Hands her a joint.)* Light it. *(She does.)* It's not the answer, I know, any more than acid, speed, THC . . . or going to the moon. But it does manage to keep me calm . . . sometimes. *(He sits.)* My nerves. My body is still depressed from all that rotten alcohol we drank last night. Put on some music . . . on the machine. Indian. *(Gets onto the floor in yoga position.)* I want to meditate . . . concentrate . . . groove . . . with something . . . spiritual.

SALLY: *(Standing over him.)* Do I have to meditate? *(She puts on Indian raga music. They sit, eyes closed, attempting meditation. After a moment.)* I can't concentrate on anything today. Somehow . . . I . . .

SAM: Shut up! Meditate . . . or just keep your trap shut! I can't talk anymore. *(They remain silent, listening to the music, passing a joint back and forth to one another. After a long moment, INGRID and HAROLD are heard by the audience moving down the corridor outside the apartment. They are pushing and shoving one another physically close to violence.)*

INGRID: *(Berating loudly, trumpeting.)* What kind of people don't put their names on the bell . . . I ask you?! *(She passes back and forth looking at various doorways.)* I think what they told us was Four-R . . . that means rear! These stairs are killing me. Maybe we should go back down . . . go have a drink somewhere by ourselves. Oh, wait. Here. *(Looking.)* There's nothing more embarrassing than knocking on the wrong door. *(She pulls out a nose popper and begins sniffing, trying to get higher.)* That man was naked and I think he was having sex in there . . . with a boy too. Sex has a very decisive, odoriferous smell I tell you. Don't you have anything to say? *(Moving close.)* I suppose you would like to have joined in or something, into the sexual act, but yet you can't raise it when it comes to me. *(At this point INGRID reaches into her handbag. She pulls out a pillbox and begins gulping pills. She offers one to HAROLD. He refuses.)* Now try to compose yourself. *(Slight pause.)* Act natural. Try not to indicate . . . to show . . . that we are having marital difficulties. It's not in good taste to wear your problems out in the open for public consumption as it were . . . this being a social situation. Now try to remember these simple rules . . . Oh . . . ha ha . . . Here we are. Hello. Hello. *(Loud. Demanding.)* Anybody home? Hello. Shhh. Shh.

SALLY: *(Disrupted.)* What's that?

SAM: *(Trancelike.)* What . . . Shhh . . . Quiet! I'm thinking . . . *(SALLY, realizing a presence, gets up and turns off the music. Puts on ballet slippers.)*

INGRID: *(A false cheerfulness.)* Uh . . . Hi — You . . . uh . . . left your door open. Can we come in? *(Examining the place suspiciously.)* You shouldn't leave your door open . . . you know, with all the murders, rapes and robberies going on . . . in the city . . . uh . . . heh . . . mmm. *(An awkward silent heavy tension takes over the room. The two couples stalk one another.)*

SALLY: *(Polite, pulling herself together, breaking the freeze.)* Oh . . . well . . . come in . . . sit down . . . wherever you can . . . there's not much room. Let me have your coat.

INGRID: Yes. *(Removes her coat and scarf. SALLY disposes of it quickly, goes to HAROLD.)*

SALLY: Harold, your jacket!

HAROLD: *(Staring downward. A tight lip.)* I prefer to keep it on . . . thank you.

INGRID: *(Moving toward the couch.)* A cold, Harold is afraid of catching a cold, aren't you Harold? *(No answer. A false merriment.)* I said to Harold . . . I bet you people forgot about having us over . . . er . . . the party . . . last night? Remember? Ha . . . ha . . . Well, we almost didn't come. *(An awkward pause.)* We had your address . . . your phone number. We were gonna call . . . first. We tried. Didn't we honey? Didn't we try?

HAROLD: *(Dull, not listening.)* Yeah.

INGRID: *(Anxious. Somewhat terrified.)* You've had your phone disconnected. I said to Harold. "I bet you forgot." It was just a casual, meaningless suggestion on your part. Just drop by. And here we are . . . Heh . . . mmm. *(Slight pause. To SAM.)* Harold would rather have his face in the TV or be screwing nuts and bolts into his machines. It was my decision to venture out. *(Cor-*

nering SALLY.) You can still renege . . . shoo us off . . . if you want to be alone. Tee . . . hee.

SALLY: *(Trying to place her guests in her mind.)* Oh . . . uh . . . no . . . uh . . . we don't mind. We were just . . . sitting . . . listening to some music . . . weren't we? Why . . . uh . . . don't you sit . . . ?

INGRID: I'll just sit down. *(Accidentally falling.)* OOooooooooooo!

HAROLD: *(Half to himself.)* The clumsy never succeed.

INGRID: *(Getting up, menacingly.)* What did you say?

HAROLD: I said . . . "The clumsy never succeed" . . . just an old saying from my mother.

INGRID: *(Angry, staring long and hard.)* Your mother! She certainly didn't teach *you* anything . . . about success in the real world. *(HAROLD moves toward her with violent intent. Abruptly, she switches her attitude to the coquette, realizing she is with "others.")* What an interesting and cute apartment you have. Ha. Ha. Very bizarre. Very interesting. I'm sure our turning up is a complete surprise . . . I said to Harold . . . it was a casual suggestion . . . on your part. *(Desperate.)* Lots of people write their names and addresses on little pieces of paper and hand them to people they meet . . . at parties . . . never really expecting . . . acknowledgement . . . or a visitation.

SALLY: It doesn't matter. We were very drunk. Part of the evening is a complete blur . . . in both of our minds. Yes? *(HAROLD walks blindly into SALLY. She stares full force at him, then breaks it off.)* Something happened which we don't remember. *(This last statement is followed by a long dead silence in which the four characters stare blankly, bewilderedly at one another. An uncomfortable tension takes over the room.)*

INGRID: *(Gazing at HAROLD and SALLY.)* Er . . . ah.

SALLY: *(Snapping her fingers nervously.)* We . . . uh . . . were having some coffee. *(Pause.)* Would anybody like some coffee . . . or something?

HAROLD: *(Following her.)* Yeah.

INGRID: *(Nervous, trying to make conversation.)* Harold doesn't say much . . . really . . . in company. *(Cornering, advancing toward SALLY in kitchen.)* We were just married . . . a year it is. We're just beginning to get used to one another . . . understand our position in relationship to one another as to who has the upper hand and all that stuff. He's a little shy . . . awkward . . . ha . . . ha . . . in a social situation. *(Slight pause. Leaves kitchen. Sits next to SAM on sofa.)* What time did you people leave last night's festivities?

SALLY: *(Moving away from HAROLD's steady advances.)* Time? What . . . time? I'm not sure . . .

INGRID: *(Angry. Sarcastic.)* We left early. Harold got sick . . . mixing the drinks. Didn't you, Harold? Didn't you get sick last night?

HAROLD: *(With controlled violence, a smirk across his face.)* Yeah.

INGRID: That's why we left early. I mean as opposed to staying on and on. Harold feels . . . that it's better to leave before things . . . people . . . become decadent as they very often do at parties. He wouldn't like it . . . *(She moves closer to SAM putting her arm around his neck seductively.)* I mean . . . if somebody tried to screw . . . I mean . . . rape me . . . made advances or anything. *(More excited.)* Harold is capable . . . I mean Harold might . . . it is within his capacity to murder someone. Didn't you say you might murder someone Harold . . . if someone . . . I mean . . . made advances on me . . . on my person . . . at a party . . . or someplace?

HAROLD: Yeah.

INGRID: *(Going into her purse.)* I carry this tear-gas gun. My Aunt Emma gave it to me . . . She sent it through the mail all the way from Kansas . . . that's where I'm from . . . mmm. You never know about men . . . she says . . . in New York City. *(She gets up and pulls out gun, points it bluntly at SAM.)* You wanna see it?

HAROLD: *(Grabs her. They wrestle for the gun.)* Gimme that!

INGRID: Harold! You're hurting me. It might go off. Harold!

HAROLD. *(Twisting her arm, throwing her down.)* Sit down!

INGRID: My arm!

SALLY: *(Ignoring the situation, trying to remain cool.)* I think coffee is ready.

SAM: *(Quietly.)* You people like music?

INGRID: *(Going up to HAROLD.)* We should apologize.

HAROLD: *(Breaking from her.)* I'll do my own apologizing if there's any to be done. *(To the rest of the room.)* What my wife, Ingrid, is trying to communicate to you all is that I have . . . a kind of . . . violent personality . . . an uncontrollable temper. When I get worked up . . . *(Pause. He sits down. Lights go dim.)* You see, I was a Marine . . . in the Marines. *(Slight pause.)* Of course . . . even as a kid . . . well . . . I'm not sure what it is. *(Slight pause.)* Back in Texas where I come from . . . a man was murdered . . . I mean to say that I don't conceal any longer this nightmare truth. I loved him . . . I guess. He was my buddy . . . in the Marines and after. We went everywhere . . . together. Well, one night . . . we shared a double bed . . . I . . . *(Slight pause.)* He was asleep. I was fooling . . . kidding around. I put a pillow over his face. He had asthma or something . . . respiration trouble. Anyway, in the fooling around . . . he stopped breathing. I took the pillow off his face. His eyes were opened . . . staring . . . at me. Later, there was an inquest you see. I was set free. It was decided that what he had had was a heart attack. Somehow, in me . . . I knew that . . .

INGRID: *(Jumping up abruptly.)* Oh . . . Stop it! Stop telling everyone you meet that morbid and ludicrous story. You don't know . . . you can't be absolutely certain that it wasn't an accident. You said that he had a heart condition . . . or something. Why continue to implicate yourself any further? This wallowing in guilt.

HAROLD: *(Still "in" the story. Moves up.)* There is . . . there was . . . an intention . . . somewhere . . . in me. There must have been. I don't understand.

INGRID: *(Quickly. Going at him like an attorney that is onto a victim.)* We understand! It is obvious . . . psychologically obvious . . . a clear deduction that you were in love with this man . . . that because of convention . . . this love . . . you could not consummate it. It turned then into hatred. You hated yourself and him for remaining unfulfilled . . . repressed.

HAROLD: *(Loud.)* Shut up!

INGRID: *(Moving in tightly.)* Why lie! You can't express . . . the truth. So you choose me with all my convenient sexual fears to share your guilt . . . to continue to support your image of manhood . . . punishing me for what was done to you by your family. I'm tired of playing the role of mother-substitute. I'm . . .

HAROLD: Shut up, I say . . . you bitch! *(He grabs her throat, pulls her to her knees and begins to strangle her with intent to kill. We hear INGRID make a gurgling sound. SAM and SALLY watch frozen in terror.)*

SAM: *(Finally.)* This will have to stop! *(SAM pulls HAROLD off of INGRID bodily forcing him to yield his grip. They are on the verge of a fist fight.)* You will both have to leave, just *leave!*

INGRID: *(Still on the floor.)* I'm sorry. Please. Let us stay. Just for a moment. Till we pull ourselves together. *(An awkward silence follows. INGRID stays on the floor for a long while. Finally she gets up. Goes to kitchen. Gets a drink. Sits back on sofa.)* Harold has vivid fantasies. He goes to an analyst three times a week. These stories . . . he . . . prefabricates them to bring attention to himself. There is no basis in truth to what has been said. *(SAM moves to the phonograph.)*

SAM: *(Nervous.)* Do . . . uh . . . you like music? I'll put on a record.

SALLY: Not now.

INGRID: *(Sitting nervously, humiliated.)* Yes . . . play it . . . anything.

(They listen through a three-minute record, Dave Clark Five, "Do You Love Me?" During the record the lights go up. INGRID swallows about seven different pills. HAROLD and SALLY stare at one another. HAROLD is attracted. SALLY is strangely drawn to his look. SAM begins to do a shaking rock and

roll dance. Each character is caught in his own private world, lost, lonely, bewildered. At the end of the record, SALLY puts on her coat and hat.)

SALLY: *(Quickly.)* Er . . . ah . . . ha . . . ha. Would . . . uh . . . you all excuse me for a moment? I think there is something I forgot at the store. *(She leaves.)*

INGRID: *(Desperate.)* Where is she going?

SAM: *(Half dazed.)* She said to the store. She sometimes leaves abruptly.

INGRID: Her leaving seemed peculiar just then. *(INGRID looks at HAROLD. He is onto the sofa laying down, legs outstretched, reading SAM's book. INGRID gets onto the floor herself. She heaves convulsively, making sounds. She has taken too many drugs. The room spins in her head. She gets half up after a long moment.)* I don't know. I'm not sure why . . . we came here. Harold . . . we must go . . . home . . . now. *(Getting her things.)* I feel a sudden panic seizing hold of me here. *(Going up to SAM.)* I am sorry. Perhaps we will see you again . . . sometime. Harold, leave one of our cards. *(They put on their things and proceed to leave.)* You invited us from the party. *(She menaces SAM a final time.)* I said to Harold earlier that you had probably forgotten. Goodbye. Come along, Harold.
(SAM waves half-heartedly with his hand, his back turned to the audience. There is a long moment in which he walks about the room examining its various sections. He goes to the phonograph but does not play it. He walks to window area (4th wall.) staring straight out. We hear traffic sounds. Finally, he lies down, exhausted. Enter slowly CHRISTOPHER in white pants and sweater. He carries a loaf of bread in pan.)

CHRISTOPHER: Er . . . ah . . . hello. *(No reply. SAM is asleep. Finally, startled by a strange presence, SAM jolts up, confronting CHRISTOPHER.)* We . . . my friend and I . . . we made some bread . . . upstairs. We just moved in. We had nothing to do today . . . so we made . . . we made some bread. *(Slight pause.)* There is a funny smell in here. Well, I'll just leave it then. *(Begins to leave.)*

SAM: *(Puzzled.)* No. Wait.

CHRISTOPHER: Yes?

SAM: *(Goes to him.)* Did you want something?

CHRISTOPHER: *(Quietly.)* No.

SAM: You moved in . . . upstairs . . . in the vacant rooms?

CHRISTOPHER: Yes.

SAM: What is your name?

CHRISTOPHER: Christopher. My friend is Joe. He's asleep.

SAM: Oh. *(Pause.)* Would you like some wine . . . or coffee?

CHRISTOPHER: *(Hesitant.)* No. I must get back. I'm a painter . . . see. I want to sort of get to bed early so I can get up . . . in the morning . . . to get the light. The skylight . . . the light here . . . upstairs . . . is the reason we took the space . . . it being on the top floor. I need it for my painting. The daylight. Well, as I said . . . I wanted to bring you down one of the loaves . . . we made two . . . see who was living underneath . . . introduce myself . . . So . . .

SAM: What do you paint?

CHRISTOPHER: *(Moving about the room, intense.)* Circles mostly. Just circles. You'll come up and see them sometime. I'm kinduv *obsessed* with circles, see. They are meant . . . I guess . . . to represent . . . ha . . . ha . . . the earth, sun, moon and all the other planets in the heavens, the solar system. I use many brilliant colors, electric colors, red, green . . . yellow . . . they hurt your eyes if you look at them too long. *(Pause.)* Well . . . we heard the music. We thought you might like some. We'll see you again . . . come back down . . . maybe . . . tomorrow you'll meet my friend. *(Exit CHRISTOPHER. There is a moment in which SAM stares at the bread. He picks it up putting it in the bread-box. Enter SALLY.)*

SAM: *(After a moment. Softly.)* Where did you go?

SALLY: I don't know . . . I just had to leave . . . get out . . . get some air. I brought back some milk. *(Puts paper bag she is carrying down.)*

SAM: They're gone.

SALLY: Yes, I see.

SAM: I don't remember ever having met them. Do you? . . . at the party?

SALLY: No . . . I . . . *(Pause.)* I don't want to talk about them . . . now.

SAM: What is it you want to do?

SALLY: I don't know.

SAM: What were you thinking about . . . what were you doing . . . what happened to you while you were out? Tell me. Talk to me. Philosophize . . . anything. I feel . . .

SALLY: *(Entering the game.)* Oh . . . not much happened . . . really. I walked around the same block two . . . three . . . times. I thought . . . if only there were someplace to go . . . to . . . to run away to. I thought . . . I would like to leave this city . . . go back to St. Louis where I came from — all the time knowing . . . inside . . . I could never go back there anymore. Backwards. I said to myself . . . "there is nowhere to go . . . nowhere left for you to run to." I passed by the newsstand . . . on the square. The headline on the evening paper glared up at me saying . . . "A Man Walks On the Moon." *(She laughs.)* It struck me as being funny somehow. Then, I ran back here . . . right then. Right away. That's all.

SAM: One day *(Lightly, in a matter-of-fact manner.)* . . . I suppose . . . as you said earlier tonight . . . there will be this community . . . a community of men who will be living on the moon in a plastic bubble . . . but it will not seem either strange or funny at all . . . to anyone who will just . . . be . . . there — in that situation. And things will not be that much different from what they are . . . right here . . . right now. The truth is none of us will really ever know anything about the deeper, darker mysteries of existence. We will never know . . . never . . . never really be certain about what it is we really are searching for in this life anyway . . . in this world. The endless questions . . . thoughts . . . that well up deep down inside of us. As of now . . . at this point in time and space we remain uncertain . . . except for having reached the moon — moo-oon. Hallelujah!

SALLY: *(Holding him — a determined, firm attitude.)* But if we could be certain . . . maybe . . . someday . . . of something more . . . than just the beating of our hearts. Listen! *(She puts his head to her breast.)* Boom. Boom. Boom. One day they will just stop pounding . . . but for now . . . they just go on . . . and on. Boom. Boom. Boom.

(Together.)

SAM:	SALLY:
BOOM	BOOM
BOOM	BOOM
BOOM	BOOM
BOOM	BOOM

CURTAIN

MONUMENTS
Diane di Prima

The Monologues that comprise this work
were among the last works performed at the Caffe Cino, in 1968

Directed by James Waring
Lights by Johnny Dodd
Stage Manager: Michael Smith

DID HE GO TO SCARSDALE?
PERFORMED BY JOHN HERBERT McDOWELL

FREDDIE'S MONOLOGUE
(FROM SPRING AND AUTUMN ANNALS)
FOR FRED HERKO, WHO DIED IN 1964
PERFORMED BY LEE FITZGERALD (A.K.A. WAHUNDRA)

ZIPCODE
PERFORMED BY DIANE DI PRIMA (STAGE NAME: MYRA MURK)

JOHN'S WORDS
PERFORMED BY JOHN BRADEN

HANDGRENADE
PERFORMED BY ALAN S. MARLOWE

BUTTERFLY SPICE
PERFORMED BY EDDIE BARTON

DID HE GO TO SCARSDALE?
for John Herbert McDowell

> Calico pie
> The little birds fly
> Out of the calico tree —

Oh, my pretty ones, I am ready to embrace you all. I am ready, quite ready
to romp on all your toes, to swallow your elbows. Do not let my red socks deter
you. I am impervious to my upbringing. The tinkling of martinis in the woods.
Glint of my mother's teeth as she smiles at me. Merry 14th Street! Take me by the
hand. Crunch. The tacos of the future. In my bed. The fruits of the earth, of the
city streets. Ramon and Edward, Paul, Philippe, and Mark. The phone is ringing,
who is at the door? My toy chest is on fire. I watch it burn. Green flame, a lurid
light on my high ceiling. Would you mind doing that again? Where are my
trousers?

> Berries from bushes
> Honey out of trees
> Up my spine so good, honey
> La.

Trick triumphs, true or false. Like playing checkers. Like showing movies
backwards on the ceiling. Like growing peaches backwards into flowers.

Do you doubt me? I scarcely believe myself. And all the pieces of me keep
coming apart. My spleen, my backbone, I juggle them in my hands. Movies on
Forty-Second Street come and go. I let them. I eat graham crackers. Cold from
my damp refrigerator. Chomp. I hang by my toes from the door jamb, whistling.
Flapping in the wind from my air conditioner. Someone is running up and down
my staircase. Is she keeping fit? His shorts are covered with forget-me-nots. I put
on my best striped towel and go to meet him.

Whose hose is up the chimney, what green tent has been pitched in the
back of my loft? Will I ever be caught? Like a fat old trout in the river I lick my
chops, wink at the seaweed as it goes drifting by. Study the bellies of logs and
alligators. Bandana on my head.

Master the light, then others shalt thou bear. La, dearie, the sounds you
made. Like a cracked bassoon. But I'm used to it, or should be. Making my bed,
four or five times in a day. Long summer afternoons. There's warm beer in the
kitchen.

Merrily, merrily shall I live now. Cracking jokes or walnuts. Eternally in the
tepid ambiance of friendship.

FREDDIE'S MONOLOGUE
(From Spring and Autumn Annals)

for Fred Herko, who died in 1964
Performed by Lee Fitzgerald (a.k.a. Wahundra)

Blasted fore & aft by cocks I stand astride in the windy park. Little birds peck at my bare toes, my staff broken off an 1890's bedstead, in my hand. Wind pulls at it, at my rags, my too-tight black lace panties under my jeans.

The sky takes care of me. I take my refuge in the hurricane. Which makes lace of my most undistinguished schmattas. I burn with the cocks that have pierced me, have poured their life into me. The assholes I have pierced form an aura about me. I am holy. I walk to Delancey Street for enchiladas. The Puerto Rican behind the counter recognizes me. He serves me quickly, salamms & makes obeisance. His dog lays back his ears against his head & growls. I lay my staff in my lap & eat a lot.

City of the sun, I walk in the night with my woman. She white, I black, in rags beneath the moon. Seeking always abandoned houses, parking lots. Pausing often to look in garbage barrels on corners. Singing in the blue light our minds have made of the air. Dancing from street to street, our arms full of rhinestones.

My rage stripped off by wind, my fat, my other face. Left behind, discarded on an abandoned roof. Like the ballet I wanted to make in a swimming pool. Like my beds and paintings, my clothes, altars, wisdom jewels. The little girls I taught. The summer sun. Never to come again to this stripped-down forehead.

I smile a lot, I am truly hollow within. Wind buoys me up, sun draws me to itself. Water caresses me. Earth enters all my pores. I say "Take care of the churches, the witches, the scattered bricks. Bejeweled zippers, the hearths. The children are dead." Or will be, soon, there is dancing, fix your teeth. Choose the best jewel for your turban. Turn backward. Make music, walking backward. WALK INTO THE EAST RIVER TO BATHE, CRYING OUT TO KRISHNA.

The horizon is opaque, made of pastels. The hills & cliffs of Jersey tiffany glass. Cast-iron bums eternally speak of lilies. Tear me loose from this love, like chunks of inedible chocolate. This new receding substance of our lives.

ZIPCODE
Performed by Diane di Prima (Stage Name Myra Murk)

Like a string of beads, my days slip from my fingers. They bounce, and roll skittering to the corners of the room. They fall so fast. They fall so fast. Will I never get away, as I promised myself I would. Never sit in a bay window in San Francisco, looking at the rain, and writing another novel? Or live in the woods at Big Sur with my new old man, large and unambitious, cutting wood and making music? As I never lived on the beach, tanned and leathery, carting home driftwood on my hip, laughing in the sun. My skin tasting of salt, and someone tasting it often.

Like a string of beads, the ones that I have loved. The faces that flash by on my way to sleep. The ones I love now, always out of reach. I sit in my hotel, behind squads of young men. All of no use to me, nor I to them. My drying skin, my heavy awkward thoughts. Colette in a wheelchair, the last of Chéri. Parallel husband beside me, never touching.

The days slip by like jewels, some grey some blue. Emeralds and moonstones, sapphires on my skin. Cool in my hands, and heavy in my hair. The faces slip like shadows out of sight. Roi, Freddie, Zella, Frank, the lightshow for this dance. I call to them in a mist which becomes smoke around me. More terrified of the soot and grey of my life than ever I was of the black and cold in the sky. The black and cold in my heart as I turned aside. Fleeing love thru the chasms and hills of California. To come up against it at last in a wooden shack. Beloveds all, who ate of my flesh, my spirit, unhand me, turn me around, I must face / in another direction.

Where I was the fisherman's daughter, by the sea. The girl who washed the towels of the kings. Where in Provence I loitered on balustrades, awaiting a voice, the long space between footsteps. Where in a cave I made soup for the revolution. Pulled mussels off the rocks, and gathered snails. Dark shops I ran, with guns hid in the back. Old anarchist presses snarling to themselves. Uncertain poolroom light from overhead falling on faces anger had made lovely. Anger and hunger. The beauty salon of the future.

Or walked the heath with a baby tied in my shawl. The songs I knew, the healing plants, the stars. Dark planet whose wandering sets all to rights. As I did then, with my hand on my man's sleeve.

A sacred frailty that is lost to me. Bright skin of former days. My hair let down, brocade I wore in Sienna. A footing on the bank of the Indus river. To breathe, to pray, to bathe in the morning wind. A hundred kinds of silk playing round my torso.

How many boats did I watch embark without me! Bright sails, the blond men moving south and west. Till my grandfather carried me here in his dark loins. Swam to this hostile shore and spat me out. And how many others? The island is peopled with them. Boys and girls come out to play / The moon doth shine as bright as day. And a green haze around it from this air.

To call you lover is to lose the game. A forties game, we stack like dominoes. As black and white, as square, as those square old movies. I move in a long gown thru these high, arched rooms. I am breathing hard, my cool is obvious. As it was on all those barstools in the fifties. The arms of painters that kept the cold night out. The cool of meeting one's lover at a party, where he came, with his wife. Leaving separately from him. Rendezvous at the Five Spot, and flowers in my hair. The dominoes clicked on the tables, the old men smoked.

Am I the priestess, or the page of cups? Whom do I wait for, there, at the edge of the sea. Blindfolded and cold as a statue, both my hands / crossed, and a sword in each. What name do I speak? Friend that I murdered in the sacred grove. Or slew on the bank of the river, by that big tree. Or fled thru Asia, hiding in my caves. Good friends, whose common dance made Europe bright. Unholy husband, wept over in Kathmandu. Your fingertips on my breastbone have turned me to ice. My skeleton smiles, my skull moves to & fro. Trembling receiver on a long, thin stalk.

JOHN'S WORDS
FOR JOHN BRADEN

Gold shimmers on the hill. It is the sparks of bonfires, thru the trees. Dark trees of the northern forests. Take my hand. Ice cracks at sea, the elf light skims the shore. Sheen of white fish which flap against the breakers. Desireless hours spent under twilight skies.

The sun travels east, just skimming the horizon. Shedding a golden light on moss and sedge. Great northern ferns turn black beneath my heels. I balance precariously on a winter wind. Which carries sea mist in, among the pines.

Is it a tale you're wanting? I'll sing you a song I'm making. I'm thinking of calling it "The Death of the Hermit."

good people you sit by your fires
you look in each other's eyes
you speak to each other for comfort
the cold winds rise

the hermit he sat by his fire
no voice could he hear but his own
the night of the forest is endless
the great trees groan

the sparks fly out of his chimney
they fall with a hiss on the snow
he whittles on wood in the evenings
and no tears flow

he looked to the sky for comfort
but clouds hid the morning star
he looked to the earth for comfort
but spring was far

he looked to the bitter holly
whose berries showed like blood
and wrapping his cloak about him
the hermit stood

and holding his light before him
he entered his hut once more
the evening star brought this wonder:
a child at the door

he laid two bowls on the table
he washed and warmed the lad
he made him a bed by the fire
his heart was glad

he wept till he slept in his corner
the sleeping child rose up
he burned one bowl in the fire
and one wood cup

he drew a knife from his waistband
he used it fast and well
with a sigh like the wind in the pine trees
the hermit fell

the child he sits by the fire
no voice does he hear but his own
the night of the forest is endless
the great trees groan

How sad beside this, my ruffs and laces. The finery I so love to affect. Shadows of great druid women loom over me. They slide in and out of my dreams like so many white wolves. Biting down. O, go to the earth for comfort. Armloads of herbs, baskets of soft wildflowers. The great birds of the southland, herons and cranes. Embracing in warm, wet gardens in the mist. Moss hanging from trees, the shape of my other dreamworld. The golden boys on gold and azure beaches. From which no boats of shell embark for elfland. Bright, garish pleasures crashing against my flesh.

Merlin leads me a merry dance from bed to bed. Hooded and grey, and always at my side. Morgan, his lady, never shuts her eyes. Her gaze is constant, directed at my heart. Which hangs like a crystal in the great ribbed halls of my chest. I shiver in the northwind, I am tired. Small, gentle people with dark eyes try to warm me. I thank them, and go my way, uncomforted. My love shines like a star behind a cloud. Something I have not seen. I swim toward it.

I feel myself sleek and furry, a water beast. Headed for home; gold hair against white gowns. Gold rings on thin white fingers, sliding loose. Lutes and great torches in the drafty halls. Or was that yesterday? I delivered papers. Scaled walls to steal the flowers of the rich. Beat back the pity that rose like gorge in my throat. Choking my lifebreath, making my thin hands tremble.

The tale is awry, I fear I've told it crooked. Another time, perhaps, I'll take you with me. Where the shafts of light thru the great trees of the north pierce you like steel and bring you to your knees. In the pitiless, white dawn . . .

HANDGRENADE
FOR ALAN MARLOWE

KAN JI ZAI BO SATSU GYO JIN HAN YA HA RA MIT TA JI SHO KEN . . .

The plastic buildings are melting around me. I set a match to them, and they collapse like celluloid. Not even any flames. Hello. Hello. What I mean to say is, that I am a poet, clearly, and in excellent physical shape. House in the country, house in town, an office or two. Thing is, I can't live in any of them. I live in the distance between one house and the other. One war and the next. A revolution comes once in a generation, lord knows, no more often than that. What are we waiting for? GRRRAAHHHHHHH!

Lady in a black veil named Madness stands at my door. Named sorrow. Void of ages, a shimmering black veil. She knocks every year or so, the door isn't locked. One day she'll discover that the door isn't locked. Pictric acid & black powder for bombs. Baby food jars are good. For barricades: mattresses, bags of cement, of salt. The enemy's line of defense will cut across Cooper Square. If you value your life, don't live near the Con Edison building. Watch out for the park, stick to your own neighborhood.

All this would be serious, if one lived only once. As often as monkeys swinging in the trees. Or our doubles take our place, all one, isn't it? To die in Benares means simply: to die in a state of grace. How much longer do you think the Taj Mahal will stand? Thank god for the bloody pavements of the future. Something to expect. Dusty roads across Asia, inheritance of my people. Mushroom and barley soup at Ratner's, a good stereo amplifier, another open car, for that it is spring. Cameras and tape machines and bell bottom trousers.

And I collect and honor men as I do my possessions. The beautiful minds, fine bodies, of my friends. Oh, the gardens I have seen, fine formal gardens of Europe! O, the wondrous houses of all my long-gone lovers! The six-masted schooner I mean to buy next year, or was it a Ferrari? Shall I go east or north? My underwear keeps getting lost at the laundry, the children tear the wallpaper on the walls, picking at the corners with their fingers. What bugs me most. My Chinese painting is warped. Plants are dying from the cold in all my windows.

It is a serious matter, but it is all nothing. A bagatelle. Form is the emptiness, and emptiness is the form. Matter for no astonishment, then, that we disappear. That no one counts our words. Nevertheless, the bright light in the sky, while Detroit was burning, while New York shall burn. That is something to live for. Like stars in the desert. Like the feel of a good horse under me, white light of meditation, white as the snow in the Alps, in the skiing season. I am as serious as Maya herself. And no more perfect.

Shell of a shell. My deads and livings whisper in my ears. I am more beautiful than they had dreamed. My long hair grows out of my shaven head. The Gemini again, taking off two ways at once. I have eaten brown rice for 24 days and nights, nevertheless I would like a chocolate éclair. My robes are hot, my jewels are glass. A sorry monk, half saint, half decoration, I look for a cooler climate in which to sport them.

Oh my loves, come with me in my Astin Martin to the edge of the sea. Negotiate these cliffs, ignore the rain. Pray for successful bombing of Seattle, and listen to the Indian chiefs turning in the earth. I am Gemini, caught in the mad crosscurrents of the year. 1968. Living in exaltation and despair. Feeling my pulsebeat in the roots of my hair. Crown chakra, shooting colors at the sky.

BUTTERFLY SPICE
FOR EDDIE BARTON

Am I a child? An owl? The air curves around me lightly as I poke my toes into the most inauspicious slippers. Silver-grey. Tootling the thinnest of flutes, and very merry, a one-eyed Pan with acne, I wave my hands like leaves above my head. All crowned as it is with mulberry leaves. I stretch full-length on a horsehair pillow. On my stomach, my chin digging in, I look at the sea. In & out it goes like a wind-up toy. A yo-yo. Making its rounds like the lines in the *Book of Changes*. Making its rounds like the milkman. Unhand me a little. I was planning to have a milkshake in Grant's, get my tea leaves read in a store-front, go to the movies. I was planning to change my shirt and study Russian. Or was that someone else? I can't keep track of the ins and outs of my head. Like breathing. Like a yo-yo. My door that opens and shuts on a regular basis. My silken skin like the skin of oranges. The bandanas of my future, a new satori.

Merrily, merrily shall I live now. Under the laundry that hangs on the bough. Tee shirts, dance belts, the paraphernalia of living. The paraphernalia of space in this apartment. Pineapple pickings pickled in lime juice. The marinated hearts of other hustlers. *Pas de bourrée en pointe*, first left, then right. Waving my hands like so many baby ducks. Seeing clear to the crystal heart of this deck of cards. The priestess and the hanged man making their rounds. With the easy, rocking motion of the tide.

Do you like those amethysts, my ankle bangles? Or watery rind of the mango, curled on my floor. Peeling back my sheets and looking at me with those eyes. Am I a child? An owl? Desire hits like starlings at my window. It swerves, it hits my wall, falls with a plop. Like the wolf falling down the chimney and into the soup. Like the thinnest of doll clothes in my closet. My granular rice cream, tapioca of the future.

He rose like a vision out of the banana split. Pirouetted on the maraschino cherry. All of three inches high, and shaking his head. Shaking his finger reprovingly at me. I mailed him to my brother. What would you do? Do you remember, love, the ancient tunes? Arching my back and falling to the floor. Looking under my pillow for all those bygone days. Feeling for them, with my hand, on my way to sleep.

St. Catherine wheels, Roman candles, burst into light in the center of my room. I lean on my elbow in bed, and look at them. Illuminating the flowers on my walls. Frightening the creatures that walk at night in all the air and spaces of this city. I point my toes, my ankles crack a little. A noise like crackerjacks. Stuffed owl with my eyes on the mantelpiece. Distressing augury, like a breath of spring. Like the first ant in your teepee, after winter.

Are you my child, my yo-yo? I am blind. Stealing marshmallow fluff in the A&P in the mornings. Living on brown rice at noon, sandalwood shavings / at dinner. Inspecting the rainbows at the ends of my socks. I shrug off the bears that come from the west to embrace me. Launching my cucumber boats on the windy brook.

Joe Cino and Michael Smith at the benefit hosted by the
Writers' Stage Theater on March 15, 1965, to fund repairs to
the Caffe Cino after the fire earlier that month

Photos by James D. Gossage

VORSPIEL NACH MARIENSTEIN
Michael Smith

by John P. Dodd, Michael Smith, and Ondine

SCENE: *Marienstein.*

CHARACTERS:

LUDWIG II
WAGNER
KUNDRY

LUDWIG: I am guilty of stifling my life, guilty.

WAGNER: I only want to be myself. *(Aside.)* Why does he always wear black?

LUDWIG: He's in mourning for his life.

> *(They part to opposite sides of the stage. They glance at each other and look away. Simultaneously.)*

LUDWIG *(Romantically)*: All my dreams come true. What am I thinking about? I think of nothing. All my friends are crazy except I don't have any friends. It's more than just funny, it's silly. It's a little dismal. Friendship is fatal — I'll take romance . . . What could he possibly want from me? Oh to be possessed! Why not a love duet before they've even met? I don't want to burden him with that kind of remorse. The thought is good, only it's not well put. *(Weeping.)* What a clumsy moment! I can't say the universe is shit. Wagner could. That's my favorite part of it. I'm not an actor. It's not hard to say these things. That was the Ludovisi nose. Madness doesn't have to relate to anything. I admire him for the right reasons. I need something concrete — that's a definite statement, but . . . My ineptness is getting in the way of my self-consciousness. If that isn't a self-conscious thought! She has the biggest tits in Leipzig. The whole thing is going to be a terrible disaster. I'm a disaster myself, and Wagner knows I'm a disaster.

WAGNER *(Challengingly)*: All right, I couldn't afford it. It should be a privilege to meet a king. Actually I'm interested. I'd like to meet anyone under those circumstances. He doesn't have a friend in the world. Maybe he'd like to buy one. I dare not . . . What could he possibly want from me? There's no reason to wait. If only I were totally subjected to the moment not realizing I *am* totally subjected to the moment. I'd like to shit in his face and get the money and go home. Why fuck around? I hate to say that, but it *is* real. He's going to fall apart eventually. This isn't an Italian opera. You have to get it together into one version, preferably the first thing that pops into your mind. I think that's a little too clear. *(Laughs cruelly.)* I hear he's a homosexual. I love that line. I know he's possessed, but he doesn't have any position except with his demons and horrors, and I have the biggest tits in Leipzig. They wander out of their own lives and say something, and all the Beethoven fans stand up and hiss. I wonder what he'd give me for my brain. Kundry has to be brought in at every possible moment, but she has to be in a thicket sleeping with the earth. Parsifal . . . Parsifal . . . *(Softly.)* Parsifal . . .

(KUNDRY appears and screams until the end of the scene.)

LUDWIG: I'd go anywhere. Oh I wish I were dead.

WAGNER: I'm always looking at the sky. Let's get on with it.

(They turn and begin moving slowly toward each other.)

LUDWIG: This is the first thing he's ever given me. I know he's my master but I don't know how to be humiliated. I'll be ravaged and divine. I'd rather serve him than die. How much of it will I get? What does he want? *(Long sigh.)* Finally I'm humiliated. No wishes, no dreams, nothing, nothing, nothing is too romantic. *(One sob.)*

WAGNER: He has to be constantly humiliated — my family make a regular ritual of it. He has to be a king or die. If I can't teach him, who can? How much will I get for it? What does he want? . . . Now we have to get very romantic. It's not the final humiliation. I passed your mother's heart and heard it die.

LUDWIG & WAGNER *(In unison):* We're both getting too far into this. I hate relating but it's far too late. Bury me in your craziness or I'll bury you in mind. Let's not talk. Kisses are the language of love.

(They stop the word with a kiss. A waterfall falls on them and they disappear. So does KUNDRY.)

CURTAIN

I LIKE IT
Michael Smith

A play in 2 short scenes

CHARACTERS:

ELEANOR: appears to be in her middle forties, turning dowdy.
PHILIP: appears to be in his early twenties, good looking.
MAID: young, attractive, also functions as a secretary.

for J. C.

SCENE: *A bedroom with an elaborate bed upstage center. At rise, ELEANOR and PHILIP, both wearing white pajamas, are in it eating breakfast.*

SCENE 1

ELEANOR: . . . and that goddam P.T.A. Fifteen years on committees, one after the other, and what have I got to show for it? Now they want me to be treasurer. I ask you. A great honor, they say. And what a show they make of it — nominations, seconds, secret ballots, everything. All because they think I'll accept the job. Of course I'm the only one of them that can add a column of figures — except a golf card or a bridge score — and they think I'm fool enough to accept the job. They've got another thing coming . . . Here, let me fix you a piece of toast. *(Feeds it to him.)* Isn't it good?

PHILIP: Mmmm. It's good.

ELEANOR: If they paid any attention at all they'd know better. Haven't I resigned from the Philharmonic board and the Ladies' Aid and the fucking Junior League? I'm not playing games, you know. You know that, God knows. Take it from me, don't join anything, because you'll have to work like hell to get loose. I've learned the hard way. Let them have their lousy agendas. They ought to argue about them and pass them and then roll them up and stuff them where they might do some good . . . Here, have another piece of toast.

PHILIP: No, I don't want any more.

ELEANOR: Of course you do, a growing boy like you.

PHILIP: I'm grown up enough. I haven't grown at all in years.

ELEANOR: Of course, but eat your toast anyway. You need your energy, for screwing, if for nothing else.

PHILIP: Mother? Why do you talk so dirty?

ELEANOR: Oh Phil, don't you like it? I thought you liked it. I'm sorry. If you say so, I won't ever do it any more.

PHILIP: I don't like it.

ELEANOR: The ayes have it then. Never again. *(Crosses her heart. They eat in silence.)* The coffee's cold again. That girl can never do anything right. Ring the bell and we'll get some more. *(PHILIP does.)* What's wrong with your eyes this morning, Philip?

PHILIP: What do you mean?

ELEANOR: They look all red. Have you been rubbing them again?

PHILIP: They always look like this lately. It doesn't matter. *(The MAID enters and stands stupidly staring.)* I haven't been sleeping right. They itch all the time.

ELEANOR: Well, keep your hands away from them.

PHILIP: Yes, I will.

ELEANOR: Promise?

PHILIP: Yes, I promise.

ELEANOR *(To MAID):* Don't just stand there gawking, you idiot. The coffee's cold.

MAID: Yes, mum.

ELEANOR: Get some more. Hot.

MAID: Yes, mum. *(Takes pot.)* Mum, there's some gentlemen downstairs.

ELEANOR: What do they want?

MAID: I don't know.

ELEANOR: You don't know *what*?

MAID: I don't know *mum*.

ELEANOR: Then find out while you're getting hot coffee. And tell them to go away. Tell them we're asleep. *(MAID goes.)* That girl is going to drive me out of my mind.

PHILIP: I don't think you should talk to her that way.

ELEANOR: Don't say 'I don't think.' Say 'I think you shouldn't.'

PHILIP: Well I do. Or I don't.

ELEANOR: She's an imbecile. How am I supposed to talk to her?

PHILIP: You could try being pleasant.

ELEANOR: I am always pleasant. I suppose they're from the P.T.A., and just when I have to pee.

PHILIP: So do I.

ELEANOR: I for one am not going to move out of this bed. I'm going to spend the rest of my life here, P.T.A. or no P.T.A. *(Squirms.)* I can wait.

PHILIP: I can't, but I'm too comfortable to move.

ELEANOR: Pee in the bed, then. I don't care.

PHILIP *(Giggles):* What would you say if I really did?

ELEANOR: I'd think it was funny.

PHILIP: All right, then, I will. *(Tries.)* I can't do it.

ELEANOR: Oh come on. Why not. You're not self-conscious, are you? Not in front of your own mother. Try harder.

PHILIP: I'm trying as hard as I can, and I can't do it. I'll bet you can't either.

ELEANOR: Of course I can. I just don't want to.

PHILIP: I'll bet you can't. I dare you. I double-dare you.

ELEANOR *(After a pause):* Sometimes you're an utter child, Philip.

PHILIP: You had asparagus for dinner, didn't you.

ELEANOR: It's easy. All you have to do is relax.

PHILIP: I'm *trying* to relax.

ELEANOR: Don't try, just let it come naturally. You never had to try to wet your diapers. *(MAID enters, unnoticed.)*

PHILIP *(Still trying):* I'm grown up now. It's different.

ELEANOR: Nonsense. It's exactly the same thing. Come on, you can do it.

MAID: Mum?

ELEANOR: You shut up.

PHILIP: No, that's all. I can't do it.

ELEANOR: You can.

PHILIP: I give up. I'll get out of bed and go to the bathroom. In a little while.

MAID: Mum, them gentlemen downstairs . . .

ELEANOR: Where's that coffee?

MAID: Here it is, mum. Them gentlemen downstairs is from the P.T.A.

ELEANOR: I knew it. Here, give me the pot. Have some more coffee, Philip, good and hot. It's all right. Don't feel bad about it.

PHILIP: Thank you, Mother.

ELEANOR: There. *(Holds cup to his lips; he drinks.)* All better now?

PHILIP: Yes, much better, thank you.

ELEANOR: Here, lean up against my shoulder. *(To MAID.)* Well, what did they want?

MAID: They said Master Philip here was your son, mum, and what was they to tell the Nominating Committee?

ELEANOR: Say to tell them I like it.

(Lights out on Scene 1; lights up immediately on:)

SCENE 2

(Everything is exactly the same as at the beginning of Scene 1.)

ELEANOR: . . . and that goddam P.T.A. Fifteen years on committees, one after the other, and what have I got to show for it?

PHILIP *(Brutally):* Shut your mouth, Mother.

ELEANOR: Now they want me to be treasurer. I ask you. *(ELEANOR stops talking. PHILIP, eating, ignores her. After a very long moment —)* Can I go on?

PHILIP: No. Shut your mouth and eat your breakfast.

ELEANOR *(Childishly):* I can't eat with my mouth shut.

PHILIP: Everybody has a problem. That's yours.

ELEANOR: Can I open my mouth if I promise not to talk? *(No reaction.)* Philip? *(No reaction. Motherly:)* Philip, I simply don't understand what's come over you lately. Some things I can tolerate — many things, in fact — but I cannot tolerate bad manners. I must insist that you show more respect for your mother.

PHILIP *(His mouth full):* Shove it.

ELEANOR: I don't know. Maybe you had the wrong environment as a child. I tried so hard to give you only the best. I've made mistakes. Oh I know I've made many mistakes. But I never tried to hurt you. You have to believe that. Everything I did, right or wrong, I did out of . . .

PHILIP *(Interrupts):* Now, Mother, that's enough. I thought we had an understanding. You know what's going to happen if you go on this way. Don't you?

ELEANOR: But Philip . . .

PHILIP: Don't you?

ELEANOR *(Chastened):* You'll get out of bed.

PHILIP: That's right.

ELEANOR: But you wouldn't really. Not really, would you? Not my sweet boy, not my darling little Phil?

PHILIP *(Starts to get up):* Here I go.

ELEANOR *(Involuntarily):* No, no. Wait, Phil. *(He settles back.)* Now look what you've made me do. You've made me spill my coffee. *(No reaction. She pours saucered coffee back into cup.)*

PHILIP: All right. Now I think we know where we stand. You know that I'll get out of bed, I really will get out of the bed if you don't behave, and I know you know. And you know I know you know. So there's no problem. You'll just have to grow up, Mother. Everything changes — people, situations, feelings, me — and you'll have to get used to it.

ELEANOR: But Philip . . . Am I allowed to speak?

PHILIP: A little, yes.

ELEANOR: Phil, I don't want anything to change. I don't want you to change.

PHILIP: I'm changed already, and I'll go on changing. You change too, and the sooner you realize it the better.

ELEANOR: I don't know what you're talking about.

PHILIP: Well T.S. on you. *(They eat in silence. PHILIP finishes breakfast.)* Ah, that was good. You'll excuse me if I get to work?

ELEANOR: Yes, of course, dear. *(PHILIP rings the bell. Immediately the MAID enters, cheerful and alert, dressed as a secretary.)*

MAID: Sir?

PHILIP: I wonder if you could bring your pad and step in for a few moments.

MAID: Yes sir. *(Goes.)*

PHILIP: I've got to get a few letters off. It won't take long. Then we can snuggle.

ELEANOR: Do I annoy you, Philip?

PHILIP: Of course not.

ELEANOR: You must understand. I'm a very affectionate person by nature. It's really nothing personal.

PHILIP: Don't be silly, Mother. Of course I understand. Of course I don't mind. I don't know what's come over you this morning. What is this compulsion to explain yourself? You know I like you best when you don't say anything. *(MAID reenters with steno pad, sits on foot of bed, and prepares to take dictation.)*

ELEANOR *(To MAID):* Dear, I wonder if you have a copy of Parents Magazine somewhere for me to read while you and Philip are working.

MAID: Of course, Madam. *(Starts to get up.)*

PHILIP *(To MAID):* No, don't bother. *(To ELEANOR.)* Mother, please.

ELEANOR: Oh, all right. Hand me my buffer then, will you? *(PHILIP does. ELEANOR buffs her nails throughout the following.)*

PHILIP: Now where were we. Oh yes. This letter goes to Bleak House, Washington. *(MAID takes it down in shorthand.)* Dear Jack, thanks for yours of whatever-it-was. I'm glad to hear that everything is working out in accordance with the plan we formulated that day Mother was asleep. Of course there are bound to be certain difficulties in the arrangement, but I'm sure you'll finally agree that the savings more than compensate for this added strain. Paragraph. Several additional points have come to mind since I last spoke to you. One: information should be disseminated to the public with the utmost caution. I'm glad to see that you have at last learned to control this without seeming to. Two: space turns out to be a wreck, what with cosmonauts, clouds, etcetera. It was nearly hopeless anyway, considering the amount of alteration that would have been necessary. You might think harder about Venus, though. Several obvious advantages there. Three: just don't worry so much. Remember, history is on our side, even if we don't know which side we're on. Paragraph. Love and kisses to the family and to you just love. Philip. *(End of letter.)* We'll need eleven copies of that. I'll give you the addresses later. I wonder if you'd read it back. It's fairly important. *(ELEANOR yawns elaborately. PHILIP deliberately ignores her.)*

MAID: Yes, sir. Bleak House, Washington. Dear Jack, thanks for yours of whatever-it-was. I'm glad to hear that . . .

PHILIP: Oh never mind. You haven't made a mistake yet. What came in for me this morning?

MAID: No mail yet, but there was a call from a Mr. Shuttlethwaite. I told him you and Madam were still in bed.

PHILIP: Who's he?

ELEANOR: That call was for me.

MAID: Yes, Madam, but I have my instructions. *(To PHILIP.)* Sir, he seemed somewhat disturbed.

ELEANOR *(To PHILIP)*: Mr. Shuttlethwaite is the president of the P.T.A. I must speak to him and tell him I can't accept the office.

PHILIP: What office?

ELEANOR: I told you, Philip. Can't you ever pay attention to me? They've elected me treasurer.

PHILIP: Oh, of course. *(To MAID.)* Call Mr. Shuttlethwaite back and tell him my mother will be honored to accept the position. *(To ELEANOR.)* We'll talk about this later.

MAID *(Makes note)*: Yes, sir. There was also a cable from Rome.

PHILIP: Read it to me.

MAID *(Does)*: Confusion here regards your intentions stop couldst clarify query stop regards John.

PHILIP: Splendid. Cable the following back to him. Dear John my message is love stop best to the girls stop I love you too stop ever. And sign it Philip. That ought to do it. One more letter, and then we'll take a few minutes off. This goes to Joe, the Sincerely Invidious Corporation, Washington.

ELEANOR: But Joe's dead, Philip.

PHILIP *(Ignores her)*: Dear Joe, I understand you have publicly expressed interest in my private life. I believe you fail to realize that I have nothing to hide. I hope you will feel free to visit me at your convenience, bearing in mind that video and audio recording of our interview will be *de rigueur.* Paragraph. I expect you would like my mother. Paragraph. I am quite certain, though, that the meeting would be more distressing to you than to me. For your own security — which I imagine interests you — I earnestly recommend that you realize that you will never understand, and just forget the whole thing. Respectfully, Philip. *(Laughs.)* How's that, Mother? Oh, one more thing. *(To MAID.)* Add a P.S. In any event, please believe that I am at least as sincere as you are. Underline the word sincere.

ELEANOR: I don't know what you're doing, Philip. Joe's been dead for years.

PHILIP: I know. *(To MAID.)* You can type the letters up and send the cable off, and we'll do some more later. Oh, and don't forget to call Mr. Shuttlethwaite.

MAID: Very good, sir. *(She goes.)*

ELEANOR: Philip, I don't want to be treasurer of the P.T.A.

PHILIP: I know, Mother, but it's important. I don't cut myself off from the life of my community, and you mustn't either. Anyway, you have to learn sometime that we can't always do just what we want. Close your eyes. *(She does.)* I'll be right back.

(He gets out of bed and very quickly goes offstage. ELEANOR opens one eye, sees that he is gone, and shuts it immediately. She begins humming a tuneless little tune a little desperately. After a moment she stops humming, opens the eye again, sees that he is still gone.)

ELEANOR *(Cries)*: Philip . . . *(Immediately he comes back onstage and climbs into the bed again.)*

PHILIP: It's all right, Mother. You know I wouldn't leave you for long. You're the only person in the world I can be sure of.

ELEANOR: I think you need a taste of your own medicine. You just see how it feels. *(She gets out of bed and starts offstage. Halfway out she stops, hesitates, then comes back to bed.)* I don't have to go now anyway. But you see what it's like.

PHILIP *(Kindly)*: Yes, Mother. Mother, I'm sorry to be so firm about the P.T.A., but it *is* important. I really think you'll enjoy it once you get used to the idea. You'll have all the meetings here, of course.

ELEANOR: Oh. I should have realized . . . Well, that's all right, then. In fact, I'm actually beginning to look forward to it. Do you know Mr. Shuttlethwaite? He's very attractive, I think, even if he does lisp.

PHILIP *(Piqued):* That's settled then. Subject closed. *(MAID enters.)*

MAID: Sir?

PHILIP: Yes, what is it?

MAID: I spoke to Mr. Shuttlethwaite, sir, and he seems to be upset. It seems to disturb him, your sleeping with your mother.

PHILIP: Yes? Well, so what?

MAID: He feels the Nominating Committee must be informed, and he wants to know what he should tell them.

PHILIP *(To ELEANOR):* Mother? . . . You remember, don't you, Mother? Go ahead.

ELEANOR: Say to tell them I . . . *(Steels herself.)* Say to tell them I like it. *(Covers her face with her hands. Sobbing.)* Oh, Philip, I can't, I can't say that.

PHILIP *(Soothing):* There now, Mother, that's all right. Everything's all right. *(To MAID, firmly.)* Say to tell them *I* like it.

CURTAIN

THE BROWN CROWN
Haal Borske

CHARACTERS:

ZEPHYRUS, The West Wind
DOCTOR RAYMOND FIELDING
THE SANDMAN
(*VOICE OF*) ECHO

The first act is done in black and white and silver. Open on: ZEPHYRUS in elaborate costume and headdress. Dim lighting with pin spot on ZEPHYRUS. Music softly over the following:

ZEPHYRUS: It's going to be another grim day! . . . Why do I bother to posture and plan, hoping the new day will bring forgiveness? Why do I hope? Why do I hope that today, Helios, the sun, will lift his shield and let his warm rays lick me again? . . . Hope is the worst purgatory! A slim chance keeps me going. That same slim chance destroyed poor brother Boreas and scattered him across the earth. Now he's just a past wind . . . I never sleep . . . Helios has probably started his ride already, but I'll see only his corona, crossing the sky, obscuring the Bull. The Heliotropes, out there, will see Helios and watch every instant of his ride; then they'll fold away and wait for the next dawn. The Heliotropes take nourishment from watching Helios's journey, but I think if they got close to their beloved, they'd burn up . . . It's lonely with everything dead and gone . . . Everything died here for lack of the sun. Apollo specified it thus, and Helios obeys like a . . . a . . . salesman! Everything died and I sang their laments, yes, I sang all their laments — in a foreign tongue, to prove I was sincere. Now, nothing is dead here; it's simply gone. The Hyenas were the last to go. I like unkillability! But I was very philosophical about it — cried my eyes out. But . . . I shouldn't dwell on it; I'm used to nothing now. Well . . . I'll get on with it . . .

(Bouncy, silly music, general dim lighting, ZEPHYRUS dances about preparing for the new day [without sunshine], takes a "shower" in silver ribbons, after removing his costume to reveal plain costume. More preparations, etc. He settles as music dims out. Picks up a botched up mess of knitting and proceeds to screw it up even more, while humming "Pace,

Pace Mio Dio," or something just as crazy. He is quite resigned and totally
unprepared for the following:
A thump is heard.)

ZEPHYRUS: What??? Someone has come to the Land of Sighs? Can it be? Is this it?
Has Apollo come to release me? Has Apollo taken pity on my sorrow? Has
my despair touched his heart? Oh, I knew they wouldn't forget me! I knew
these centuries of wailing and moaning would not go unnoticed! Helios!
Was it you, who . . . No, of course not . . . You can't look down to earth. If
your gaze wavered for an instant, you'd lose control of the chariot and crash
the sun . . . But, who??? . . . I guess Apollo remembered that a specified time
has passed, and he's come to release me! Ai! I don't need this any more!

He throws his centuries' work of knitting about, unraveling it around the
stage.

ZEPHYRUS: He's coming closer! I'm freed! Ai! It hurts! Here he comes! . . . I'm
relieved . . . !

(DOCTOR RAYMOND FIELDING enters. He's in white, glasses, uptight. A
very sniffy Doctor type.)

FIELDING: *(After spotting ZEPHYRUS.)* What is this?

ZEPHYRUS: Where's Apollo?

FIELDING: Who? I'm alone . . . I'm a scientist . . .

(ZEPHYRUS groans and tries to salvage his knitting. Then, confronting
FIELDING.)

ZEPHYRUS: Who are you, and what do you want?

FIELDING: I'm Dr. Raymond Fielding. I've come to investigate a scientific
phenomenon of nature here . . . uh . . . who are you?

ZEPHYRUS: *What* are you, and *who* do you want?

FIELDING: I just told you . . . Dr. Fielding. . . investigate scientific phenomenon
of nature . . . uh . . . who are you?

(ZEPHYRUS strikes a Greek pottery pose.)

ZEPHYRUS: Look closely . . . can't you tell?

FIELDING: No.

ZEPHYRUS: Don't lie to me. My likeness is on countless numbers of mosaics and
pots!

FIELDING: I'm a Doctor. I can help you.

ZEPHYRUS: You've come to torment me!

(ZEPHYRUS runs from FIELDING. FIELDING turns to fiddle in his bag. He
fiddles around in his bag, draws out telescope and peers through it, scien-
tifically.)

ZEPHYRUS: *(Still turned away.)* I'm Zephyrus. The West Wind . . . in exile . . .
Didn't you hear me, Bub?

FIELDING: *(Still busy with telescope.)* What? Oh, yes. Zephyrus, the West Wind. I'm afraid I've had my nose in too many Technical books. I haven't had much time for you artists.

ZEPHYRUS: Artists??!!

(FIELDING is still busy. ZEPHYRUS is curious and rummages through FIELDING's bag. Quite bewildered, he pulls out an enema bag. He inspects it from all angles, pulls off tube and blows into bag like a balloon, making a rude noise.)

FIELDING: Hey! Put that down!

ZEPHYRUS: *(Flinging bag away . . . FIELDING frantically retrieves it.)* You mean you haven't heard about the scandal? The . . . ugh . . . Hyacinthus Affair?

FIELDING: Scandal? I'm afraid I don't . . . What are you talking about? West Wind? . . . I don't believe you.

ZEPHYRUS: *You* don't believe *me*? Hah! *(He turns away.)*

FIELDING: There is no West Wind. The other winds blow by west, and the North Wind is a past wind. There is *no* West Wind.

ZEPHYRUS: I know! I've been *here* for centuries! Ai! Ai!

FIELDING: . . . What was that about a scandal?

ZEPHYRUS: Ai! Ai! Well . . . It all started with Hyacinthus . . . *That Rat-Prick!!!* Well . . . My brother Boreas and I were so tired of servicing horses and dolphins and swans, and you know how reasonable it is to give your heart of hearts to a beautiful young boy . . . Young? He was sixteen if he was a day! Well . . . one day, Boreas brought me to see what someone had written on the Parthenon wall: "Hyacinthus takes it in the ass!" . . .

FIELDING: He probably wrote it himself.

ZEPHYRUS: *(Ignoring this.)* Well . . . This Hyacinthus sounded intriguing, like just what we needed. And a mortal too! Mortal buttocks are so . . . impermanent; like theatre . . .

(FIELDING feels his own buttocks, gingerly. ZEPHYRUS notices.)

ZEPHYRUS: Well . . . we wanted to find out what all the fuss was about, so we lurked about the city, trying to get a peek at him . . .

FIELDING: This is disgusting! I don't want to hear any more! . . . Do you mean to say you considered having sexual relations with a member of your own sex?

ZEPHYRUS: Have you ever made love to a swan?

FIELDING: A what? A swan? Of course not! I never . . . What????

ZEPHYRUS: *(Plucking imaginary feather from his mouth.)* Well . . . one day we saw that wretch, Hyacinthus . . .

FIELDING: I'll bet he was silly, and cheap, and snotty, and prissy, and . . .

ZEPHYRUS: How dare you! I ought to strangle you! He was beautiful. His arms were marble . . . His feet were large . . . his eyes were cornflowers . . . his fingers were long and straight . . . his jawbone had definition!

FIELDING: I'm sorry . . . I thought you said he was a wretch.

ZEPHYRUS: His fingers were long . . . and straight . . .

FIELDING: In what way?

ZEPHYRUS: *(Ignoring him.)* We loved him, and I can't even see the flower he became.

FIELDING: I'm sorry. Go on, please . . .

ZEPHYRUS: It was the typical, mythical love affair; a few days of bliss and the usual twisted ending.

FIELDING: But? What? How? Who? . . . What?????

ZEPHYRUS: *(All in one breath.)* Apollo fell in love with him. One day while throwing quoits, Boreas and I, out of jealousy, caused the quoit thrown by Apollo to strike Hyacinthus on the head, killing him instantly. He bled on the ground. A beautiful flower sprang therefrom, which still bears his name.

FIELDING: *GOOD GOD!* . . . . Oh, I get it! Apollo got peeved . . .

ZEPHYRUS: Peeved?!!!

FIELDING: . . . and banished you here and caused the sun not to shine on you.

ZEPHYRUS: *Dear* Doctor Fielding.

FIELDING: Gosh, I'm really sorry, Mr. Wind. And I do believe you . . . it's the only scientific explanation for this dead place. I mean it. I'm really sorry, and I'd like to be your friend and help you . . .
(No reaction.)
I've led kind of a rough life myself. When I was a kid, my mother never let me . . . Well, all the other kids . . . then, later on . . . I mean . . . well . . . I always wanted to be an actor.

ZEPHYRUS: Oh, shut up!

FIELDING: *(After a few moments.)* What have you been doing here all these years?

ZEPHYRUS: Knittin' and writing my memoirs, of course.

FIELDING: Memoirs . . . of course . . . Has no one been here all this time?

ZEPHYRUS: The animals, of course. But they're gone . . . The Hyenas were the last to go, of course . . .

FIELDING: Hyenas? Ugh!

ZEPHYRUS: What? The Hyenas were my friends, Chum!

FIELDING: Oh? Well, I always thought they were, you know, sort of, well . . .
pretentious.

ZEPHYRUS: Pretentious???? Pigs call peacocks pretentious. Peacocks call other
peacocks pretentious. Hyenas go about their business with no hysteria, and
you call *them* . . . ?

(ZEPHYRUS snatches enema bag.)

ZEPHYRUS: . . . And what do you call this???? David? Mario????

*(ZEPHYRUS slings enema bag at FIELDING. Slinks into following soliloquy
accompanied by special lighting and soft melancholy music. FIELDING
takes comfort with his enema bag.)*

ZEPHYRUS: . . . My Hyenas . . . my precious . . . I never noticed them when I was
a big wind. I swept over them and ruffled their fur, but my mind was always
elsewhere . . . playing with kites . . . turning pinwheels . . . kissing little children under their clothes . . . when the trees died, and the little animals, and
the big ones too; I remember remarking to myself; how neat everything
was . . . not at all smelly. Then I noticed that the Hyenas were going about
their ghastly work, quietly and with excellent manners. I gulped and realized that they knew their own doom, but they did what was required . . .
with dignity, Doctor.

(Pause.)

They didn't like to be lonely, so they traveled with their brothers and lovers
and all who would share their fortune. Finally, there were two Hyenas
left . . . the only things left with me in the Valley of Woe. They were brothers; anyone would know it . . . the bravest of them . . . They had no pas-
times, no rituals or ceremonies! Now they were alone with me . . . Neither
one of them ever had a hobby!!! They sat with me all the time . . . they
hoped I would die. They hoped I would die, so that they could go on for a
little while more . . . and maybe something would happen.

(Pause.)

They knew one of *them* would die and the other would be alone . . . After a
while . . . days . . . one of them looked at his brother, and then looked away
and gave a little howl. The other joined in, and they howled and howled. At
the height of this one of them looked at me and then fell to the ground . . .
He pretended he was dead, and while the other went about his feeding, he
carried it off, all the way to the end. He showed no emotion, Doctor, and
carried it off to the end.

(Pause.)

The last one came to me and put his snout in my lap for a while, and just
looked at me . . . for a long time . . . then he went away.

(Pause.)

Do you have any comments, Doctor?

(FIELDING, who has been contemplating a name for his enema bag, hasn't heard a word of the preceding. He holds up the enema bag to ZEPHYRUS.)

FIELDING: Mario???

(ZEPHYRUS, infuriated, snatches the enema bag, and beats FIELDING with it during the following:)

ZEPHYRUS: When I was frivolous, and nothing mattered, I wouldn't have noticed such things. But when I did my first absolutely wrong thing, I came here for punishment and found out! I found out that being found out is out, and finding out is found, and found is finding out, and out is finding, and finding is out of finding, and out of finding is out and out of finding found is finding found finding outs and out of finding out of founds is finding out finds . . .

(ZEPHYRUS gives FIELDING a final wallop . . . hard.)

FIELDING: . . . I needed that.

(Pause.)

There's nowhere for me to go from here, but to fall in love with you, right?

ZEPHYRUS: Do you have any comments, Doctor?

FIELDING: No.

(Pause.)

ZEPHYRUS: *Are* you in love with me?

FIELDING: Yes, but I'll do what you want me to do, anyway.

ZEPHYRUS: Permit me to give you this precious jewel.

(ZEPHYRUS gives FIELDING the precious jewel.)

Who ever accepts a fifty without thanks, has stolen the gift.

FIELDING: Oh, you'll get it back, after putting me through endless tortures. I'm beginning to see that that's what love is; a twisted game of give and give.

ZEPHYRUS: Do you like the jewel? . . .

FIELDING: Torments, like making lanyards, and going to Sweet Shoppes.

ZEPHYRUS: It's Hyacinthus's heart . . .

FIELDING: . . . and buying you presents . . . that *I* like . . .

ZEPHYRUS: Tiny, ain't it? . . .

FIELDING: . . . and waiting for you in places . . .

ZEPHYRUS: . . . I use it to cut diamonds.

FIELDING: . . . and hoping you'll do me a favor . . .

ZEPHYRUS: Will you do me a favor?

FIELDING: Lover's demands are sacred.

ZEPHYRUS: I want you to find Apollo, and tell him . . . beg him . . . throw ourselves at his mercy . . .

FIELDING: Take your thin story, and punch it up enough for him to forgive you and let Helios, the sun, shine once more on you? You want me to take a flimsy tale . . . make it sound important, and hope he'll forgive you? Is that what you want me to do?

ZEPHYRUS: Yes.

FIELDING: I'll do it, but first; can I kiss you?

ZEPHYRUS: Uh, yes . . .

FIELDING: Can I fondle you? Can I put my hands on yours? Can I wash up and sit around waiting for you? Can I hope you like me? Can I work and make apologies for you? Can I endure you and wait for a discharge?

ZEPHYRUS: Uh, I'm too tired.

FIELDING: Can I care?

ZEPHYRUS: Uh, I don't feel like it . . .

FIELDING: I *will* find Apollo. I will find him and remind him of his duty. I'll plead for you. I'll do anything I don't believe in because I believe in believing in you.

ZEPHYRUS: Go, my Doctor! . . . Er, I love you . . .

FIELDING: Kiss me goodbye! Take off my clothes and look at me . . . one of my socks has a hole in it. I didn't know I'd fall in love today . . . Please?

ZEPHYRUS: Now that we're lovers, you have a *duty*! I can't let *us* stand in our way. Go!

FIELDING: Lovers? But we haven't . . .

ZEPHYRUS: You're beautiful when you're angry.

FIELDING: What??? Now that we're lovers, *you* have a duty.

ZEPHYRUS: I have a bellyache.

FIELDING: A kiss goodbye?

ZEPHYRUS: Of course . . . *(Blows a kiss.)* There.

> *(FIELDING exits muttering about "back alley affairs," etc. He pops back on and holds up the enema bag.)*

FIELDING: Hey! I'm going to call it "Zephyrus!"

> *(FIELDING exits.)*

ZEPHYRUS: I never liked scientists but that one's different. It's been so long. I'm frightened.

(ZEPHYRUS crosses to center and kneels. Special pin spot light. Sneak up despair music which will cross fade to "I'm all alone in the world" type music. Dim out before the last few lines of the following:)

ZEPHYRUS: I know that nobody's listening, but; I'm lost here, and can't seem to find a way.

(Pause.)

I made so many pin-wheels turn! I scattered seeds. I tickled so many children, and made them laugh. I worked . . . So many ladies were in danger of succumbing to beasts . . . I blew a cool breeze cross their foreheads and put an end to a dreary initiation. And how many ladies were with true lovers? Experts, because they loved? I blew warm gusts, and fanned them, bringing fever and thunder to a painful joy! I kissed swimmers and dried them! I made so many pin-wheels turn! I tickled so many children . . . I never sleep . . . I'm so lonely . . . I've made so many people laugh, and I can't sleep. I'm so lonely and scared and I can't find a way, and made children laugh and I'm lonely and afraid and I can't seem to find my way. I'm so scared I can't find children or laugh because I'm lonely . . . it's so Shelley here!! . . . I feel so bad . . . I can't sleep . . . It hurts . . .

(ZEPHYRUS remains with arms outstretched and head up, eyes glassy. Special magic lighting dims up. A lullaby is heard dimming up. The SANDMAN appears behind ZEPHYRUS, who doesn't notice. The SANDMAN sprinkles magic sand which glitters up the stage, ZEPHYRUS rubs his eyes, yawns and goes to sleep a la Shirley Temple. Music to crescendo. Lots of glitter making the air sparkle. Music and lights quickly dim to out.)

(INTERMISSION if possible.)

(The next part is done in FULL color. Portentous type music up. Spots on ZEPHYRUS and SANDMAN. SANDMAN does conjuring type action and ZEPHYRUS rouses from his first sleep in centuries. He does not see SANDMAN. He listens to impending music for a moment.)

ZEPHYRUS: Something is going to happen!

(Lights to full. [The sun rises.] Spring in bloom type music. Flowers, etc. Bliss and happiness and all that kind of hoopla, which goes on for awhile, with the SANDMAN enjoying it all. ZEPHYRUS finally spots SANDMAN.)

ZEPHYRUS: Who are *you?* Who cares! Get out! This is *my* redemption scene. This is *my* happiness. Get out! How dare you!

(The SANDMAN exits sadly.)

ZEPHYRUS: I'm so happy I won't even cry or laugh! . . . What should I do now? I can't think of a funny way of putting it, but I'll go out and see what's what. I'll put two and two together, so to speak . . . but I'll go incognito, of course. I hope they haven't lost the art of disguise. And more important; the art of ignoring disguises . . . but which disguise? Remember — it's been Eeeeeeeeeeeeeeeons . . .

(Pause.)

A Soothsayer of course! Mystery. Intrigue. They'll always believe the unbelievable and make believe it's all make-believe.

(Putting on soothsayer garb he's plucked from nowhere.)

A soothsayer can get away with anything. Just make sure they know you're a soothsayer, and not a poet.

(He's now dressed in elaborate costume. Magic wand, funny hat.)

Now I'll go out and see if rewards are in order or spankings.

(To the sky.)

I presume I retain my ranking? Hello? Hello? Helios, is the bloodshed over? It's all so rhythmical here . . . But of course . . . when one goes from one medium to another, one naturally vibrates in sympathy with the other . . . I sound like Doctor Fielding, with a quirk . . . ?? Has the oracle come true? What Oracle? What am I talking about? Now I sound like crazy Narcissus.

(Pause.)

So as a Soothsayer I go. There will be no tests for them . . . But they'd better pass it! I wonder who that was during my redemption? Sprinkling beauty???? No time to think of it . . . Goodbye, dead Hyenas; I have to go now. I'll remember all of this. I'll come back and see this again, of course. I'll see all of this again, won't I? Of course. I have to go now.

(Prepares for the grandest exit of all time. Indicates the outer world:)

I think they've forgotten greatness! All the more reason to remind them of it!

(Exiting:)

The best things about gods is they never *really* get their come-uppance.

(ZEPHYRUS exits. Blackout.)

(Lights up and Birdy music on the new DOCTOR FIELDING. He is in colorful costume and quite loose. Possibly on a flower-decked swing. This is the "outside world." FIELDING is chirping and grooving on the whole scene.)

FIELDING: It's going to be another nice day! Children are laughing. I helped them fly their kites today. I ran and giggled with them . . . I made love with a soldier today. I drank Wah-wah from his hands! We ate oranges and our lips stuck together; and we inhaled . . . and made love. My cellophane gland has completely dissolved! There was a time when all of my body's discharges came out in little cellophane packages! Hygienic. Very sanitary . . . but that's all over now . . . I even sweat! My soldier, today smelled me . . . and liked it!

Nature is so cool and fresh! I like to look at things and feel them with my hands . . . I am *so* happy

(ZEPHYRUS enters. They see each other at the same time.)

TOGETHER: I have to thank you!!

FIELDING: *(With an intake of breath.)* Uhhhhh! I forgot! I forgot to find Apollo!

ZEPHYRUS: You . . . ?

FIELDING: Forgot to find Apollo and tell him about you! . . . How did you get here?

ZEPHYRUS: . . . I'll tell you later.

FIELDING: Well, I did find out that Apollo is a croupier in Las Vegas.

ZEPHYRUS: A what? In what? What???

FIELDING: A croupier in Las Vegas, and while I was going there, I accidentally had sex with a boy in Morocco . . .

ZEPHYRUS: Hmmmm . . . High Russian?

FIELDING: Mmmmmmm! . . . Well anyway . . . I threw away my enema bag, and then I heard there was a beauty contest in Boy's Town, and then I discovered nature, and lost my cellophane gland and learned how to swim, and, and today I made love with a soldier . . . and . . . and . . . here I am. I'm sorry!

ZEPHYRUS: Come here.

FIELDING: Are you going to hit me?

ZEPHYRUS: Come here!

> *(An Argentine tango plays. They both fling off their cloaks and do a brief but well executed dance, with snorting and gasping. It ends suddenly. They are both satisfied. After a moment:)*

FIELDING: By the way, I also found out that Helios doesn't drive the sun chariot any more. Yes, a mortal drives the sun . . . Well, it's not funny; but it's true.

> *(ZEPHYRUS looks at the sky, then at FIELDING, incredulous. In a moment he swings his hip and bumps FIELDING off stage. We hear a scream and a splash and FIELDING is never seen again.)*

> *(ZEPHYRUS, confused, staggers off stage.)*

> *(Enter the SANDMAN. He delivers the following to the mortal who is driving the Sun Chariot.)*

SANDMAN: Whoever you are, driving the sun chariot . . . I know what I've done is unforgivable, and I guess you don't want me to be the Sandman any more . . . but . . . Gosh . . . I didn't want Zephyrus to see how they behave in their temples; like clubhouse gangs. I didn't want him to find out that people don't love and then fret about it. I didn't think he should find out that

Helios has left off driving the sun and that a mortal has taken over now . . . I didn't want him to see ART . . . When I discovered that he was the only one left who could remember beauty, I kept him there. There . . . where he could remember. I thought he shouldn't sleep . . . and dream . . . Dreams are pastel nightmares! . . . I should know; I dream! I thought Zephyrus would be better off with memories, honest. I didn't know those memories would swirl into loneliness . . . I didn't know he'd start weeping! Honest, I didn't know. Well, he started weeping and I just didn't know. Honest.

(Pause.)

Well, I guess that's it.

(Pause.)

After a long hard day, there's nothing quite as refreshing as a soliloquy!

(End music. Blackout.)

(Lights up. Enter ZEPHYRUS on same location. Wanders around. Sees stilled wind chime. He lovingly blows it to make it ring. The voice of ECHO is heard.)

ECHO: Zephyrus! Is that you?

ZEPHYRUS: Huh?

ECHO: Zephyrus! It is you! You snake-in-the-grass; where have you been?

ZEPHYRUS: Huh?

ECHO: It's me, Echo!

ZEPHYRUS: Echo?

ECHO: Yes. We've all been wondering what happened to you.

ZEPHYRUS: Apollo banished me, don't you remember?

ECHO: You're such a camp! . . . But of course we remember. But he forgave you ages ago. Matter of fact he's not even around any more . . . Las Vegas, you know.

ZEPHYRUS: He forgave me? But why didn't Helios shine on me?

ECHO: Oh, Helios doesn't drive the sun chariot any more. He's a beach-boy in California.

ZEPHYRUS: But . . . but . . . how???

ECHO: Oh, some mortal drives the sun chariot now. I don't know who, but the sun rises every day . . . and who cares, you know? The Heliotropes died of course, but we made plastic ones, of course.

ZEPHYRUS: Of course . . .

ECHO: We're all having such a good time! Everything is such fun! I'm learning how to yodel.

ZEPHYRUS: Where are the others?

ECHO: Well, Venus is a snake-charmer in Rangoon . . .

ZEPHYRUS: I was present at her birth!

ECHO: You sound bitter.

ZEPHYRUS: What of Ares?

ECHO: Ares has been in a trance for years.

ZEPHYRUS: In a trance?

ECHO: Yes. He's a playwright.

    (ZEPHYRUS screams.)

ECHO: You're getting shrill.

ZEPHYRUS: And Zeus?

ECHO: Politician.

    (ZEPHYRUS shrieks and falls to the ground.)

ECHO: We were worried about Eros. He kept wringing his hands over us.

ZEPHYRUS: *(Raising himself.)* Ahhhh . . . Eros . . .

ECHO: We changed him into an octopus, and he wrung himself to death.

ZEPHYRUS: What? Is Eros dead?

ECHO: You're such a camp!

ZEPHYRUS: *Is Eros dead*!!

ECHO: It's not funny, but it's true.

    (ZEPHYRUS, weak and swooning staggers off.)

ECHO: He's such camp! Taxi!!

    (Blackout.)

    (Bright lights up on ZEPHYRUS, alone and weeping at his lowest. Back in the Land of Sighs.)

    (Enter the SANDMAN who delivers the following to the despairing ZEPHYRUS. During this ZEPHYRUS gradually raises himself and listens.)

SANDMAN: There's danger in being you. I've seen it. I've seen the pine trees reach for you. I've seen the ocean's waves try to drag you out with them . . . to hold you. The sky sends hot fingers down to caress you. The willows would strangle you in their embrace. The flowers would smother you in their eagerness. The little fishes would tear you to pieces; to have a part of you. The air would bloat you with too much of itself. The rivers would batter you on their rocky bottoms, just to take you with them . . . You can't go rummaging around in people's hearts. You could be killed . . . for love . . . The Pleiades saw you crying and went out of focus . . . I saw you weeping and made assumptions . . . There's danger in being you.

(ZEPHYRUS takes the SANDMAN's hand and kisses it. Then he rises. They look at each other, then to the sun and then back at each other a few times.)

ZEPHYRUS: *(Grimly.)* I wonder what would distract a mortal? *(Looking at the sun.)* I wonder what would make a mortal look down to earth and lose the reins and tumble the sun into the sea . . . I wonder?

(The SANDMAN whispers to ZEPHYRUS shyly.)

ZEPHYRUS: Of course! The same thing that distracts me! The same thing that has distracted men and gods since time began.

(ZEPHYRUS deliberately whisks off the SANDMAN's cloak and reveals a very nice looking young man.)

ZEPHYRUS: Beauty!!!

(A whirring noise is heard after a moment . . . then a cracking up noise . . . the sounds of doom.)

ZEPHYRUS: It worked! The sun chariot is doomed. Who is the mortal who dared become a god???

(Sound of Marlene Dietrich singing "Easy Come, Easy Go." We see with lighting the sun falling and hear it splash into the sea. Silence and darkness. Whoops! Lights come back up and we hear the last determined few notes of the song . . . then darkness and silence. The rest of the play is done in blues and dimness.)

(Icicles begin to form. We see snow flurries.)

SANDMAN: What have you done?

ZEPHYRUS: What have we done?

SANDMAN: What have *we* done? What did they do?

ZEPHYRUS: Nothing!

SANDMAN: We're like Hyenas. Cowards!

ZEPHYRUS: We must put the world to sleep. It's terrible to die of the cold! We must put the world to sleep!

SANDMAN: They've been asleep for centuries.

ZEPHYRUS: Messages yet! Hurry, I hear moaning! You scatter the sand, and I'll blow it across the lands and seas.

(The SANDMAN holds magic sand in hands and ZEPHYRUS blows it about. They stand quietly looking at each other.)

SANDMAN: We'll be the only ones left! We'll have to look at each other forever. Forever! There'll be nothing left.

ZEPHYRUS: Except the cockroaches, of course.

SANDMAN: . . . Of course . . . and the crickets, of course.

ZEPHYRUS: Of course . . . And you, of course . . .

SANDMAN: . . . Of course . . . What is there to worry about? . . .

ZEPHYRUS: . . . You, of course . . .

SANDMAN: . . . Of course.

> *(The entire world turns to ice with appropriate music and lighting. Very slow dim to out.)*

CURTAIN

theatre

By Edward Albee

ICARUS'S MOTHER

A play by Sam Shepard, presented through Sunday by and at the Caffe Cino, 31 Cornelia Street. Directed by Michael Smith.

November 25, 1965

For those of you who are busy people, facts first, implications later. (And by facts I mean, of course, nothing closer to the truth than my opinions.) Sam Shepard is one of the youngest and most gifted of the new playwrights working off-Broadway these days. The signature of his work is its unencumbered spontaneity—the impression Shepard gives of inventing drama as a form each time he writes a play. His new theatre piece, "Icarus's Mother," is presently on view at the Caffe Cino. Sad to say, it gives the impression of being a mess. . . .

The value of off-Broadway and its café adjuncts lies not only in its enthusiasm for sustaining plays without which the uptown theatre is unreal and preposterous—the work of Beckett, Genet, Pinter, Claudel, deGhelderode, for example—but, as well, in offering new, experimental playwrights (such as Sam Shepard) a proper ambiance in which to try things out, overreach, fail and, if they have the stuff, finally succeed.

If Shepard's new theatre piece, "Icarus's Mother," fails to please, by which I mean fails to engage one, the failure is of no importance so long as the piece is merely one random experiment, one spontaneous throw-off, one way-stone on the path toward the creation and recreation of theatre. If, on the other hand, this play signals, as I have the disquieting suspicion it does, the beginnings of a premature crystallization of Shepard's theatre aesthetic, then the failure of the play is a good deal more serious.

Review reprinted by permission of The Village Voice; *photographer of Sam Shepard snapshot, circa 1965, unknown*

Both provided through the courtesy of Robert Patrick

ICARUS'S MOTHER
Sam Shepard

Icarus's Mother was first produced at the Caffe Cino on November 16, 1965, directed by Michael Smith, with the following cast:

BILL	John Kramer
JILL	Lee Worley
PAT	Cynthia Harris
HOWARD	James Barbosa
FRANK	John A. Coe

SCENE:

The stage is covered with grass. A low hedge upstage runs the width of the stage. Behind the hedge is a pale blue scrim. Center stage is a portable barbecue with smoke rising out of it. The lighting is bright yellow. On the grass down left is a tablecloth with the remnants of a huge meal scattered around it. BILL lies on his back down left staring at the sky. HOWARD lies up left, JILL up right, PAT down right and FRANK center stage — all in the same position as BILL and staring at the sky. Before the lights come up the sound of birds chirping is heard. The sound lasts for a while. The lights come up very slowly as the sound fades out. The lights come up full. A long pause, then all the people start belching at random. They stop.

BILL: *(Still staring at the sky.)* Does he know there's people down here watching him do that?

JILL: Sure.

PAT: It's skywriting.

HOWARD: No, it's not skywriting. It's just a trail. A gas trail.

PAT: I thought it was.

FRANK: It's gas.

BILL: I don't like it. I don't like the looks of it from here. It's distracting.

FRANK: It's a vapor trail. All jets do it.

BILL: I don't like the way he's making it. I mean a semicircle thing like that. In a moon shape.

JILL: I like it.

BILL: If he knows what he's doing, that means he could be signaling or something.

FRANK: Jets don't signal.

PAT: It's gas, Bill.

BILL: You mean that whole long stream of cloud is just excess gas?

HOWARD: Right.

BILL: He has no other way of getting rid of it?

HOWARD: Nope!

(BILL stands, looking up at the sky.)

BILL: And he's spreading it all over the sky like that?

HOWARD: That's right.

BILL: He's staying in the same general area, though. How come he's not moving to some other areas? He's been right above us for the past hour.

FRANK: He's probably a test pilot or something.

BILL: I think he sees us. I don't like the looks of it.

HOWARD: He's a million miles up. How could he see us?

BILL: He sees our smoke and he's trying to signal. *(Yelling at the sky.)* Get away from here! Get out of our area!

(HOWARD stands, looking up at the sky.)

HOWARD: He can't hear you, Bill. You'll have to be louder than that.

BILL: Hey! Get your gas away from here!

FRANK: Sit down.

BILL: We don't know what you want but we don't want you around here!

JILL: He can't hear you. What's the matter with you?

HOWARD: He can see us, though. He knows we're looking at him.

BILL: If you need help you'll have to come down!

HOWARD: *(Yelling at the sky.)* We ate all the food so we can't give you any!

FRANK: Sit down, you guys.

BILL: Get away from the picnic area! Go somewhere else! Go on! Get away from the park.

JILL: Will you guys cut it out? Leave the poor guy alone. He's just flying. Let him fly.

HOWARD: He's not just flying. If he were just doing that it would be all right. But he's not. He's signaling.

JILL: Who would he be signaling to?

HOWARD: His mother, maybe. Or his wife.

BILL: He could be signaling to anybody.

FRANK: Not likely.

PAT: What if he is? So what?

BILL: So, someone should be told about it. The community should know.

PAT: Let him signal his wife if he wants to. He's probably been away for a while and he just got back. Let him show off a little.

HOWARD: But he's right above us. His wife isn't down here.

JILL: I'm his wife.

BILL: Are you his wife, Jill?

JILL: That's right.

BILL: Then we should tell him, so he doesn't have to waste any more time.

HOWARD: Come on down! Your wife's down here.

BILL: Come on down here!
    (JILL stands and yells at the sky.)
JILL: Come here, honey! Here I am!

BILL: Come and get her!
    (FRANK stands and yells at the sky.)
FRANK: Come and get your wife, stupid!
    (The following lines should happen on top of each other, with whistling and ad-lib shouts from all the actors.)
HOWARD: Come on! Land that thing!

JILL: Here I am, sweetheart! *(Throwing kisses.)*

FRANK: You'd better hurry!
    (PAT stands and yells at the sky.)
PAT: Come on down! Here we are! Yoo hoo!

BILL: Your other wife's here, too!

FRANK: Two wives!

PAT: Come on, sweetie! Where have you been!

JILL: We've been waiting and waiting!

FRANK: Two ripe juicy wives waiting for you!

HOWARD: Come on!

BILL: You've been up there too long, mister.

FRANK: We can see you! Come on down!

BILL: Land that thing!

PAT: Come to me, boobsy! Boobsy, boobsy, boobsy.
  (JILL and PAT start shimmying around the stage.)

HOWARD: We've got your wives, mister pilot! You'd better come down or we'll
  take them away.

BILL: We'll use them ourselves! There's three of us here!

FRANK: He's leaving! Look! Hey!

HOWARD: Hey don't! Come back here!

JILL: He's leaving us! Stop!

PAT: Darling! The children.

BILL: You're running out on your kids!
  (They all yell and shake their fists at the sky.)

JILL: Don't leave us! Come back here!

HOWARD: You're no good, mister pilot!

PAT: Come back! The children!

JILL: Don't leave us, darling!
  (They all boo loudly.)

BILL: What a rotten guy!
  (They stop booing and just stare at the sky.)

FRANK: He's gone.

HOWARD: That makes me sick.
  (A pause as they all stare at the sky.)

PAT: Well, when do they start this thing?

FRANK: Are you in a hurry?

PAT: No. I just want to know so I could take a walk or something in the meantime.

BILL: They don't start till it gets dark.

FRANK: Where are you going to walk to?

PAT: Just down the beach or something. To rest my stomach. That was a big
  meal, you know.

FRANK: Walking doesn't rest your stomach. When you're full and you walk, that
  just irritates it.

JILL: He's right.

PAT: All right! I'll walk just to loosen my legs up or something. I'm not going to lie around here waiting for it to get dark, though.

HOWARD: What happens if they start while you're on your walk?

JILL: That'd be terrible, Pat.

PAT: They shoot them in the sky. I can watch fireworks while I'm walking just as easy. It isn't hard. All I have to do is tilt my head up and watch and continue walking.

BILL: You may trip, though, and there you'd be unconscious on the beach somewhere and we'd have to go looking for you.

JILL: Yeah.

HOWARD: Then we'd miss the fireworks just on account of you, Pat.

FRANK: We'd be looking all over. Through the bushes and up and down the beach for hours. Everyone would miss everything.

JILL: Then maybe someone else would trip while they were looking for you and we'd have two missing people on the beach unconscious instead of just one.

BILL: We might all trip and be there on the beach for weeks unconscious.

PAT: All right!
    (She sits; the rest remain standing and close in on her, slowly forming a circle.)

HOWARD: You can walk if you want to, Pat. While it's still light. We don't mind.

JILL: We don't want to wreck your fun, Patsy.

BILL: But you have to get back before it gets dark. Because that's when the fireworks start. And you don't want to miss them.

FRANK: You don't want to be lost on the beach by yourself and suddenly hear loud booming sounds and suddenly see the sky all lit up with orange and yellow and blue and green and purple and gold and silver lights.
    (They gather around PAT in a circle, looking down at her as she remains seated.)

JILL: That'd be scary.

HOWARD: You might run and fall and scream. You might run right into the ocean and drown or run right into the forest.

BILL: They'd have to send helicopters out looking for you.

JILL: Or jets.

BILL: Your husband in the jet would find you.
    (PAT stands suddenly.)

PAT: Shut up! I don't have a husband in a jet and neither does Jill! So stop kidding around! If I want to walk, I will! Just to walk! Just to walk down the

beach and not come back till after dark. To loosen my legs up after a big
dinner like that.

FRANK: We were just kidding, Pat.

(*They all sit slowly around PAT.*)

PAT: Boy! That's something. Trying to scare me into not walking. What a group.

FRANK: We were kidding.

PAT: Shut up, Frank! Jesus. All of a sudden picnics are localized events. We all
have to hang around the same area where we eat. We can't even walk. We
eat a big steak and we can't walk it off.

(*HOWARD stands and grabs PAT's hand; he starts pulling her stage left.*)

HOWARD: Let's walk! Come on, Pat. Here we go walking. Where do you want to
walk to? (*The rest remain seated.*)

PAT: Cut it out! Let go! Let go of my hand!

(*He holds her hand tightly, staring at her.*)

HOWARD: I would like very much to take a walk. You're absolutely right about
the steak. We need to walk it off.

PAT: Let go, Howard, or I'll kick you.

BILL: Let her go, Howard.

HOWARD: But she's right. We should all walk after steak dinners. The stomach
works best when the whole body's in motion. All the acid gets sloshed
around.

(*PAT struggles violently to get away. HOWARD grabs her other arm and
holds her tightly, they face each other.*)

PAT: Let me go! Let go of my arm, Howard! I'll kick you! I really will.

FRANK: Come on. Let her go.

HOWARD: But she's right, Frank.

FRANK: Her husband may come back in his jet plane and see what you're doing.
Then you'll be in trouble.

PAT: Very funny.

BILL: He might.

JILL: Then he'll land and do you in with a ray gun or a laser beam.

HOWARD: But we'll be way up the beach. Jets can't land on a little strip of
beach. We'll be under some bushes even. He won't even see us. Will he, Pat?

(*He shakes her.*)

Will he, Pat?

PAT: He might.

JILL: See?

HOWARD: Pat's lying, though. Jets fly at an altitude of approximately five thousand feet and move at a minimum of approximately five hundred miles an hour with an air velocity of approximately — and a wind velocity and the pilot can't even hear or see or anything. He's just hung in space and he can't hear or see. Can he, Pat?

(He shakes PAT more violently. PAT gives no resistance.)

Can he or can't he? No he can't. Oh yes he can! He can see fireworks because fireworks explode at an altitude of approximately five hundred feet and give off powerful light rays and make swell patterns in the sky right under his keen old plane! Right? Beautiful. Just think how beautiful, Pat. We'll be down here on the grass and he'll be way, way up in the air. And somewhere in between the two of us there'll be a beautiful display of flashing fireworks. I can hardly wait for nighttime.

(He lets go of PAT. She moves downstage slowly, then turns and walks slowly upstage; she stands upstage staring at the scrim. HOWARD and the others watch her.)

HOWARD: Of course you have to let yourself go into aeronautics gradually, Pat. You can't expect to grasp the sensation immediately. Especially if you've never been up before. I mean in anything bigger than a Piper Cub or a Beachcraft Bonanza. Single — or double-propeller jobs of that variety usually don't get you beyond say a sore ear or two sore ears from the buzzing they make. The booming of a jet is something quite different.

JILL: She knows that.

HOWARD: Of course the sound isn't all of the problem. Not at all. It's something about being in the cockpit surrounded by glass and knowing the glass is solid, yet it's something you can see through at the same time. That's the feeling. You know what I mean, Pat? Looking through this glass enclosure at miles and miles of geometric cow pastures and lakes and rivers. Looking through and seeing miles and miles of sky that changes color from gray to blue, then back to gray again as you move through it. There's something to look at all around you. Everywhere you turn in the cockpit you have something to see. You have so much to see that you want to be able to stop the plane and just stay in the same position for about half an hour looking all around you. Just turning your seat from one position to the other until you take it all in. Even then you get the feeling that you'd like to spend more than just half an hour. Maybe a whole hour or two hours or maybe a whole day in that very same position. Just gazing from one side to the other.

(He crosses up to PAT slowly and stands behind her.)

Then up, then down. Then all the way around until you realize you don't have enough eyes for that. That maybe if you had a few more eyes you could do that but not with just two. Then you get kind of dizzy and sick to the tum tum and your head starts to spin so you clutch the seat with both hands and close your eyes. But even inside your closed eyes you can see the same thing as before. Miles and miles of cow pasture and city and town. Like a movie. Lake after lake with river after river running away from the lake and going to the ocean. House after house turning into city after city and town after town. So you quick open your eyes and try to fix them on the control panel. You concentrate on the controls and the dials and the numbers. You run your hands over the buttons and the circles and the squares. You can't look up now or around or from side to side or down. You're straight in front straining not to see with peripheral vision. Out of the sides of your eyes like a bird does but straight ahead. But the sky creeps in out of the corner of each eye and you can't help but see. You can't help but want to look. You can't resist watching it for a second or two or minute. For just a little bitty while.

(JILL stands.)

JILL: All right! Leave her alone!

HOWARD: Sorry.

(He crosses back down left and sits; JILL crosses up to PAT and stands beside her, patting her on the back.)

JILL: We're all going to see the fireworks together. So there's no point in getting everyone all excited. Pat's going to see them with us and nobody's going to walk anywhere.

FRANK: Oh, thanks a lot.

(He stands; BILL and HOWARD remain sitting.)

Thanks for the consideration, Jill. My stomach happens to be killing me. I could use a walk. And besides I'd like to see the beach.

BILL: We can walk later. After the fireworks.

FRANK: I can't wait and besides I have to pee too. I really do.

JILL: Well go ahead.

HOWARD: Pee here.

FRANK: No!

HOWARD: Pee in your pants.

FRANK: Look, Howard —

BILL: You can pee in front of us, Frank. It's all right. Pee your heart out.

HOWARD: We don't mind. Really. We're all friends.

JILL: We'll close our eyes, Frank.

FRANK: I would like very much to take a nice little walk and pee by myself, alone. Just for the enjoyment of peeing alone.

BILL: Well go ahead.

FRANK: Thank you. *(FRANK goes off right.)*

HOWARD: How's the girl?

JILL: She's all right. All she needs is some rest.

BILL: Listen, Pat, why don't you and Jill go up the beach with Frank and pee together under the bushes?

HOWARD: And we'll stay and wait for it to get dark.

> *(At this point the lights start to fade, almost imperceptibly, to the end of the play.)*

BILL: Pat?

HOWARD: We'll wait here, Pat, and save you a place. We'll save all of you a place to sit.

BILL: How does that sound, Patricia?

HOWARD: It would give you time to rest and settle your stomach and empty your bladder and loosen your legs. What do you think?

BILL: You could take as much time as you wanted.

HOWARD: You could even miss the display altogether if you want to do that. I mean it's not mandatory that you watch it. It's sort of a hoax, if you really want to know the truth. I mean if it's anything at all like the one they had last year.

BILL: Last year's was a joke.

HOWARD: That's right, Pat. Most of them didn't even work. The city spent thirty thousand dollars for twenty-five hundred fireworks last year and fifteen hundred of them exploded before they even got off the launching pad. They just made a little pop, and a stream of smoke came out, and that was it. A joke.

JILL: Some of them were beautiful.

BILL: Some of them were beautiful. The big gold and silver ones with sparklers on the ends. Then they had rocket ones that went way up and disappeared and then exploded way out over the ocean. They'd change into different colors. First orange, then blue, then bright yellow. Then this little parachute came floating down very softly with a tiny silver light on it. We just watched it slowly falling through the air hanging from the parachute. It went way out and finally sank into the water and the light went out. Then they'd shoot another one.

PAT: *(Still facing upstage.)* I'm not going to miss the display. I've seen every one of them for the past ten years and I'm not going to miss this one.

JILL: Of course not, Pat. *(She strokes her hair.)*

PAT: They get better and better as the years go by. It's true that some of them didn't work last year and that the city got gypped by the firecracker company. But that doesn't mean it will happen again this year. Besides, as Bill said, some of them were beautiful. It's worth it just to see one beautiful one out of all the duds. If none of them work except just one, it will be worth it to see just that one beautiful flashing thing across the whole sky. I'll wait all night on my back, even if they have to go through the whole stack without one of them working. Even if it's the very, very last one in the whole pile and everybody who came to see them left and went home. Even if I'm the only one left in the whole park and even if all the men who launch the fire-crackers go home in despair and anguish and humiliation. I'll go down there myself and hook up the thing by myself and fire the thing without any help and run back up here and lie on my back and wait and listen and watch the goddamn thing explode all over the sky and watch it change colors and make all its sounds and do all the things that a firecracker is supposed to do. Then I'll watch it fizzle out and I'll get up slowly and brush the grass off my legs and walk back home and all the people will say what a lucky girl. What a lucky, lucky girl.

JILL: We'll see them, Patty. Don't worry.

BILL: Jill, why don't you take Pat up the beach for a little walk? We'll wait for you. It would do you both good.

JILL: Do you want to walk, Patty?

PAT: Will we be back in time?

JILL: Sure. We'll just take a short walk and come right back.

(PAT turns downstage.)

PAT: All right. But just a short one.

BILL: That's a girl.

(JILL leads PAT by the arm; they go off right.)

HOWARD: Take your time and we'll save your places.

(BILL and HOWARD look at each other for a second, then they both get up and cross to the barbecue. HOWARD picks up the tablecloth and drapes it over the barbecue, BILL holds one side of the tablecloth while HOWARD holds the other, they look up at the sky, then they lift the tablecloth off the barbecue and allow some smoke to rise; they replace the tablecloth over the barbecue and follow the same procedure, glancing up at the sky; they do this three or four times, then FRANK enters from left in bare feet and carrying his shoes.)

FRANK: What a beach!

(HOWARD and BILL turn suddenly to FRANK and drop the tablecloth on the ground.)

It's fantastic! The beach is fantastic, you guys.

(They just stare at FRANK.)

You ought to go down there. No beer cans, no seaweed, no nothing. Just beach and water and a few rocks. It's out of the question. We ought to go down there and sit. That'd be the place to watch fireworks from. Right on the sand. We could move our stuff down there. What about it?

HOWARD: There's flak and little particles that fly off in those explosions. It gets in your eyes.

FRANK: Well, it would get in our eyes up here just as easy.

HOWARD: Not likely. We're above sea level here.

FRANK: So what?

HOWARD: So the air is denser above sea level and the flak and shrapnel and — well, it's just safer up here. Besides there's waves to contend with at sea level. And there's sand and we're away from the smell up here. There's a nice little breeze up here.

FRANK: I'd like to be down there myself.

(He crosses upstage and stares over the hedge as though looking down at a beach.)

BILL: Why don't you go?

FRANK: I'd like to. It'd be nice lying there with the waves right next to me and explosions in the air.

HOWARD: Go ahead, Frank. We'll stay here.

FRANK: Well we could all go. Like an expedition or an exploration. We could all find out what there is to know about the beach before it gets dark.

BILL: There's nothing to know. The beach is composed of sand which is a product of the decomposition of rock through the process of erosion. Sand is the residue of this decomposition which, through the action and movement of tides controlled by the location of the moon in relation to the position of the other planets in the hemisphere, finds itself accumulating in areas which are known to us as beaches.

FRANK: But it stretches so far out. It'd be nice to walk to the end of it and then walk back.

HOWARD: Go, then! Nobody's stopping you! Have fun! Go roll around in it.

(FRANK turns downstage.)

FRANK: Boy! You guys are really something. It interests me to know that I've been living in this community for ten years and never knew about this beach. I mean I never knew it was so clean. I expected trash all over and a huge stench from dead fish. But instead I find a long old beach that seems to go out to some kind of a peninsula or something. That's nice to see. I'd like to try hiking out there some day. That's an interesting thing to know. That you could spend a day hiking with a nice group of friendly neighborly neighbors and pack a lunch and make a weekend of it even. Or maybe two weekends' worth, depending on the weather and the friendliness of the neighbors and the cost of the baby-sitters involved.

BILL: That sounds very nice, Frank.

FRANK: I think so.

BILL: We'll have to try that.

FRANK: Where are the girls?

HOWARD: They left. They said they were going to look for you.

BILL: They wanted to tell you something.

FRANK: What?

BILL: They wouldn't say. Something important.

FRANK: They're just kidding.
  (He crosses down left.)

HOWARD: No. It was something big, though, because they wouldn't tell us even. We asked them what it was and they said they could only tell you.

FRANK: Something big?

HOWARD: Some kind of secret.

FRANK: Did they giggle about it?

BILL: Yeah but they wouldn't tell. We even threatened them. We told them we'd take them home before the fireworks started if they didn't tell.
  (FRANK crosses down right.)

FRANK: And they still didn't tell?

BILL: Nope. Something exciting, they said.

FRANK: But they giggled a lot?

BILL: Yep.

FRANK: I bet I know what it is.

HOWARD: You do?

FRANK: If it's what I think it is I'll kill both of them. Do you want to know what I think it is?

HOWARD: No. They said it was top secret. We don't want to know until you find out first.

FRANK: Well, I already know.

HOWARD: Not for sure. Go find out for sure, then come back and tell us.

FRANK: Okay, but it's really a joke if it's what I think it is. And if it is what I think it is they're going to be in real trouble.

HOWARD: Go find out.

FRANK: Which way did they go?

   (HOWARD and BILL both point off right.)

FRANK: Thanks a lot. I'll see you later. *(He goes off right.)*

BILL: Good luck.

   (BILL and HOWARD pick up the tablecloth and drape it over the barbecue again; they look up at the sky, then lift the tablecloth. They do this a couple of times, then JILL and PAT enter from left, laughing hysterically and slapping each other on the back; they are in bare feet and carry their shoes. BILL and HOWARD drop the tablecloth and turn to the girls.)

JILL: Too much! What a nut!

   (They both double over with laughter as BILL and HOWARD watch them. PAT falls on the ground and rolls around laughing and holding her sides; JILL stands over her.)

PAT: Oh my side!

JILL: Do you know — do you know what this idiot did? Do you know what she did! She — we're walking on the beach, see — we're walking along like this. *(She walks very slowly with her head down.)* Very slowly and dejected and sad. So suddenly she stops. We both stop and she says, Guess what? And I said what? She says I really do — I really do have to pee after all.

   (They both break up.)

So I said all right. I'm very serious with her, see. I say all right, Patsy dear, if you have to you have to. So then she said I have to pee so bad I can't even wait. I have to go right now. Right this very minute. So we're in the middle of the beach with nothing around but sand. No bushes or nothing. So she whips down her pants and crouches right there in the middle of the beach very seriously. And I'm standing there looking around. Sort of standing guard. And do you know what happens?

   (They crack up.)

All of a sudden I have to pee too. I mean really bad like she has to. So I whip my pants down and crouch down right beside her. There we are sitting side by side on the beach together.

   (She crouches down in the position.)

Like a couple of desert nomads or something. So. You know how it is when you have to pee so bad that you can't pee at all?

   (BILL and HOWARD nod their heads.)

Well, that's what happened. Neither one of us could get anything out and we were straining and groaning and along comes our friend in the jet plane. Except this time he's very low. Right above our heads. Zoom! So there we were. We couldn't stand up because then he'd really see us. And we couldn't run because there was nowhere to run to. So we just sat there and pretended we were playing with shells or something. But he kept it up. He kept flying back and forth right above our heads. So do you know what this nut does?

(HOWARD and BILL shake their heads.)

She starts waving to him and throwing kisses. Then he really went nuts. He started doing flips and slides with that jet like you've never seen before.

(She stands with her arms outstretched like a plane.)

He went way up and then dropped like a seagull or something. We thought he was going to crash even. Then I started waving and the guy went insane. He flew that thing upside down and backwards and every way you could imagine. And we were cracking up all over the place. We started rolling in the sand and showing him our legs. Then we did some of those nasty dances like they do in the bars. Then we both went nuts or something and we took off our pants and ran right into the water yelling and screaming and waving at his plane.

PAT: *(Lying on her back and staring at the sky.)* Then he did a beautiful thing. He started to climb. And he went way, way up about twenty thousand feet or forty thousand feet. And he wrote this big sentence across the sky with his vapor trail. He wrote "E equals MC squared" in huge letters. It was really nice.

BILL: Are you sure he saw you?

JILL: Well, he wasn't doing all those tricks for nothing.

BILL: But are you sure it was the same guy?

JILL: Of course.

HOWARD: It couldn't have been anyone else?

JILL: Not a chance.

HOWARD: Because Frank told us that guy crashed.

   (PAT stands suddenly.)

HOWARD: He said that he saw that very same jet go down in the middle of the ocean.

PAT: When?

HOWARD: Just before you came back.

JILL: So where did Frank go?

BILL: To get some help. They're trying to fish him out right now.

PAT: You mean he crashed into the water?

BILL: That's what he told us. It could be a different guy, though.

JILL: I doubt it.

HOWARD: The plane exploded just before it hit the water.

PAT: No!

BILL: That's what Frank said.

JILL: Well let's try to find him, Pat.

BILL: He went that way. *(He points off right.)*

PAT: Are you guys coming?

HOWARD: We'll wait here.

JILL: Come on, Pat.

(She pulls PAT by the arm, they go off right. HOWARD and BILL pause to look at the sky, then grab the tablecloth quickly; they are about to drape it over the barbecue when FRANK enters slowly from left. He seems to wander around the stage undeliberately and staring blankly in front of him. HOWARD and BILL drop the tablecloth and watch FRANK.)

HOWARD: Frank?

(FRANK continues to walk as he speaks; he moves all over the stage in a daze as HOWARD and BILL watch.)

FRANK: Boy, oh boy, oh boy, oh boy. You guys. You guys have missed the fireworks altogether. You should have seen — this is something to behold, this is. This is the nineteenth wonder of the Western, international world brought to you by Nabisco Cracker Corporation for the preservation of historians to come and for historians to go by. This is. If only the weather and the atmospheric conditions had been better than they were it would have beaten the Hindenburg by far more than it did.

(The lights by this time have become very dim, so that the scrim takes on a translucent quality.)

By that I mean to say a recognized world tragedy of the greatest proportion and exhilaration to make the backs of the very bravest shudder with cold sensations and the hands moisten with the thickest sweat ever before known, ever. And the eyes to blink in disbelief and the temples swell with pounds and the nose run with thick sticky pus. Oh, you guys should have come, you guys should have. What a light!

(There is a tremendous boom offstage, followed in a few seconds by flashes of light onstage changing from orange to blue to yellow and then returning to the dim lighting of before; the flashes should come from directly above them. This all occurs while FRANK continues, oblivious to everything but what he's saying; HOWARD and BILL remain in their positions.)

And to happen while walking head down looking at your toes and counting your steps. To happen under private conditions on sand. To be thinking about killing your baby boy or your baby girl or your wife or your wife's sister or your pet dog. And to come to a standstill.

(Another boom followed by the same lighting and returning to the dim; the sound of a vast crowd of people starts faintly and builds in volume to the end of the play.)

To stop still in your tracks, thinking about the night to come and how long it takes to build a beach given the right amount of sand and the right amount of time and the right amount of water to push everything up. Bigger bodies of water with more rain and less sun. More water than land ever. In volume, in density, in the stratospheric conditions. And to hear a sound so shrieking that it ain't even sound at all but goes beyond that into the inside of the center of each ear and rattles you up so you don't know exactly or for sure if you'll ever hear again or if it actually exactly matters. And it pulls your head straight up off your shoulders in a straight line with the parallel lines of each leg and so each tendon leading to your jawbone strains to its utmost.

(Another boom followed by the lighting; the crowd increases.)

So your eyes bob back and roll around in their sockets and you see the silver-sleek jet, streamlined for speed, turn itself upside down and lie on its back and swoop up, then give itself in so it looks like it's floating. Then another boom and it falls head down just gliding under its own weight. Passing cloud after cloud and picking up its own speed under its own momentum, out of control. Under its own force, falling straight down and passing through flocks of geese on their way back from where they came from. Going beyond itself with the pilot screaming and the clouds breaking up.

(Another boom and light.)

And the windows cracking and the wings tearing off. Going through seagulls now, it's so close. Heading straight for the top of the flat blue water. Almost touching in slow motion and blowing itself up six inches above sea level to the dismay of ducks bobbing along. And lighting up the air with a gold tint and a yellow tint and smacking the water so that waves go up to five hundred feet in silver white and blue. Exploding the water for a hundred miles in diameter around itself. Sending a wake to Japan. An eruption of froth and smoke and flame blowing itself up over and over again. Going on and on till the community comes out to see for itself.

(Another boom and light.)

Till the houses open because of the light, they can't sleep. And the booming goes on. And the porches are filled with kids in pajamas on top of their fathers shielding their eyes. And their mothers hold their fathers with their mouths open and the light pouring in and their cats running for cover.

(The booming sounds come closer together now and the lighting keeps up a perpetual change from color to color in bright flashes; the crowd noise gets very loud. FRANK moves faster around the stage, almost shouting the lines; HOWARD and BILL hold hands and stand very close together.)

And the sound keeps up and the doors open farther and farther back into the city. And the whole sky is lit. The sirens come and the screaming starts. The kids climb down and run to the beach with their mothers chasing and their fathers chasing them. Oh what a sight to see with your very own eyes. How lucky to be the first one there! And the tide breaks open and the waves go up!

BILL: Stop it, Frank!

FRANK: The water goes up to fifteen hundred feet and smashes the trees, and the firemen come. The beach sinks below the surface. The seagulls drown in flocks of ten thousand. There's a line of people two hundred deep. Standing in line to watch the display. And the pilot bobbing in the very center of a ring of fire that's closing in. His white helmet bobbing up and bobbing down. His hand reaching for his other hand and the fire moves in and covers him up and the line of two hundred bow their heads and moan together with the light in their faces. Oh you guys should have come! You guys should have been there! You guys —

(He staggers off left. HOWARD and BILL stand very still, facing out to the audience and holding hands. JILL rushes on from right.)

JILL: Come on, you guys! The plane went down. Come and look! Come on!

HOWARD: Get away from here!

JILL: Everybody's down there! It's fantastic. The plane crashed, Bill! It really did!

BILL: Get away from the picnic area!

JILL: All right. But you guys are missing out.

(She runs off right, HOWARD and BILL stand very still, the crowd noise becomes deafening, the lights dim slowly out, the sound stops.)

CURTAIN

NOW SHE DANCES!
Doric Wilson

a fantasia on the trial of Oscar Wilde
in two acts
for then
Richard Barr, Joe Cino, and Charles Loubier
and now
Barry Childs, Mark Finley, and Robert Locke

Around the time *And He Made a Her* showcased at the Cherry Lane theater (1961), I was arrested for sexual (I was innocent) whatever. The producer Richard Barr bailed me out of jail and I ran to the safety of the Caffe Cino, sat at a table and wrote (just like in the movies) *Now She Dances!* (I should have dedicated it to the cop who entrapped me, and who, years later, encountered me in a leather bar, leered, and suggested maybe he and I might . . . but that's another scene in another play.)

Now She Dances! began as a response to the hilarious histrionics and fruity language of Lord Douglas's translation of Oscar Wilde's *Salome*. Written with overwhelming earnestness in no-doubt equally florid French, Wilde's play has become a touchstone for decadence, equating lavender eau de cologne and slavering smears of silver eyeshadow with degeneracy. I decided to rewrite it as "The Importance of Being Salome" (Richard Barr later found the right title in one of the last lines of the play). The resulting play became an angry, ironic, nightmare metaphor for the trial of Oscar Wilde (the quintessential closet queen, Wilde was determined to establish his heterosexuality in court, which led to his fatal second trial).

Now She Dances! is my most fiercely autobiographical play. Painfully private and highly sensitive details of my youth are shattered, stitched back together and scattered liberally throughout the play. No, they are not the ones you think they are.

Now She Dances! was first presented as a one-act play at the Caffe Cino in August of 1961.[1] Produced by Joe Cino, directed by William Ashley, the Cino cast was as follows:

---

[1] Extensive rewrites and successful productions ensued, and Mr. Wilson reports that the original Cino script is lost. What appears here is the final final version of *Now She Dances!* Concerning rights to this play, contact Doric Wilson TOSOS II, 506 Ninth Avenue, 3FN, New York, NY 10018, phone 212.563.2218, email doricw@nyc.rr.com.

```
LANE ..................................... Thomas Lawrence
BILL ..................................... William Galarno
GLADYS ................................ Jane Lowry
MISS SALOME........................ Lucretia Simmons
LADY HERODIAS................... Zita Jenner
SIR HEROD, K.C.B ................ John Bevan
PRISONER ............................ Doric Wilson
```

CHARACTERS:

LANE, a butler with references from another play
GLADYS, a maid with references from many other plays
BILL, the new footman
SIR HEROD, K.C.B., a judge of the highest court
LADY HERODIAS, his dowager sister
The Hon. MISS SALOME, her diffident daughter
The PRISONER in the summerhouse

TIME:

now and then

SETTING:

a performance space

Shortly after *The Importance of Being Earnest* premièred in 1895, Oscar Wilde brought legal proceedings for slander against the Marquis of Queensberry. This determination to establish his heterosexuality before the bench caused the public scandal which led to his to his degrading second trial and imprisonment.

Operating on three main levels, *Now She Dances!* is a metaphor for this trial, blending characters from Wilde's *Salome* and *Earnest* with a Post-Modernist America. The denizens of Herod's decayed and corrupt court discover themselves constrained in the lace and frippery of a polite Victorian comedy of manners where they sit in judgement on a contemporary stand-in for Wilde.

The proceedings of this play are ruled over by Moloch, a deity who demanded of parents that their children be burnt in sacrifice.

ACT ONE

(An empty stage lit by a work light. Scattered about is shabby rehearsal furniture and a rack with costumes to be used later in the play. During the preset BILL enters from offstage and, acting as a stagehand, begins removing the furniture.)

(BILL, the new footman, is heartily young and blatantly American. Self-centered in his narrow sense of masculinity, he corresponds with the Young Syrian in Wilde's Salome. *He wears Levi's and a T-shirt reading: "Nuke 'em All.")*

(As BILL exits offstage with the next to last load of furniture, the house lights dim and the ACTRESS who will play MISS SALOME and the ACTOR who will play SIR HEROD enter down the aisle.)

(The ACTOR is an aging matinee idol deteriorated into a rouged and rugged roué. His wardrobe is frayed foppish, he wears his topcoat casually draped over his shoulders. Later, as SIR HEROD he is Algernon well past his prime.)

(Dressed in anticipation of fame and fortune, the ACTRESS is an ingénue with a future. Later, as MISS SALOME, she is an uneasy blend of Gwendolen and the ecdysiast of the New Testament — on the surface, a diffident daughter of propriety, in her soul, a carnivorous priestess of Moloch.)

(As the ACTOR and the ACTRESS reach the foot of the aisle, the play-within-a-play-within-a-play begins.)

ACTRESS: *(Disdainful of her surroundings.)* Is this —?

ACTOR: *(Arms wide.)* A theater!

ACTRESS: Disgusting.

ACTOR: Atmospheric.

ACTRESS: Claustrophobic.

ACTOR: *(Attending her with smirking lechery.)* Intimate.

ACTRESS: *(Looking around as she ascends to the stage.)* Not at all what I was lead to expect . . .

ACTOR: I think it's what they term experimental!

ACTRESS: *(Doubtful.)* I sincerely hope not —

ACTOR: *(Grabbing for her hand.)* You're here, I'm here — we can still make this a meaningful experience.

ACTRESS: *(Pulling away.)* Save it for later.

ACTOR: What need have you and I for flimsy make-believe? *(Falling to his knees.)* Deep in my heart —

ACTRESS: I said later.

(BILL enters from offstage to remove the last of the rehearsal furniture.)

ACTOR: *(To BILL.)* You're new.

BILL: *(Defensive.)* What's it to you?

ACTOR: *(To the ACTRESS, insinuating.)* Another "new" one.

ACTRESS: *(Crossing to the costume rack.)* Five in the last month.

ACTOR: *(Following the ACTRESS.)* Whatever does Lane do with them all?

BILL: Five what?

ACTOR: My costume hasn't been cleaned.

BILL: Not my job.

ACTRESS: *(Examining the hem of her SALOME costume.)* What precisely is your job?

(LANE, temporarily acting as stage manager, enters from offstage, carrying a clip board. A butler with excellent references from The Importance of Being Earnest, *LANE is smug and guarded — the quintessential closet queen. He wears pinstriped trousers and a work apron. The rest of his butler's rig — vest, stiff collar and swallow tailed coat — wait on the costume rack.)*

LANE: *(As he enters, protective of BILL.)* William will know his duties all in good time.

(BILL exits offstage with the last of the rehearsal furniture.)

ACTOR: *(To LANE.)* My costume —

LANE: We couldn't afford to send it out.

ACTOR: *(To the ACTRESS.)* With all due respect to you, m'dear — *(To LANE.)* — we seem to have found the funds to clean hers.

ACTRESS: Mine are never soiled. *(To LANE, indicating an exuberant red-feathered fan.)* What is this?

LANE: Your mother acquired it yesterday —

ACTOR: *(To LANE, a throwaway.)* — from Pick-n-Pay?

LANE: *(To ACTOR, a throwaway.)* A traveling Gypsy.

ACTRESS: She intends to use it?

LANE: In Act Two.

ACTOR: It's in character.

ACTRESS: I wouldn't know. I never rely on props. *(To LANE.)* You might suggest to dearest Mamma —

LANE: I've given her fair warning.

ACTRESS: *(Shades of SALOME.)* Are you interrupting me?

LANE: Anticipating.

ACTRESS: *(Sweetly.)* — you might suggest to dearest Mamma, ever so nicely, that, in my final scene, should I notice even a flick of this fan, I shall throttle her where she sits.

ACTOR: Before we commence our little comedy, would you care to nip by my dressing room for a dram of Madeira, m'dear?

ACTRESS: You truly are, aren't you?

ACTOR: Dashing? Dauntless? Debonair?

ACTRESS: Wholly and altogether without redeeming social content.
    (The ACTRESS exits backstage toward her dressing room.)

ACTOR: Hopelessly in love with me. They always are, all the ingénues. The price one pays for possessing a profile.

LANE: Might I remind you she is your daughter.

ACTOR: *(Tightly.)* We've only my sister's word for that.

LANE: *(Disapproving.)* But surely —

ACTOR: We both know how Herodias tends to muddle everything . . . *(Before LANE can object.)* . . . should, in fact, the dear child be less kith than kin, we would do well to remember "the times they are a changing." One must be au courant.

LANE: Au contraire, one must be —

ACTOR: *(As SIR HEROD.)* Servants do not speak French.

LANE: *(As the butler.)* Very well, milord.

ACTOR: And spare me epigrams that snicker at incest.

LANE: As you say, milord.

ACTOR: A tone of censure? From you, Lane? *(An innuendo.)* What did happen to the last one?

LANE: *(In all innocence.)* The last one what?
    (BILL enters from offstage.)

ACTOR: His "predecessor."

LANE: — proved unsatisfactory. *(To BILL.)* William, stand by to bring on the set.
    (BILL exits to the scene dock as GLADYS enters from the lobby. A maid with references from many other plays, she is arbitrary in her commitment to this one. A single woman of uncertain age, GLADYS is sister to Miss Prism. Dressed in contemporary street clothes, she carries her make-up kit, a PBS tote bag and her maid's costume on a hanger.)

GLADYS: *(To the audience, as she enters.)* Please, I'm late . . . which way is the rose garden? The rose garden, where is it?

LANE: Up here, Gladys.

GLADYS: *(Hurrying down the aisle.)* Yes! Indeed! Up there you are, the evil-doer and the evil-done-unto! Problem is, which is which?

ACTOR: You're late.

GLADYS: We've already established that.

LANE: Very late.

GLADYS: *(Climbing onto the stage.)* You're lucky I made it here at all. You won't believe the public transit in this burgh. This one creep in a trench coat —

ACTOR: *(Correcting.)* Not "transit — "

LANE: — tram.

ACTOR: *(Patronizing.)* Please try to remember, this is a period piece.

GLADYS: And so are you, dearie. *(To the audience.)* Ain't he a picture of days gone by, what with his wavy rug and cheeks of rouge? Used to be a matinee idol, he was. Before electricity. *(To the ACTOR.)* Had hair and teeth and everything, didn't you? Practically everything.

LANE: *(Censuring.)* Gladys —

GLADYS: *(To the audience.)* This one here's the butler. Very pompous he is, our Lane.

LANE: Gladys!

GLADYS: *(To the audience.)* And the terror of the footmen. *(Tweaking LANE under the chin.)* Grabs them above the knee in the pantry.

LANE: Gladys, that will do!!

ACTOR: Costumes are not to be removed from the theatre.

GLADYS: Took it back to my digs to wash it. Felt one of us should attempt to maintain some semblance of personal hygiene.

LANE: You'd best go in and change.

ACTOR: Tardy as you are.

GLADYS: *(Looking around the stage.)* Where's the set? Finance company repossess it? Fire Department find it too inflammatory? National Endowment revoke our grant?

LANE: *(As the butler.)* The French doors lead from this rose garden into the London townhouse of Sir Herod, K.C.B.

GLADYS: *(Still uncertain.)* French doors—?

ACTOR: *(To GLADYS.)* You, however, use the servants' entrance —

LANE: *(Indicating upstage right.)* — back by the compost pile.

GLADYS: *(To LANE.)* I don't need this job, you know. I've played more maids in more plays than you've had arrests for moral turpitude in Piccadilly tea-rooms.

(GLADYS exits downstage left, establishing a nonconforming attitude toward entrances and exits she will maintain throughout the play.)

ACTOR: *(To LANE, a general to his aide.)* The preparations—?

LANE: — are proceeding.

ACTOR: Tricky business seduction, requires the same meticulous attention to detail as a military campaign.

LANE: I've been briefed with tonight's battle plan.

ACTOR: The troops—?

LANE: Deployed.

ACTOR: The artillery—?

LANE: Primed.

ACTOR: The lady in question—?

LANE: — unsuspecting.

ACTOR: My technique l'amour is derived entirely from the principles of armed conflict as delineated by Attila the Hun.

LANE: I might never have guessed.

ACTOR: Not much of a gentleman, that barbarian, but a damned fine strategist, romantically speaking.

LANE: The combatant's Kama Sutra?

ACTOR: As my friend the Marquis of Queensberry is wont to say, "the female of the species must always be treated as a treacherous adversary."

LANE: Sporting of him.

ACTOR: Lull the wench into a false sense of security with moonlight and music and when she lowers her drawbridge, mount your assault, rapier in hand!

LANE: The charge of the light brigade?

ACTOR: The ladies love it.

LANE: *(Under his breath.)* Whatever gets you off.

ACTOR: Music is mandatory.

LANE: *(Evading.)* There will be music.

ACTOR: *(Licentiously.)* Ravel's *Valses Nobles et Sentimentales*?

LANE: As you requested.

ACTOR: Tape or CD?

LANE: Long-play record.

ACTOR: *(Crossing to the costume rack.)* Damned nuisance those musician chaps, demanding to be paid.

LANE: Fancy actors behaving so unprofessionally.

ACTOR: *(Taking his costume.)* We can hardly expect Miss Salome to dance a cappella.

LANE: Assuming she condescends to dance at all.

ACTOR: Not dance? Don't be preposterous. It's expected . . . it's a matter of tradition . . . it's . . . it's in the script.

LANE: Then you need not worry.

ACTOR: *(Almost an afterthought.)* As for the blood —

LANE: The blood will be authentic. Thick . . . warm . . . red . . . and most convincing.

ACTOR: Yes . . . well . . . jolly good.

    (The ACTOR exits offstage to his dressing room carrying his costumes.)

BILL: *(Coming to the edge of the stage.)* Lots of junk back here.

LANE: Start handing it out.

BILL: *(Returning to the scene dock.)* What do you want first?

LANE: *(Checking his clipboard.)* Flora. Let's set up the undergrowth.

BILL: *(Offstage.)* Trees? Flowers? Shrubs?

LANE: William, bring on garden.

    (BILL enters from the scene dock with a wing flat, which LANE and he position downstage left. As the scene progresses, they will set the stage to represent the rose garden of SIR HEROD's London townhouse.)

    (The scenery, when in place, is patched and peeling and flatly two-dimensional. Pictorially Victorian, it is lushly painted with indolent begonias and overblown roses intertwined in a sinister mesh of excessive ferns and convoluted vines. Through a gap in this strangle of shrubbery is glimpsed SIR HEROD's stately home. Ornamental steps, flanked by fuchsia laden urns, lead to French doors and within.)

BILL: *(As he enters.)* Whose blood?

LANE: *(Assisting BILL.)* Not your concern. *(Reminiscing.)* I remember as if it were yesterday my coming into the employ of this house. Palestine Walk it was known as in those days. My father — he was head eunuch — brought me in to amuse the boys. Young master Philip, young master Archelaus and young master Herod — "Antipas" we called him below the stairs. As the old earl — Herod Antipater — was notoriously lethal toward children, we were confined to the tower. *(His eyes misting over.)* The tower. What fond memories. There were rafters in the tower and chains and manacles and assorted other implements of persuasion. On rainy days the young masters were forever devising recreation, which inevitably was me. Boys being boys, I was frequently . . . well, I doubt they meant me permanent harm. *(With malicious pleasure.)* Philip was the first to go. Done in by a fetish for the sea. A grappling hook to the thorax. A bit fishy, as he was discovered in his own bath, nearly a hundred miles from the nearest merchant marine. Archelaus was next to meet his maker. It was Christmas Eve. The family was in the drawing room playing charades. Archelaus was acting out King Edward the Second, somebody had tampered with the poker. Most unfortunate. Authentic as hell. At the time Sir Herod was blamed as he had been observed, not a moment before, stoking the Yule log. *(As a portent.)* Now Herod himself, the last of the line . . .

BILL: *(Referring to HEROD.)* He's a big shot?

LANE: *(Back to here and now.)* Sir Herod is a lord justice of the highest court, a peer of the realm, a personage of ancient lineage, staggering debts and impeccable prominence.

BILL: Says who?

LANE: Debrett's.

BILL: What's that?

LANE: A book which tells you who's who.

BILL: *(As he exits to the scene dock.)* My mom doesn't approve of books.

LANE: She's illiterate?

BILL: *(Offstage.)* Naw, she's been married seven times.
   (BILL enters from the scene dock with a second wing flat. LANE helps him place it downstage right.)

LANE: Where did she acquire her antipathy to literature?

BILL: Grade school.

LANE: Prodigious of her.

BILL: Mom says books pervert the mind.

LANE: *(Fascinated.)* Your mother's an authority on perverts?

BILL: We had a whole library of books in our town, but mom got all the church ladies together and they cleaned it out. *(As he exits to the scene dock.)* Except for the Bible.

LANE: You're a student of scripture?

BILL: *(Offstage.)* I have a friend in Christ.

LANE: Then you'll feel right at home in our little scenario, it's vaguely Biblical.

(BILL enters from the scene dock with a third wing flat. LANE helps him place it stage left.)

BILL: *(As he enters.)* I've been born again.

LANE: How uncomfortable.

BILL: Have you been saved?

LANE: From what?

BILL: Eternal damnation.

LANE: Probably not.

BILL: *(Making a fist.)* You deny Jesus?

LANE: Nothing personal. He goes his way, I go mine.

BILL: Refuse salvation, I'll punch you in the face.

LANE: Threatening me bodily harm?

BILL: Only cause I love you.

LANE: *(Charmed.)* William.

BILL: I'm a Christian, I love all creatures great and small. Except the humanists.

LANE: *(Intrigued.)* And punching me in the face is how you express affection?

BILL: *(As he exits to the scene dock.)* If it'll save your soul.

LANE: How came you to our "sceptred isle?"

BILL: *(Offstage.)* Where?

LANE: How did you arrive in England?

BILL: *(Offstage.)* I hitch-hiked.

(BILL enters from the scene dock with a fourth wing flat. LANE helps him place it stage right.)

LANE: Wanderlust?

BILL: Nah, an itch to travel.

LANE: To see the world?

BILL: To get away from my stepdad.

LANE: Unsympathetic was he?

BILL: Nah, he kicked me out.

LANE: What did he catch you doing?

BILL: Failing.

LANE: At what?

BILL: Nothing in particular.

LANE: An all-around underachiever?

BILL: *(With pride.)* School, sports, selling used cars — you name it, I'm unsuccessful at it.

LANE: *(With an ulterior motive.)* Are you currently fiancéd?

BILL: Beg pardon?

LANE: Have you a girlfriend?

BILL: Don't you?

LANE: You must miss her.

BILL: Not as much as I miss my best buddy.

LANE: This "buddy" of yours, why didn't he accompany you on your travels?

BILL: He got married.

LANE: To your girlfriend.

BILL: *(Impressed.)* How'd you know that?

LANE: Intuition.

BILL: So I'm working my way to the Holy Lands.

LANE: A pilgrimage.

BILL: Nah, to join the Marines and sock it to the infidels.

LANE: Which infidels in particular?

BILL: Arabs, Jews, liberal Democrats . . . all them Godless heathens.

LANE: How romantic.

BILL: *(Sneering.)* Romance is woman's stuff.

LANE: What would you call running off to the Foreign Legion to nurse a broken heart?

BILL: Real men don't get broken hearts, they have coronaries.

LANE: You'll look most impressive in uniform.

BILL: Yeah, I know.

LANE: You definitely have the physique for it.

BILL: *(Flexing.)* I do, don't I?

LANE: Awesome musculature.

BILL: Wanta feel my biceps?

LANE: *(Tempted.)* This hardly seems the time or the place —

BILL: *(Ingenuous.)* Ah . . . come on . . . It's just between us guys.

LANE: *(Uncomfortable.)* The possibilities are most intriguing.

BILL: *(Flexing.)* Grab a hold of this.

LANE: *(About to succumb.)* The probability fraught with —

(Before LANE can make his move, GLADYS pops out from behind the just placed stage right flat. She wears her maid's costume and a dust cap, carries an immense transistor radio, street variety, and an old fashioned phonograph horn.)

GLADYS: *(As she enters.)* Hope I'm not intruding.

LANE: *(Rapidly moving away from BILL.)* Not at all.

GLADYS: *(To BILL.)* Why hello there.

BILL: Howdy.

GLADYS: *(Vamping.)* Where has Lane been keeping you?

LANE: Busy.

GLADYS: *(To BILL.)* My friends call me Gladioli Glad.

LANE: William is occupied. As you should be, Gladys.

GLADYS: *(To BILL.)* Don't talk much, do you?

LANE: When he has something to say.

GLADYS: *(To BILL.)* The strong silent type?

BILL: Yep.

GLADYS: *(Offering the radio and horn to LANE.)* Before you go all red in the face and start stomping about in a snit, I'm well aware this phonograph isn't strictly period so I scrounged around in the attic and found this old morning-glory horn — isn't it a hoot?

LANE: *(Horrified.)* A transistor radio?

GLADYS: Or as they say in the vestibule, a ghetto blaster. I liberated it from a nubile number in pink spandex who almost ran me down on his ruby red roller skates.

LANE: *(Returning the radio and horn to GLADYS.)* This is in no way suitable.

GLADYS: Sure it is. *(Trying to attach the horn to the radio.)* We simply insert . . . jam this into here — *(The radio complains loudly.)* — and we have an almost plausible facsimile Gramophone, circa here and now, by which I mean then and — *(Frustrated, she gives the radio and horn to BILL.)* — there, you're male, you're mechanically inclined.
  (GLADYS exits hastily to the wings. A baffled BILL exits to the scene dock trying to figure out how to connect the horn to the radio as LADY HERODIAS, a dowager dreadnought, enters full steam down the aisle. Bracknell deranged, LADY H is dressed for the boulevards of 1895. She carries a beaded reticule, her hat is a fantastic bird of prey.)

LADY H: *(Barging down the aisle.)* I came the back way through the streets. I felt it best to avoid scrutiny. *(To the audience.)* I can not with clear conscience recommend the streets. The people one encounters on them are revolting. Actively. *(As she climbs onto the stage.)* Indeed, I've a maxim for you. Curb your every inclination toward pedestrianism — it only puts you in proximity with the wrong people.

LANE: *(Conspiratorially.)* Did you accomplish your mission?

LADY H: *(Warily.)* My swine of a brother?

LANE: Sir Herod is feeding the falcons.

LADY H: You mean he's stumbling into his costume between swigs from the bottle. He better stay sober tonight. *(A sudden thought.)* He isn't . . . he hasn't —

LANE: He suspects nothing.

LADY H: And my diffident daughter? My guileless little girl?

LANE: Miss Salome is in the music room, whittling.

LADY H: *(As Mata Hari.)* Step aside.
    (Before LANE can comply, BILL enters from the scene dock with the flat depicting the facade of the house. Guiltily, LANE and LADY H quickly separate. LANE helps BILL position the flat upstage center.)

LADY H: *(For BILL's benefit.)* The garden is pulling itself together quite nicely. *(Indicating the foliage depicted on the wing flats.)* Look, hemlock in full bloom and it's only May. And foxglove . . . and there, deadly nightshade . . . and here, look, dainty belladonna . . . how I do prefer the domestic poisons. They take me back to when I was but a sprig of a thing — a silly miss — gathering me banewart where I might.

BILL: *(Alarmed.)* Poison?

LANE: Roses and begonias, all very benign. *(To LADY H.)* You're overloading the metaphor.

BILL: *(Still suspicious.)* What's a metaphor?

LADY H: You are. *(To the audience.)* Years ago Lane brought home this languid lad with aesthetic posture and creative hair who designed our set for us and then was seen no more. *(To LANE.)* Did we ever recover the family silver?

BILL: If this Herod guy's such a hot shot —

LANE: Yes, William?

BILL: — how come he doesn't have real plants?

LADY H: *(Nonplused.)* Qu'est-ce que c'est "real?"

BILL: You know, plastic — like they have on TV.

LADY H: *(Affronted.)* Television?

BILL: That's my big ambition. To be on the tube.

LANE: You aspire to fame and fortune?

BILL: Nah, I want to crash cars and kill people.

LADY H: *(To LANE, a throwaway.)* Wherever did you pick up this one? No, I'd
   rather not know. *(To BILL, as before.)* Young man, are you reliable?

BILL: What's in it for me?

LANE: *(To LADY H.)* He's colonial.

LADY H: Nonsense. They never put Americans on the stage. Not even in America. *(To the audience.)* I've played Masterpiece Theater, I know of what I
   speak. *(To BILL.)* Young man, tonight, here in the garden, Lane and I are
   planning an intimate tête-à-tête — nothing actually outré, but should the
   proceedings turn a trifle —

LANE: *(Warning.)* M'lady —

LADY H: Shouldn't he be in on it?

BILL: In on what?

LANE: Nothing which concerns you.

LADY H: *(To BILL.)* Young man, I've a maxim for you. Delve not.
   (A puzzled BILL exits to the scene dock.)

LANE: *(Pulling LADY H aside.)* Did you accomplish your mission?

LADY H: *(Referring to the streets.)* Out there in the streets is anarchy. Fuzzy
   fiscal policies stalking the better shops, radicals running riot, left to right,
   close personal acquaintants hanging from the lampposts — but for the
   sake of you and your silly mission I gathered my skirts about me and perse-
   vered, when suddenly, to my horror, there, before me, was . . . was . . .
   was —

LANE: *(Skeptical.)* "What?"

LADY H: A hand.

LANE: A hand?

LADY H: Your usual five fingers. Nothing out of the ordinary. No, now that I
   recall, there was an ink smudge near the knuckle of the third digit from the
   thumb. Or was it the first digit from the pinkie?

LANE: *(Losing patience.)* Had this hand a face?

LADY H: I daren't look. There stood I, there stood the faceless hand — the both
   of us poised on the precipice of an impasse. And then I saw it. The anonymous appendage with the ominous ink stain was proffering to me a piece of
   paper.
   *(BILL enters from the scene dock with a step unit which he places at the
   French doors.)*

LANE: A piece of —?

LADY H: — 8½ by 11-inch rag bond with miscellaneous mimeography on it.
   Which I instantly disposed of in the proper receptacle. *(LANE reaches out*

his hand.) It may have inadvertently slipped into my reticule. *(Producing the piece of piece of paper.)*

(As LANE reaches for the paper, GLADYS appears from the wings and intercepts it.)

GLADYS: *(Snatching the paper.)* A flyer!

LANE: A circular of protest?

LADY H: Such a polite, well-groomed young man. You'd never guess he was a dirty Bolshevik, bent on circulating protest.

LANE: I thought you didn't see him.

LADY H: I didn't.

BILL: What's he protesting?

LADY H: Me. They're always protesting me.

LANE: *(To GLADYS, curious about the cause.)* Save the whales? Ban the bomb? Free the Standard and Poor's 100?

GLADYS: *(Perusing the flyer.)* It's something about the G.D.F. . . . . *(As she comprehends.)* . . . Ha! Lady Herodias, avert your eyes!

LADY H: It's off-color?

GLADYS: Depravity, pure and simple.

BILL: Porno?

GLADYS: *(Offering the flyer to LANE, a gleam in her eye.)* This, I think, is addressed to you.

LANE: *(Reaching for the flyer.)* Me?

LADY H: *(Intercepting the flyer.)* What would Lane want with obscenity?

LANE: *(Attempting to retrieve the flyer.)* Mine, milady.

LADY H: *(Examining the flyer front and back.)* I see no depravity. *(To GLADYS.)* Gladys, you were titillating us. Oh . . . here it tells what "G.D.F." stands for. *(Reading.)* "Gay Defensive Front."

LANE: *(Under his breath.)* Peachy.

LADY H: *(Looking to LANE.)* Gay? Happy? I don't understand. Why be defensive about being happy?

BILL: If they're so happy, why run around protesting?

LANE: *(Dismissing BILL.)* William —

BILL: I'm on a break.

LANE: *(Pushing BILL toward the scene dock.)* The grownups need to talk.

BILL: *(Reluctantly exiting.)* Just when it starts to get interesting.

LADY H: *(Flyer in hand.)* Will somebody explain this to me?

LANE: *(On the spot.)* I . . . er . . .

GLADYS: *(Enjoying LANE's discomfort.)* It's a euphemism.

LADY H: A euphemism for what?

LANE: A euphemism for a euphemism.

LADY H: To be happy?

GLADYS: The synonym.

LADY H: Gay?

LANE: Does milady chance to remember Oscar Wilde?

LADY H: Mr. Oscar Wilde is not a fit subject for conversation. Certainly not in a family entertainment.

GLADYS: The circular comes from one of them.

LADY H: One of whom?

LANE: Mr. Wilde's progeny.

LADY H: They don't have progeny.

GLADYS: *(Still needling LANE.)* We throw 'em all in jail.

LANE: We seem to have missed one or two.

LADY H: *(Staggered by the thought.)* You mean to say out there in the streets I was placed in juxtaposition with a . . . with a . . .

GLADYS: "Sodomist!"[1]
  (BILL enters from the scene dock with an urn.)

BILL: *(As he enters.)* A sodo-what?

LANE: *(Taking the urn from BILL.)* An unlicensed proctologist.
  (BILL exits back to the scene dock.)

LADY H: I might have been molested.

LANE: *(Placing the urn next to the step unit.)* I sincerely doubt it.

LADY H: *(Waving the flyer.)* This is an omen.

LANE: It is nothing of the sort.

LADY H: The writing's on the wall, I tell you. There . . . above our heads . . . "Mene Mene Tekel Upharsim!"[2] Mimeographed.

LANE: That particular message was meant for Belshazzar.

GLADYS: It's all in the family.

  (BILL enters from the scene dock with the second urn which he places next to the step unit.)

---

[1] See The Trials of Oscar Wilde.
[2] The writing on the wall.

LADY H: Whatever is this country coming to?

GLADYS: Perversion lurking in every byway?

LADY H: Are none of us safe?

GLADYS: Shall we all be murdered in our beds by bad Judy Garland impersonations?

LANE: *(To LADY H, unaware of BILL.)* I entrusted you with an errand of the utmost importance, some street queen gives you a flyer and you go all unglued. You return the back way, empty handed.

LADY H: *(As a drug transaction.)* The password?

LANE: Cut the flummery.

LADY H: *(To GLADYS, as she extracts a parcel from the folds of her costume.)* Gladys, keep a peeled eye.

LANE: *(Eagerly.)* You managed to score?

LADY H: It had to be arranged.

LANE: *(Snatching the parcel and tearing it open.)* How much arranged?

LADY H: Our usual source was not available.

LANE: *(Revealing a long-playing record album.)* As long as it's legitimate.

LADY H: I paid more than the going price.

LANE: *(Reading the album title.)* Holy Mother of Moloch!

LADY H: What?

LANE: *(Returning the album with great disdain.)* Beginner's Burlesque?

LADY H: *(Reading from the liner notes.)* "Bump your way out of the daily grind?"

GLADYS: *(Snatching the album from LADY H, reading the notes.)* "Flesh and how to flash it?"

BILL: *(Sneaking a peek at the cover.)* Hot damn!
       (LANE glares at BILL, causing him to exit to the scene dock.)

LANE: *(To LADY H.)* You seriously expect Miss Salome to frolic about the shrubbery in her all together accompanied by snare drums and slide trombones?

LADY H: I naturally expect my dear daughter to — *(The horrible realization hits home.)*

LANE: Precisely.

LADY H: We're dead meat.

GLADYS: T'ain't missing tonight's shindig for nothing. *(She hums a bump and grind rendition of The Snake Charmer's Dance while doing a Sally Rand fan dance with the album cover.)* I see Paris, I see France, I see Salome's underpants —

LADY H: *(Retrieving the album from GLADYS.)* Steady, Gladys!

LANE: *(To LADY H.)* Take it back.

LADY H: Take it back?

LANE: Explain to the clerk that this is not the noble and sentimental waltzes of Ravel.

LADY H: Unhappily —

LANE: Simply demand he make an exchange.

LADY H: I doubt he'll still be operating from the same street corner.

GLADYS: Street corner?

LANE: But surely —

GLADYS: Milady's made a bum connection.

LADY H: I've been hornswoggled.

LANE: What am I to tell Sir Herod?

LADY H: *(Giving the album to LANE.)* I've a maxim for you. Make do.

LANE: *(Appalled.)* "Make do?"

LADY H: We all know who's behind this sabotage. *(Brandishing the flyer.)* The Gay Defensive Front. This is their doing. Oscar Wilde's revenge. A conspiracy of Ganymedes. Well, they shan't get away with it. I will see them hang! Drawn and quartered! Vasectomized! *(As she exits, a rogue caribou.)* Herod?! Herod, dear brother?! Debauched . . . debased . . . I've been undone!

GLADYS: His lordship'll have apoplexy.

LANE: *(Looking for somewhere to hide the album.)* His lordship need never know.

GLADYS: As for the kid, she'll have a conniption.

LANE: Miss Salome is no kid.

(The ACTRESS enters upstage right, wearing a dressing gown.)

ACTRESS: *(To GLADYS, as she enters.)* You.

GLADYS: Yeah?

ACTRESS: "Yeah?"

GLADYS: *(As a proper maid.)* Yes, Miss, I'm sure.

(LANE takes advantage of the ACTRESS's distraction to hide the album behind one of the urns.)

ACTRESS: *(Watching LANE out of the corner of her eye.)* I'm not at all sure.

GLADYS: No, Miss.

ACTRESS: I've seen you somewhere before.

GLADYS: I've worked for a lot of other plays.

ACTRESS: *(With a lethal smile.)* It's unlikely we frequent the same plays.

GLADYS: Yes, Miss.

ACTRESS: It's even less likely we frequent the same playwrights.

GLADYS: No, Miss.

ACTRESS: *(Sweetly.)* My costumes?

GLADYS: Immediately.
> *(GLADYS gathers the SALOME costumes from the rack and exits upstage right toward the dressing room.)*

ACTRESS: *(To LANE, referring to LADY H's exit.)* Have we degenerated into improvisation?

LANE: Not if I can prevent it.

ACTRESS: I could hear Mamma's histrionics all the way to my dressing room.

LANE: A slight deviation in the narrative.

ACTRESS: *(A warning.)* I abhor melodramatics.

LANE: As well you might.

ACTRESS: Almost as much as I detest spontaneity.

LANE: Nothing for you to worry your pretty head about.

ACTRESS: I intend to file a grievance with Actors' Equity.

LANE: *(Nervous about the music.)* Which violation in particular?

ACTRESS: Production values.

LANE: If you refer to —

ACTRESS: *(Pretended innocence.)* Music?

LANE: There's a perfectly good explanation —

ACTRESS: I am referring to the shabby set —

LANE: *(Relieved.)* Hopefully the moonlight will minimize —

ACTRESS: *(Stopping dead in her tracks.)* No moon.

LANE: But considering what's to transpire here tonight —

ACTRESS: No moon.

LANE: The moon is symbolic.

ACTRESS: *(Nicely.)* No moon.

LANE: It's your show.

ACTRESS: You bet your sweet ass it is.

(The ACTRESS exits upstage right to change into her SALOME costume as BILL enters from the scene dock with a pedestal.)

BILL: *(As he enters.)* Where do you want this?

LANE: The Holy Perch. Hand it to me. Reverently.

(BILL gives the pedestal to LANE and exits to the scene dock.)

LANE: *(Placing the pedestal.)* What else is back there?

BILL: *(Offstage.)* Not much. Lanterns . . . a box of empty bottles . . . the furniture for Act Two . . . some kind of a — ouch! — hatchet —

LANE: The headsman's axe.

BILL: *(Offstage.)* Sharp S.O.B. *(Continuing his inventory.)* — croquet mallets . . . a cannon . . . the sphinx —

LANE: The summerhouse!

BILL: *(Offstage.)* What's it look like?

LANE: Large —

BILL: *(Offstage.)* No.

LANE: Octagon —

BILL: *(Offstage.)* Nope.

LANE: Overwrought with wicker.

BILL: *(Offstage.)* Not back here.

LANE: We can not possibly proceed without it.

(GLADYS enters downstage left.)

GLADYS: You butlers slay me. You take everything so seriously.

LANE: Have you forgotten the importance of the summerhouse? *(Indicating the back of the auditorium.)* It must stand there at the bottom of the garden.

GLADYS: Fake it.

LANE: Misrepresent?

GLADYS: *(To BILL, offstage.)* Bill, what's back there by way of a substitute?

BILL: *(Offstage.)* The box of bottles?

LANE: Keep rummaging.

BILL: *(Offstage.)* Hey, guess what I found?

GLADYS: What?

BILL: *(Offstage.)* The moon.

LANE: No moon.

GLADYS: Yes!

LANE: No.

GLADYS: *(To BILL, offstage.)* Bill, bring it here.

LANE: *(To BILL, offstage.)* William, the lanterns?

GLADYS: *(To LANE.)* I'm very partial to moonlight.

LANE: No whimsy.

GLADYS: I'll keep it out of sight.

> *(BILL enters from the scene dock with a carton of Chinese lanterns which he places on the floor. He exits back to the scene dock for the ladder.)*

GLADYS: Please, Lane, for me?

LANE: We've been specifically instructed to exclude it.

GLADYS: *(Furious.)* Just you remember one thing, a maid never forgets. Never ever. Not in a thousand years.

> *(SIR HEROD enters from the wings dressed as a dandy of the period.)*

HEROD: *(To LANE, as he enters.)* Everything is —?

GLADYS: *(Peeved.)* Hunky dory.

HEROD: Unfortunately, I must go out.

LANE: *(Crossing to the costume rack.)* Before dinner, milord?

HEROD: A deranged sodomist is running amuck, pillaging the womenfolk.

GLADYS: *(Gleefully.)* A sodomist?

LANE: *(Doubtful.)* The womenfolk?

HEROD: This deviant undid the dignity of my sister. He also sold her some bum goods.

LANE: *(Gathering HEROD's cape, cap and cane.)* Shouldn't your usual woman-izer want to have — if only as a point of departure — some interest in women?

HEROD: Who can say with certainty just where sexual misdirection will ulti-mately lead a chap?

> *(BILL enters with a ladder and begins hanging the lanterns.)*

GLADYS: *(Out for revenge.)* Suppose, Lane, you were the pervert in question.

HEROD: *(Reconstructing the crime.)* Yes, there you are, loitering in the twilight of the street of no return —

LANE: I stay off the streets.

GLADYS: *(Joining in.)* — genetically you're unbalanced.

LANE: *(Conscious of BILL.)* Still waiting for the lab report on that.

HEROD: A product of improper toilet training.

LANE: Leave my sainted mother out of this.

GLADYS: A paucity of adequate role models.

LANE: Pseudopsychological hogwash foisted on the gullible public by a Viennese quack with a marked tendency toward misogyny.

HEROD: The moon is full.

LANE: *(A throwaway.)* No moon.

HEROD: *(A throwaway.)* No moon?

GLADYS: *(A throwaway.)* Ain't it a cheat?

HEROD: *(To LANE, resuming the reconstruction.)* You are transfigured by lust.

LANE: Not in recent memory.

GLADYS: Possessed of unbridled passion.

LANE: Perhaps in the privacy of my pantry.

HEROD: In short, you're horny.

LANE: Mildly aroused.

GLADYS: *(An evangelist.)* Moloch has entered unto you.

HEROD: He walks with you —

GLADYS: — and he talks with you —

HEROD: — urging you ever onward to your moral martyrdom.

GLADYS: Your carnal comeuppance.

HEROD: Your *auto da fé.*

LADY H: *(Suddenly appearing from the wings.)* Me!

GLADYS: Lady Herodias.

HEROD: Innocently coming the back way through the streets.

LADY H: A vessel of consternation.

GLADYS: *(To LANE.)* Your cup runneth over.

LANE: *(Helping HEROD into his cape.)* Poppycock.

HEROD: It only remains for me to catch the culprit.

LADY H: I'll identify him.

LANE: You didn't see him.

GLADYS: When you've seen one, you've seen 'em all.

LADY H: He'll be charged with perversity! With playing footsy with the wrong feet. With . . . with mimeography!
(LADY H exits stage left.)

HEROD: I pity the poor chap his punishment.

LANE: Will it be severe?

HEROD: *(With foreboding.)* Civilized.

    (GLADYS and LANE shudder at the thought.)

HEROD: *(Instructing LANE for later, a complete change of tone.)* Devotions first, I think. Here in the garden —

LANE: The Holy Perch is in place.

HEROD: — then inside for dinner and . . . *(Suggestively.)* . . . out again for the . . . er . . . the . . .

LANE: *(Hopefully.)* A nice rubber of bridge?

HEROD: Don't be preposterous.

LANE: *(Resigned.)* Ravel.

GLADYS: Digitally remastered.

HEROD: The phonograph record . . . I want to hold it . . . feel it . . . fondle its grooves.

LANE: *(Handing HEROD his deerstalkers cap.)* First things first, milord.

HEROD: *(To GLADYS.)* When my niece does begin to . . . er . . .

GLADYS: Trip the light fantastic?

HEROD: You might slip out to the lobby and lock the doors. We wouldn't want the guardians of public morality —

LANE: *(Handing HEROD his walking stick.)* The Vice Squad's been taken care of.

HEROD: *(Starting up the aisle through the audience.)* Should I not return —

GLADYS: — your understudy's in the bar across the way —

LANE: — standing by.

HEROD: *(From the aisle.)* I have my sword stick.

    (SIR HEROD exits through the lobby in pursuit of the sodomist as GLADYS and LANE wave him on his way.)

GLADYS: Tallyho.

LANE: *(To GLADYS, through gritted teeth.)* "Suppose, Lane, you were the pervert in question?"

GLADYS: I'll go in and finish the dusting.

    (GLADYS makes a hasty exit stage right.)

LANE: *(Muttering to himself as he crosses to the costume rack.)* The wrong music . . . no summerhouse . . . a dubious gramophone . . . fractious fairies making spectacles of themselves on the public thoroughfares. *(Reminiscing to BILL, as he puts on his butler's livery.)* . . .

BILL: Can I help?

LANE: Sweet of you, William, to offer. Perhaps during the interval. *(Calling to the light booth.)* Gary, kill the worklights and bring up dimmers one . . . eight . . . nine . . . and five . . . *(The light booth complies.)* . . . and check the gel on the decapitation special. The severed head's been looking overly lurid. *(To BILL.)* As for us, there is naught we can do but hope. And see to the escargot.

> *(LANE exits behind the house flat taking the costume rack as GLADYS peeks around the stage right flat.)*

GLADYS: *(To BILL.)* Pssst!

BILL: Me?

GLADYS: *(Still making mischief.)* Lane did it.

BILL: Did what?

GLADYS: *(Entering.)* Lane is the man with the ink-stained hand.

BILL: You mean he's the sodo-whatchamacallit?

GLADYS: He used an alias.

BILL: Lane?

GLADYS: That's also an alias.

BILL: *(Uncertain.)* Naw.

GLADYS: *(Blocking him.)* Thanks to him the entire *deus ex machina* is in dire jeopardy.

BILL: Figured something was up.

GLADYS: Later tonight Sir Herod will draw Miss Salome aside. She will finger her tassels, he will clear his throat, she will tap her toe . . .

BILL: *(So what.)* Yeah?

GLADYS: Absolute darkness.

BILL: So?

GLADYS: You try constructing a seduction without moonlight.

BILL: *(Shocked.)* Touching and stuff?

GLADYS: Complete with X-rated choreography.

BILL: This Miss Salome —?

GLADYS: — is being lead down the garden path. Minus the atmospheric lighting.

BILL: Somebody should warn her.

GLADYS: *(Hinting.)* Pity this play hasn't a hero.

BILL: I volunteer.

GLADYS: *(Pretending surprise.)* You?

BILL: Why not?

GLADYS: You're only a secondary story line.

BILL: I'll pad my part.

GLADYS: They'll throw you in the summerhouse.

BILL: We didn't put up the summerhouse.

GLADYS: *(Indicating the back of the auditorium.)* The summerhouse is there at the end of the garden where it's always been.

BILL: *(Astonished.)* But how did it . . . ?

GLADYS: *(Pleased with herself.)* Always remember, Gladys is your friend.

BILL: *(Fascinated by the sudden appearance of the summerhouse.)* If you say so.

GLADYS: Always remember, Lane is not your friend.

BILL: *(Confused.)* But —

GLADYS: What I just confided in you?

BILL: About the damsel in distress?

GLADYS: Mull it over, Galahad.

> *(GLADYS starts to exit upstage right.)*

BILL: Miss Gladys, ma'am, wait!

> *(BILL makes a hurried exit to the stage left wings to retrieve the moon as a satisfied GLADYS waits.)*

> *(The French doors open revealing MISS SALOME dressed in a high-necked teagown of pale lace sashed and bowed in pink satin. GLADYS sees her and backs to a nervous exit downstage right. BILL returns from the wings with a rusty moon shaped tray.)*

BILL: *(As he enters.)* I know how much you wanted this so I —

> *(BILL sees MISS SALOME, stops short, instinctively hiding the tray behind his back.)*

SALOME: *(To the audience as she descends the stairs.)* I usually enter side-saddle, riding a giant purple peacock, proceeded by a hundred naked Nubians blowing fanfares on long, lovely golden horns. It's very musical.

BILL: *(Love at first sight.)* I'll bet.

SALOME: Direct me to the garden.

BILL: This is it.

SALOME: I don't much care for it.

BILL: *(Backing to the ladder.)* Come back when it's finished. There'll be fancy paper lanterns all over the place, there was even gonna be —

SALOME: Are you he?

BILL: "He" who?

SALOME: The degenerate.

BILL: I'm the footman. Bill. *(Reconsidering.)* William.

SALOME: A degenerate molested Mamma today. Uncle Herod's gone out to catch him.

BILL: You're not supposed to know about that.

SALOME: I do know about it.

BILL: *(Hiding the tray in the lantern carton.)* Figured you must.

SALOME: I know everything.

BILL: Don't be scared.

SALOME: I never am.

BILL: You're safe.

SALOME: Am I?

BILL: I'll protect you.

SALOME: You will?

BILL: *(Climbing the ladder.)* I work here.

SALOME: So you said.

BILL: *(Preening.)* I'm responsible for —

SALOME: Hanging the lanterns.

BILL: *(Hanging the lanterns.)* Among my many other duties.

SALOME: Unskilled labor fascinates me.

BILL: It does?

SALOME: From afar.

BILL: Hanging lanterns is a lot more difficult than it looks.

SALOME: It must be.

BILL: It takes . . . *(Fumbling with a lantern.)*

SALOME: Manual dexterity?

BILL: Naw, you just have to be good with your . . . *(dropping a lantern)* — hands.

SALOME: I admire expertise.

BILL: You won't believe this but my mom has a ceramic lamp by her bed that's the spitting image of you. When I was a kid — before mom met up with my stepdad — I'd crawl in under the cover with her and if I was a good boy —

SALOME: *(Bored.)* She'd let you touch it?

BILL: *(Retrieving the lantern.)* Yeah.

SALOME: When do we eat?

BILL: After church.

SALOME: Church?

BILL: Devotions.

SALOME: I'm hungry.

BILL: I'll find Lane.

SALOME: You'll do nothing of the sort.

BILL: But, Miss Salome —

SALOME: I am a nameless woman.

BILL: *(Impressed.)* You are?

SALOME: And famished.

BILL: I could sneak down to the kitchen.

SALOME: What's down in the kitchen?

BILL: Food.

SALOME: *(Interested.)* What kind of food?

BILL: I know where they keep the cookies.

SALOME: Forget it.

BILL: I could swipe you a glass of milk.

SALOME: Beef. Pork. Venison.

BILL: They don't feed us that.

SALOME: I wish you were the degenerate.

BILL: You do?

SALOME: *(Pointing her finger gun-like at BILL.)* I'd take a gun and shoot your head off.

BILL: *(Envious.)* You got a gun?

SALOME: I'm a girl. Girls don't play with guns.

BILL: Then you couldn't shoot my head off.

SALOME: Then I'd be at your mercy.

BILL: *(A fantasy come true.)* Just like on TV.

SALOME: You concealed something behind your back.

BILL: *(Cautious.)* I did?

SALOME: When I made my humble entrance.

BILL: Behind my back?

SALOME: And then you slipped it into that carton when you thought I wasn't looking.

BILL: I didn't . . . I was just . . .

SALOME: Is it a secret?

BILL: Sort of.

SALOME: Is it a present?

BILL: Yeah. No. I . . . *(Not sure what to say.)*

SALOME: For me?

BILL: For Miss Gladys.

SALOME: Never heard of her.

BILL: You know, the one who does the dusting.

SALOME: *(Realizing.)* Just plain Gladys.

BILL: Yeah, her.

SALOME: Gladys isn't permitted presents.

BILL: She isn't?

SALOME: *(Hinting.)* Seems a shame to waste a perfectly good present.

BILL: That's the breaks.

SALOME: I'm partial to presents.

BILL: Who isn't?

SALOME: *(About to lose her patience.)* You have a superfluous gift on your hands, I haven't been the recipient of a gift in who-knows how long —

BILL: Give it to you?

SALOME: It's a thought.

BILL: You wouldn't want it.

SALOME: How will I know unless I see it?

BILL: *(Retrieving the tray.)* It's kinda dirty.

SALOME: It's all rusted red.

BILL: *(Offering her the tray.)* I can clean it off.

SALOME: *(Hands behind her back.)* Yuck.

BILL: Maybe a Brillo pad.

SALOME: I don't think I like it.

BILL: It's supposed to be the moon.

SALOME: *(Recoiling in horror.)* Away from me with that. Get rid of it. Now. Dispose of it before it can cause even more damage.

BILL: *(Holding the tray like a waiter.)* But it's only an old tray.

SALOME: Tray?!! You fool! You idiot!! You . . . you lunatic!!! *(Trying to control herself.)* Will dinner be served from that?

BILL: *(Laughing.)* No. *(Less certain.)* No.

SALOME: *(Sweetly.)* Then throw the . . . *(About to say moon.)* . . . "tray" away.

BILL: But —

SALOME: I, Salome, order it.

BILL: You —

SALOME: I lost my namelessness.

   (BILL hesitates, then throws the tray into the wings.)

SALOME: The whole garden is improved.

BILL: It is?

SALOME: I like you.

BILL: You do?

SALOME: Are all Americans handsome?

BILL: Most.

SALOME: Which tribe are you?

BILL: Tribe? *(Laughing.)* Oh . . . "tribe" . . . no, see —

SALOME: When did you say dinner would be?

BILL: I didn't.

SALOME: Are all Americans retarded?

BILL: I —

SALOME: You're not. You're wonderful.

BILL: *(Confused.)* I —

SALOME: And you like me, don't you?

BILL: I'm not so sure.

SALOME: Are you trifling with me? Am I some toy for you to play with and then dispose of like you did with the . . . *(Catching herself.)* . . . like uncle Herod did with poor Mamma?

BILL: I guess I like you.

SALOME: You "guess?"

BILL: You shouldn't be here.

SALOME: Says who?

BILL: Any minute now it all starts to thicken.

SALOME: The plot?

BILL: You said it, sister.

SALOME: What's the denouement?

BILL: Say what?

SALOME: Who's the victim?

BILL: You.

SALOME: Me?

BILL: Afraid so.

SALOME: Whatever will I do?

BILL: Hide.

SALOME: Where?

BILL: *(Indicating the wings.)* Over there . . . the scene dock —

SALOME: And miss dinner?

BILL: They're conspiring to commit . . .

SALOME: What?

BILL: *(Having difficulty with the word.)* Love.

SALOME: In the vernacular?

BILL: Nah, here in the garden.

SALOME: And all the time I was under the impression it was only dinner with
    maybe a drink or two after.

BILL: We can escape.

SALOME: To America?

BILL: Mom'll love you.

SALOME: I intend to report you.

BILL: Report me?

SALOME: To uncle Herod. For speaking to me.

BILL: You talked to me first.

SALOME: Prove it.

BILL: You like me.

SALOME: Fat chance.

BILL: But you said —

SALOME: I also intend to report your larceny.

BILL: Larceny?

SALOME: You attempted to pawn off on me a glass of burgled milk.

BILL: You're nuts.

SALOME: I also intend to report your vandalism. You deliberately destroyed property belonging to the house of Herod.

BILL: I did not.

SALOME: Willfully did you discard a precious Mesopotamian tray, middle period, one of a matched pair.

BILL: You ordered it.

SALOME: Unlikely.

BILL: It wasn't precious.

SALOME: Irreplaceable.

BILL: It was all rusted red.

SALOME: Terra cotta.

BILL: I'll go find it.

SALOME: You have not been dismissed.

BILL: You didn't mean what you said.

SALOME: What did I say?

BILL: About —

SALOME: Liking you?

BILL: Yeah.

SALOME: Dare you say I didn't mean it. I like you. I like all footmen. And I am grateful you warned me. Although you were mistaken. Never was the victim meant to be me.

(The lights fade as MISS SALOME exits through the French doors.)

ACT TWO

(The lanterns are hung, the Holy Perch is strung with garlands, the fake phono sits on a pedestal. A white wicker table waits off to the side.)

(Down the aisle comes a religious procession. MISS SALOME leads, scattering purple flower petals. She has replaced her pink sash with one of blood red. GLADYS follows, clanging diminutive cymbals. She now wears a frilly apronette and frou-frou. Next comes LANE, caped in the ritual robes of a high priest of Moloch. He wears a mask depicting the more vicious visage of the God. BILL follows, sheltering LANE with the Holy Umbrella. He wears an altar boy's surplice over his Levi's. Last is LADY HERODIAS, mater dolorosa, rosary clenched in her folded hands. She has changed into a scarlet evening dress of decadent décolletage.)

LANE: *(As they come down the aisle.)* Blessed be Moloch.

THE OTHERS: Blessed be Moloch.

LANE: Blessed be Bush the Belligerent.

THE OTHERS: Scourge of Saddam Hussein!

LANE: Blessed be Big Barbara.

THE OTHERS: Mother of Bionics.

LANE: Blessed be their begotten son.

THE OTHERS: Little Georgie.

LANE: Defender of the Profit Motive.

THE OTHERS: Avenging sword of the oil cartels!

LANE: Blessed be the Holy Ghost of the National Rifle Association.

THE OTHERS: Bang, bang.

>   *(The procession reaches the stage. LANE officiates in front of the Holy Perch. The others prostate themselves according to their faith.)*

LANE: Mighty Moloch of repression.

>   *(As LANE intones, the others repeat.)*

LANE: Deliver us from objectivity. Deliver us from self-analysis. Deliver us from secular humanism. Deliver us from retroactive abortion. Deliver the disciples of abortion unto capital punishment.

THE OTHERS: For such is the right to life.

LANE: Protect and defend family values.

GLADYS: *(With evangelical fervor.)* Praised be the missionary position!

LANE: Protect and defend us from marauding mimeographers.

LADY H: Drive some nails in that closet door!

LANE: Protect and defend Thy man children. Make them strong of limb, red of blood, with narrow waists and broad shoulders and tattoos of panthers running up and down their hairy forearms.

GLADYS: *(Trying to restrain him.)* Er . . . Lane . . . ?

LANE: *(Unheeding.)* Endow them with bountiful genitalia straining the seams of their sweat-stained athletic supporters.

LADY H: Lane.

LANE: *(Coming out of his rapture.)* What? Oh . . . yes . . . sorry. *(Perfunctorily.)* As for girls, make them submissive, feminine and good homemakers.

SALOME: *(Under her breath.)* For Christ's sake.

LANE: For Thine is the kingdom

GLADYS: — and the power —

ALL: — and the glory.

LADY H: *(Flagellating herself with her rosary.)* Mea culpa, mea culpa, mea maxima culpa.

(They start to rise.)

LANE: And — *(They return to their knees.)* — omnipotent Moloch, protect and defend Sir Herod, K.C.B., who has yet to return from the darkness of Thy night and the uncertainty of Thy streets.

(They rise. LANE places the mask of Moloch on the Holy Perch.)

SALOME: When do we eat?

LADY H: With Herod lost, gone, never to return?

GLADYS: Sure puts a crimp in the climax.

LANE: Gladys, away to the greenhouse.

LADY H: *(To GLADYS.)* Pick a brave bouquet.

(GLADYS exits upstage left behind the house.)

BILL: *(Shedding the surplice.)* Shouldn't we call the cops?

LADY H: And disturb their slumber?

LANE: *(To BILL.)* The garden chairs?

(BILL exits downstage right.)

SALOME: I'm going in.

LADY H: You'll stay put until dinner is served.

LANE: *(Formally.)* Dinner is served.

LADY H: Perhaps that's for the best.

(LADY HERODIAS and MISS SALOME exit through the French doors as GLADYS enters from upstage left with a bouquet of exaggerated flowers.)

GLADYS: *(As she enters.)* If there was any money in the family, I'd say the old boy absconded.

LANE: *(Placing the table stage center.)* Unless he actually apprehended the miscreant —

GLADYS: — and they're hot at it in a motel somewhere.

(SIR HEROD enters down the aisle, his costume disheveled, his swordstick bent.)

HEROD: *(In the aisle.)* Have I missed devotions?

GLADYS: Milord, you're safe.

HEROD: *(Climbing onto the stage.)* Barely.

LANE: You caught the culprit?

HEROD: I caught someone.

GLADYS: You're not positive if it's the deviant in question?

HEROD: It was getting dark, I had to take what I could find.

(BILL enters downstage right with two wicker garden chairs.)

LANE: He confessed?

HEROD: Poor chap, he didn't seem to know what was happening to him.

GLADYS: I'll be off to the ladies with the glad tidings.
       (GLADYS exits through the French doors.)

HEROD: *(To LANE.)* They're already at the table?

LANE: *(Arranging the flowers in a vase.)* They're already in the aspic.

HEROD: *(Starting for the French doors.)* Keep an eye on the summerhouse.

LANE: You locked him in there?

HEROD: You might see that he has fresh water.
       (SIR HEROD exits through the French doors.)

LANE: *(As a cue.)* Now it all begins.

BILL: *(Putting an 18th century livery coat over his T-shirt.)* I don't understand.

LANE: You're not expected to. *(Repeating the cue.)* Now it all begins.

BILL: He caught the wrong man?

LANE: It is never the wrong man. *(Repeating the cue.)* Now it all begins.
       (GLADYS enters from downstage left, a champagne glass in hand.)

GLADYS: *(Referring to the flowers.)* What lovely expositions and how nicely you are arranging them.

LANE: You missed your cue.

GLADYS: *(Giving the glass to LANE.)* Here's the first champagne glass. *(GLADYS exits downstage right.)*

LANE: *(Calling after GLADYS.)* One glass? Surely you're not planning to bring them on one at a time.

BILL: Lane is your real name, isn't it?

LANE: Whatever do you mean?

BILL: It isn't an alias, is it?

LANE: William, have you been smoking the flora?

BILL: *(Attaching a lace jabot around his neck.)* I'm getting mighty suspicious.

LANE: *(Referring to GLADYS.)* As am I.

BILL: *(TV tough guy.)* You and me, we need to talk.

LANE: And we shall. Later.

BILL: Man to man.

LANE: Absolutely.

BILL: Now.

LANE: You do pick the most inconvenient times.
       (GLADYS enters from downstage left, a second champagne glass in hand.)

GLADYS: *(Giving the glass to LANE.)* Here is the second champagne glass. *(GLADYS exits downstage right.)*

LANE: *(Calling after GLADYS.)* Stop making entrances if you're not intending to play the scene.

BILL: *(To LANE.)* There's something fishy going on around here.

LANE: Only the caviar.

BILL: Look, pal, let's lay our cards on the table.

LANE: You first.

BILL: I'm onto you.

LANE: Are you?

BILL: I know all about the whole conspiracy.

LANE: *(Alarmed.)* Which conspiracy in particular?

BILL: The garden path . . . the missing moonlight . . . the distressed damsel —

LANE: *(Calling offstage right.)* Gladys, get out here!

BILL: I figured it out all by myself.

LANE: Cunning of you.

BILL: When I took this job, I didn't know I'd be implicated in a . . . in a . . .

LANE: Love scene?

BILL: If the folks back home find out . . . well, it'd kill mom.

LANE: It's not your love scene.

BILL: There's guilt by association.

LANE: Nobody invited you to associate.

BILL: I can't just stand by and watch it happen.

LANE: *(An attempt at damage control.)* Trust me, William, tonight. *(GLADYS enters from downstage left, a third champagne glass in hand.)*

GLADYS: *(As she enters.)* . . . is fraught with significance. Farce fencing force over tea, tragedy triumphantly tripping through the petit fours, life leaping over the Christopher Wren balustrade, cucumber sandwich in hand. *(To the audience.)* This moment of purple prose was brought to you by Exxon in hopes that a nice smear of culture will keep your mind off the mess they're making of the environment.

LANE: What have you been telling William?

GLADYS: *(Giving the glass to LANE.)* Here is the third and final champagne glass. *(GLADYS exits downstage right.)*

LANE: *(Calling after GLADYS.)* Gladys?! *(To BILL, fearing the worst.)* This "conspiracy theory" of yours, has it had wide circulation?

BILL: Miss Salome, but only to warn her.

LANE: "Warn her"?

BILL: She was to be the victim.

LANE: "Was to be?"

(LADY HERODIAS enters through the French doors, napkin and fork in hand.)

LADY H: I slipped away from the table unnoticed.

LANE: There's a revolt brewing among the footmen.

LADY H: Squelch it. The film —?

LANE: *(Handing the red feathered fan to LADY H.)* — is in the camera.

LADY H: *(Pleased.)* And the camera is hidden in the handle of the fan! How fortunate for us you've had such wide experience with blackmail.

LANE: *(Conscious of BILL.)* Milady.

LADY H: When my cad of a brother debauches my diffident daughter, we document the whole unsavory episode with my handy Instamatic and you and I are set for life.

BILL: Blackmail?

LADY H: Faithful family retainers and faded females of fashion must fend for themselves as best as they can.

(LADY HERODIAS exits through the French doors.)

BILL: *(Disgusted.)* Her own daughter.

LANE: You're to stay out of this.

(GLADYS enters downstage left with a small silver tray on which there are bags that look as if they might contain tea.)

GLADYS: *(Giving the tray to LANE.)* Here are the champagne bags.

LANE: *(As he exits offstage right.)* Pity, she was a great maid in her day.

BILL: *(Impressed.)* You were in show business?

GLADYS: *(Including the audience.)* If only you could have been there for my debut. Oh, I'd had some experience . . . a bit of dusting in Act One, answering the phone in Act Two . . . but this was my first big break . . . my first big formal sit-down dinner. There were many, many courses, but the entrance was soup. Back in the wings I stood, soup in hand. Pea soup in hand. Split pea soup in hand. I tried to concentrate. To prepare. What is soup? What is the essence of soup? What are the social implications? What would Stanislavski say? I tried to recall my earliest encounter with soup. Soup de jour. Soup kitchens. Mother's soup. This soup, here, now, in the tureen I saw before me. How did I feel about this soup? How did this soup feel about me? I stepped out into the golden, fervent light. I paused. I took one step . . . my thoughts racing back . . . another step . . . back to years of study . . . another step . . . hard years . . . step . . . sad years . . . step . . . making the rounds . . . step . . . parts I never got . . . step . . . dinners I never served . . . step . . . years that brought me here . . . step . . . tonight . . . step . . . would they like me . . . step . . . would they understand . . . step . . . would I ever get there . . . step . . . once I got there . . . step . . . would they like the soup? I put the soup on the table. Next day I came down with hepatitis and had to leave the show.

(GLADYS exits downstage right almost colliding with LANE who enters carrying a champagne bucket in a stand.)

BILL: *(To LANE.)* What happened to theatre?

LANE: Died, in your country, from overeating.

GLADYS: *(Popping her head out from the downstage right wings.)* Something tingling with excitement is about to take place.

LANE: *(Taking his position by the French doors.)* William, to your post.

BILL: Here's the plan. I need a helicopter, a fast car — the kind that converts into a speed boat, some plastic explosives, an Uzi, a cigarette lighter that is really a top secret anti-satellite device. You cause a diversion, I grab the girl, we make a run for it.

LANE: You'll do nothing of the sort.

BILL: But —

LANE: To your post.

(BILL reluctantly takes his position.)

LANE: *(Announcing.)* The honorable Miss Salome.

(The Chinese lanterns flare, the French doors fling open, MISS SALOME stands in the doorway.)

SALOME: Not a very good dinner, no potatoes.

BILL: You're in danger.

SALOME: Lane, restrain your minion.

LANE: *(To BILL, warning.)* William.

SALOME: How dark it is tonight.

LANE: You gave specific instructions

SALOME: Let's get cracking around here. Let us commence the festivities. Let there be music!

BILL: No!

SALOME: Lane, I asked for music.

LANE: I . . . er . . . your Mamma . . . we —

SALOME: The footman's right. We want quietude. Save the violins for later.

LANE: *(Under his breath.)* Not to mention the snare drums.

SALOME: Why is the door to the summerhouse locked?

LANE: Is it, miss? I hadn't noticed.

SALOME: I have every confidence in you, Lane.

LANE: I have even greater confidence in you.

SALOME: That's something a footman can't be expected to understand.

BILL: You gotta listen to me.

SALOME: Can you see me?

BILL: *(Unsure.)* Yes.

SALOME: What do you see?

BILL: What should I see?

SALOME: An innocent lamb being led to slaughter?

BILL: Yeah!

SALOME: Never again are you to see me as mutton. Lamb is mutton. To be served. I am not a lamb. I am not a sea gull. I am not a wild duck. Nor the Christmas goose. Nor a goat named Sylvia. I am none of those symbolic animals. I am a little girl. A shy lithe girl. Unworldly, undemanding, desperately in need of a drink.

LANE: The water is icing.

SALOME: That hardly satisfies my thirst.

> *(As LANE starts for the bell pull, GLADYS enters downstage left with a pitcher of ice water.)*

GLADYS: You rang?

LANE: *(Taking the pitcher from GLADYS.)* I would have.

> *(GLADYS exits downstage right. During the following speech, LANE fills a champagne glass with water.)*

SALOME: Why must everyone complicate everything? Mamma and "uncle" Herod sit in there all hunched over the Queen Anne table, puffing on their panatellas, scribbling figures and percentages and prorates on the damask and haggling, haggling, haggling. Do they care about me? Do they consider my feelings? They toss and throw me back and forth like dice.

> *(LANE brings the glass and a champagne bag to MISS SALOME.)*

SALOME: *(Reading the tag on the champagne bag.)* A good year. A very good year. Disappointing country. *(Dunking the champagne bag in the glass of water.)* Why is it so difficult to find a good year and a decent country in the same bag? I recall . . . was it Rome? Carthage? No, that odd island in the Aegean where those martial ladies kept that athletic girls school — he's locked in the summerhouse, isn't he?

LANE: Who, miss?

SALOME: Don't dissemble.

LANE: The prophet?

SALOME: Prophet?

LANE: Meant to say prisoner.

SALOME: Pervert.

LANE: Has that been proven?

SALOME: The "alleged" pervert. Mamma's friend. The guy with the leaflets . . . locked in the summerhouse.

LANE: I wouldn't know.

SALOME: You would know.

LANE: Drink your wine.

SALOME: *(To LANE.)* Let him out.

LANE: *(To SALOME.)* Impossible.

BILL: *(To LANE.)* Forget the fast car.

SALOME: *(To LANE.)* Liberate the libertine.

BILL: *(To LANE.)* A bicycle will do.

LANE: Might we return to the plot at hand?

SALOME: Let him out.

LANE: No.

SALOME: Release him.

LANE: Impossible.

BILL: Miss Salome, please, no.

SALOME: Let the misogynist out!

BILL: For your protection.

SALOME: *(Laughing.)* My protection?

LANE: His protection, then.

BILL: He's dangerous.

SALOME: *(To BILL.)* Surely you can protect me from a sissy. *(To LANE.)* Are you making me wait? I don't like to wait. When I wait, I become bored . . . when I become bored, I tend to look less than ravishing . . . Lane, I am not looking pretty. I'm very insecure, Lane. When I have reason to doubt my allure, I become nasty. Very nasty.

GLADYS: Maids never open doors, so don't ask me.

SALOME: What do you mean maids never open doors?

GLADYS: It's an Equity rule.

SALOME: Any hand that dusts a table can open the door to the summerhouse.

GLADYS: Shows how much you know.

SALOME: Your fingers itch for that handle.
   (GLADYS hides her hands behind her.)

SALOME: You're simply pagan with door opening tendencies.

GLADYS: No!

SALOME: Solidarity, sister, sorority.

GLADYS: Unfair!

SALOME: As one woman to another.

GLADYS: Never!

LANE: Brava, Gladys.

GLADYS: I almost weakened. I don't often get included in the female gender.
   (GLADYS exits USR.)

SALOME: Bill?

LANE: *(Warning.)* William.

SALOME: Brave Bill.

BILL: No way.

SALOME: Manly Bill. Tomorrow, at high tea, when I make my humble entrance, walking, without the benefit of naked trumpeters, I shall smile. That smile, Bill . . . blue eyed, blonding Bill . . . shall be for you.

BILL: I won't open that door.

SALOME: I might even drop my glove.

BILL: *(Weakening.)* Your glove?

SALOME: You can retrieve it for me.

BILL: *(To LANE.)* Her glove?

SALOME: My white, right glove.

LANE: *(Warning.)* William.

SALOME: Both gloves!

BILL: I can keep them?

SALOME: You may do with them as you please. Whatever you please. Wherever you please. With whatever pleases you.

LANE: And you'll grow hair on the palm of your hand.

SALOME: Butt out, Lane.

BILL: Both gloves?

SALOME: And one stocking.

> *(BILL jumps from the stage, hurries up the aisle to the summerhouse.)*

LANE: *(To BILL.)* No, stay away from that door!

SALOME: *(To LANE.)* You may leave us.

LANE: You wish.

SALOME: Ten minutes alone with him.

LANE: I'd rather watch.

SALOME: A voyeur.

LANE: An innocent bystander.

SALOME: Five minutes. I'll make it worth your while.

LANE: The other stocking?

> *(BILL leads the PRISONER down the aisle. The PRISONER's hands are bound behind him with raw-hide, his shirt is torn. He is an attractive, personable, contemporary gay male, dressed for Saturday night on West Street.)*

SALOME: *(To the PRISONER.)* Hello . . . come up here . . . pay no mind to the functionaries.

> *(The PRISONER and BILL are on the stage.)*

SALOME: *(To the PRISONER.)* . . . watch your step . . . here . . . come . . . sit down. *(To BILL.)* Thank you, William, that will be all. *(To the PRISONER.)* Hello.

PRISONER: Where am I?

SALOME: Sit down.

PRISONER: I'll stand.

SALOME: You'll sit.

PRISONER: What's going on here?

SALOME: You must be shaky.

PRISONER: Why are my hands tied?

SALOME: You look shaky.

PRISONER: What the fuck's going on here?

BILL: Watch your language!

SALOME: Your hands are trembling. Is the rawhide too tight?

PRISONER: Is this some kind of a game?

SALOME: Game?

PRISONER: A fantasy trip with me as the sex object?

SALOME: You want to play games? *(To LANE.)* Set up the hoops. *(To the PRISONER.)* I challenge you to croquet.

PRISONER: Unreal.

SALOME: Would you prefer badminton?

PRISONER: Is this a garden?

SALOME: Are you a horticulturist?

PRISONER: This must be a dream.

SALOME: Are you asleep?

PRISONER: Or a bad trip. Sure, that's it! You're one 'lude too many.

SALOME: Are you an addict?

PRISONER: Not after this.

SALOME: Already I've influenced your rehabilitation.

PRISONER: This is a stage, isn't it?

SALOME: Are you an actor?

PRISONER: I seem to be under arrest.

SALOME: What did you do?

PRISONER: I'm innocent.

SALOME: Of what?

PRISONER: How should I know?

SALOME: You don't know why you're here?

PRISONER: I don't know where I am.

SALOME: Will that be your defense?

PRISONER: Then this is a jail?

SALOME: Did you do it?

PRISONER: No, I did not.

SALOME: What didn't you do?

PRISONER: I was innocently walking along West Street

SALOME: I thought you people called it cruising.

PRISONER: Right . . . it's funny . . . I'm laughing. *(To LANE.)* Is there a telephone here?

SALOME: I said sit down. No? Stand, do precisely as you please. Should you wish to sit down, these are chairs. Lane, function, give our guest some champagne.

PRISONER: No thanks.

BILL: *(To SALOME.)* Want me to put him away now?

SALOME: Fine, don't have champagne. *(To LANE.)* I'll have some, he can share from my glass.

(LANE takes glass, refills it.)

SALOME: *(To the PRISONER.)* My name's Salome.

PRISONER: *(To LANE.)* I asked to use a telephone.

SALOME: And you?

PRISONER: Me what?

SALOME: Your name.

PRISONER: *(To BILL.)* Where's the phone?

BILL: Come near me, I'll bust you in the face!

SALOME: Are you a phone freak?

PRISONER: I'm allowed one phone call.

SALOME: Why won't you tell me your name?

PRISONER: *(To BILL.)* Untie me.

BILL: No.

PRISONER: Why not?

BILL: You're a prisoner.

PRISONER: Am I? It seems I am. I'm not sure I know what kind of jail this is.

SALOME: You've had experience with incarceration?

PRISONER: Only on pig night at the Lure.

SALOME: If I loosen your bondage, will you tell me your name?

PRISONER: Try it and find out.

SALOME: *(Untying him.)* Our only interest is making you comfortable.

PRISONER: *(To LANE.)* What are you supposed to be? The butler?

LANE: On occasion.

PRISONER: I've seen you somewhere before.

LANE: *(Uncomfortable.)* It's hardly likely.

PRISONER: Sure . . . some piss elegant bar on the Upper East Side.

LANE: You're mistaken.

PRISONER: *(To LANE.)* Ah . . . yes . . . I understand.

LANE: I would prefer you didn't.

PRISONER: *(To BILL.)* What are you supposed to be?

BILL: I warned you once.

PRISONER: I'm only being friendly.

BILL: I know what you are.

PRISONER: You're not enjoying this as much as she is.

BILL: You ready to go back now?

PRISONER: *(To BILL.)* Want to tell me what this is all about?

SALOME: Are you ignoring me?

PRISONER: I'm talking to him.

SALOME: You're talking to me.

PRISONER: *(To BILL.)* They won't let you talk?

SALOME: He can talk. Talk, William.

PRISONER: William? Bill? Which do you prefer?

LANE: He seems to have nothing to say.

SALOME: *(To the PRISONER.)* And your name?

PRISONER: Any name will do.

SALOME: Are you ashamed of your name?

PRISONER: *(To LANE.)* You seem to be the power behind the throne here.

LANE: Don't include me in this.

PRISONER: It may be too late.

LANE: For you.

PRISONER: We're in this together.

LANE: How naïve.

PRISONER: Each man for himself?

BILL: *(With contempt.)* Ha!

PRISONER: *(To BILL.)* What name would you like me to have?

SALOME: Name yourself!

PRISONER: I am Jokanaan. *(Optional substitute: John the Baptist.)*

SALOME: Don't be irreligious.

PRISONER: Alexander the Great?

SALOME: Don't be pretentious.

PRISONER: Achilles.

SALOME: Such self-delusions.

PRISONER: Antinous?

SALOME: You aren't cute enough.

PRISONER: Richard the —

SALOME: — Wasn't lion-hearted in the least. He was a sniveling little . . .

PRISONER: Socrates.

SALOME: Are you going to trot them all out? Michelangelo? Marlowe? Bacon? Shakespeare?

LANE: How about Horatio Alger?

PRISONER: How about George Washington?

BILL: Watch it!

PRISONER: Sorry, Bill.

SALOME: You're not shocking me.

PRISONER: *(To LANE.)* I'll have that drink now.

SALOME: Lane, champagne.

PRISONER: I'd rather have a beer.

LANE: Budweiser?

PRISONER: Sure.

SALOME: We still haven't settled on your name.

PRISONER: Alfred Taylor.

SALOME: Is that your real name?

PRISONER: No, but it'll do.

> *(LANE brings the wine bucket and stand to the table, removes a can of Bud, serves it to the PRISONER without a glass.)*

SALOME: I don't like it.

PRISONER: Sorry.

SALOME: I shall call you Bruce.

PRISONER: *(To LANE.)* I want out of here.

SALOME: So you can hurry back to the old G.D.F.?

PRISONER: Fifth amendment.

SALOME: You know Mamma. You met her on the street today.

PRISONER: I stay off the streets.

SALOME: I thought you were innocently walking along West Street.

PRISONER: Nope.

SALOME: Because you were cruising and you aren't innocent. Oh, you didn't do anything to Mamma, nobody ever does anymore. Maybe you gave her a leaf-let. But you are in no way innocent.

PRISONER: Certain of that?

SALOME: I know one when I see one.

PRISONER: One what?

SALOME: What you are.

PRISONER: What am I?

SALOME: I don't blame you for being ashamed of it.

PRISONER: I'm not.

SALOME: Humiliated?

PRISONER: No.

SALOME: You disgust decent people.

PRISONER: No more than they disgust me.

SALOME: Who do you think you are?! *(To LANE.)* Lane, tell Bruce the story about
the pederast and —

PRISONER: *(Wearily.)* — the Boy Scout?

LANE: *(To SALOME.)* I don't think he's interested.

SALOME: Tell him!

LANE: To earn his merit badge for fishing, the Boy Scout went hiking backwards
through the bus station with his fly unbuttoned —

PRISONER: *(With pained patience.)* — trolling for queers.

LANE: *(To SALOME.)* He may have already heard it.

SALOME: *(Enjoying the PRISONER's discomfort.)* Then tell him the one about
the fluff who fell in love with the handsome doctor

PRISONER: *(His patience strained.)* — who specialized in disorders of the
alimentary canal.

LANE: *(To SALOME.)* I'd really rather not.

SALOME: Lane?

LANE: This is hardly the place or time —

SALOME: Tell him!

LANE: *(Not comfortable.)* The fluff flitted into the surgery of the handsome
doctor complaining of a blockage. The doctor extended his arm some distance up the orifice in question where indeed he did encounter an impedi-
ment, which the doctor extracted, which, to his amazement, was one dozen
long stemmed red roses, to which the fluff said —

PRISONER: *(With carefully constrained rage.)* "Read the card."

BILL: I don't get it! Was something written on the card?

PRISONER: *(Referring to LANE.)* Have him explain it to you.

SALOME: I'll bet you'd love to get your hands on my coiffure.

PRISONER: No.

SALOME: Want to decorate my apartment?

PRISONER: No.

SALOME: Want to wear one of my dresses?

PRISONER: I doubt it'll fit.

SALOME: Lane, put some Bette Midler on the boombox. *(Update accordingly.)*

PRISONER: Enjoying yourself?

SALOME: You and I seem to have gotten off on the wrong foot. You were innocently cruising . . . excuse me . . . walking along West Street.

PRISONER: I was at home.

SALOME: Whose home?

PRISONER: In bed.

SALOME: With whom?

PRISONER: Alone.

SALOME: You people live such lonely lives, don't you? No, forget I said that. I don't know what makes me say things like that. I'm not spiteful by nature. *(To the audience.)* Really, I'm not. *(To the PRISONER.)* You were at home, alone, in bed.

PRISONER: You got it.

SALOME: You lie! Herod would never take you in your own home.

PRISONER: He didn't even knock.

BILL: He should have kicked your door in!

PRISONER: He did!

BILL: Good for him!

PRISONER: I was beaten.

SALOME: With what?

BILL: A baseball bat?!

PRISONER: A golf club.

SALOME: Herod wouldn't hurt a fly.

PRISONER: He hurt me.

SALOME: *(To the PRISONER.)* Did you bleed?

PRISONER: Yes.

SALOME: Badly?

PRISONER: Yes.

SALOME: I don't see any blood.

PRISONER: They cleaned me up.

LANE: They cleaned you up?

PRISONER: When they found out I was coming up here.

LANE: People only get hurt when they deserve it.

PRISONER: Is that so?

LANE: No one ever clubbed me.

PRISONER: Yet.

LANE: Are you threatening me?

SALOME: *(To the PRISONER.)* No wonder you get hurt.

PRISONER: *(To BILL.)* Bill, I don't know how you got mixed up in whatever is going on up here. I don't know how I got mixed up in it. I seem to be staying around for a while. You should get your ass out of here.

BILL: My ass ain't any of your business.

SALOME: *(To the PRISONER.)* Why are you so hostile to me?

PRISONER: I'm not.

SALOME: You should be guilt-ridden. Your very existence is a denial of my femininity.

PRISONER: *(To BILL.)* Look, Bill, I like you.

BILL: You what?!

SALOME: He "likes" you.

BILL: *(To the PRISONER.)* Take that back! *(Making a fist.)* I mean it, fruit!

SALOME: *(To the PRISONER.)* William seems to be rejecting you.

BILL: *(To the PRISONER.)* Come on, fight like a man.

SALOME: *(To the PRISONER.)* Fight like a man, Bruce.

PRISONER: *(To BILL.)* No.

BILL: You shouldn't say stuff like that, people will get the wrong idea.

PRISONER: Let them.

BILL: *(To SALOME.)* Please, Miss Salome, I did nothing to lead him on.

SALOME: *(To the PRISONER.)* You're proud of what you are, aren't you?

PRISONER: Why not?

LANE: He's probably had his consciousness lifted.

PRISONER: *(Correcting.)* "Raised" . . .

LANE: *(To SALOME, referring to the PRISONER.)* He's probably above compromise.

SALOME: How selfish.

LANE: It's even likely he's dedicated to his own pleasure.

SALOME: Unnatural.

LANE: He fancies himself better than the rest of us.

SALOME: The rest of whom?

LANE: Those of us who prefer the cool, clean, dark air of the closet.

PRISONER: Mothballs and mushrooms.

LANE: I'd rather be standing here, safe and secure in my Gucci's, than stomping around in your boots on a collision with calamity.

SALOME: Closets? What has this to do with closets?

PRISONER: Everything.

LANE: Friend — may I call you friend? Like it or not, maybe we do have a lot in common. We have even more that is not in common. You're committed, I've never found commitment pays my bill at Bloomingdale's. You're an activist, I go to the Opera. You're involved, I rely on opiates.

SALOME: Drugs?

PRISONER: Whatever turns you on.

LANE: Which is to say, whatever turns you off. Personally, I prefer Dewar's.

SALOME: *(To the PRISONER.)* Stop and consider the harm you do. Sodom and Gomorrah, burned to the ground, thanks to you. You and your ilk pushed the Roman Empire over the brink. I've even been told that buggery is the cause of earthquakes.

PRISONER: Why not throw in gasoline prices?

SALOME: I am concerned for your soul. I offer myself to you as the receptacle of your repentance, the repository of your repudiation.

PRISONER: Fine. I repudiate, I repent, now put me back.

SALOME: *(To the PRISONER.)* Repent what?

PRISONER: Whatever you say.

SALOME: Word of honor?

PRISONER: You allow me honor?

LANE: You should be guilt-ridden.

SALOME: And self-hating.

LANE: *(Sweetly.)* And self-destructive.

SALOME: *(To the PRISONER.)* What kind of a life do you have?

PRISONER: A life.

SALOME: A life? Is that all?

PRISONER: It's the best place to begin.

SALOME: Without so much as a pardon my dust?

PRISONER: What kind of a life do you have?

SALOME: You think I didn't notice your hair.

PRISONER: What about it?

SALOME: It's long.

PRISONER: *(Laughing.)* It is not.

SALOME: It isn't a crew cut.

PRISONER: It's my hair.

SALOME: You're free to wear your hair that way.

PRISONER: How liberal of you.

SALOME: I'm free to find it repugnant.

BILL: Me, too.

SALOME: *(To the PRISONER.)* Don't get me wrong, I like you.

BILL: You what?!

LANE: She likes him.

BILL: But . . . !

SALOME: *(To the PRISONER.)* I said I like you.

PRISONER: *(To BILL.)* Put me back in the summerhouse.

SALOME: Lane says you're a prophet.

LANE: Slip of the tongue.

BILL: *(To SALOME.)* You don't like him, you like me!

SALOME: *(To the PRISONER.)* Give me a prophecy.

PRISONER: *(To BILL.)* You took me out, put me back.

SALOME: I can see you now, standing in some dark bar somewhere on the
    waterfront, absolutely convinced you know who you are. Well you don't
    know who you are. Not until I decide to tell you who you are. I define you.
    And you're not special at all. Or you won't be, not when I cut your hair.

LANE: *(Blocking her.)* Wrong play, Miss Salome.

SALOME: *(To BILL.)* William . . . Bill . . . in the drawing room . . . my sewing
    kit . . . the scissors . . .

LANE: *(Restraining SALOME.)* No!

SALOME: *(Struggling to free herself, to BILL.)* . . . there on the table . . . the
    butter knife . . . give me that knife . . . *(To LANE.)* . . . unhand me!
    (BILL takes a butter knife from the garden table.)

LANE: *(Shaking SALOME.)* Cool it, Delilah!

SALOME: *(Dazed.)* I . . . I . . .

LANE: Remember who you are!

SALOME: But . . .

LANE: Where you are!

SALOME: *(Looking around her.)* Where . . . who . . . ?

LANE: You've got the wrong climax going for you.

SALOME: Where are we?

LANE: Not among the Philistines.

(LADY H and HEROD enter laughing through the French doors USC.)

HEROD: Salome, my dear child

LADY H: It's all been settled!

HEROD: The contract has been signed.

LADY H: *(To SALOME.)* — You get everything!

SALOME: It has not been settled. Mamma, Herod, go back inside and wait.

HEROD: But —

LADY H: *(To the PRISONER.)* Oh . . . Hello, there . . . we meet again.

SALOME: *(To HEROD and LADY H.)* I'm not kidding. Go back off stage and wait.
    (LADY H and HEROD exit confused through the French doors USC.)

SALOME: *(To the PRISONER.)* Now, sir, come to me.

BILL: No!

SALOME: Yes.

PRISONER: Why?

SALOME: I am your lover.

BILL: No, Miss Salome, me!

SALOME: *(To the PRISONER.)* Look at me!

BILL: Don't fight it, it's you and me.

SALOME: You're the footman.

BILL: I'll go to business school.

SALOME: *(To the PRISONER.)* Sir, as I was saying before we were so rudely
    interrupted . . .

BILL: Without you, I'll . . . I'll . . .

SALOME: What? Without me you'll what?

BILL: Die.

SALOME: *(Laughing.)* Silly boy.

LANE: William, don't be a fool!

BILL: I will!

SALOME: Prove it.

BILL: Die?

LANE: I think not.

SALOME: He offered.

PRISONER: *(To BILL.)* Don't let her manipulate you.

SALOME: It seems his offer was not in good faith.

BILL: *(Butter knife in hand.)* I will.

PRISONER: *(To LANE.)* Hadn't you better disarm him?

LANE: Interfere?

BILL: When it's too late, when I'm lying dead on the floor, then you'll appreciate
     me.

SALOME: Maybe. Maybe not. *(To the PRISONER, unbuttoning her bodice.)* In
     years to come, when you talk of this, and you will, be kind.

PRISONER: Bill, give me that knife.

BILL: *(To SALOME.)* Look at me!

LANE: *(Nervous.)* William, you'd best leave the theatrics to your elders.

BILL: Look!

     (To his own surprise, BILL stabs himself.)

LANE: William!

SALOME: Now what have you done?!

BILL: Stabbed myself.

LANE: *(Scandalized.)* In the garden?

SALOME: For me?

BILL: For . . . for . . . *(He collapses.)*

LANE: *(Catching BILL, cradling him.)* William?

PRISONER: Quick, open his shirt!

SALOME: Are you a doctor?

PRISONER: No, but . . .

SALOME: Then stay out of this —

BILL: *(Weakly.)* I . . . You . . .

SALOME: I what?

BILL: You didn't mean it. *(BILL dies.)*

PRISONER: *(To LANE.)* Let me help you.

LANE: *(Bitterly.)* Haven't you done enough?

PRISONER: You set the stage.

SALOME: *(To LANE.)* Is he?

LANE: Yes.
    (GLADYS enters DSL with a broom and dust pan.)

PRISONER: *(The game is over.)* Dead?

GLADYS: *(As she enters.)* You rang?

SALOME: I dropped one of my props.

LANE: And it broke.

SALOME: *(Advancing on the PRISONER.)* You, Mr. No-name, you should know
    the poem even better than I. *(She quotes.)* "But I am love —"

PRISONER: *(Backing away from SALOME in disgust.)* Love? *(He starts back
    toward the summerhouse.)*

SALOME: *(Quoting.)* "— and I was wont to be alone in this fair garden." Say it
    with me! "I am true love I fill the hearts of boys and girls with mutual
    flame."
    *(In her advance on the PRISONER, MISS SALOME daintily steps over the
    body of BILL.)*

GLADYS: *(To SALOME.)* Your skirt's trailing in the blood.

SALOME: *(To the PRISONER.)* You're so proud of it, say it with me. "— then
    sighing, said the other . . ." You know the words.

PRISONER: *(Starting up the aisle.)* "— then sighing, said the other, 'have thy
    will, I am the love that dare not speak its name.'"
    (The PRISONER has gone back to the summerhouse.)

SALOME: My hand, sir, take it. Look into my eyes. There is a planetarium in my
    eyes. I've most of the big dipper in my left eye; in my right eye, you have a
    good go at the morning star. Keep out of that summerhouse! You locked
    the door, didn't you? I heard the click. Do you want me to come back there
    and break that door down? You like that, don't you — breaking down
    doors. Come out. Come out come out come out. We'll have a party to wel-
    come you. Waltzing does a lot for the soul. One, two, three; come, two,
    three; out, two, three. La . . . sir . . . La, if you think you have the right to re-
    fuse propriety. I dish out the rights around here. I shan't be the poor loser
    in a contest won by a summerhouse. Not I, sir. *(To LANE .)* Lane, tell an
    amusing story.

LANE: *(BILL still cradled in his arms.)* Once upon a time, there was a young
    footman . . .

SALOME: Never mind, Lane, things are quite funny enough. *(To the summer-
    house.)* Do you hear that in there? I think your hilarious attitude is in bad

taste. You tire me. I am finished with you. *(Calling offstage.)* Herod?! Mamma?! Everybody on stage.

(HEROD and LADY H enter USC through the French doors.)

HEROD: It's about time!

LADY H: No footman to announce us?!

HEROD: Only two chairs, where will . . .

LADY H: *(Coming upon BILL's body.)* Rise, sir, from that completely recumbent position.

SALOME: He can't, Mamma, he butter-knifed himself to death.

HEROD: Who's responsible for this carnage?

SALOME: The butler did it.

LADY H: Not another one.

HEROD*: (To LANE.)* Remove it.

LANE: *(With a dark look toward the summerhouse.)* If Miss Salome is finished with it.

SALOME: Quite finished, thank you, Lane.

(GLADYS and LANE pull BILL's body to the side. LANE covers it with the cape of Moloch. LANE and GLADYS exit SR, unobtrusively.)

SALOME: *(To HEROD and LADY H.)* Have you any idea how long you've kept me waiting out here?

HEROD: My dear child . . .

LADY H: You sent us back in.

SALOME: *(To HEROD.)* You and Mamma have talked it over, yes?

LADY H: Herod and I . . .

SALOME: Yes or no?

HEROD: We did happen to discuss . . .

SALOME: To what conclusion?

LADY H: The conclusion is up to you.

SALOME: In other words, I'm to be it.

HEROD: I wouldn't put it . . .

SALOME: I am up to here with answers! Before I enter into any relationship with a male . . .

LADY H: *(Fanning herself.)* Salome, please, the "opposite sex!"

SALOME: *(To HEROD.)* Before I contract with you, corporate or carnal . . .

HEROD: The necessary papers have been . . .

LADY H: We're rich!

HEROD: Your mother, acting as your agent —

SALOME: I'm adding a rider to the contract.

LADY H: He hasn't anything left.

SALOME: *(With a look toward the summerhouse.)* Oh, yes, he has.

HEROD: What do you want?

SALOME: *(To HEROD.)* You desire me?

HEROD: *(Looking for LANE.)* Where's the Ravel?

LADY H: *(Helping herself to champagne.)* We can dispense with the music.

SALOME: *(To HEROD.)* You crave and covet me?

HEROD: I'm very fond of you . . . where is Lane?

SALOME: And you will give me anything I ask?

HEROD: *(Falling to his knees.)* Miss Salome, deep in my heart —

SALOME: Get up.

HEROD: *(Rising.)* You're taking the romance out of it.

SALOME: Answer my question.

HEROD: What is it that you want?

SALOME: Just give it to me.

HEROD: Aren't you expected to dance?

SALOME: Later maybe. There's a little waltz step I'm warming up right now.

LADY H: Then it's settled! *Quelle surprise.* What an alliance. *(Lifting a glass to SALOME and HEROD.)* To the both of you.

SALOME: No, Mamma, it is not settled.

HEROD: But —

SALOME: As soon as I've been given what I want.

HEROD: Then tell me what it is.

SALOME: *(To the summerhouse.)* Him.

LADY H: Who?

SALOME: I want him. In there. He who rejected me.

HEROD: He isn't mine to give.

LADY H: He belongs to justice.

HEROD: To this summerhouse and those to follow.

LADY H: And you don't want him — who knows where he's been?

SALOME: Fair enough. I consent to settle for his head.

HEROD: Do you know what you're asking for?

SALOME: From here up!

LADY H: My dear child . . .

SALOME: When little girls start asking for heads, they're no longer addressed as child.

HEROD: Anything else . . . the sun . . . the stars . . . the —

SALOME: No moon!

HEROD: *(Opening his jacket, displaying a cache of jewels.)* Could I interest you in a few precious gems — the black pearl of Poseidon . . . the Queen of Sheba's sapphire . . . the diamond diadem of Dido . . . Rasputin's ruby . . . the emerald of Montezuma . . . Donald Trump's digital watch?

SALOME: I lust for a head; give it to me, Herod!

LADY H: I swoon!

SALOME: Whatever you think best, Mamma.

HEROD: He hasn't had his trial yet.

SALOME: Try him here, now, guilty.

HEROD: We'd need a jury.

SALOME: I am your jury.

LADY H: Not in the face of history.

SALOME: Bother history.

HEROD: I'll not have history slandered, not in my garden.

SALOME: Stop procrastinating, Herod, throw the lions to the Christians.

LADY H: Dear, you've got that back to front.

SALOME: No, Mamma, I haven't.

HEROD: Court will come to order.

SALOME: Are we ever out of order?

HEROD: The accused?

SALOME: Your guess is as good as mine.

LADY H: You want his head and you don't even know his name?

SALOME: He has hundreds of names. Hundreds of thousands.

HEROD: His crime?

SALOME: You must know, you locked him up.

HEROD: After careful deliberation, we find the defendant —

LADY H: Guilty!

SALOME: Then give me his head.

HEROD: It's yours.

SALOME: How do I get it off?

HEROD: Not my jurisdiction.

SALOME: *(Demurely.)* Antipas, my sweet . . .

HEROD: Not on your tintype.

SALOME: Twiddle, I should have saved Bill. *(Looking toward LADY H.)*
Mamma —

LADY H: Surely you jest.

SALOME: Where is Lane?

(GLADYS enters USL. She has changed, is dressed as she was at the start of the play. She is jumping ship.)

SALOME: Gladys, bring me his head.

GLADYS: Are you for real?

SALOME: Sir Herod gave it to me.

GLADYS: *(With chilly courtesy.)* Nice of you to try to include me in the action. *(To the audience as she exits DSR.)* Hell, I seldom last beyond the first ten minutes of the play. Let's face it, there aren't that many plays left with maids in them.

SALOME: If somebody doesn't do as I ask, I shall hold my breath until I . . .

(LANE enters down the aisle with the tray from Act One. On it is the PRISONER's head, covered with a colorful tea cozy.)

LANE: I found the tray thrown away in the shrubbery.

SALOME: *(In awe.)* Is this?

LANE: *(Climbing onto the stage, giving the head to SALOME.)* I put a tea cozy on it to keep it warm. Bill has been revenged.

SALOME: A wonderful head!

(The fake phono sputters to life with the "severed head" motif from the opera Salome *by Richard Strauss.)*

SALOME: *(To the head.)* You did come to me, sir. I have in my hands, on a precious middle-period Mesopotamian tray, under the cozy auntie deFarge crocheted for me, a head. Bad country, miserable year, but a good head. An anonymous head. *(Tweaking it under the chin.)* Aren't you sorry you never told me your real name? Now you'll never get proper credit. We must celebrate. We must sing and laugh and dance . . . dance! Yes! We must dance! *(A sleazy bump-and-grind rendition of Maurice Ravel's* Valses Nobles et Sentimentales *is heard.)* Herod, we're going to a ball.

LADY H: *(Producing a hat fit for Ascot from out of nowhere.)* Not without a hat.

SALOME: *(Handing head to Sir HEROD.)* Careful, don't drop it.

LADY H: *(Giving the hat to SALOME.)* Then you are happy?

SALOME: *(Putting on the hat.)* Delirious. We're going all the way to France, Mamma. I'll tell Louis and Marie you send your love.

LADY H: Do that, dear. And should you chance to drop in on Caesar after the ball, give him one for me.

SALOME: *(Retrieving the head from Sir HEROD.)* A young lady may well do without the benefit of naked trumpeters, if first, she takes special care to master the intricacies of the waltz. *(She begins a slow waltz with the head.)*

HEROD: "Now She Dances!"

LANE: But with her hat on.

LADY H: — like the proper girl I raised her to be.

SALOME: Take solace from that as I exit waltzing.

(Ravel's Valses Nobles et Sentimentales mutates into an insane and energetic distortion of a Waltz, the music swells as the lights BLACKOUT.)

CURTAIN

ACKNOWLEDGMENTS

Even in the midst of the generosity of spirit for which theatre people are renowned, a few people have stood out with extraordinary offers of information, introductions, resources, and very hard work.

ROBERT PATRICK has unfailingly (and, contrary to his frequent descriptions of himself, cheerfully) responded to hundreds of emails and phone calls concerning everything from how to track down Sandy Bigtree to who took which photo. Without his devotion to the memory of the Caffe Cino, and his generous spirit, this volume would have been a much smaller and more modest endeavor.

JAMES D. GOSSAGE was by far the most prolific chronicler of events at the Caffe Cino, and he maintains a library of photographs that deserve to be published in a big, showy volume. But such displays do not seem to interest him. Instead, he has donated all of his Cino images to the New York Public Library for the Performing Arts, where they reside in the Billy Rose Theatre Collection at Lincoln Center.

ELLEN STEWART has been a guardian angel throughout the preparation of this book, although, as the Director of La Mama E.T.C., she is a very busy woman. She was, from what we can gather, Joe Cino's most trusted friend. She agreed to let us interview her, but not for a published "interview" — only to provide background information and to keep us from wasting our time tracking down people and resources readily available through her vast network.

MICHAEL STRICKLAND joined this project as a copy editor and stayed to become a cherished friend. His commitment to the preservation of endangered plays, his wide-ranging knowledge, and his commitment to excellence have inspired us.

PAUL SAGAN volunteered to proofread the manuscript and contributed a level of professionalism and thoroughness, combined with a cheerful spirit, that calmed our nerves as the final deadline approached. Having directed the work of two Cino playwrights, he brought extensive and invaluable knowledge of the theatre, and of off-off-Broadway history and culture, to the task.

Many of the contributors refused to accept honoraria for the work that appears in this volume. Their generosity has enabled us to produce a higher-quality book, and to make more copies available at a reasonable price, than otherwise would have been possible.

THE EDITORS

THE EDITORS

GEORGE BIRIMISA *(right)* was the first openly gay playwright to receive a Rockefeller Foundation Grant, for the 1969 London production of *Mr. Jello* at the International Theatre Club. He later won the *Drama-Logue* Award for his 1978 play *Rainbow in the Night*. *Daddy Violet,* the 1967 play included in this collection, opened at the Caffe Cino and went on to tour college campuses in the U.S. and Canada. *Village Voice* drama critic Ross Wetzsteon wrote of the 1968 play *Georgie Porgie,* "Birimisa's considerable talent [is] as fluid as it is raw, as passionate as it is brutal." The founder and director of Inter-generation Writing Workshops in San Francisco, George won the Harry Hay award in 2005 as ". . . noted playwright, teacher and cherished inspiration across the generations of the LGBT community." He lives with his pussycat Sweetheart, and as we go to press he is doing final revisions to his twenty-fifth play, *Hackberry Tree, a Memoir.*

STEVE SUSOYEV *(left)* is the founder and editor-in-chief of Moving Finger Press. He writes for the legal community on the child-custody rights of gay and lesbian parents and other human rights issues. His bestselling memoir, *People Farm,* won a 2004 Writer's Digest Culture Award. The *White Crane Journal* calls him "An example of the gay man as seeker, as victim, as redeemed and redeemer." Steve practices law in San Francisco, specializing in the needs of people with life-threatening conditions. He spends part of every summer with the Squaw Valley Community of Writers.

Photo by James T. Eilers, 2005

INDEX AND REFERENCE MATERIALS

Photo by James D. Gossage

BIBLIOGRAPHY AND SELECTED RESOURCES

Bottoms, Stephen J. *Playing Underground: A Critical History of the 1960s Off-Off-Broadway Movement*. Ann Arbor: University of Michigan Press, 2004.

Crespy, David A. *Off-Off-Broadway Explosion: How Provocative Playwrights of the 1960s Ignited a New American Theater*. New York: Backstage Books, 2003.

Dominic, Magie. *The Queen of Peace Room, a Memoir*. Ontario, Canada: Wilfrid Laurier University Press, 2002.

Esslin, Martin. *The Theatre of the Absurd*. New York: Vintage Books, 2004, Third Edition.

Eyen, Tom with Feingold, Michael. S*arah B. Divine and Other Plays* (indexed in many catalogues as *Sarah B. Devine...)* New York: Winter House Limited, 1971.

Eyen, Tom. *Ten Plays*. New York: Samuel French Inc., 1971 (edited by Michael Feingold).

Harbin, Billy J., Marra, Kim, and Schanke, Robert A., eds. *The Gay and Lesbian Theatrical Legacy, a Biographical Dictionary of Major Figures in the American Post-Stonewall Era*. Ann Arbor: University of Michigan Press, 2005.

Helbing, Terry, ed. *Directory of Gay Plays*. New York: JH Press (Gay Theatre Alliance), 1980.

Hoffman, William M., ed. *New American Plays*. (Vols. 1-4) New York: Hill and Wang, 1968-1971.

McDonough, Jimmy. *The Ghastly One: The Sex-Gore Netherworld of Filmmaker Andy Milligan*. Chicago: Chicago Review Press (A Cappella Books), 2001.

Orzel, Nick and Smith, Michael, eds. *Eight Plays from Off-Off Broadway*. New York: Bobs Merrill, 1966.

Patrick, Robert. *Cheep Theatricks*. New York: Winter House Limited, 1972.

Patrick, Robert. *Untold Decades: Seven Comedies of Gay Romance*. New York: St. Martin's Press, 1988.

Mailman, Bruce and Poland, Albert. *The Off, Off Broadway Book: The Plays, People, Theatre*. Indianapolis: Bobbs-Merrill Co., 1972. [Out of print; ISBN: 0672517531].

Smith, Michael, ed. *The Best of Off-Off Broadway*. New York: E. P. Dutton, 1969.

Smith, Michael, ed. *More Plays from Off-Off Broadway*. New York: Bobbs-Merrill Co., Inc., 1972.

Stone, Wendell C. *Caffe Cino: The Birthplace of Off-Off-Broadway*. Carbondale, IL: Southern Illinois University Press, 2005.

Wetzsteon, Ross, ed. *The Best of Off-Broadway: 8 Contemporary Obie-Winning Plays*. New York: Penguin Group, 1994.

Williams, Philip Middleton. *A Comfortable House: Lanford Wilson, Marshall W. Mason, and the Circle Repertory Theatre*. Jefferson, NC: McFarland & Company, 1993.

Collections and Archives:

La Mama E.T.C. Archives, 74A East 4th St., New York, NY 10003, telephone 212.475.7710

New York Public Library for the Performing Arts
 The Billy Rose Theatre Collection at Lincoln Center
 40 Lincoln Center Plaza, New York 10023-7498, telephone 212.870.1630:
  Caffe Cino papers
  James D. Gossage Photographs, 1965-1975
  Robert Patrick papers, 1940-1984
  George Birimisa papers, 1966-2005

Ohio State University, Jerome Lawrence & Robert E. Lee Theatre Research Institute,
 1430 Lincoln Tower, 1800 Cannon Drive, Columbus, OH 43210-1230,
 telephone 614.292.6614: *The Tom Eyen Collection*

Rutgers University, Alexander Library, 169 College Ave, New Brunswick, NJ 08901, telephone
 732.932.7851:
 Paul Foster Collection, Theatrical papers 1957-1991
 Robert Heide Collection, Theatrical papers 1964-1986

WEB ARCHIVE maintained by La Mama Experimental Theatre Club, indexing productions
 since the closing of the Caffe Cino: http://www.lamama.org/archives/year_lists/1969page.htm

WEB PAGES maintained by Robert Patrick, with hundreds of photographs from the Caffe Cino,
 other early off-off-Broadway venues, and up-to-date information on the pioneers. Enter
 through: http://hometown.aol.com/rbrtptrck/Dailypage1.html

WEB PAGES maintained by Doric Wilson include full scripts from Mr. Wilson's body of work, a
 memoir of his time at the Caffe Cino, and links to the current projects of the Tosos II theatre
 company, the re-initiation of the theatre company he co-founded in 1974.[1] Enter through:
 http://www.doricwilson.com/caffecino.asp and http://www.tosos2.org/

WEB PAGE maintained by Michael Smith includes off- and off-off-Broadway history, the full text
 of Mr. Smith's plays, links to ongoing projects, and Mr. Smith's blog. Enter through:
 http://www.michaeltownsendsmith.com/

---

[1] Among the many treasures available from Cino pioneers is a voice recording of Joe Cino, circa 1961, making his nightly announcement: "And now, before closing, a basket will be passed to accept any contributions for the performers." The recording is available on a CD of an original cast recording of Doric Wilson's *And He Made a Her* included with an edition of the play published in November 2006 by United Stages. http://www.unitedstages.com

APPENDIX
Partial and Not Entirely Accurate List
of Work Performed at the Caffe Cino[1]

Arthur Adamov
  As We Were .... June 1962
Søren Agenoux
  Charles Dickens' Christmas Carol .... December 1966–January 1967
  Donovan's Johnson .... May 1967
  Speak, Parrott .... November 1966
Michael Alaimo's Commedia del Arte Troupe .... April 1964
Ross Alexander
  A New Place .... December 1963
Robert Woodruff Anderson
  Tea and Sympathy .... May 1960
Jean Anouilh
  Antigone .... August 1961
David Antin and Jerome Rothenberg
  A Poetry Reading .... April 1960
Aristophanes
  Lysistrata 1960
Owen G. Arno
  The Street of Good Friends .... 1959 & March 1964
Fernando Arrabal
  The Two Executioners .... September 1962
Bill Ashley and Jerry Kahn
  Write the Real Mavis Pugh Please (A Myopic Fable) .... December 1961
Johann Sebastian Bach
  Chromatic Fugues .... May 1960
Paula Ballan and Ron Rosoff, Guitarists .... January 1964
Glenn Barrett
  Every Bomb Shelter Has One .... June 1963
James M. Barroe
  The 12-Pound Look .... April 1963
Matt Baylor
  Civil War .... April 1965

---

[1] Originally compiled by Leah D. Frank for the 1985 Exhibition "Caffe Cino and Its Legacy" at the Vincent Astor Gallery, hosted by the Library & Museum of the Performing Arts at Lincoln Center, New York Public Library. This list has been revised extensively by Robert Patrick and Wendell Stone. Please see Mr. Patrick's disclaimer at the end of the Appendix. In spite of any gaps or inaccuracies due to the passage of time and the Cino's inherent eccentricities, the list conveys the extraordinary scope of the work performed on a plywood platform in a Greenwich Village coffee-house.

Samuel Beckett
   Embers .... March 1963
Michael Benedict
   The Vaseline Photographer .... March 1966
George Birimisa
   Daddy Violet .... June 1967
Haal Borske
   The Brown Clown .... December 1967
Mary Boylan and Robert Dahdah
   A Christmas Show .... December 1964
Breton, Claudel and Michaux
   Reading of Works in Translation .... April 1960
Josef Bush
   French Grey .... September 1967
Albert Camus
   The Fall .... January 1963
Truman Capote
   A Christmas Memory .... February 1959
   From Truman Capote (readings) .... July 1963
   My Side of the Matter .... November 1961
Jerry Caruana
   If I Had a Heart .... April 1963
   The Implied Rejection .... February 1963
   Mannikins .... May 1962
   Melancholia .... November 1962
John Chace
   The Devil and the Good Lord (Adaptation from Sartre) .... May 1960
   The Egg (The System Adaptation from Felicien Marceau) .... October 1960
The Chamber Theatre / Chamber Players
   French Surrealist Poetry 1959
   Potpourri, Comedy and Mime .... April 1959
   Stories and Tales from Jewish Life .... February 1959
Lonnie Chapman
   The Buffalo Skinner .... May 1961
Paddy Chayefsky
   The Mother 1960
Anton Chekhov
   The Boor .... April 1960 / 1962
   The Cherry Orchard 1961
   The Marriage Proposal .... November–December 1967
   On the Harmfulnes of Tobacco .... May 1961
   Swan Song .... December 1962
Joe Cino and Neil Flanagan
   Two One-Acts .... April 1963
Daniel Haben Clark
   The Singing Lesson .... July 1964
P. Winthrop Clark
   On a Park Bench .... August 1962
Jean Cocteau
   The Human Voice .... February 1962

Ronald Colby
   Episode .... July 1962 / November 1963
   Vignette .... September 1962
Comic Book Productions
   Archie and his Friends 1967
   Goethe's Faust 1967
   The Secret of Taboo Mountain (Concept: Donald L. Brooks) .... December 1966
   Wonder Woman 1967
E. T. Conlin
   Minnie Field .... April 1962
Noel Coward
   Ave A Banahnah .... October 1962
   Blithe Spirit 1961
   The Cat's Cradle 1960
   Fumed Oak .... March 1963
   Still Life .... March 1963
Robert Dahdah
   Angel in the Pawnshop (999 Words/Adapted from Abraham B. Shiffrin) 1960
Kelly Davis
   Flywheel .... October 1963
Michael deGhelderode
   Escurial .... August 1962
Diane di Prima
   Monuments [1] .... March 1968
   Poet's Vaudeville .... March 1965
B. L. Dorr and Do Cox
   Doe, Doe, Doe .... March 1964
John Dunn
   Didelum Algit: A Fugue .... September 1963
Lord Dunsany
   The Glittering Gate .... January 1961
George Economou and Armand Schwerner
   A Poetry Reading .... March 1960
T. S. Eliot
   The Cocktail Party 1962
   Murder in the Cathedral 1962
   Sweeney Agonistes .... November 1962
   The Waste Land 1962
Joseph Eppert
   Dark Night of the Soul .... August 1964
Tom Eyen
   Eyen on Eyen .... August 1966
   Frustrata (Cino at La Mama) .... March 1964
   The White Whore and The Bit Player .... December 1965 / January 1967
   Who Killed My Bald Sister Sophie? .... February 1968
   Why Hanna's Skirt Won't Stay Down .... November 1965 / April 1966 / December 1966
Neil Flanagan
   Candide (adaptation of Voltaire) .... May 1962 / June 1963

---

[1] The final production at the Caffe Cino.

Paul Foster
Balls .... November 1964
Hurrah for the Bridge .... September 1963
The Recluse .... March 1965

Ketti Frings
Look Homeward, Angel .... June 1960

Christopher Fry
A Phoenix Too Frequent .... March 1960 / October 1962

Jean Genet
Deathwatch .... October 1961
The Maids .... July 1961

William Gibson
Two for the Seesaw .... October 1960

Andre Gide
David and Bathsheba .... August 1961
Philoctètes .... August 1961

Jean Giraudoux
The Apollo of Bellac .... April 1962
The Madwoman of Chaillot .... February 1960

Lady Gregory
Glittering Gates 1964
Hyacinth Halvey .... 1959 / November 1960

Group / Various Authors
Palm Sunday Spectacular / Easter All Star Spectacular: More! More! I Want More!
Benchley Monologue
Songs
Dance
Wandering
Tidy Passions
    (Michael Smith; Remy Charlip; John Dodd; Robert Benchley;
    Al Carmines; Deborah Lee; Robert Dahdah; Lanford Wilson;
    H. M. Koutoukas) .... April 1966
Potluck .... June 1967
Surprise 1967
Vorspiel Nach Marienstein
    (Johnny Dodd; Ondine; Michael Smith) .... June 1967
Thanksgiving (Jury Duty) Horror Show .... November 1966

John Guare
A Day for Surprises .... August 1965
The Loveliest Afternoon of the Year .... October or November 1966
Something I'll Tell You Tuesday .... October or November 1966

Barbara Guest
The Office .... March 1963

Oliver Hailey
Animal (A Monologue.) .... June 1965
The Picture (A Demonstration.) .... June 1965

George Haimsohn
Psychedelic Follies (Music: John Aman) .... October 1966

George Haimsohn and Robin Miller
Dames at Sea or *Golddiggers Afloat (Music: Jim Wise)* .... May–June 1966

Holworthy Hall and Robert Middlemass
The Valiant .... October 1960
Peter Hartman
Vistas of the Heart Unveiled .... March 1966
Robert Heide
The Bed .... June–July 1965 / September 1965
Moon .... February 1967 / February 1968
Lillian Hellman
The Lark .... July 1960
Rose Hennessey
The Candles .... December 1961
Jack Hirschman
Poetry Reading .... May 1960
William M. Hoffman
Good Night, I Love You .... September 1965
Saturday Nite at the Movies .... September 1965
Thank You, Miss Victoria .... August–September 1965
James Howard
Flyspray[1] .... Summer 1960
Improvisation (anonymous)
Commedia Dell'Arte .... April 1964
William Inge
Glory in the Flower .... November 1960 / 1964
The Tiny Closet 1961
To Bobolink, For Her Spirit 1961
Eugène Ionesco
The Bald Soprano .... Dates unknown
The Chairs .... August 1962
Jack, or The Submission .... Dates unknown
The Lesson .... January 1963
Scenes from The Bald Soprano and Jack .... May 1962
Alan Lysander James
Dearest of All the Boys .... August–September 1966
Fairies I Have Met .... December 1965
G.B.S.'s A.B.C.'s .... November 1966
Oscar Revisited (adaptation) .... December 1962
Sunflower Lily and Green Carnation .... October 1966
Triumphs and Tragedies by Oscar Wilde .... October 1965
The World of Oscar Wilde (adaptation) .... October 1962
Lee Kalcheim
The Morning After .... January 1963
Party for Divorce .... October 1963
George S. Kaufman
If Men Played Cards as Women Do .... July 1962
Jan Kelley
The Weak Spot .... August 1963
Robert Kelly and George Economou
Poetry Reading .... May 1960

---

[1] Believed to be the first original work written for production at the Caffe Cino.

Robert Kelly and Frank Kuenstler
Poetry Reading .... April 1960

Charles Kerbs
Phaedra .... August 1967
The Sleeping Gypsy .... October 1967

H. M. Koutoukas
A Letter From Collette or Dreams Don't Send Valentines .... February 1966
All Day For a Dollar or Crumpled Christmas .... December 1965
Cause Celebre 1966
Cobra Invocations .... November 1966
Medea or Maybe the Stars Will Understand or Veiled Strangers .... October 1965
Michael Touched Me 1967
Only A Countess May Dance When She's Crazy .... December 1964
Tidy Passions .... *Dates unknown*
View From Sorrentino .... *Dates unknown*
With Creatures Make My Way .... May 1965

Ruth Krauss
The Cantilever Rainbow (Cino at La Mama) .... April 1965
Newsletters .... March 1966
38 Haikus .... September 1964

Donald Kvares
Filling The Hole .... June 1964
What Did You Say To Me In The Last Scene? .... April 1964

Tom La Bar
Empire State .... January 1968

Edith Laurie
The War vs. Women .... May 1964

Stephen Leacock
Laugh with Leacock — A Musicaless Revue .... December 1962

G. Roy Levin
Henry and Henrietta .... October 1963

Michael Locascio
I'm in Love with W.S. .... May 1962

Larry Loonin
Our First Gobi Fossils .... Summer 1965
Run To The Sea .... May 1964

Larry Loonin and Yvonne Rainer
Incidents .... June 1964

Federico García Lorca
Don Cristobal .... November 1963
The House of Bernarda Alba 1962

Maurice Maeterlinck
The Death of Tintagiles .... March 1966

Edgar Lee Masters
Spoon River Anthology .... September 1966

Edna St. Vincent Millay
Aria Da Capo .... April 1960

A. A. Milne
Miss Marlowe at Play .... October 1960
Once Upon an Ugly .... January 1963

Mary Mitchell
Who Put That Blood On My Long-Stemmed Rose? .... *Dates unknown*
Molière
The Affected Young Ladies 1961
Cervantes and Others .... February 1962
Molière, Cervantes, and others
Repertory of Plays .... February 1962
Phoebe Mooney
Alice in Wonderland (adaptation of Lewis Carroll) .... January 1962
John Mortimer
The Dock Brief .... April 1963
John Madison Morton
Box and Cox .... July 1960
Tad Mosel
All My Sons .... June 1962
Impromptu .... May 1962
David Mueller
Eugenia Wore An Evening Gown .... December 1963
Claris Nelson
The Carders .... December 1964
The Clown .... September 1962 / April 1967
The Girl on the BBC 1965
Medea (A New Version) 1965
Neon in the Night .... November 1962
A Road Where Wolves Run .... September–October 1964
The Rue Garden .... July 1962
Sean O'Casey
Bedtime Story .... August 1963
Tom O'Horgan
A Masque .... September 1963
Love and Variations: A Masque .... September 1963
Love and Vexations: A Masque and *The Masters: A Curtain Raise* .... September 1963
Eugene O'Neill
Before Breakfast .... July 1962 / October 1963
Sally Ordway
A Desolate Place Near A Deep Hole .... August 1965
Anthony Osnato
The Apple Tree and I: A Musical .... September 1963
Abe Paconofsky
Caldwell Corners 1961
The Tycoon 1960
Pagoon Kang Wouk
Among Dummies .... October 1962
Between Yesterday and Tomorrow .... June 1964
Tales of Thieves .... *Dates unknown*
Dorothy Parker
Well, Here We Are![1] .... December 1958

---

[1] First documented Caffe Cino play production.

Robert Patrick
Cornered .... January 1968
Halloween Hermit .... October 1966
The Haunted Host .... November 1964
Indecent Exposure .... September 1966
New Works: Lights; Camera; Action .... June 1967
The Warhol Machine .... September 1967

S.J. Perelman
S.J. Perelman Carnival .... July 1960

Jim Perkinson
A Recollection of Cabbage Roses .... August 1963
To Angels on Sunday .... June 1963

Harold Pinter
The Dumb Waiter 1962
A Slight Ache .... December 1962

Pirandello
The Man with a Flower in his Mouth .... April 1961

Jean Racine
Phaedra 1962

Terrence Rattigan
Separate Tables .... July 1960 / 1961

Reginald Rose
Crime in the Streets .... March 1963

J. D. Salinger
For Esmé with Love and Squalor .... May 1963
Just Before the War with the Eskimos 1960
Pretty Mouth and Green My Eyes 1960

William Saroyan
Hello Out There .... January 1961 / March or April 1962

Jean-Paul Sartre
No Exit .... February 1960 / December 1960 / May 1963

Arthur Schnitzler
A Country Day in the Quiet .... August 1962

William Shakespeare
An Evening of Shakespeare .... March 1961
As You Like It .... May 1963
Love (Merchant of Venice excerpts) .... March 1964
Romance D'Amore (For Valentines)
Scenes from Shakespeare
   (E. Rostand, A. de Musset and Solomon) .... February 1963
Two for Shakespeare .... September 1961

George Bernard Shaw
A Village Wooing .... February 1962
G. B. Shaw's ABC's from Annihilation to Ziegfeld,
   A Shavian Kaleidoscope .... November 1966

Sam Shepard
Icarus's Mother .... November 1965

David Shumaker
A Field of Poppies .... November 1965

Roberta Sklar
The Flight into Egypt .... December 1963
Michael Smith
I Like It .... June 1963
(with Johnny Dodd and Ondine:) *Vorspiel Nach Marienstein* .... June 1967
Terry Alan Smith
God Created Heaven and Earth, But Man Created Saturday Night .... March 1967
Charles Stanley
Faust .... Date unknown
Opening July 4th for Joe .... July 1967
Snow White & the 7 Dwarfs 1967
Vultures Over Miami 1967
David Starkweather
The Family Joke .... January 1965 / January 1966
The Love Affair .... May 1963
The Love Pickle .... February 1963
So, Who's Afraid of Edward Albee? .... February–March 1963 / September 1966
You May Go Home Again .... February 1963 / June 1965
Gertrude Stein and Alice B. Toklas
Three Kinds of Murder .... *Dates unknown*
Florence Stephenson
Heart of Gold .... January 1961
Wallace Stevens
Carlos Among the Candles .... March 1966 / July 1967
Robert Stock
Why I Live at the P.O. (adaptation of Eudora Welty) .... May 1962
August Strindberg
Creditors .... April 1964
Miss Julie .... July 1963
Peter Symcox
An Anthology of Love .... June 1963
Francis Medicine Story Talbot
Herrengasse .... February 1961 / 1963
Sometime Jam Today .... February 1966
Ronald Tavel
Vinyl .... October–November 1967
James Thurber
Case of Dimity Ann .... October 1960
Unknown Plawrights
And the Dead Cry Lonely .... April 1960
Goodbye Mama 1960
Laughter, Love, Lunacy .... March 1964
Religious Accordion Music .... April 1962
Surprise Package .... May 1961
What (An Intimate Revue) .... September 1960
Jean-Claude van Itallie
America Hurrah (Cino at La Mama) .... April 1965
Pavane (Cino at La Mama) .... April–May 1965
War .... March 1965
Margaret Variadis
Fables, Fantasies, & Fitzgerald .... June 1960

Fred Vassi
　The Re-Enactment .... January 1966

Stanley Wallace
　Miss Julia (from Strindberg's *Miss Julie*) .... July 1963

Sidney Shubert Walter
　For Esmé With Love and Squalor .... May 1963

Ed Weingold
　The Keys .... January–February 1964

Jeff Weiss
　A Funny Walk Home .... February 1967

Eudora Welty
　Petrified Man .... July 1963
　Why I Live at the P.O. .... May 1962

Oscar Wilde
　The Importance of Being Earnest .... February 1959 / October 1960
　The Little Prince 1962
　Salome .... February–March 1964
　The Picture of Dorian Gray 1961
　Triumphs and Tragedies .... October 1965

Thornton Wilder
　The Happy Journey 1960

Tennessee Williams
　Auto Da Fé .... March 1962 / April 1964
　Camino Real 1961
　The Case of the Crushed Petunia .... September 1960
　The Dark Room .... Winter 1960 or Spring 1961
　The Enemy Within .... October 1961
　A Field of Blue Children 1961
　The Glass Menagerie 1961
　Hello, From Bertha .... December 1964
　I Rise in Flames, Cried the Phoenix .... October 1961
　In the Winter of Cities 1961
　The Lady of Larkspur Lotion .... June 1960 / June 1962
　The Last of My Solid Gold Watches 1961
　One Arm .... July 1962
　A Perfect Analysis Given by a Parrot .... September 1962
　The Rose Tattoo 1961
　Talk To Me Like the Rain .... August 1960 / March 1961 / July 1962
　This Property is Condemned .... June 1960
　The Unsatisfactory Supper .... September 1960

Doric Wilson
　And He Made a Her .... March 1961
　Babel, Babel Little Tower .... June 1961
　Now She Dances! .... September 1961
　Pretty People .... November–December 1961

Lanford Wilson
A New Untitled Work .... October 1963
Days Ahead .... January 1966
Home Free .... January 1964 / August 1964
Ludlow Fair .... February 1965 / April–May 1967
The Madness of Lady Bright .... May 1964 / Frequent Revivals
No Trespassing .... January 1964
The Sandcastle .... 1965 / 1966 / 1967
Sex Is Between Two People .... January 1966
This is the Rill Speaking .... August 1964, July 1965, May 1967
So Long At the Fair .... August 1963

Sandy Wilson
The Boy Friend .... August 1960 / 1963

William Butler Yeats
The Land of Heart's Desire .... April 1960
Purgatory .... January 1962

R. L. Yorck
Lullabye for a Dying Man .... February 1964

*Robert Patrick has asked to add the following
disclaimer to this Appendix:*

The above list, certainly incomplete and presumably in some part inaccurate, is based on (1) a list compiled by Leah D. Frank for the 1985 Exhibition "Caffe Cino and its Legacy" at the Vincent Astor Gallery, hosted by the Library & Museum of the Performing Arts at Lincoln Center, New York Public Library, (2) Wendell Stone's research for his book *Caffe Cino: The Birthplace of Off-Off-Broadway* (see Bibliography), and (3) generous contributions of information *and* supposition from Caffe Cino participants. While an attempt has been made to place shows in the proper months, precise dates are uncertain in the extreme because *Village Voice* ads (the principal source of dates) had to be placed ahead of time and often do not reflect actual programs. There are many dozens of other productions which people say they saw or participated in for which the month or even the year cannot be determined. Any corrections, additions, and documentation will be welcomed.

ROBERT PATRICK

INDEX

Also available from Moving Finger Press:

Tools of the Writer's Craft by Sands Hall

"Reading this book is like learning how a juggler juggles. It will be invaluable for writers new and old, and for anyone giving or taking a writing workshop."

Lynn Freed, author of
The Curse of the Appropriate Man

People Farm by Steve Susoyev

"The raw, gut-wrenching power of this personal and eyewitness testimony shows through clearly as a warning to the seductive embrace of overly close-knit and controlling groups.... A compelling tell-all which is very hard to put down."

The Midwest Book Review

The Moving Finger writes; and, having Writ, moves on: Nor all your Piety nor Wit shall lure it back to cancel half a Line, nor all your Tears wash out a Word of it.

The Rubáiyát of Omar Khayyám

Moving Finger Press

SAN FRANCISCO
WWW.MOVINGFINGERPRESS.COM

Manufactured by Falcon Books, San Ramon, California